Is Everyone Really Equal?

An Introduction to Key Concepts in Social Justice Education

THIRD EDITION

Robin DiAngelo and Özlem Sensoy

Series Foreword by James A. Banks

Published by Teachers College Press,® 1234 Amsterdam Avenue, New York, NY 10027

Copyright © 2026 by Teachers College, Columbia University

Front cover art and design by Katherine Streeter

All rights reserved. No part of this publication may be reproduced or transmitted in any form or by any means, electronic or mechanical, including photocopy, or any information storage and retrieval system, without permission from the publisher. For reprint permission and other subsidiary rights requests, please contact Teachers College Press, Rights Dept.: tcpressrights@tc.columbia.edu

Library of Congress Cataloging-in-Publication Data

Names: DiAngelo, Robin, 1956– author | Sensoy, Özlem author
Title: Is everyone really equal? : An introduction to key concepts in social justice education / Robin DiAngelo and Özlem Sensoy.
Description: Third edition. | New York, NY : Teachers College Press, [2026] | Series: Multicultural education series | Previous edition: 2017. | Includes bibliographical references and index. | Summary: "This is the long-awaited third edition of the bestselling, multi-award-winning introduction to foundational concepts in social justice education. Accessible to students from high school through graduate school, this comprehensive resource addresses the most common stumbling blocks to understanding social justice. In response to the deep divides in public discourse, this edition provides a framework for reaching common ground on issues of justice within a pluralistic democracy. The authors have updated statistics, research, and examples, and revised discussion questions and extension activities to guide classroom dialogue and engagement with today's complex issues. New topics include the science of sex and gender, and the political backlash against equity and racial justice efforts. The authors trace the roots of white supremacy globally in the history of colonialism. Concepts such as oligarchy, kleptocracy, and capitalism's relationship to democracy are introduced and discussed"— Provided by publisher.
Identifiers: LCCN 2025041321 (print) | LCCN 2025041322 (ebook) |
  ISBN 9780807787786 paperback | ISBN 9780807787793 hardcover |
  ISBN 9780807783443 ebook
Subjects: LCSH: Educational sociology | Social justice—Study and teaching | Teaching—Social aspects | Racism in education | Critical pedagogy
Classification: LCC LC191 .S38 2026 (print) | LCC LC191 (ebook)
LC record available at https://lccn.loc.gov/2025041321
LC ebook record available at https://lccn.loc.gov/2025041322

ISBN 978-0-8077-8778-6 (paper)
ISBN 978-0-8077-8779-3 (hardcover)
ISBN 978-0-8077-8344-3 (ebook)

Printed on acid-free paper

Manufactured in the United States of America

MULTICULTURAL EDUCATION SERIES
James A. Banks, Series Editor

Is Everyone Really Equal? An Introduction to Key Concepts in Social Justice Education, 3rd Ed.
Robin DiAngelo & Özlem Sensoy

Race, Curriculum, and the Politics of Educational Justice
Wayne Au

Fostering School–Family Relationships in Multicultural Communities
Matthew Knoester, Maura G. Robinson, & Touorizou Hervé Somé

Affirming Student Ethnic Identities: How Teachers Can Create Welcoming Classrooms
André J. Branch

Critical Theory, Methods, and Design in Educational Research
Lois Weis & Michelle Fine

Critical Ethnic Studies and the Global Pursuit of Justice
James Wright

Let's Talk About DEI: Productive Disagreements About America's Most Polarizing Topics
Shaun Harper

Why Historically Black Colleges and Universities Matter: 25 Years of Historical Research for Justice
Marybeth Gasman

Hidden in Blackness: Being Black and Being an Immigrant in U.S. Schools and Colleges
Chrystal A. George Mwangi & Adaurennaya C. Onyewuenyi

"To Remain an Indian": Lessons in Democracy from a Century of Native American Education, 2nd Ed.
K. Tsianina Lomawaima and Teresa L. McCarty

From Foster Care to College: Navigating Educational Challenges and Creating Possibilities
Royel M. Johnson

Achieving Equal Educational Opportunity for Students of Color: Disrupting Structural Racism—An American Imperative
Richard R. Valencia

Critical Multicultural Education: Theory and Practice
Christine E. Sleeter

Race and Media Literacy, Explained (or Why Does the Black Guy Die First?)
Frederick W. Gooding Jr.

Whiteness in the Ivory Tower: Why *Don't* We Notice the White Students Sitting Together in the Quad?
Nolan L. Cabrera

Culturally Sustaining Policymaking in Indigenous Communities: Partnering to Promote Lasting Change
Aprille J. Phillips

Educating for Equity and Excellence: Enacting Culturally Responsive Teaching
Geneva Gay

Speculative Pedagogies: Designing Equitable Educational Futures
Antero Garcia & Nicole Mirra, Eds.

Seeing Whiteness: The Essential Essays of Robin DiAngelo
Robin DiAngelo

Becoming an Antiracist School Leader: Dare to Be Real
Patrick A. Duffy

The Hip-Hop Mindset: Success Strategies for Educators and Other Professionals
Toby S. Jenkins

Education for Liberal Democracy: Using Classroom Discussion to Build Knowledge and Voice
Walter C. Parker

Critical Race Theory and Its Critics: Implications for Research and Teaching
Francesca López & Christine E. Sleeter

Anti-Blackness at School: Creating Affirming Educational Spaces for African American Students
Joi A. Spencer & Kerri Ullucci

Sustaining Disabled Youth: Centering Disability in Asset Pedagogies
Federico R. Waitoller & Kathleen A. King Thorius, Eds.

The Civil Rights Road to Deeper Learning: Five Essentials for Equity
Kia Darling-Hammond & Linda Darling-Hammond

Reckoning With Racism in Family–School Partnerships: Centering Black Parents' School Engagement
Jennifer L. McCarthy Foubert

Teaching Anti-Fascism: A Critical Multicultural Pedagogy for Civic Engagement
Michael Vavrus

Unsettling Settler-Colonial Education: The Transformational Indigenous Praxis Model
Cornel Pewewardy et al., Eds.

Culturally and Socially Responsible Assessment: Theory, Research, and Practice
Catherine S. Taylor, with Susan B. Nolen

For a complete list of series titles, please visit www.tcpress.com/MCE

(continued)

MULTICULTURAL EDUCATION SERIES, *continued*

LGBTQ Youth and Education
  CRIS MAYO
Transforming Multicultural Education Policy and Practice
  JAMES A. BANKS, ED.
Critical Race Theory in Education
  GLORIA LADSON-BILLINGS
Civic Education in the Age of Mass Migration
  ANGELA M. BANKS
Creating a Home in Schools
  FRANCISCO RIOS & A. LONGORIA
Generation Mixed Goes to School
  RALINA L. JOSEPH & ALLISON BRISCOE-SMITH
Indian Education for All
  JOHN P. HOPKINS
Racial Microaggressions
  DANIEL G. SOLÓRZANO & LINDSAY PÉREZ HUBER
City Schools and the American Dream 2
  PEDRO A. NOGUERA & ESA SYEED
Measuring Race
  ROBERT T. TERANISHI ET AL.
Transformative Ethnic Studies in Schools
  CHRISTINE E. SLEETER & MIGUEL ZAVALA
Why Race and Culture Matter in Schools, 2nd Ed.
  TYRONE C. HOWARD
Just Schools
  ANN M. ISHIMARU
"We Dare Say Love"
  NA'ILAH SUAD NASIR ET AL., EDS.
Teaching What *Really* Happened, 2nd Ed.
  JAMES W. LOEWEN
Culturally Responsive Teaching, 3rd Ed.
  GENEVA GAY
Music, Education, and Diversity
  PATRICIA SHEHAN CAMPBELL
Reaching and Teaching Students in Poverty, 2nd Ed.
  PAUL C. GORSKI
Deconstructing Race
  JABARI MAHIRI
Transforming Educational Pathways for Chicana/o Students
  DOLORES DELGADO BERNAL & ENRIQUE ALEMÁN JR.
Un-Standardizing Curriculum, 2nd Ed.
  CHRISTINE E. SLEETER & JUDITH FLORES CARMONA
Global Migration, Diversity, and Civic Education
  JAMES A. BANKS ET AL., EDS.
Reclaiming the Multicultural Roots of U.S. Curriculum
  WAYNE AU ET AL.
We Can't Teach What We Don't Know, 3rd Ed.
  GARY R. HOWARD
Diversity and Education
  MICHAEL VAVRUS

Mathematics for Equity
  NA'ILAH SUAD NASIR ET AL., EDS.
Race, Empire, and English Language Teaching
  SUHANTHIE MOTHA
Black Male(d)
  TYRONE C. HOWARD
Race Frameworks
  ZEUS LEONARDO
Class Rules
  PETER W. COOKSON JR.
Achieving Equity for Latino Students
  FRANCES CONTRERAS
Literacy Achievement and Diversity
  KATHRYN H. AU
Understanding English Language Variation in U.S. Schools
  ANNE H. CHARITY HUDLEY & CHRISTINE MALLINSON
Latino Children Learning English
  GUADALUPE VALDÉS ET AL.
Asians in the Ivory Tower
  ROBERT T. TERANISHI
Diversity and Equity in Science Education
  OKHEE LEE & CORY A. BUXTON
Forbidden Language
  PATRICIA GÁNDARA & MEGAN HOPKINS, EDS.
The Light in Their Eyes, 10th Anniversary Ed.
  SONIA NIETO
The Flat World and Education
  LINDA DARLING-HAMMOND
Educating Citizens in a Multicultural Society, 2nd Ed.
  JAMES A. BANKS
Culture, Literacy, and Learning
  CAROL D. LEE
Facing Accountability in Education
  CHRISTINE E. SLEETER, ED.
Talkin Black Talk
  H. SAMY ALIM & JOHN BAUGH, EDS.
Improving Access to Mathematics
  NA'ILAH SUAD NASIR & PAUL COBB, EDS.
Beyond the Big House
  GLORIA LADSON-BILLINGS
Improving Multicultural Education
  CHERRY A. MCGEE BANKS
Transforming the Multicultural Education of Teachers
  MICHAEL VAVRUS
Learning to Teach for Social Justice
  LINDA DARLING-HAMMOND ET AL., EDS.
Learning and Not Learning English
  GUADALUPE VALDÉS
Multicultural Education, Transformative Knowledge, and Action
  JAMES A. BANKS, ED.

*To all those whose shoulders we stand on and lean on—
may ours be as steady for the next generation.*

Contents

Series Foreword James A. Banks	xiii
Acknowledgments	xix
Preface	xxi
What Is Critical Social Justice?	xxi
Chapter Summaries	xxiii
Prologue	xxvii
A Parable: Hodja and the Foreigner	xxvii
Layers of the Parable	xxviii
1. How to Engage Constructively in Courses That Take a Critical Social Justice Approach	1
An Open Letter to Students	3
A Story: The Question of Planets	5
Guideline 1: Strive for Intellectual Humility	6
Guideline 2: Everyone Has an Opinion. Opinions Are Not the Same as Informed Knowledge	9
Guideline 3: Let Go of Anecdotal Evidence and Examine Patterns	11
Guideline 4: Use Your Reactions as Entry Points for Gaining Deeper Self-Knowledge	13
Guideline 5: Recognize How Your Social Position Informs Your Reactions to Your Instructor and the Course Content	15
Grading	17
Conclusion	20

    Discussion Questions   21
    Extension Activity   21

2. About Knowledge   22
    Knowledge as Socially Constructed   22
    Research on Knowledge as Socially Constructed   26
    Applying Critical Theory   29
    Finding Common Ground   33
    Discussion Questions   36
    Extension Activities   36
    Patterns to Practice Seeing   37

3. Culture and Socialization   38
    What Is Culture?   39
    What Is Socialization?   39
    Cultural Norms and Conformity   43
    Implicit Bias   44
    You in Relation to the Groups to Which You Belong   48
    Discussion Questions   53
    Extension Activities   53
    Patterns to Practice Seeing   55

4. Prejudice and Discrimination   56
    What Is Prejudice?   57
    What Is Discrimination?   61
    All Humans Have Prejudice and Discriminate   62
    Discussion Questions   64
    Extension Activities   64
    Patterns to Practice Seeing   65

5. Oppression and Power   66
    Social Stratification   67

Contents

    Understanding Power   69
    What Is Oppression?   71
    Understanding the "Isms"   75
    Internalized Dominance   81
    Internalized Oppression   82
    Discussion Questions   88
    Extension Activities   88
    Patterns to Practice Seeing   89

6. Understanding Privilege Through Ableism   **90**
    What Is Privilege?   91
    External and Structural Dimensions of Privilege   92
    Internal and Attitudinal Dimensions of Privilege   98
    Common Dominant Group Misconceptions About Privilege   106
    Discussion Questions   109
    Extension Activities   110
    Patterns to Practice Seeing   110

7. Understanding the Invisibility of Oppression Through Sexism   **111**
    What Is an Institution?   112
    Sex/Gender and Science   113
    An Example: Sexism Today   118
    What Makes Sexism Difficult to See?   121
    Dominant Discourses of Sexism as Empowerment   126
    Discussion Questions   137
    Extension Activities   137
    Patterns to Practice Seeing   138

8. Understanding the Structural Nature of Oppression Through Racism   **139**
    What Is Race?   141

A Brief History of the Social Construction of Race in the United States	141
A Brief History of the Social Construction of Race in Canada	142
What Is Racism?	144
Two Key Challenges to Understanding Racism	145
Racism Today	148
Dynamics of White Racial Superiority	151
Dynamics of Internalized Racial Oppression	155
Racism and Intersectionality	157
Common White Misconceptions About Racism	161
Discussion Questions	168
Extension Activities	169
Patterns to Practice Seeing	169
9. Understanding the Global Organization of Racism Through White Supremacy	**170**
Whiteness and White Supremacy	171
White Supremacy in the Global Context	174
Discussion Questions	189
Extension Activities	189
Patterns to Practice Seeing	190
10. Understanding Intersectionality Through Classism	**191**
Mr. Rich White and Mr. Poor White Strike a Bargain	191
What Is Class?	193
Common Class Terms	203
Class Socialization	210
Common Misconceptions About Class	212
Understanding Intersectionality	219
Examples of Everyday Class Privilege	221
Common Classist Beliefs	222

Contents   xi

       Discussion Questions   226
       Extension Activities   226
       Patterns to Practice Seeing   227

11. **"Yeah, But . . .": Common Rebuttals**   **228**
       Claiming That Schools Are Politically Neutral   229
       Dismissing Social Justice Scholarship as the Personal Opinions of Woke Radicals   230
       Citing Exceptions to the Rule   230
       Arguing That Oppression Is Just Human Nature   231
       Appealing to a Universalized Humanity   232
       Insisting on Immunity From Socialization   232
       Ignoring Intersectionality   233
       Refusing to Recognize Structural and Institutional Power   234
       Denying the Politics of Language   235
       Invalidating Claims of Oppression as Oversensitivity   236
       Positioning Social Justice Education as Something "Extra"   237
       Being Paralyzed by Guilt   238
       Discussion Questions   240
       Extension Activity   240
       Patterns to Practice Seeing   241

12. **Putting It All Together**   **242**
       Recognize How Relations of Unequal Social Power Are Constantly Being Enacted   243
       Understand Our Own Positions Within Relations of Unequal Power (Intersectionality)   246
       Think Critically About Knowledge   250
       Act in Service of a More Just Society   254
       Discussion Questions   258
       Extension Activities   259
       Patterns to Practice Seeing   261

References	**263**
Glossary	**291**
Index	**301**
About the Authors	**321**

Series Foreword

Since publication of the second edition of this visionary, practical, and engaging book, a number of events in the United States and around the world have stimulated the rise of xenophobia, institutionalized racism, and the quest for social cohesion and nationalism (J. A. Banks, 2024, 2026; Johnson & Harper, 2024). These events include the election of Donald Trump as president of the United States in 2024, and his inauguration in January 2025. Shortly after his inauguration, Trump issued several executive orders that targeted the elimination of DEI (diversity, equity, and inclusion) programs and the teaching about race and diversity in the nation's schools, colleges, and universities. He issued Executive Order 14151 on January 20, 2025, "Ending Radical and Wasteful DEI Programs and Preferencing," and Executive Order 14190 on January 29, which demands an end to "radical indoctrination in K–12 schooling" and promotes "patriotic education" that includes the "celebration of America's greatness." A March 27, 2025, Executive Order (14253), "Restoring Truth and Sanity to American History," asserts that the Smithsonian has "come under the influence of a divisive, race-centered ideology."

The executive orders issued by President Trump assume that DEI programs discriminate against Whites and that teaching about diversity and racism in American history victimizes White students and makes them uncomfortable. His executive orders are designed to silence the shameful parts of U.S. history and to erase the history and cultures of African Americans and other ethnic groups of Color. Since Trump's second inauguration, White racism, nationalism, and authoritarianism have flourished (Salajan & Jules, 2025; Vavrus, in press). Some states had begun to eliminate or modify DEI programs before he was inaugurated. Florida enacted a "Stop Woke" Act in July 2022 that restricted workplace diversity and inclusion (Sorkin et al., 2022). At least 22 states have either banned or modified DEI programs in schools, colleges, and universities (Bolstad, 2024; Saul, 2024). Consequently, the publication of this book is timely and needed to give teachers and policymakers visions, theories, and strategies for resisting the targeted, funded, and effective attacks on DEI programs in schools, colleges, and universities.

Martin Luther King Jr. said, "The arc of the moral universe is long, but it bends toward justice" (King, 1965). The chilling and pernicious attacks on DEI do not necessarily invalidate the belief that the quest for social justice is long and "bends toward justice." However, they exemplify the major thesis of Arthur W. Schlesinger Jr.'s (1986) illuminating book, *The Cycles of American History*, in which he argues that during the past 2 centuries of American history periods of social justice and idealism have rotated with periods of pragmatism and conservative backlash. The election of Donald Trump as president of the United States after Barack Obama had engineered the passage of progressive legislation related to health care and the environment during his 8-year occupancy of the White House epitomizes Schlesinger's thesis.

The dismal and toxic "cycle" of American history that has been initiated by the Trump administration and the White nationalism that it has sanctioned since his second inauguration underscores the continuing legacy of racism in the United States (Anderson, 2016; Painter, 2016) and the need for the third edition of this informative, visionary, and helpful book. Teachers, like other Americans and Canadians, will be influenced by the disconcerting and dispiriting racial climate in the United States and in many other nations today (J. A. Banks, 2017, 2024; Salajan & Jules, 2025). These developments require multicultural and progressive teacher educators to work more diligently to promote social justice and equality today than was perhaps the case when the second edition of this book was published.

This trenchant and timely book is written to help both preservice and practicing teachers attain the knowledge, attitudes, and skills needed to work effectively with students from diverse groups, including mainstream groups. A major assumption of this book is that teachers need to develop a critical social justice perspective in order to understand the complex issues related to race, gender, class, and exceptionality in the United States and Canada and to teach in ways that will promote social justice and equality.

One of the most challenging things that those of us who teach multicultural education courses to teacher education students experience is resistance to the knowledge and skills that we teach. This resistance has deep roots in the communities in which most teacher education students are socialized as well as in the mainstream knowledge that becomes institutionalized within the academic community and the popular culture, which most students have not questioned until they enrolled in a multicultural education or diversity course. DiAngelo and Sensoy—who have had rich and successful experiences teaching difficult concepts to teacher education students—thoughtfully anticipate student resistance to many of the concepts discussed in this adept and skillfully conceptualized book. They respectfully and incisively convey to readers the important difference between opinion and informed knowledge. They also convincingly describe why informed and reflective knowledge is essential for effective teaching in diverse schools and classrooms. The authors also provide vivid and compelling examples, thought experiments, and anecdotes to help their readers master challenging and complex concepts related to diversity, social justice, and equity.

DiAngelo and Sensoy draw upon their years of experience working with predominantly White teachers and their deep knowledge of diversity issues to construct explicit definitions of complicated concepts such as racism, sexism, classism, ableism, and internalized oppression. Another important feature of this book is the wide range of issues and groups with which it deals, including race, gender, exceptionality, and social class. The authors also present an informative discussion of intersectionality and how the various concepts related to diversity interrelate in complex and dynamic ways that create institutionalized and intractable forms of marginalization.

This well-written and practical book will help practicing educators deal effectively with the growing ethnic, cultural, and linguistic diversity within U.S. society and schools. Although students in the United States are becoming increasingly diverse, most of the nation's teachers are White, female, and monolingual. Race and institutionalized racism are significant factors that influence and mediate the interactions of students and teachers from different ethnic, language, and social-class groups (Ladson-Billings, 2024; Love, 2019; Suárez-Orozco, in press) The growing income gap between adults (Stiglitz, 2012)—as well as between youth that are described by Putnam (2015) in *Our Kids: The American Dream in Crisis*—is another significant reason why it is important to help teachers understand how race, ethnicity, gender, and class influence classroom interactions and student learning and to comprehend the ways in which these variables affect student aspirations and academic engagement (Suárez-Orozco et al., 2008).

Schools in the United States are more diverse today than they have been since the early 1900s, when a multitude of immigrants entered the United States from Southern, Central, and Eastern Europe (C. A. M. Banks, 2005). American classrooms are experiencing the largest influx of immigrant students since the beginning of the 20th century. Approximately 21.5 million new immigrants—documented and undocumented—settled in the United States in the years from 2000 to 2015. Less than 10% came from nations in Europe. Most came from Mexico and nations in South Asia, East Asia, Latin America, the Caribbean, and Central America (Camarota, 2011, 2016). The influence of an increasingly diverse population on U.S. schools, colleges, and universities will continue to be enormous, despite the ways in which immigration will vary during changing policy cycles and presidential administrations.

The major purpose of the Multicultural Education Series is to provide preservice educators, practicing educators, graduate students, scholars, and policymakers with an interrelated and comprehensive set of books that summarizes and analyzes important research, theory, and practice related to the education of ethnic, racial, cultural, and linguistic groups in the United States and the education of mainstream students about diversity. The dimensions of multicultural education, developed by J. A. Banks (2004) and described in the *Handbook of Research on Multicultural Education* and in the *Encyclopedia of Diversity in Education* (J. A. Banks, 2012), provide the conceptual framework for the development of the publications in the Series. The dimensions are content integration, the knowledge construction process, prejudice reduction, equity pedagogy, and an empowering institutional culture and social structure. The books in the Series provide research, theory, and practical knowledge about the behaviors and learning characteristics of students of Color (Conchas & Vigil, 2012; Lee, 2007), language minority students (Gándara & Hopkins, 2010; Valdés, 2001; Valdés et al., 2011), low-income students (Cookson, 2013; Gorski, in press), and other minoritized population groups, such as students who speak different varieties of English (Charity Hudley & Mallinson, 2011) and LGBTQ youth (Mayo, 2022).

Several books in the Multicultural Education Series complement this book because they describe ways to reform teacher education to make it more responsive to social justice issues and concerns. They include *We Can't Teach What We Don't Know: White Teachers, Multiracial Schools* by Gary R. Howard (2016); *Why Race and Culture Matter in Schools: Closing the Achievement Gap in America's Classrooms* by Tyrone C. Howard (2020); *Learning to Teach for Social Justice*, edited by Linda Darling-Hammond, Jennifer French, and Silvia Paloma García-Lopez (2002); and *Walking the Road: Race, Diversity, and Social Justice in Teacher Education* by Marilyn Cochran-Smith (2004).

The first two editions of this influential and best-selling book helped teacher education students and practicing teachers to acquire the knowledge, skills, and perspectives that enabled them to work more effectively with the rich and growing student diversity in U.S. and Canadian schools. This third edition has been enriched by extensive updating, including the chapter summaries, discussion questions, extension activities, and citations. Students will find the third edition of this excellent and visionary textbook challenging, enlightening, and empowering.

—James A. Banks

REFERENCES

Anderson, C. (2016). *White rage: The unspoken truth of our racial divide*. Bloomsbury.

Banks, C.A.M. (2005). *Improving multicultural education: Lessons from the intergroup education movement*. Teachers College Press.

Banks, J. A. (2004). Multicultural education: Historical development, dimensions, and practice. In J. A. Banks & C.A.M. Banks (Eds.), *Handbook of research on multicultural education* (2nd ed., pp. 3–29). Jossey-Bass.

Banks, J. A. (2012). Multicultural education: Dimensions of. In J. A. Banks (Ed.), *Encyclopedia of diversity in education* (Vol. 3, pp. 1538–1547). SAGE Publications.

Banks, J. A. (Ed.). (2017). *Citizenship education and global migration: Implications for theory, research, and teaching*. American Educational Research Association.

Banks, J. A. (Ed.). (2024). The global quest for educational equity. *Daedalus, 123*(4), 1–319 (special issue).

Banks, J. A. (Ed.). (2026). *Standing strong in undemocratic times: Supporting diversity and enhancing democracy in education*. Teachers College Press.

Bolstad, E. (2024, June 14). Backlash against DEI spreads to more states. *Stateline*. https://stateline.org/2024/06/14/backlash-against-dei-spreads-to-more-states/

Camarota, S. A. (2011, October). *A record-setting decade of immigration: 2000 to 2010*. Center for Immigration Studies. https://cis.org/2000-2010-record-setting-decade-of-immigration

Camarota, S. A. (2016, June). *New data: Immigration surged in 2014 and 2015*. Center for Immigration Studies. https://cis.org/New-Data-Immigration-Surged-in-2014-and-2015

Charity Hudley, A. H., & Mallinson, C. (2011). *Understanding language variation in U.S. schools.* Teachers College Press.

Cochran-Smith, M. (2004). *Walking the road: Race, diversity, and social justice in teacher education.* Teachers College Press.

Conchas, G. Q., & Vigil, J. D. (2012). *Streetsmart schoolsmart: Urban poverty and the education of adolescent boys.* Teachers College Press.

Cookson, P. W. Jr. (2013). *Class rules: Exposing inequality in American high schools.* Teachers College Press.

Darling-Hammond, L., French, J., & García-Lopez, S. P. (Eds.). (2002). *Learning to teach for social justice.* Teachers College Press.

Gándara, P., & Hopkins, M. (Eds.). (2010). *Forbidden language: English language learners and restrictive language policies.* Teachers College Press.

Gorski, P. C. (in press). *Reaching and teaching students in poverty: Strategies for erasing the opportunity gap* (3rd ed.). Teachers College Press.

Howard, G. R. (2016). *We can't teach what we don't know: White teachers, multiracial schools* (3rd ed.). Teachers College Press.

Howard, T. R. (2020). *Why race and culture matter in schools. Closing the achievement gap in America's classrooms* (2nd ed.). Teachers College Press.

Johnson, R. M., & Harper, S. R. (2024). *The big lie about race in America's schools.* Harvard Education Press.

King, M. L., Jr. (1965, February 26). *Sermon at Temple Israel of Hollywood.* https://www.americanrhetoric.com/speeches/mlktempleisraelhollywood.htm

Ladson-Billings, G. (2024). How pedagogy makes the difference in U.S. schools. *Daedalus, 153*(4), 96–110.

Lee, C. D. (2007). *Culture, literacy, and learning: Taking bloom in the midst of the whirlwind.* Teachers College Press.

Love, B. L. (2019). *We want to do more than survive: Abolitionist teaching and the pursuit of educational freedom.* Beacon Press.

Mayo, C. (2022). *LGBTQ youth and education: Policies and practices* (2nd ed.). Teachers College Press.

Painter, N. I. (2016, November 16). What Whiteness means in the Trump era. *The New York Times.* https://www.nytimes.com/2016/11/13/opinion/what-whiteness-means-in-the-trump-era.html

Putnam, R. D. (2015). *Our kids: The American dream in crisis.* Simon & Schuster.

Salajan, D. D., & Jules, T. V. (2025). Academic freedom under siege: The global fallout of US authoritarianism and its threats to comparative and international education. *Comparative Education Review, 69*(3), 371–541.

Saul, S. (2024, April 12). With state bans on D.E.I., some universities find a workaround: Rebranding. *The New York Times.* https://www.nytimes.com/2024/04/12/us/diversity-ban-dei-college.html

Schlesinger, A. M., Jr. (1986). *The cycles of American history.* Houghton Mifflin.

Sorkin, A. R., Giang, V., Gandel, S., Hirsch, L., Livni, E., & Gross, J. (2022, August 19). Florida's 'stop WOKE' act gets pushback in court. *The New York Times.* https://www.nytimes.com/2022/08/19/business/dealbook/florida-desantis-stop-woke-act.html

Stiglitz, J. E. (2012). *The price of inequality: How today's divided society endangers our future.* Norton.

Suárez-Orozco, C. (in press). Culturally responsive pedagogy for immigrant-origin students. In J. A. Banks (Ed.), *Standing strong in undemocratic times: Supporting diversity and enhancing democracy in education.* Teachers College Press.

Suárez-Orozco, C., Suárez-Orozco, M. M., & Todorova, I. (2008). *Learning a new land: Immigrant students in American society.* Harvard University Press.

Valdés, G. (2001). *Learning and not learning English: Latino students in American schools.* Teachers College Press.

Valdés, G., Capitelli, S., & Alvarez, L. (2011). *Latino children learning English: Steps in the journey.* Teachers College Press.

Vavrus, M. (in press). Rise of fascism in the United States: A critical multicultural anti-fascist response. In J. A. Banks (Ed.), *Standing strong in undemocratic times: Supporting diversity and enhancing democracy in education.* Teachers College Press.

Acknowledgments

We begin this text by acknowledging that we have conducted our scholarship and teaching on the unceded ancestral territories of various Indigenous peoples, lands today identified as Canada and the United States. It can be easy for us to dismiss the idea that events from the past could matter to us here in the present. But studying the history of colonialism—the cultural, emotional, and physical genocide of peoples around the world—reminds us that to understand the injustices of today we must recognize their connection to injustices of the past. We offer our deepest respect to Elders and knowledge keepers both past and present.

We extend our heartfelt thanks to the friends and colleagues who have supported us with this project, especially those who so generously gave their time and expertise to read and offer feedback to the various editions of the book.

Big thanks to our amazing research assistant Sabrina Ngo, whose careful work double-checking our references and helping update the statistics was invaluable support in the creation of this third edition.

Thank you to Katherine Streeter for her artwork on each edition of our book, which brings joy and meaning to the text.

Thank you to Brian Ellerbeck and the entire publication team at Teachers College Press for over a decade of support of this book. A special thanks to Lori Tate and Nancy Mandel for their meticulous editing.

And finally, we extend our deepest appreciation to James Banks for his trust in us to produce a text worthy of joining the Multicultural Education Series, for his mentorship, and for his lifelong courage and commitment to building a more just world.

Map of Indigenous Communities Throughout North America

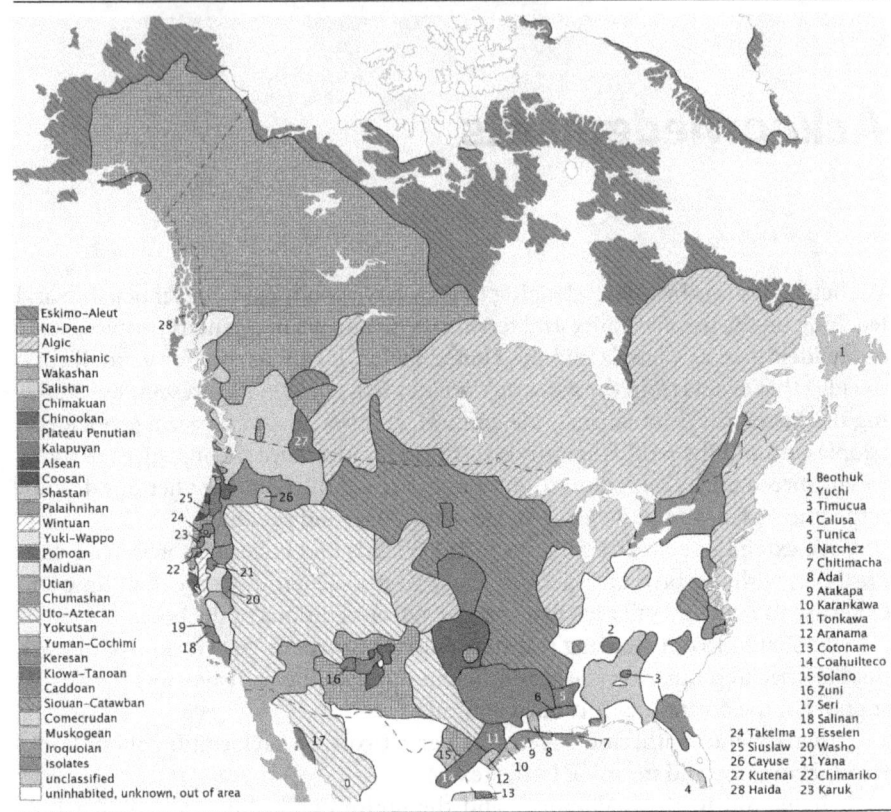

Source: https://www.en.wikipedia.org/wiki/Indigenous_languages_of_the_Americas#/media/File:Langs_N.Amer.svg

Preface

We are educators who collectively bring decades of experience conducting research, teaching, writing, leading workshops, and facilitating discussions in the study and practice of social justice. We have led this work with elementary and high school students, undergraduate and graduate students, preservice and inservice teachers, and in the workplace for employees of government, university, nonprofit, and for-profit organizations. We have presented our research at national and international conferences, and within the disciplines of education, social work, cultural studies, women's studies, ethnic studies, and Middle East studies.

Through our experiences with wide-ranging audiences, we consistently see predictable gaps in people's understanding of what social justice is and what might be required to achieve it. We think of these gaps as a form of social justice illiteracy and argue that this illiteracy is not due to a lack of information alone. Rather, social *in*justice depends on this illiteracy; it is not benign or neutral, but is actively nurtured through many forces and serves specific interests.

Social justice illiteracy prevents us from moving forward to create a more equitable society; if we cannot recognize injustice we cannot remedy injustice. Thus the primary objective of this book is to provide a foundation for social justice literacy for a wide range of readers, using accessible language, addressing the most common misinformation, and providing vignettes, definitions, exercises, and reflection questions.

WHAT IS CRITICAL SOCIAL JUSTICE?

Most people have a working definition of *social justice*; it is commonly understood as the principles of *fairness* and *equality* for all people and respect for their basic human rights. Most people would say that they value these principles. Yet seldom are the following questions discussed, and even less often are the answers agreed upon: What are those basic human rights? Have we already achieved them? If not, why not? How do we go about achieving them, if we agree on what they are and why they haven't yet been achieved? From whose perspective is something fair and equitable? Might something be fair for one person while actually having an unfair outcome for another? What does *respect* actually mean in practice? While some say it is to treat others as *we* would like to be treated, some say that it is to treat others as *they* would like to be treated. Thus the *definition* itself is our first challenge.

The second challenge surfaces when we consider what it means to *practice* social justice. Generally, because most people see themselves as valuing social justice, they also see themselves as acting justly in their lives. In response to questions about how they practice social justice, many would say that they treat everyone the same without regard to differences, and therefore their actions are aligned with their values.

While conceptualizing social justice as treating others with "fairness" and "equality" is common, it is woefully inadequate. Indeed, a great deal of scholarship in social justice studies is focused on the gap between the *ideals* of social justice and the *practices* of social justice.

To clarify our definition, let's start with the concept. While some scholars and activists use the term *social justice*, in this book we prefer to talk about *critical social justice*. We do so in order to distinguish our standpoint from mainstream standpoints. A critical approach refers to specific theoretical perspectives that recognize that society is *stratified* (i.e., divided and unequal) in significant and far-reaching ways along social group lines. These groups include race, class, gender, sexuality, and ability. Critical social justice recognizes inequality as deeply embedded in the fabric of society (i.e., as structural) and actively seeks to change this.

The definition we proceed from is rooted in a critical theoretical approach. While this approach applies to a broad range of fields, there are some important shared principles:

- All people are individuals, but they are also members of social groups.
- These social groups are valued unequally in society.
- Social groups that are valued more highly have greater access to the resources of a society.
- Social injustice is real, exists today, and results in unequal access to resources between groups of people.
- Those who claim to be for social justice must be engaged in self-reflection about their own socialization into these groups and must strategically act from that awareness in ways that challenge social injustice.
- This action requires a commitment to an ongoing and lifelong process.

Based on these principles, a person engaged in critical social justice practice must be able to:

- Recognize that relations of unequal social power are constantly being enacted at both the micro (individual) and macro (structural) levels.
- Understand our own positions within these relations of unequal power (positionality, intersectionality).
- Think critically about knowledge: what we know and how we know it.
- Act on all of the above in service of a more just society.

Our goal in writing this book is to deepen our readers' understanding of the complexity of these principles and inspire readers to actively engage in critical social justice practice. We call this blend of understanding and action *critical social justice literacy*.

We have brought together key concepts necessary for beginning to develop critical social justice literacy. Drawing on examples from Canada and the United States, the chapters are intended to be accessible to both Canadian and U.S. readers. We provide many familiar examples and have kept in-text citations to a minimum. We open each chapter with a statement that captures a familiar misconception we will address. The chapters are written to be building blocks; because each builds upon the previous, they are best read in sequence. The issues are complex, political, and often emotionally charged, and if readers have difficulty understanding a key idea from one chapter, they may have difficulty carrying the idea forward into the next. For these reasons, the book has the following features:

- Definition Boxes in which we define key terms
- Stop Boxes to serve as reminders of key ideas from previous chapters and to help with difficult or challenging concepts
- Perspective Check Boxes to draw attention to alternative standpoints on examples used in the text and to respond to superficial "both-sides" rebuttals
- Discussion Questions and Extension Activities for those who are using the book in a class, workshop, or study group
- A Glossary of terms used in the book

CHAPTER SUMMARIES

Chapter 1: How to Engage Constructively in Courses That Take a Critical Social Justice Approach guides students using the book in a course context. We address some of the common challenges and present five guidelines or dispositions that can help ensure a constructive learning experience in the social justice classroom. These guidelines include how to reframe student beliefs and expectations about course grading and assessment.

Chapter 2: About Knowledge explains what it means to think critically about social justice. We explain the theoretical perspective known as *Critical Theory* and provide a brief sketch of key ideas relevant to our approach. The concept of *knowledge construction* is introduced. This chapter clarifies the difference between the *opinions* that readers already hold on a topic and the *informed knowledge* that we wish to provide and foster. We explain the importance of setting aside one's opinions and engaging with humility when encountering content that is personally challenging or politically charged. Given the increased polarization in public discourse, in this 3rd edition we offer a framework for finding common ground on difficult issues.

Chapter 3: Culture and Socialization. This chapter explains what *culture* and *socialization* are and how they work. We introduce the relationship between being an individual and being a member of multiple social groups (such as race, gender, and class). The chapter explains how important it is for us to understand that our ideas, views, and opinions are not objective and independent, but rather the result of myriad social messages and conditioning forces. We take the reader beyond the common conception of parents and families as the sole forces of socialization and describe how other institutions work to form our worldviews. Examples are provided to illustrate the power of socialization and how it works as an unconscious filter shaping our perceptions.

Chapter 4: Prejudice and Discrimination unravels common misunderstandings of two key interrelated terms: *prejudice* and *discrimination*. The chapter examines prejudice as *internal*—thoughts, feelings, attitudes, and assumptions—and its relationship to discrimination, which is *external*—prejudice occurring in action. We explain that prejudice and discrimination cannot be humanly avoided; we all hold prejudices and we all discriminate based on our prejudices. We argue that the first step in minimizing discrimination is to be able to identify (rather than to deny) our prejudices.

Chapter 5: Oppression and Power explains how prejudice and discrimination are not the whole story. We move beyond individuals and take readers on an examination of prejudice and discrimination at the group level. We introduce the concept of *power*, which transforms group prejudice into oppression, and define terms such as *dominant group* and *minoritized group.* This chapter also explains the difference between concepts such as *race prejudice,* which anyone can hold, and *racism,* which occurs at the group level and is only perpetuated by the group that holds social, ideological, economic, and institutional power. The chapter explains the "ism" words (for example *racism, sexism, classism*) and how these words allow us to capture structural power as it manifests in particular forms of oppression.

Chapter 6: Understanding Privilege Through Ableism explains the rights, benefits, and advantages automatically received by being a member of the dominant group, regardless of intentions. From a critical social justice perspective, *privilege* is systemically conferred dominance and the institutional processes by which the beliefs and values of the dominant group are made "normal" and universal. The key is not how big your group is, it is whether your group holds social and institutional power. This chapter also explains related concepts such as *internalized oppression* and *internalized dominance,* and offers examples of how these dynamics work to hold existing relations of power in place.

Chapter 7: Understanding the Invisibility of Oppression Through Sexism traces a specific form of oppression—sexism—in order to illustrate how our ideas, views, and opinions are shaped by interlocking and ongoing social messages. We describe how such interlocking messages serve as barriers to seeing oppression and as such are central to how oppression is normalized. This 3rd edition includes a substantial discussion on the science of sex and gender, an overview of gender-related language, and an analysis of common dominant discourses of sexism as empowerment. The chapter addresses the dynamics that make sexism difficult to see.

Chapter 8: Understanding the Structural Nature of Oppression Through Racism traces a specific form of oppression in depth. *Racism* is discussed within the U.S. and Canadian contexts and explained as White racial and cultural prejudice and discrimination, supported intentionally or unintentionally by institutional power and authority. Racism is illustrated through an examination of economic, political, social, and cultural structures, actions, and beliefs. We offer an in-depth understanding of racism as an entry point into building an in-depth understanding of how all oppressions are structural. We emphasize that racism—as with all systems of oppression—is highly adaptive and hard-won gains can always be revoked. Thus social justice gains require ongoing protection. We identify some of the progress that has been reversed since the 2nd edition. The chapter ends by addressing common misconceptions about racism.

Chapter 9: Understanding the Global Organization of Racism Through White Supremacy explores White supremacy in the global context by tracing the history of imperialism and colonialism and how that history formed the divisions between the Global North and the Global South. The chapter connects the legacies of imperialism and colonialism to industrialization, resource extraction, and labor exploitation globally. We examine how White supremacy defines humanity and civilization, who is civilized and who is savage, where civilization is located, and by doing so, maps these definitions onto the Global North/Global South. This core binary is still with us today and organizes our world and how we understand global conflicts, economics, and politics.

Chapter 10: Understanding Intersectionality Through Classism begins with an examination of class oppression. We explain current economic relations of power, address concepts such as capitalism, democratic socialism, oligarchy, kleptocracy, wealth and income, and prison labor, and review common terms. The chapter also addresses the concept of *intersectionality* as an important theoretical development for understanding the multidimensional nature of oppression. We identify elements of class privilege, name common misconceptions about class mobility, and speak back to common classist narratives.

Chapter 11: "Yeah, But...": Common Rebuttals. Based on our experiences teaching critical social justice in a variety of forums, we can predict that readers will raise certain questions, objections, and rebuttals. This chapter addresses the most common ones we hear. Drawing on all that has been discussed in previous chapters, we briefly but directly speak back to these "Yeah, buts."

Chapter 12: Putting It All Together summarizes what social justice means in action. The chapter reviews four arenas of action. We must be able to recognize how relations of unequal social power are constantly being negotiated at both the micro (individual) and macro (structural) levels; understand our own positions within these relations of unequal power; think critically about knowledge; and act from this understanding in service of a more just society. This final chapter reviews key principles of critical social justice and offers some concrete suggestions for action. Readers are offered specific actions for critical social justice skill development.

Looking head-on at injustice can be painful, especially when we understand that we all have a role in it. However, making our roles more visible is not about assigning guilt or blame. At this point in society, guilt and blame are not useful or constructive; no one reading this book had a hand in creating the systems that hold injustice in place. But each of us does have a choice about how to proceed once that injustice is visible to us; there is no neutral ground.

Prologue

A PARABLE: HODJA AND THE FOREIGNER

Once upon a time, a foreign scholar and his entourage were passing through a town in Anatolia. The scholar asked to speak to the town's most knowledgeable person. The townsfolk immediately called Nasreddin Hodja to come to meet the foreign scholar.

The foreigner did not speak Turkish, Persian, or Arabic, and Hodja did not speak any European languages, and so the two wise men had to communicate with signs while the townsfolk and the entourage watched in fascination.

The foreigner used a stick to draw a large circle in the sand. Hodja took the stick and divided the circle into two halves. The foreigner drew a line perpendicular to the one Hodja drew, and the circle was now split into four. He moved the stick to indicate first the three quarters of the circle, then the remaining quarter. In response, Hodja made a swirling motion with the stick on the four quarters. Then the foreigner made a bowl shape with his two hands held together side by side, palms up, and wiggled his fingers. Then, Hodja responded by cupping his hands with his palms down and wiggling his fingers.

When the meeting was over, the members of the foreigner's entourage asked him what they had talked about. "Nasreddin Hodja is a very learned man," he said. "I told him that the Earth was round and he told me that there was an equator slicing it in half. I told him that three-quarters of the Earth was water and one-quarter of it was land. He said that there were undercurrents and winds. I told him that the waters warm up, vaporize, and move toward the sky, and to that he replied that they cool off and come down as rain."

The people of the town were also curious about how the conversation went. They gathered around Hodja. "This stranger has very good taste," Hodja explained. "He said that he wished there was a large tray of baklava. I said that he could only have half of it. He said that the syrup should be made with three parts sugar and one part honey. I agreed and said that they all had to be well mixed together. Next, he suggested that we should cook it on blazing fire. And I added that we should pour crushed nuts on top of it."

LAYERS OF THE PARABLE

This story is from the tales of Nasreddin Hodja, a 13th-century Sufi sage. His wisdom stories often use humor to point out human failings and misunderstandings. What is relevant about this story for our purposes is the way it captures some of the key concepts in critical social justice literacy:

- Each of us has a culturally based worldview.
- We hold a common assumption that others share our worldview.
- We often assume that what we intend to communicate is what is received.

Because Hodja and the foreigner do not speak the same verbal language, they move to a form of sign language and assume that they share the same understanding of what is being signed. Both men leave the exchange feeling satisfied, but we realize that they have completely misunderstood each other. If we go deeper, we might also see that they had completely different ways of organizing the world and what they valued within it. For the foreigner, the emphasis was on the elements of the Earth; he had a more scientific orientation. For Hodja, the emphasis was on sharing a meal; he had a more community orientation.

As their ideas about each other form and are communicated to their respective groups (the foreigner to his entourage and Hodja to his fellow townspeople), consider now that one of them is in the position to enforce his worldview upon the other; that is, consider what might happen when we add *power* to the encounter. Imagine the foreigner and his entourage are not just passing through, they are in town because their nation has just invaded Hodja's. The foreigner has been installed to govern Hodja's town and he now controls all of the land—land that Hodja and the townfolk have lived on and raised their food on all of their lives, as did their ancestors before them. But now Hodja must pay the foreigner large fees to use this land. The foreigner moves in and appoints his own people to key positions of government and sets up rules and norms for society that are based on *his* worldview. The foreigner imposes these new rules and norms upon Hodja and the townspeople.

Which one of these men is going to need to learn to understand the perspective of the other? While they each have their own worldview and neither worldview is inherently superior, only one of them is in a position of power that enables him to impose his worldview on the other. Hodja and his community's ability to work and feed their families now depends upon learning and accommodating the foreigner and his customs, language, and traditions. Conversely, the foreigner does not have to learn or accommodate Hodja's customs, language, or traditions. Indeed, the foreigner, who now controls all of the resources needed for Hodja's livelihood, will profit from Hodja's and the community's labor without ever having to learn to understand their perspective.

Now fast-forward from the 13th century to the 21st. Centuries of domination of the town and resultant conflicts have occurred. The descendants of the foreigner, who continue to control the town, benefit from the resources and power they have accumulated. Meanwhile, the descendants of the townsfolk have had to change their entire way of life, customs, and even language in order to survive. The townsfolk try to pass their traditions on to their young children, but the children see little value in cultural traditions that don't seem to get them anywhere in society. Many of the foreigners' descendants are also frustrated. They can't understand why some townsfolk are so angry—after all, *they* weren't the ones who invaded the town centuries ago, and they don't see why the townspeople can't just get over it and assimilate so they can all live together in peace.

As we can see, there are many layers of complexity in this story, layers that have built up and been left unaddressed over generations. The foreigner's descendants see the situation as simple: Hodja's descendants should just let go of the past and move on. Hodja's descendants, however, see the situation as much more complicated. Until the historical, cultural, and ideological aspects of the foreigner's domination are addressed, no one can just "get over it." Indeed, they recognize that far from being over, the domination continues in newer forms. The suggestion that they could just move on reveals how little the foreigner's descendants understand the history of their town and their current position within society, based on that history.

This story is meant to illustrate many of the complex issues that must be understood in order to develop critical social justice literacy. An issue that we will highlight in Chapter 3 is how we might find common ground from which to move forward within our current context. Finding common ground is not the same as "both-sides-ing"; we don't have to give away our values or "go along to get along." Rather, it is part of working for a more socially just society without losing sight of the other side's humanity. In the cultural moment in which we find ourselves, holding one another's humanity is more important than ever, and is at the heart of social justice.

CHAPTER 1

How to Engage Constructively in Courses That Take a Critical Social Justice Approach

> The struggle has always been inner, and is played out in outer terrains. Awareness of our situation must come before inner changes, which in turn come before changes in society. Nothing happens in the "real" world unless it first happens in the images in our heads.
>
> —Gloria Anzaldúa (2009, p. 310)

> **Vocabulary to practice using:** anecdotal evidence; platitude; ideology; mainstream society; peer review; objective; subjective

If you are reading this book, you are likely enrolled in a course that takes a critical stance. A *critical stance* is an approach within academic fields that proceeds from the premise that knowledge is not neutral, and that education is a political project that can either reproduce or interrupt inequality.

> **Critical stance:** An academic perspective that proceeds from the understanding that there is no human objectivity and works to uncover the politics and interests underlying knowledge production.

Throughout your course, you will likely be studying key concepts such as *socialization, oppression, privilege,* and *ideology* and doing coursework that challenges your worldview by suggesting that you may not be as open-minded as you may have thought. You are encountering evidence that inequality not only exists but is deeply structured into society in ways that secure its reproduction. You are also beginning to realize that, contrary to what you have always been taught, categories of difference (such as gender, race, and class), not merit alone, *do* matter and contribute significantly to people's experiences and life opportunities.

When confronted with evidence of inequality that challenges our identities, we often respond with resistance; we want to deflect this unsettling information and protect a worldview that is more familiar and comforting. This is especially true if we believe in justice and see ourselves as living a life that supports it. Forms that resistance takes include silence, withdrawal, immobilizing guilt, feeling overly hopeless or overly hopeful, rejection, anger, sarcasm, and argumentation. These reactions are not surprising. Mainstream narratives reinforce the idea that society overall is fair, and that all we need to overcome injustice is to be nice and treat everyone the same. Yet while comforting, these platitudes are woefully out of sync with scholarly research about how society is structured. The deeply held beliefs that inform our emotional responses make studying and teaching from a critical stance very difficult.

> **Platitude:** A point or phrase intended to have moral meaning but has been used so often in so many different contexts it has become empty or meaningless. For example, "Everything happens for a reason!" or "I was taught to treat everyone the same. I don't see color."

In addition to asking us to question ideology that is deeply internalized and taken for granted, critical engagement rarely provides concrete solutions. This ambiguity can lead to frustration, for our K–12 schooling (especially in Canada and the United States) has conditioned us to seek clear and unambiguous answers. Still, we offer an overall framework for critical engagement. We draw on research and our years of practice teaching social justice content and share the vignettes and guidelines that have been most effective for our own students. A list of key terms can be found at the beginning of this chapter. Practice incorporating these terms into your academic vocabulary.

> **Ideology:** The big, shared ideas of a society that are reinforced throughout all of the institutions and are very hard to resist or avoid absorbing. These ideas include the stories, myths, representations, explanations, definitions, and rationalizations that are used to justify inequality in society. *Individualism* and *meritocracy* are examples of ideology.

AN OPEN LETTER TO STUDENTS

Courses that address social justice and inequality through a critical lens often challenge mainstream understandings and thus bring to the surface patterns and tensions that other courses do not (Gallavan, 2000; Kincheloe, 2008). There are two key reasons for this.

The first is that many of us are *underprepared to engage in the course content in scholarly ways*. Basic study habits, reading comprehension, writing skills, vocabulary, and critical thinking are often underdeveloped in college students. Ironically, much of this is due to structural inequalities that courses like these try to address. For example, political and economic pressures on schools to focus on standardized testing have resulted in moves away from intellectual curiosity, critical thinking, and engagement with ambiguity and toward creating conforming and compliant students who can memorize the "one right answer" to pass the test. Differences in the kinds of schooling we receive and the differential futures they prepare us for are based on structural inequalities related to our race, class, gender, and other social locations. These differentials affect our preparation for college and university-level engagement. The ultimate goal of social justice education is to enable us to recognize structural inequalities in ways that prepare us to change them. However, the sociopolitical context of schooling makes critical engagement challenging for many students, and this challenge is heightened when the topics under study are politically and emotionally charged.

This leads to the second reason that courses that address social justice and inequality bring to the surface patterns and tensions that other courses do not: *Most of us have very strong feelings and opinions about the topics examined in social justice courses* (such as racism, sexism, and homophobia). These opinions often surface through claims such as:

> "People should be judged by what they do, not by the color of their skin."
> "I accept people for who they are."
> "I see people as individuals."
> "It's focusing on difference that divides us."
> "My parents taught me that all people are equal."
> "I always treat everyone the same."
> "I've been discriminated against so I don't have any privilege."
> "Our generation is more open-minded."
> "I have friends from all races and we are all fine with each other."
> "I don't think race and gender make any difference—as long as you work hard."
> "It's White males who are the minority now."
> "Women are just as sexist as men."

While these opinions are deeply held and appear to be commonsense truth (and not opinion at all), they are predictable, simplistic, and misinformed, given the large body of research examining social relations. The relentless repetition of these ideas in the mainstream makes them *seem* true and allows us to form strongly held opinions without being particularly educated on the issues. Indeed, where we are members of dominant groups (e.g., if we are male, White, cisgender, nondisabled), our opinions will almost certainly be superficial, because a superficial level of understanding is all that is made available to us in mainstream education—if these issues are addressed at all. Where we are members of minoritized groups (e.g., if we are women, peoples of Color, transgender, people with disabilities), we may have a deeper personal understanding of social inequality and how it works, but may not have the language to discuss it in an academic context.

Further, it is a rare individual who is dominant in all key social groups, or conversely is minoritized in all key social groups. Yet messages that circulate in mainstream society do not prepare most of us to conceptualize or develop the language to discuss our intersecting identities in any depth. Take, for example, the intersection of race and class and consider a White woman who lives in poverty. While she will face many *class* barriers, she will not face *racism*. Yet a poor White woman—while not facing *racism*—will face barriers related to her gender—*sexism*—that a poor White *man* will not. For example, she will be more likely to be held responsible for the care of her children than a man, she will be likely to earn less, and she will be more at risk for male violence, all of which increase the burden of poverty. Yet mainstream culture tends to present poverty as if there is a collective and shared experience of "the poor."

Without practice and study beyond what we absorb in our daily living, we are ill prepared to understand social group injustices. Therefore, our perspectives on issues like poverty and social inequality are necessarily lacking—and especially so if we ourselves are not poor. These perspectives include the idea that if we don't believe in social inequality, then we don't participate in it. Mainstream culture prevents us from understanding a central tenet of social justice education: Society is structured in ways that make us all somehow complicit in systems of inequality; there is no neutral ground. Thus, an effective critical social justice course will challenge our baseline views about ourselves and what we know about society, how it works, and our place in it.

Unfortunately, when we are new to the examination of social relations, we only know one way to respond to ideas studied in the course: "If the professor is saying that I participate in systems of injustice (such as racism), they are saying that I am a bad person (a racist)." Later, we should come to understand that this is *not* what our professors are saying, and that binary ways of conceptualizing these issues (good/bad, racist/not-racist) are part of what prevents us from seeing them in their complexity.

In sum, the combination of underdeveloped academic skills, difficult theoretical concepts, and highly charged political content can make these courses challenging. Yet basing our knowledge on such sources as personal opinions, self-concepts, anecdotal evidence, hearsay, intuition, family teachings, popular platitudes, limited relationships, personal experiences, exceptions, and mainstream media is insufficient for understanding and responding constructively to social injustice.

Therefore, to maximize your learning of social justice content, we offer the following guidelines:

1. Strive for intellectual humility.
2. Recognize the difference between having an opinion and being informed.
3. Let go of personal anecdotal evidence and look at broader societal patterns.
4. Notice your own defensive reactions and attempt to use these reactions as entry points for gaining deeper self-awareness.
5. Recognize how your social perspective (such as your race, class, gender, sexuality, ability status) informs your reactions to the course content, your instructor, and the individuals whose work you study in the course.

Below we explain these guidelines in more depth and how they can help you engage constructively with social justice content.

A STORY: THE QUESTION OF PLANETS

Imagine: You are in a course that fulfills a university science requirement. The professor holds a PhD in astronomy. He has written several books, is widely published in academic journals, and has a national reputation in his field. The course objectives include defining terms used in modern astronomy and exposure to the practices, methodology, and concepts of the discipline. The professor is reviewing the assigned readings, which present the most established theories in the field. He overviews the scientific community's discussion of the number of planets and states that based on the current criteria for what constitutes a planet, only eight planets are officially recognized in our solar system.

One of the students raises his hand and insists that there are actually nine planets. That is what he learned in school. He has seen many books with pictures of the planets, and there are always nine. As further evidence, he recites the mnemonic he learned to pass all his science tests: "My Very Educated Mother Just Served Us Nine Pizzas." He states that he had a map of the sky in his bedroom as a child and it showed nine planets. Further, he says, his parents taught him that there were nine planets and many of his friends also agree that there are nine. He spent his childhood camping out and looking up at the sky and identifying constellations, so he has experience in astronomy. The professor tries to explain to the student that to engage with the planet controversy one must first demonstrate understanding of the criteria for what constitutes a planet, but he is cut off by the student, who declares, "Well, that's your opinion. My opinion is that there are nine."

The professor tries once more to explain that what he presents in regard to the number of planets is not his opinion, but based on the scholarly community's established criteria for what defines a planet. Although at one time astronomers believed that Pluto qualified as a planet, as with all disciplines, their knowledge evolved. With the discovery of new information and further study they now understand that Pluto doesn't meet the criteria of a planet, in large part due to its shape. This is not an opinion, the professor repeats, but astronomical theories that have resulted from ongoing research and study. The student replies, "I don't care if Pluto is square, diamond-shaped, or shaped like a banana, it's a planet, and there are nine planets."

How likely is it that the majority of the class thinks our hypothetical astronomy student is raising a credible point? Would the class admire him for standing up to the professor and expressing the same understanding they had (but were too hesitant to bring up)? Even if his peers were to share his view, that would not make his argument valid. In any case, it is more likely that they will see him as having some academic challenges, as somewhat immature, and perhaps even as disrespectful. They may even assume that he will have trouble passing the class.

GUIDELINE 1: STRIVE FOR INTELLECTUAL HUMILITY

Our hypothetical student is representative of many students we encounter: He has not done the readings or he has trouble understanding what he's read; he has limited information but is resistant to increasing it; he clings to the same worldview he came into the course with; and he is overly confident about his position. Scholars have referred to these patterns as a form of *willful ignorance* (Baker, 1990; Dei et al., 2004; Schick, 2000). In our experience, students who have trouble understanding what they read seldom either reread, slow down, look up new words, or ask their professors to explain difficult passages. Standardized testing and the punishment and reward system of grades are major contributors to these habits, as they have created a school culture that encourages conformity and single correct answers over intellectual curiosity and risk-taking. Critical social justice education demands a different kind of engagement than most of us have been prepared for in our previous schooling.

Another challenge to intellectual humility is that many of us see social science content as *soft science* and therefore *value-laden* and *subjective*. On the other hand, the natural sciences such as astronomy are seen as *hard science* and therefore *value-neutral* and *objective*. Because of the presumed neutrality of the natural sciences, we are unlikely to argue with astronomy findings until we have some mastery in the field—knowing that we might not fully understand the concepts and theories presented. We are more likely to focus on gaining a basic understanding and not on whether we agree or disagree. If we perform poorly on tests, we might feel frustrated with the professor or material as being too hard but still recognize our own lack of understanding as the primary cause of the poor performance.

Yet in the study of the social sciences—and particularly when the topic is social inequality—the behavior of our imaginary astronomy student is not unusual. In fact, it can be common for students to argue with professors prior to achieving mastery of the concepts and theories presented. Furthermore, students frequently cite anecdotal evidence to support their arguments and dismiss course content prior to engaging with the research. And, unfortunately, a student who disagrees with social justice content *is* often taken seriously by classmates—even seen as a kind of hero for speaking up to the professor. Seeing the study of social inequality as a form of subjective scholarship, these students put its findings on par with their own personal opinions and dismiss it out of hand.

In academia (including the social and natural sciences), in order for an argument (e.g., how many planets there are, or whether racism exists) to be considered legitimate it must stand up to scrutiny by others who are specialists in the field. This scrutiny is called *peer review*. Peer review is the process by which theories and the research they are based on are examined by other scholars in the field who question, refine, deepen, challenge, and complicate the arguments, expanding the collective knowledge base of the field. Just as the astronomy professor's teachings are more than his personal opinions, social justice professors' teachings are more than their personal opinions. Both instructors are presenting concepts that have undergone peer review. The overall evidence, theories, arguments, and analysis presented in class are rooted in the peer review process.

> **STOP:** When we say that peer review makes an argument *legitimate*, remember that we mean this for academic contexts (such as a college or university course you might be taking). There are other forms of evidence that are legitimate (such as a person's lived experience, or collective community stories). However, academic arguments such as those we present in this book must stand up to peer review.

Most of us have seldom previously encountered—much less understood enough to disagree with—the scholars we initially read, especially in introductory critical social justice courses. Although some of us may bring important firsthand experiences to the issues (such as being a member of a particular group under study), we too can benefit from grappling with any theoretical framework before debating that framework. For the beginner, grappling with the concepts of a framework is the first step. To facilitate doing so, practice the following:

- Read the assigned material carefully. Look up vocabulary words and terminology that are new to you (e.g., if there are terms used in this chapter that you do not know, start with the book's glossary). Accept that you may need to read all or part of the material more than once. Consider reading passages out loud or taking notes of key points as you read. Practice using new terms in class.
- If there are terms or concepts you are still unsure about, ask in class. It is likely that you are not alone in your uncertainty. Assume that your instructors appreciate questions that demonstrate engagement and

curiosity, rather than apathy and silence that make it difficult to assess and address student needs.
- Strive to see the connections to ideas and concepts already studied. This will help with your recall, critical thinking (for example, by comparing and contrasting), and ability to see the big picture.
- Focus on understanding rather than agreement. Consider whether "I disagree" may actually mean "I don't understand," and if so, work on understanding. Remember, understanding a concept does not require that you agree with it.
- Practice posing questions. Because most students have been socialized to care more about getting the answers right and less about comprehension, we may fear that asking questions will reveal that we don't know the answers. Thus, we may make bold statements that lack intellectual humility. These statements could be more usefully framed as questions.
- Be patient and willing to grapple with new and difficult ideas. To "grapple with" ideas means to receive, reflect upon, practice articulating, and seek deeper understanding of them; grappling is not debate or rejection. The goal is to move us beyond the mere sharing of opinions and toward more informed engagement.

One place where grappling often falls short is in small-group work. For most instructors, the goal of small-group work is much more than students simply sharing their ideas or opinions about some subject. Rather, it's an opportunity for students to spend time critically thinking through difficult ideas with the support of others in order to deepen understanding, identify, question, and share insights. In addition to the specific prompts and questions that the instructor has given, all of the following could be taken up in small-group work:

- Asking clarifying questions of each other
- Making connections to other readings
- Identifying key concepts and defining terms
- Generating examples that illustrate the concepts under study
- Identifying patterns
- Developing questions
- Questioning relationships between concepts
- Discussing the implications for your own life and work
- Practicing articulating the ideas introduced in the course using your own words, in order to clarify and increase your comfort discussing them with others
- Identifying and discussing challenging passages

Yet instructors often encounter small groups who are merely reinforcing their previous opinions, have moved on to engage in off-topic social banter, or are sitting in silence, scanning media, or texting friends because they are "finished" discussing the topic at hand. From an academic perspective, a small group should never be "done" talking about any topic they are given. Scholars have spent their careers developing these concepts, and a limited number of class minutes is not adequate to finish working through and understanding them. If you find yourself at a standstill, work through the bulleted list above, or ask your instructor for some prompts and check in about how you are doing in your comprehension.

GUIDELINE 2: EVERYONE HAS AN OPINION. OPINIONS ARE NOT THE SAME AS INFORMED KNOWLEDGE

One of the biggest challenges to attaining Guideline 1—intellectual humility—is the emphasis placed in mainstream culture on the value of opinion. Mainstream culture has normalized the idea that because everyone has an opinion, all opinions are equally valid. For example, local news and radio shows regularly invite callers to share their opinions about questions ranging from "Do you think so-and-so is guilty?" to "Should immigration be restricted?" Reality shows invite us to vote on the best singer or dancer, implying that our opinions are equal to the opinions of professional dancers, singers, choreographers, and producers. While we *might* have an informed opinion, our response certainly does not depend on one. Thus we can easily be fooled into confusing having an *opinion* (which everyone has) with *being informed* (which few are without ongoing study).

Because of this socialization, many of us unwittingly bring the expectation for opinion-sharing into the academic classroom. However, in academia, *opinion is the weakest form of intellectual engagement*. When our comprehension is low and critical thinking skills underdeveloped, expressing our opinion is the easiest response. All of us hold opinions on a topic before we enter a course (as our astronomy student did), and these opinions don't require us to understand the issues or engage with the course readings at all. Therefore, expressing our opinions simply rehearses what we already think and doesn't require us to expand or question our ideas. If we aren't interested in reading what we have been assigned, or do not understand what we have read, the easiest thing to do is to point to a passage in the text and give a personal opinion about it (e.g., "I loved it when the author said that research has shown that men dominate because it reminded me of an experience I had. . . .") or use personal experience or opinion to reject the reading out of hand (e.g., "The author said White people have privilege. I totally disagree with that because I know someone who didn't get a job because he's White!").

Simply having an opinion is not predicated on any accounting for new information or understanding of complexity; popular opinions tend to be superficial and anecdotal and do not require that we understand an issue at all. Although someone might disagree that social injustice exists, to be credible they must root their argument in an understanding of what has already been established and demonstrate how their opinion brings new evidence for consideration. From a scholarly perspective, offering anecdotal evidence that social injustice does not exist (e.g.,

"In today's society, everyone has an equal opportunity to succeed, regardless of race, class, or gender.") is equivalent to the claim "I looked out my window and the Earth doesn't look round to me."). To argue that there is no longer social injustice and have validity, one must be aware of existing knowledge in the field. From an academic perspective, claims must stand up to scrutiny by peers who are specialists in the subject. Claims about social injustice made within the academic community have undergone this process. Although there are debates within this community, peer scholars have found the arguments to be relevant and worthy of engagement.

We would not use opinion in astronomy class to disagree with Stephen Hawking. Yet in the social justice classroom, scholars such as W.E.B. Du Bois, Paulo Freire, and bell hooks are regularly disagreed with well before their work is mastered. Consider how our astronomy student's understanding of planets—as well as his understanding of science as an ever-evolving field—could deepen if he was able to engage with current theories even if he did not yet fully understand them.

Because of these tendencies, professors who teach from a critical social justice stance sometimes "shut down" opinion-sharing (Sensoy & DiAngelo, 2014). This curtailing of the sharing of opinions in class is often perceived as breaking a social rule: "I have the right to my opinion and denying me that right is unfair." Of course we have a right to our opinions. But our classroom goal is not simply to express our preexisting opinions; our goals are to engage with scholarly ideas and develop the tools with which to gain a more complex understanding of social phenomena. Let us be clear: We *do* want students to offer opinions in order to *reflect on and examine* them; examining one's opinions is not the same as simply expressing them.

In order to move beyond your opinions, practice the following:

- Reflect on your reasons for pursuing higher education. Many students would say they are going to university or college in order to secure a good career. However, your longevity and success in that career will depend on your critical thinking skills and the depth and breadth of your general knowledge base. How might allowing your worldview to be stretched and challenged actually serve your future career interests?
- Recognize that you do not have to agree with concepts under study in order to learn from them. Let go of the idea that you must agree with a concept you are studying in order for it to be valid or worth learning.
- Practice posing open-ended questions rather than closed questions that invite yes/no responses or debate. Closed questions often begin with "Should" or "Do you agree" (e.g., "Should schools ban soda machines?" or "Do you agree that opportunity is not equal?"). The limitation of these questions is that the debate format does not leave much room for examining grey areas or grappling with complexities. Closed questions can also be answered with an easy yes or no, which prevents a nuanced engagement with complex issues.
- Practice developing quality questions. For example, using John Taylor Gatto's idea of the "seven-lesson schoolteacher" (2002), strong questions

could include: "Consider Gatto's argument that all teachers teach the seven lessons. On a continuum from 'Yes, absolutely' on one end, to 'No, absolutely not' on the other, position yourself in relation to his argument. Explain why you have positioned yourself there." Use phrases such as "Under what conditions" and "To what extent" when you ask questions. For example, "Under what conditions might we avoid teaching Gatto's lessons?" "To what extent does the school curriculum influence teacher autonomy?" Respondents would have to use the course readings to support their position. Questions connected to texts should require familiarity with the text to answer. For example, "Identify two of Gatto's seven lessons and find examples you have seen in schools." If someone can respond to the question without ever having read the text, it is not a strong question. Questions may also ask people to reimagine existing conditions. For example, "Using the readings, design the ideal classroom. Describe the guidelines for student engagement in this ideal classroom. How would the curriculum and pedagogical activities be organized? How would you assess your goals?"

GUIDELINE 3: LET GO OF ANECDOTAL EVIDENCE AND EXAMINE PATTERNS

Anecdotal evidence is evidence drawn from hearsay or personal experience, and thus anecdotal evidence is superficial, limited to interpretation, and not generalizable. For example, many of us have heard something similar to, "My cousin tried to get a job, but they hired an unqualified minority instead because they had to fill a diversity quota." Because mainstream education and media seldom teach us how social inequality works, most of the evidence we rely on to understand issues of social justice is anecdotal. But the goals of college and university classes are to expand one's ability to make sense of everyday events, issues, and incidents; in other words, to offer new and more complex sense-making systems. One of the more important academic skills we can develop is the ability to apply a new sense-making framework to something we currently make sense of using another framework.

To illustrate this concept of frameworks, imagine that you have pain in your leg and go to your doctor. Your doctor would likely examine your leg, feel the bones and muscles, and perhaps take X-rays to identify the source of the pain. If, however, you went to an alternative (from a Western perspective) medical practitioner, such as a doctor of Traditional Chinese Medicine (TCM), she might have a completely different way of examining your body and identifying the source of the pain. She may begin by looking at your tongue and examining other parts of your body. A chiropractor might not examine your leg at all but instead begin work on your spine.

If we are taking a course studying how humans understand the body and conceptualize healing, we are less interested in which practitioner is "right" and which is "wrong" in their approach to identifying the source of your pain. We are more interested in the various frameworks each practitioner uses, the scholarly community that informs the ideas that practitioner draws on, and what each framework offers us in terms of understanding how the body works and how humans conceptualize illness and healing. Just as the TCM doctor offers a new way of understanding how your body works, the critical social justice framework offers us a new way of understanding how society works.

Another popular approach many of us take when we encounter a new and unfamiliar framework is to focus on one or two exceptions in order to undermine the framework under study. For example, when reading scholarship describing racism as structural, we may cite sensational examples such as former U.S. president Barack Obama as proof that "anyone can make it." We may also use personal stories to "prove" that structural oppression doesn't exist (or has now "reversed" direction), such as in the story above about the cousin who didn't get a job and believes this is because the company had to fill a racial quota. Although it is a common White myth that peoples of Color must be (unfairly) hired over Whites, it is false and problematic for at least three reasons. First, it's misinformed because hiring quotas are actually illegal. Affirmative Action in the United States and Employment Equity in Canada are not hiring requirements, but *goals for the hiring of qualified people who are underrepresented in a given field*. Second, all of the evidence demonstrates that peoples of Color are *discriminated against* in hiring, not preferred (Alexander, 2010; Bertrand & Mullainathan, 2004; Dechief & Oreopoulos, 2012). Third, the story above rests on an embedded racist assumption that the only reason a person of Color *could* have been hired over the cousin is because of a quota and not because the person of Color was in fact more qualified, or equally qualified and brought a needed perspective that the cousin did not.

Focusing on exceptions or unanalyzed personal experiences prevents us from seeing the overall, societal patterns. While there are always exceptions to the rule, exceptions also illustrate the rule. Yes, people from oppressed groups occasionally rise to the top in dominant society. But the historical, measurable, and predictable evidence is that this is an atypical occurrence. If we focus exclusively on those exceptional occurrences, we miss the larger structural patterns. Focusing on the exceptions also precludes a more nuanced analysis of the role these exceptions play in the system overall.

The following questions offer a constructive way to engage with the course content and support Guideline 3:

- How can using a critical framework expand my understanding of these phenomena? For example, let's say you are White, are from the United States or Canada, and have spent time abroad. You have enjoyed the food and cultures of places such as China, Mexico, or Morocco, but have also felt discriminated against (ignored, stereotyped, made fun of) because you are a foreigner. Why, you might wonder, aren't the locals more open to you when you are being so open to them—maybe even learning a bit of their language? You offer this anecdote as an example that illustrates that everyone is racist in some ways. Now imagine that you are grappling with a new framework to make sense of your experience. You are studying key concepts such as Whiteness, globalization, and hegemony. How can using this framework help you contextualize your experience within larger macrodynamics and apply academic concepts?

- Am I able to identify the larger group patterns at play in any individual situation? For example, if my best friend lives with a disability, I may assume that I am outside of ableism because I am open to this friendship when others are not. Yet rather than make me exempt from ableism, how can my friendship provide me with a view into the barriers faced by persons with disabilities? How can considering overall patterns help me recognize how my friendship is situated in relation to broader social dynamics—dynamics that intentions and individual practices alone do not overcome?
- Do I recognize that when I claim that my friend's disability is not an issue in our friendship, that I am sharing my own limited perspective, because my experiences are interpreted from my perspective as someone who is considered a person without disability? What might the risks be for my friend to disagree with me or try to give me feedback on unaware ableist assumptions I may be making? Do I have the skills to respond to this feedback without defensiveness and denial? Using another example, we often hear heterosexual students make claims such as, "There was one gay guy in our school and no one had an issue with him." Yet that "one gay guy" likely has a very different memory of school. Indeed, when we have students in our classes from minoritized groups, they invariably tell us of the misery of high school and all of the unconscious attitudes and behaviors from the dominant group that they had to endure. Our anecdotes are not universal, they are from a particular perspective; they will necessarily be filtered through our blind spots and thus are not sufficient evidence.

GUIDELINE 4: USE YOUR REACTIONS AS ENTRY POINTS FOR GAINING DEEPER SELF-KNOWLEDGE

Because social justice courses directly address emotionally and politically charged issues, they can be upsetting. For many of us, this is the first time we have experienced a sustained examination of inequality—especially where we are in dominant groups. Further, much of what is presented is counter to everything we have previously been taught. In addition, these courses typically ask us to connect ourselves personally to the issues under study, triggering patterns of resistance such as those previously discussed. For those of us who have experienced inequality in key dimensions of our lives, it can be painful to see the explicit resistance and hostility of our classmates.

Although the frameworks used in these courses do not claim that people in dominant groups are "bad," many of us hear it that way because our current sense-making framework says that participation in inequality is something that only bad people do. Until we have a critical social justice framework—which requires a whole new paradigm of sense-making—we often find it difficult to remain open, especially if we are a member of a dominant group under study. Defensiveness, cognitive dissonance, and even feelings of guilt, shame, and grief are not uncommon. In some ways, these kinds of feelings indicate movement and change, and although unpleasant, they are not necessarily problematic. The key to whether these feelings play a constructive or destructive role lies in what we do with them. We can, of course, use them as "proof" that the class content and approach is "wrong" and reject all that we are being taught. But there is no growth for us in this reaction. Rather than allow these emotions to block our growth, we can use them as entry points into greater self and content knowledge.

Conversely, where we belong to minoritized groups, these courses can surface emotions for different reasons. Feelings such as anger, frustration, shame, grief, and the sense that we are under a spotlight are common and can also get in the way of our academic development. However, the analysis, evidence, and conceptual language offered by social justice education can provide the tools with which to challenge the relations of oppression that lead to these feelings. Indeed, the evidence and analysis presented should reveal that the challenges you have faced are not due to your own individual shortcomings but are in large part the product of socially organized structural barriers. As such, these barriers can be identified and acted against. In this way, rather than reinforcing a sense of hopelessness and immobilization, courses such as this have the potential to empower people to make change.

Returning to our astronomy student, we can see that upon receiving information that challenged his worldview, he was unable to use his emotional reactions constructively. Instead, he categorically rejected the information, ending with a somewhat nonsensical claim that Pluto was still a planet, even if it was shaped like a banana. This is the equivalent to claiming that "I treat people the same regardless of whether they are red, yellow, green, purple, polka-dotted, or zebra-striped." Simplistic platitudes often surface when we are faced with evidence that fundamentally challenges our worldviews. For example, that racism not only exists but is systemic and implicates everyone is a difficult idea for many of us. But popular platitudes such as "I don't care if you're purple" are problematic for at least two reasons: First, colorblindness is not actually possible—we *do* in fact see race and it *does* have social meaning and consequences. Second, people do not come in these colors and so claims about green, purple and polka-dotted people render discussions about race ridiculous and trivialize the realities of racism.

Social justice content can trigger strong reactions, but these reactions can be constructive if we use them as entry points to deeper self-awareness, rather than as exit points from further engagement.

Practice the following approaches to the course content in support of Guideline 4:

- How does considering the course content or an author's analysis challenge or expand the way I see the world?

- How have I been shaped by the issues the author is addressing? For example, if the author is talking about the experiences of the poor and I was raised middle-class, what does the contrast between our experiences help me see about what it means to have been raised middle-class?
- What about my life in relation to my race/class/gender might make it difficult for me to see or validate this new perspective?
- What do my reactions reveal about what I perceive is at risk were I to accept this information?
- If I were to accept this information as valid, what might be ethically required of me?

GUIDELINE 5: RECOGNIZE HOW YOUR SOCIAL POSITION INFORMS YOUR REACTIONS TO YOUR INSTRUCTOR AND THE COURSE CONTENT

Positionality is the concept that our perspectives are based on our place in society. Positionality recognizes that where you stand in relation to others within a stratified society shapes what you can see and understand about yourself in relation to others. For example, if I am considered a person without disability, my position in a society that devalues people with disabilities limits my understanding of the barriers people with disabilities face. I simply won't see these barriers, in large part because I don't have to—society is structured to accommodate the way I use my body.

> **Positionality:** The recognition that where you stand in relation to others within a stratified society shapes what you can see and understand about yourself in relation to others. Positionality recognizes the power of socialization and considers our standpoint from the group—or collective—perspective, rather than regarding our perspective as simply personal or unique.

Guideline 5 addresses the *perception* that the content of this class, or any class covering social science or controversial matters, is subjective, value-based, and political, while the content of other courses (like science or math) is objective, value-neutral, and nonpartisan. We discussed this perception under Guideline 3 as it relates to common views on the social sciences. Here we want to consider this perception using the lens of positionality as it relates to the instructors of these courses. Because instructors of critical social justice content are more likely to *name* their positionality and encourage students to do the same, they are often seen as biased. Mainstream courses rarely if ever name the positionality of the texts they study (for example, the idea that Columbus discovered America is from the colonizer's perspective, but certainly not from the perspective of Indigenous peoples). Unfortunately, because acknowledging one's positionality is a rare occurrence in mainstream courses, doing so in courses on critical social justice reinforces students' perceptions of mainstream courses as objective and critical social justice courses as subjective. Yet all content is taught from a particular perspective; the power of dominant knowledge depends in large part on its presentation as neutral and universal (Kincheloe, 2008).

In order to understand the concept of knowledge as never purely objective, neutral, and outside of human interests, it is important to distinguish between discoverable laws of the natural world (such as the law of gravity) and knowledge, which is framed by the ideologies, language, beliefs, and customs of human societies. Even the field of science is subjective (the study of this subjectivity is known as the sociology of science). Consider scientific research and how and when it is conducted. Which subjects are funded and which are not (e.g., the moon's atmosphere, nuclear power, wind power, atmospheric pollution, or stem cells)? Who finances various types of research (private corporations, nonprofits, or the government)? Who is invested in the results of the research (e.g., for-profit pharmaceutical companies, the military, or nonprofit organizations)? How do these investments drive what is studied and how? How will the research findings be used? Who has access to the benefits of the research? As you can see, these are not neutral questions—they are always political, and they frame how knowledge is created, advanced, and circulated. Because of this, knowledge is never value-neutral.

Many educators use the metaphor of a fish in water to capture the all-encompassing dimensions of culture. A fish is born into water and so simply experiences the water as one with itself; a fish has no way of knowing that it is actually separate from the water. Although the fish *is* separate, it still cannot survive without water. In the same way that a fish cannot live without water, we cannot make sense of the world without the meaning-making system that our culture provides. Yet this system is hard to see because we have always been "swimming" within it; we just take for granted that what we see is real, rather than a particular perception of reality. Social justice educators name our positionality—the currents and waters we swim in—in order to make the political nature of knowledge visible and to challenge the claim that any knowledge is neutral. Yet, ironically, that naming is often used to reinforce the idea that social justice content and those who present it are driven by personal agendas and special interests, and thus less legitimate.

Because instructors who teach critical social justice courses often belong to minoritized groups and because they name these groups, they can be perceived as having a personal bias; they are viewed as if they only teach these courses because they are "minorities" and have an "axe to grind." When instructors can be dismissed as simply "pushing their personal agendas," students often feel more comfortable to explicitly disagree with the curriculum and pedagogy. Indeed, this challenge further illustrates how unimaginable our example of the astronomy student is. The instructor in our scenario is most likely a White male, as is the vast majority of higher education faculty (Espinosa et al., 2019; Henry, 2015; Kobayashi, 2018; Mohamed & Beagan, 2019). White males overall hold more social authority and are seen as more objective, and thus students are less likely to argue with them

(Griffin, 2020; La Salle et al., 2020). That, along with the presumed neutral content of a subject like astronomy, means students respond to this instructor and the course as though they were value-neutral. In contrast, because the positionality of a woman of Color professor who teaches a social justice course is named, both she and the course are presumed to be value-driven.

One or two courses in our college or university schooling are not enough to brainwash us or deny us the ability to think freely. In fact, the opposite is true: The more depth, perspective, and complexity we can bring to bear on how we and others view and understand the world, the clearer, more nuanced, and ultimately freer our thinking can become. Returning to our astronomy student, it isn't necessary for his positionality to align with the instructor's in order for him to consider the framework the instructor is using.

The following practices support Guideline 5:

- Identify your social positionality (e.g., your race, class, gender) and stay attentive to how it informs your response to the course context. What limitations of awareness might you have as a result of that positionality? What are the things you can and can't see based on the social positions you hold or don't hold?
- Recognize the perspectives embedded in all texts (such as textbooks, newspaper articles, and TV news), especially those that don't explicitly name them. Are the ideas presented as if they have no perspective and apply universally to all people, regardless of social positionality? If so, practice seeking out and considering alternative perspectives informed by a range of positionalities.
- As you study the content of your course, it is important for you to continuously consider the interplay between your positionality and that of your instructor. If the instructor represents perspectives from key minoritized groups (women, peoples of Color, persons with disabilities, LGBTQ+ people), you could welcome the opportunity to hear perspectives seldom represented in mainstream education. Support the course for the opportunity it offers, rather than undermining it because the concepts are unfamiliar, uncomfortable, or difficult.

GRADING

Grading in a course whose primary goal is to challenge social stratification is not without irony. Activist and scholar Audre Lorde (1984) captures this irony when she says, "The master's tools will never dismantle the master's house." By this she means that in using the tools of the system we are more likely to uphold that system than to challenge it. As instructors, we recognize that by grading we are upholding an institution that ranks students hierarchically—and such hierarchies are what we seek to challenge. Still, many of us choose to work within systems despite their constraints, so that we may better challenge them. The traditional grading system is one of those constraints we must work within.

Mainstream schooling places a tremendous emphasis on grades, and the prevalence of high-stakes testing has only intensified this emphasis. Grades convey powerful ideas about our presumed intellectual abilities, and these ideas influence what education we will have access to (through tracking into gifted or special programs and ability grouping). We are placed into academic tracks as early as 1st grade and these tracks have very real consequences for the kinds of careers we will have access to later in life (Anyon, 1981; Oakes, 1985). Thus an understandable but regrettable outcome of tracking based on grades in K–12 schooling is that we may care more about the grades we receive than about the learning we achieve.

The focus on grades often shapes our very identities and sense of self-worth, further complicating the dynamics of grading. This identity is often reinforced outside of school as we earn praise or punishment from our families based on our grades. While some students who have not been successful within this system come to feel fortunate just to earn a C, students who have generally been successful by the measure of grades often feel entitled to As. It is not uncommon for these students to claim, "I am an A student!" Students with such an identity may feel frustrated—even personally slighted—when receiving grades that challenge this identity.

Although we as instructors are aware of the complexities and contradictions of grading, we are also deeply invested in student comprehension of the course concepts. The grading system is one of the primary tools we must use to both measure and communicate our assessment of this comprehension. We encourage students to keep the following in mind when considering the dynamics of grading:

In Order to Grade Comprehension, Instructors Must See Demonstration of Comprehension. Whether in assignments or in class participation and discussion, we must *demonstrate* understanding. Comprehension can be demonstrated in written, verbal, and active forms (such as presentations and projects).

Assessing comprehension verbally is generally done through class discussions and question and answer sessions. However, assessing comprehension verbally can be challenging for instructors if students don't speak up in class. For example, how many times have you witnessed your instructor posing a question to the whole class only to be met by silence? Looking out into a room full of students, most of whom are not responding, instructors are left to assume that these students cannot answer the question. Students sometimes say later that they did not respond because the answer was "so obvious" that it did not require a response. Yet how can our instructors know that we understand if we do not respond when questions are posed in class, even if the answers to those questions seem obvious?

Another common explanation for silence is that someone has already said what we were thinking. Yet from an instructor's perspective, it is fine to repeat (or better yet, to build on) an idea that another student has already stated. No two people will say it exactly alike, and it is important to practice articulating these concepts in your own words in order to develop your critical social justice literacy. Any statement can be expanded, deepened, or in other ways supported. At the minimum, if students build on what others have said, instructors can gain a sense of how many students are thinking similarly or struggling with understanding key ideas. This is valuable information for instructors in terms of assessing the collective understanding of the group as well as the comprehension levels of individual students. For these reasons, we encourage students to give some kind of verbal response when asked questions in class, even if it is to say that one does not know, is not sure, or only has a partial answer.

In regard to demonstrating understanding in written work, we evaluate this work by assessing how well written, organized, and clear it is, and how well the submitted work meets the goals of the assignment. The work should at minimum be proofread for errors, avoid colloquialisms, conform to a standard style of citation, use inclusive language, and stay within the guidelines of the assignment description. These are all baseline indicators of the degree of student achievement in a written assignment. Perceptive integration of course readings and lectures in a student's own words, relevant use of examples, and insightful connections can transform an adequately written assignment into an excellent (or "A") assignment. These criteria are usually communicated to students in either the course syllabus or assignment description. In order to most accurately grade comprehension, we must see evidence of comprehension in both verbal participation and written work.

Effort Is Not the Same as Understanding. When students are worried about their grades or are making a case for the grade they believe they should receive, they often claim that they "worked really hard." These students feel that they should be rewarded for that hard work with an A. The reason this argument rarely makes much headway with instructors is because we are grading student *demonstration* of understanding of content, not the perceived degree of effort expended to achieve it.

Consider this analogy: I am taking swimming lessons. My goal is to compete in an upcoming match. I see myself as putting in a lot of effort by making the time to show up for practice, following my coach's instructions, and swimming the number of laps I am assigned. My coach, however, expects that I will attend lessons and complete my practice sessions; thus, they are focused on other things, such as how I hold my body while swimming, my breathing pattern, hip and shoulder movements, smoothness of stroke, and speed. In the end, my coach will determine whether I am ready to compete. This determination will be made based on my demonstrated ability that I am ready, regardless of the degree of effort it takes me to reach that point, and certainly not on the mere fact that I showed up for my lessons and got in the pool.

Some students feel that showing up to class, listening, and handing in assignments are evidence of a level of effort that should be rewarded with an A. For instructors, this level of effort qualifies as the minimum expectation for all students. Still, we are not grading on how hard a student works but on the outcome of that work.

The following are common student rationales we hear for why they should get a grade higher than what was assessed:

> "I worked really hard."
> "I am an A student."
> "I came to all the classes."

"I listened."
"I spent hours doing the readings."
"I talked in class discussions."
"I handed in all my assignments."
"I have never thought about these things before."
"I'm really interested in these issues."
"I've had other courses like this one so I already know all this."
"I have to get a good grade or I will have to drop out."
"I have been going through a lot of personal issues this semester."
"I learned so much in this class."

Student rationales such as these are familiar to many instructors, and we understand that they are driven by genuine anxieties about grades. However, we urge our students to challenge this anxiety because it thwarts the process of authentic learning.

A final note on grading: Students often believe that the reason they received a poor grade was because the instructor didn't like something they said in class, or because they disagreed with the instructor. Every institution has an appeal process for students who feel they have not been graded fairly by an instructor. This makes it very difficult to lower a student's grade just because of something they said. While classroom assessments have some degree of subjectivity, an instructor must be able to account for a grade they gave in terms of guidelines for the assignment, as well as in terms that are clear to a mediating third party. Because of this accountability requirement, an instructor's grading criteria are usually clearly stated in the syllabus or on assignments.

CONCLUSION

Many college and university courses provide opportunities that are rare in any other dimension of life: critical engagement with new ideas; opportunity to hear and consider multiple perspectives; expansion of our capacity to understand and talk about complex social issues; guidance in the examination of our identities, socialization, and meaning-making frameworks; and tools to work toward a more just society. A fixation on grades minimizes these opportunities. We find that students who let go of their attachment to grades and put their energy into sincerely grappling with the content tend to do well. Worrying about grades detracts from the ability to focus on content and can become a kind of self-fulfilling prophecy. The following reflection questions may be useful in lessening this attachment:

- Am I willing to consider that I may not be qualified to assess my performance in a course, especially one in which new concepts are being introduced?
- Do I expect an A in all of my courses, and if so, why? Is it because I have always received As, or is it because I demonstrate mastery of course concepts?

- When I ask my instructor, "How am I doing?" am I asking them to provide me with valuable feedback about what my performance conveys about my comprehension and how it might be improved, or am I asking them to tell me what grade I will receive?

We sincerely hope that our students find our courses valuable in terms of the knowledge and insight gained. It has been our experience that this is most likely achieved when students focus more on mastery of content than on the final grade.

DISCUSSION QUESTIONS

1. If I weren't worried about my grade, how would my engagement in this course change?
2. Which of the various guidelines detailed in this essay are the most challenging to me, and why? How can I meet these challenges?
3. What degree of responsibility am I willing to take for getting the most out of this course (e.g., coming to class prepared and having completed the reading, engaging in large-group discussions, not dominating discussions, asking questions for clarity, and using academic rather than colloquial discourse)?
4. What degree of responsibility am I willing to take to support my peers in getting the most from this course (e.g., engaging in discussions, not dominating discussions, listening respectfully when others speak and building on their ideas, taking the small-group discussions seriously, coming to class prepared and having completed the reading)?
5. Many students think about higher education solely as a stepping stone to employment, and thus the only content deemed worthwhile is what is directly connected to getting a job. We ask you to consider what other kinds of skills higher education can provide, and how these skills are also connected to future employment. If you think beyond a strictly vocational approach, what skills do citizens in a global democracy need? How are these skills also important to any future work you do?

EXTENSION ACTIVITY

Read the October 24, 2024, *New York Times* article by Matt Kaplan, "How Many Continents Are There? You May Not Like the Answers" (https://www.nytimes.com/2024/10/30/science/earth-continents-geology-research.html). In your own words, explain how the problem of defining the continents illustrates why what we learned in the past and the opinions we formed based on that information are not sufficient evidence.

CHAPTER 2

About Knowledge

"I know it's true, I saw it on the news."
"Antifa is just as violent as the KKK."

The word critical *has negative connotations in everyday speech. But in academia it has a very specific and useful meaning. We begin this chapter with an introduction to the concept of knowledge as* socially constructed. *We then describe "critical" as used in academia to refer to knowledge and thinking. We explain the theoretical perspective known as "Critical Theory" and its relationship to social justice. We close with a discussion of applying these concepts in practice.*

> **Vocabulary to practice using:** ideology; critical theory; social stratification; positionality; socially constructed; positivism

Many of the concepts we present in this book are politically and emotionally charged. In order to help readers engage with these concepts most effectively, this chapter will review what it means to take a critical (as opposed to layperson's) perspective.

KNOWLEDGE AS SOCIALLY CONSTRUCTED

Knowledge is never neutral. In other words, knowledge is *socially constructed*. Consider a question asked by many philosophers: *How do you know what you know?* Take a moment to reflect on or write down how you would answer that question yourself. If you can ask the people around you for their answers, see if you notice any themes or patterns.

It is likely that phrases like "I know how to X because I was taught by my parents" or "The meaning of X is something I learned in school" come up for most people. Perhaps you also notice the terms "read," "watched," or "experienced." But we cannot make sense of what we read or experience without the meaning-making frameworks taught to us early in life. For example, you might discover through experience that people die from cancer, or through observation that the sun rises and sets in predictable ways. But the meaning you make from that experience or observation has consequences, and those consequences vary depending on the meaning you make. If, for example, you think the sun is a deity that must be worshipped to ensure it provides its life-giving power, that will shape your daily actions and rituals. Consider the difference between knowing that prayer *can* cure cancer and knowing that prayer *can't* cure cancer. These ways of knowing profoundly shape our responses to cancer and the outcomes that result. Another common response to the question of how we know what we know will be "I read about it" or "I studied it." But of course what we read or study is not neutral. Is my source for how I think about cancer the King James Bible or *Prevention Magazine*?

Even what we think of as facts are dependent upon the belief systems of a time and place. The authors of this textbook were taught that there were nine planets, and that was a fact. Today students are taught that there are eight, and that is a fact. The presence of the celestial body we call Pluto did not change, but the criteria for what constitutes a planet—what Pluto *means*—did. Those criteria are human-made, but whether Pluto is or isn't a planet is still considered a fact. Of course, this fact is also subject to a particular cultural viewpoint.

As another example, the authors are writing this edition of your textbook from two different time zones. So is it 9:00 a.m. right now, or 5:00 p.m.? Which fact is true? Both are, depending on the place in which they are measured. Even the measurement itself—specific increments of minutes and hours—represents a particular framework of meaning, in this case a Western industrial one.

> **STOP:** To understand knowledge as socially constructed is not the same as descending into meaninglessness wherein nothing is real or matters. The point is that the lens you apply to a problem will shape how you see the problem and the strategies you use to address it, and that these lenses are connected to our social positions in society and must be taken into account.

Our answers to the question *How do you know what you know?* illustrate an important concept—that knowledge is *produced*, not static or unchanging. Given that the transmission of knowledge is an integral activity in schools, critical scholars in the field of education have been especially concerned with *how* knowledge is produced and whose interests that production serves. These scholars argue that the claim that some knowledge is objective, neutral, and universal while other knowledge is subjective, biased, and singular is one key way that injustice is reproduced. They question the idea that objectivity is even desirable, much less possible. The term used to capture this way of thinking about knowledge is to believe that knowledge is *socially constructed*. When we refer to knowledge as socially constructed we mean that knowledge reflects the values and interests of those who produce it and is tied to a social context.

Teaching from an understanding that knowledge as socially constructed is often described as engaging with "critical" forms of teaching—critical thinking, critical pedagogy, critical social justice. The term *critical* has several meanings. The mainstream usage is *to find fault*, to judge, or to criticize. However, in academic uses, *critical* refers to the skill of analysis. *Critical thinking* means to think with complexity, to go below the surface when considering an issue. *Critical theory* (as an academic field of study you may have heard of) refers to a specific body of scholarship that is foundational to the ability to think critically. Critical theory offers various frameworks for analyzing social conditions within their historical, cultural, and ideological contexts so that we might find more effective and nuanced solutions to social problems.

From this foundation, critical educators guide students along at least three fronts:

1. *Critical analysis* of knowledge claims that are presented as objective, neutral, and universal; for example, that Christopher Columbus discovered America
2. *Critical self-reflection* about their own social perspective and subjectivity; for example, how the Columbus myth and the teacher's racial identity influence what they know and teach about the history of North America
3. *Critical action* through the development of the skills needed in order to contribute to a more equitable society; for example, have students rewrite existing school lesson plans or curricula to reflect the complexities of the myth of discovery and the political investments in this myth

In these ways educators who teach from a critical perspective guide their students in an examination of the relationship between who they are and what they know. Of course this is no easy task because for many Westerners the ideal of *positivism* (that European science follows rules and thus its findings are objective and indisputable) is deeply entrenched.

> **Positivism:** A paradigm that views the scientific method as objective, neutral, and value-free, and thus the only credible way to study the world.

It is challenging to guide people in a critical examination of knowledge that they have assumed was beyond question. Thus critical educators often begin with a reflection on students' own social positions and the relationship between those positions and the perspectives they have on knowledge claims. As discussed in Chapter 1, this form of reflection is termed *positionality* and is the recognition that what we know is dependent upon a complex web of cultural values, beliefs, experiences, and social positions. Positionality is a key entry point into understanding how knowledge is socially constructed. For example, a student's perspective on whether their grade is fair is likely to be different from the perspective of the teacher who grades them. A doctor trained in Western allopathic medicine is likely to have a different perspective on the effectiveness of acupuncture than a doctor trained in traditional Chinese naturopathic methods.

James Banks is a scholar in education who has made significant contributions to the understanding of how knowledge is socially constructed. Banks (1996) explains that the knowledge we create is influenced by our experiences within various social, economic, and political systems. Thus who we are (as knowers) is intimately connected to our group socializations (including our gender, race, class, and sexuality). For example, consider the Columbus story. Whose racial perspective is reflected in the idea that the continent was "discovered"? Which racial groups may be invested in this story? Which racial groups may be invested in challenging it? Asking questions such as these develops a clearer picture of how *what* you know is connected to *who* you are and *where* you stand.

Banks's knowledge typology has become a classic framework used by critical educators to help unravel how knowledge is validated. According to Banks, there are five types of knowledge:

Personal and cultural knowledge refers to the explanations and interpretations people acquire from their personal experiences in their homes, with their family and community cultures. Personal and cultural knowledge is transferred both explicitly, as in direct lessons taught by family members on what constitutes politeness (e.g., "make eye contact with your elders"), as well as implicitly through messages such as what isn't talked about (e.g., race or money).

Popular knowledge refers to the facts, beliefs, and various character and plot types that are institutionalized within television, movies, social media, and other forms of popular culture. Concepts such as the ideal family, normal relationships, and which kinds of neighborhoods are dangerous are all standardized through ongoing representations in popular culture. Because popular knowledge is widely shared, it serves as a common vocabulary and reference point. For instance, you might remember what hobbies and activities you engaged in during the COVID-19 pandemic and the global shutdown. If you asked someone what they did during that time, many people would know what you were referring to and be able to answer your question.

Mainstream academic knowledge refers to the concepts, paradigms, theories, and explanations that make up established knowledge in the behavioral and social sciences. This type of knowledge is based on the belief that there is an objective truth and that with the right procedures and methods it is possible to attain this truth. For example, many university courses teach theories that explain the psychological, physical, and intellectual development of children as a cohesive group. This development is said to occur through predictable stages that can be named, studied, and applied to all children, regardless of socioeconomic status, race, or gender identity.

School knowledge refers to the facts and concepts presented in textbooks, teachers' guides, and other aspects of the formal curriculum designed for use in schools. School knowledge also refers to teachers' interpretations of that knowledge. A critical component of school knowledge is not only what *is* taught, both explicitly and implicitly, but also what *is not* taught. School knowledge can also be thought of as *canonized knowledge* that has been approved or officially sanctioned by the state, for example, through textbooks or standardized tests. Many students are socialized not to question the textbook, but rather to accept it uncritically. Questioning school knowledge is often penalized by school authority figures. These penalties, via lower grades, test scores, tracking, reprimand, and other forms of censure and punishment, have deep and lasting consequences.

Transformative academic knowledge refers to the concepts and explanations that challenge mainstream academic knowledge and that expand the canon. Transformative academic knowledge questions the idea that knowledge can ever be outside of human interests, perspectives, and values. Proponents of transformative academic knowledge assume that knowledge is not neutral and that it reflects the social hierarchies of a given society. Transformative academic knowledge recognizes that the social groups we belong to (such as race, class, and gender) necessarily shape our frame of reference and give us a particular—not a universal—perspective. Therefore, each of us has insight into some dimensions of social life but has limited understanding in others.

RESEARCH ON KNOWLEDGE AS SOCIALLY CONSTRUCTED

Let's examine knowledge construction through a specific example. In what is considered to be a seminal study on social class, Jean Anyon (1981) asked elementary-aged students to respond to variations on the simple question *What is knowledge?* Their answers revealed that their definitions were largely dependent on which social class positions they held (see Figure 2.1).

Children who attended schools that served primarily poor and working-class families most often said that knowledge was "remembering things," "answering questions," and "doing pages in our workbooks." Children who attended affluent schools serving primarily upper-class families said things such as "you think up ideas and then find things wrong with those ideas," "it's when you know things really well," and "figuring out things."

As can be seen from these responses, how these students conceptualized knowledge was shaped by the intersection between their social class and the institution of schooling. This institution provides students with very different education based on their position in society and the resources they have access to. This is profoundly significant because the kind of knowledge we receive in schools has concrete implications for our later positions in life (Hunt & Seiver, 2017; Yendell et al., 2024).

As these children's answers reveal, what we know and how we know it are not fixed or universal. What we know is socially constructed. In turn, the lens we use to view a problem—such as the persistence of social inequality—will shape how

About Knowledge

Figure 2.1. Jean Anyon Study

Question	Working-class schools	Middle-class schools	Affluent professional schools
What is knowledge?	"To know stuff." "Doing pages in our books and things." "Worksheets." "You answer questions." "To remember things."	"To remember." "You learn facts and history." "It's smartness." "Knowledge is something you learn."	"You think up ideas and then find things wrong with those ideas." "It's when you know something really well." "A way of learning, of finding out things." "Figuring out stuff."
Where does knowledge come from?	"Teachers." "Books." "The Board of Ed." "Scientists."	"Teachers." "From old books." "From scientists." "Knowledge comes from everywhere." "You hear other people talk with the big words."	"People and computers." "Your head." "People—what they do." "Something you learn." "From going places."
Could you make knowledge, and if so, how?	No. (15) Yes. (1) Don't know. (4) One girl said, "No, because the Board of Ed makes knowledge."	No. (9) Yes. (11) "I'd look it up." "You can make knowledge by listening and doing what you're told." "I'd go to the library." "By doing extra credit."	No. (4) Yes. (16) "You can make knowledge if you invent something." "I'd think of something to discover, then I'd make it." "You can go explore for new things."

we see that problem and the strategies we use to address it. What scholarly research on knowledge as socially constructed has offered is a way to trace the workings of society from the past into the present (to see its roots) and based on that understanding, offer ways it might work better for more of us; to see, for example, who's been included and who hasn't, and to ask how we can remedy that exclusion.

From a critical social justice perspective, there are typically two dimensions of thinking critically about knowledge: first, assessing new information as it is revealed, and second, placing that information in a sociocultural and historical context—in other words, working to understand what *meaning* different groups of people give to that knowledge and what the consequences of that meaning are. This determination includes assessing the investment various groups may have in furthering or challenging those meanings in any particular historical moment. For example, there was a time when it was not widely understood that the Earth is round. Common sense might tell us that it is flat, and anyone looking out over a vast landscape would have this sense confirmed. Yet when scientific reasoning and more accurate technological methods for measuring the Earth emerged, the knowledge or "fact" that the Earth is flat was rewritten so that now we teach students that the Earth is spherical—or round.

Thus one dimension of thinking critically about knowledge is *the acquisition* of new information that may challenge our common sense (such as looking out the window and seeing what we believe is a flat landscape). In other words, to think critically means to continuously seek out the information that lies beyond our commonsense ideas about the world. Yet knowledge also involves understanding *the meaning* given to information (such as the meaning given to the journeys of explorers such as Columbus that are presumed to have debunked the idea of a flat Earth). We must understand what the political investments are in that meaning—in other words, who benefits from that knowledge claim and whose lives are limited by it?

Thus, thinking critically not only requires constantly seeking out new knowledge, but also understanding the historical and cultural context in which knowledge is produced, validated, and circulated. For example, while many might believe (and were perhaps taught in school) that people thought the Earth was flat until Columbus set sail for India, the reality is that many civilizations knew the Earth was round prior to Columbus. These civilizations included the ancient Greeks, Muslim astronomers, early Christian theologians, ancient Indian scholars, and Maya, Aztec, and Inca Indigenous peoples of what is today known as North, Central, and South America. Why, then, are we so familiar with the idea that everyone believed in a flat Earth until Columbus set sail? What are the cultural, political, and social investments in fostering this idea?

Considering the first dimension of thinking critically (acquisition of new information), we would first seek new knowledge about other societies and their contributions (such as ancient Indigenous, Indian, and Islamic scientists). Now considering the second dimension of thinking critically (the meaning given to that "flat Earth until Columbus" knowledge), we would ask questions about the social and historical context of that knowledge. For example, in what contexts has the knowledge of societies other than European been hidden? Critical thinkers might argue that obscuring this knowledge promotes the idea of progress as a line moving from ancient and non-European societies (Indigenous, Indian, Islamic) to European and then to North American societies.

Practicing thinking critically helps us see the role of ideology in the construction of knowledge about progress. It challenges the belief that knowledge is simply the result of a rational, objective, and value-neutral process, one that is removed from any political agenda. The notion of value-free (or objective) knowledge was central to rationalizing the colonization of other lands and peoples that began in the 15th century. For example, if we believe that Columbus was simply an explorer and trader, we reinforce the idea of discovery as outside of political and economic interests. The promotion of this idea has allowed dominant culture to ignore the genocide of Indigenous peoples and the transatlantic slave trade that his "discoveries" set in motion.

Just as our commonsense understanding would have had us convinced that the Earth is flat (validated by looking out our windows), many of the arguments that we make in this book may also counter commonsense understandings. For example, common sense would tell us that because we do not believe in discrimination, we do not engage in it. However, most discrimination is unconscious and takes place whether we intend to discriminate or not, despite genuinely held beliefs in fairness and equity. If we think critically about this idea that we do not discriminate, we will discover that this belief is inaccurate. There is a great deal of research in the dynamics of discrimination that demonstrates again and again the power of discrimination to elude conscious awareness (Dovidio et al., 2005; Greenwald & Krieger, 2006). Were we to consider the impact of the idea that we do not discriminate, we might discover that this idea actually allows discrimination to continue. Thus those who benefit from societal patterns of discrimination may be invested in not understanding the actual nature of discrimination.

APPLYING CRITICAL THEORY

Mastery of critical theory requires ongoing study and practice. However, even a preliminary understanding of its principles can offer tools for thinking critically about knowledge.

When we are ready to apply critical thinking to a specific social problem—for example, "If so many of us believe everyone is equal, why is inequality so persistent?"—we will need a set of tools or lenses. Academics have developed just such a set of lenses termed *critical theory*.

Critical theory refers to a body of interdisciplinary scholarship (from sociology, psychology, philosophy, political science) that examines how society works, and is a tradition that emerged in the 1930s from a group of mostly Jewish scholars at the Institute for Social Research in Frankfurt, Germany (because of this, the origin of this body of scholarship is sometimes called "the Frankfurt School"). These theorists set out to examine how society worked and to offer a productive critique that was engaged with questions about social betterment (Celikates & Flynn, 2023). Their work was guided by the belief that society should work toward the ideals of equality.

Many influential scholars worked at the Institute, and many other influential scholars came later but worked in the Frankfurt School tradition. You may recognize the names of some of these scholars, such as Max Horkheimer, Theodor Adorno, Jürgen Habermas, Walter Benjamin, and Herbert Marcuse. Their scholarship is important because it is part of a body of knowledge that builds on other social scientists' ideas: Emile Durkheim's research questioning the infallibility of the scientific method, Karl Marx's analyses of capital and social stratification, and Max Weber's analyses of capitalism and ideology. All of these strands of thought "talked to" and built on one another. For example, scientific method (sometimes referred to as "positivism"—the idea that everything can be rationally observed without bias) was the dominant contribution of the 18th-century Enlightenment period in Europe. Positivism itself was a response and challenge to religious or theological explanations for reality. It rested on the importance of reason (not just blind faith) as a principle of rational thought, the infallibility of close observation, and the discovery of natural laws and principles governing life and society. Critical theory developed in part as a response to the dominance and presumed infallibility of scientific method, and asked questions about whose rationality and whose presumed objectivity underlies scientific methods.

> **STOP:** From a critical social justice framework, informed knowledge does not refer exclusively to academic scholarship but also includes the lived experiences and perspectives that marginalized groups bring to bear on an issue, due to their insider standing. However, scholarship can provide useful language with which marginalized groups can frame their experiences within the broader society.

Efforts among scholars to understand how society works weren't limited to the Frankfurt School; French philosophers (notably Jacques Derrida, Michel Foucault, Pierre Bourdieu, and Jacques Lacan) were also grappling with similar questions (this broader European development of critical theory is sometimes called "the continental school" or "continental philosophy"). As many of the Jewish scholars of the Frankfurt School worked in exile during World War II at universities in the United States, their works were taken up by English-speaking scholars. Their ideas on concepts such as alienation, ideology, injustice, and oppression merged in the North American context of the 1960s with antiwar, feminist, gay rights, Black Power, the Indigenous Peoples' Red Power Movement, the Chicano Movement, disability rights, and other movements for social justice and human rights (Celikates & Flynn, 2023).

Many of these movements initially advocated for a type of liberal humanism (individualism, freedom, and peace) but quickly turned to a rejection of liberal humanism. The logic of individual autonomy that underlies liberal humanism (the idea that people are free to make independent rational decisions that determine their own fate) was viewed as a mechanism for keeping the marginalized in their place by obscuring larger structural systems of inequality. In other words, it fooled people into believing that they had more freedom and choice than societal structures actually allow, and that if they did not rise up in society, it was simply due to their own choices rather than any structural barriers. These activists critiqued societal structures and argued that social institutions were organized in ways that perpetuated the marginalization of women and of Black, Indigenous, Chicano, disabled, and LGBTQ+ peoples. They were primarily led by young revolutionaries, and their ideas were in part informed by the theoretical and scholarly literature they were studying in universities. The politics of the social justice movements aligned with academic research showing that society is structured in ways that marginalize some to the benefit of others.

> **STOP:** "I'm looking out the window and there's a rock there. What do you mean there's no human objectivity? A rock is a rock. I see it with my eyes." Yes, you see a rock, but the meaning, placement, and function of the rock are dependent upon human subjectivity—what you believe about what a rock is and where it should be; what you have been taught about rocks. For example, when is a rock an expensive gem and when is it something you toss aside to clear a path? When does a rock add beauty to your home and when does it make your home dirty?

This broad-brush sketch of critical theory is not the whole story. Critical theory neither begins in Europe nor ends in the United States. Critical theory's attention to analyzing how society works continues to expand and deepen as theorists from Indigenous, postcolonial, racialized, and other marginalized perspectives add layers to our collective understanding. It is actually the objective of critical theorists to contextualize social movements, to trace their trajectory across history and time, and to respond to ongoing cultural changes and phenomena. To examine and explain social movements doesn't require one to agree with or support them, but asks us to seek to deepen and expand our understanding of what is going on in a particular cultural moment, why, and what the consequences might be. For example, early theorists grappled with the worldwide rise of fascism and critical theorists today grapple with the worldwide rise of White nationalism worldwide. To engage in a study of society from a critical perspective, one must move beyond common sense–based opinions and begin to grapple with all the layers that these various, complex, and sometimes divergent traditions offer.

Many people outside of academia find theory—critical or otherwise—uninteresting. Theory often seems unnecessarily dense and abstract, far removed from our everyday lives. But, in fact, all of us operate from theory. Whenever we ask "how" or "why" about anything, we are engaged in theorizing; theory can be conceptualized as the learned cultural maps we follow to navigate and make sense of our lives and new things we encounter. Everything we do in the world (our actions) is guided by a worldview (our theory).

> **STOP:** Some may say, "Liberal universities are part of the problem. They've become too focused on identity politics and teaching students to hyper-focus on their victimhood rather than on knowledge and skills they need for life and work." Of course, universities exist within societies (not outside of them) and thus are not infallible nor immune from problematic social acts. However, while it may be a convenient talking point and easy strategy to dismiss critical ideas by calling them simple identity politics or "wokeness," these ideas come from generations of scholarly study and as such deserve respectful consideration (not necessarily agreement). What might it mean to see society structured in the way critical theorists suggest?

If you are a teacher, you might believe that theory is irrelevant to your practice, but let's consider a common scenario: Several students regularly come to school without a lunch. Your response will depend on where you see the problem located and what you see as your role in the problem (that is, how you theorize, or make sense of, what's going on). If you theorize that the problem is about a lack of family values—not caring enough about their children to bother giving them a lunch—you might take a punitive approach and report the parents to social services. If you theorize that the students' lack of a lunch is an income problem (because a family doesn't have the resources to meet its children's needs), you might direct the students to the free and reduced lunch program. If you theorize that the problem is a structural problem (because raising healthy children benefits everyone in society, and meals are an investment in society), you might advocate for policy change at the governmental level. In fact, we have free and reduced lunch programs today because people understood the problem as structural and worked on policies that address the structural aspects of childhood hunger.

Consider the theoretical distinction between locating the problem in values, resources, or structures. These frameworks will result in very different ways of seeing and responding to an issue. None are neutral, but all will have profoundly different impacts (for example, some more collectivist countries, such as Finland and Japan, automatically provide a school lunch for all children, not just to low-income children. In so doing, they remove the stigma associated with special programs).

The way we make sense of our world (or our theories about the world) is often invisible to us. But we cannot address issues of critical social justice without first examining the maps we are using to identify the problem and conceptualize its solutions. Further, awareness of our theoretical maps can lead to fundamental change in our behaviors. This is why understanding theory is not only relevant but also essential for social change to occur.

FINDING COMMON GROUND

There is a level of polarization and ideological entrenchment in society today that did not seem as deep when we wrote the first edition of this book over a decade ago. At that time in politics, for example, the concept of multi- or bipartisanship was the norm. *Multipartisanship* is the recognition that there are typically at least two sides to any societal issue, and if the issue is to be addressed, all sides will need to negotiate in good faith to reach a compromise and find solutions. Today, we don't see compromise as the expected outcome. Rather, we see a rise in refusal to dialogue and negotiate, threats to shut the process down, and calls for retribution and "payback." People who don't agree with us are often cast as literal enemies that are "evil" and "must be destroyed." This entrenchment in an either/or binary further divides society and is antithetical to the goals of social justice. Yet how can we compromise on issues that seem so clearly right or wrong, true or false; for example, whether abortion should be legal or whether the disproportionately high incarceration rate for Black men in the United States is due to systemic racism?

There are of course some moral agreements that we would not advocate compromise on, such as whether torture is wrong or whether some groups of people are naturally inferior to others. These agreements are codified in most societies through policies such as the United Nations Declaration on the Rights of Indigenous Peoples, the Canadian Charter of Rights and Freedoms, and the Constitution of the United States. While not infallible, such documents are intended to reflect a society's foundational values. But that aside, when we *can* find common ground, we believe we *must*. As we close out this chapter, we offer a process for finding pathways to working towards common ground that we hope will guide the rest of your engagement with this text and your commitments outside the classroom. This process has four parts that can be worked in different sequences and steps used or returned to as needed.

Part 1: Define terms. Before dialogue on an issue can move forward, we need, together, to be sure we are using the same terms in the same ways. If when I say *racism* I mean a system and when you say *racism* you mean individual prejudices, we are not going to understand each other, much less find common ground. So to move us away from "your opinion" versus "my opinion" about the meaning of terms, scholars rely on shared definitions developed over time through ongoing research. In this book, we use scholarly definitions as our shared starting point. But even if your context isn't a scholarly one, it is constructive to begin by simply asking, *What do you mean when you say X?*

Part 2: Identify immediate goals. Even highly charged issues such as abortion have aspects that most people can agree on, even if their reasons are not the same.

For example, most people would agree that at the minimum, lowering the abortion rate is a good goal. For one group this may be because fewer abortions mean fewer women have unwanted pregnancies and the physical, emotional, medical, and economic complications that go with them. This group is focused on the life and health of the mother. For another group, a desire to lower the rate may be because they believe life begins at conception and they see abortion as immoral because it ends a life that is unable to defend itself. This group's focus is on the life and health of the baby. Yet regardless of the reasons, establishing a shared goal is foundational to the process and the ability to find common ground in order to move forward.

Part 3: Seek evidence. It is rarely the case that any one person or group sees the entire picture on an issue. Imagine that the issue under discussion is the opening of a safe drug injection site in your neighborhood. You might be concerned that having supervised consumption of drugs near schools, parks, or stores puts the public at risk. Or, on the other hand, you might believe that neighborhoods are engaging in NIMBYism (not in my back yard). But what does the evidence actually show about safety when there are safe consumption spaces versus when there is open use that is unsupervised? How might social resources be best allocated, and offer greater return for public investment in safety and in healthcare? What have other jurisdictions around the world discovered through their policies? And so on. We are often led to taking a position on issues prior to a diverse and thorough consideration of the evidence available to us.

Part 4: Pivot. This turn could be a step forward, a step back, or a step to the side. The point is not to think of the question at hand in terms of right or wrong but to incorporate the evidence into your perspective and take action that breaks the polarization and allows for movement. For example, Professor of Public Policy Robert Reich tells the story of meeting with a group of students to talk about what was happening in Israel and Gaza (Reich, 2023). The tensions were high and positions entrenched between those who identified themselves as pro-Israeli or pro-Palestinian. Yet identifying shared moral principles created a shift. While the students did not solve the conflict, the common ground they found allowed them to pivot away from a right/wrong position. In so doing, the climate was radically changed and an entrenched group became a unified coalition willing to continue to dialogue, and to work together to find a way forward.

Now let's apply these four steps to a highly charged issue that may seem intractable: whether abortion should be legal. For example, we might all agree on the outcome that "fewer abortions is better than more abortions," even if our reasons for agreeing with this may differ. So if we agree that we all want to get there, then what is necessary to get there? What evidence would be useful to get us to fewer abortions (i.e., what do we know or what can we find out about what has actually impacted the rates of abortion?).

Part 1: Defining terms. We should be able to come up with a basic and broad definition of one key term, "abortion," as: The elective termination of a pregnancy, whether for medical or other reasons. This definition leaves out questions that will likely arise when applying the subsequent steps—such as whether there are any "legitimate" elective reasons such as the life of the mother (we may need to come to consensus on what is legitimate and not), or whether there are points during the timeline of pregnancy at which abortion is more or less acceptable (so what terms might be important to identifying this timeline: weeks from conception? or other markers of development?).

Part 2: What immediate goals can we agree on? The time and place in which you have this discussion will already have made abortion legal (as in Canada) or illegal (as in a number of U.S. states). Given that we are seeking common ground and not a yes-or-no, right-or-wrong outcome, it seems reasonable to assume that most people could agree that—albeit for different reasons—at the minimum, lowering the abortion rate as much as possible and as soon as possible would be a good outcome and thus a shared goal.

Part 3: What does the evidence show? In the case of abortion, if we have agreed that our shared goal is fewer abortions, what does the evidence show actually achieves that goal? We have to be prepared for the evidence to surprise us, because it can often be at odds with what we see as common sense. Does sex education in schools prevent unwanted pregnancies? What about the opposite—does keeping sex education out of the classroom help prevent unwanted pregnancies? What effect does poverty have on rates of unwanted pregnancies? How does access to contraception impact the rates? What about ease of access to abortion clinics, parental involvement laws, mandatory waiting periods, or reductions in funding (Austin & Harper, 2019; K. M. Jones & Pineda-Torres, 2024; Joyce et al., 2020; Lindo et al., 2020)? We must be prepared to ask, when these circumstances lead to lower abortion rates, do they also correspond to lower unwanted pregnancies? What about abstinence-only versus comprehensive sex education? Is one or the other of these approaches more effective at preventing unwanted pregnancies (Bradley, 2024; Paton et al., 2020; Society for Adolescent Health & Medicine, 2017)? Whose perspectives on this issue are available to us, and whose must we still seek out to get a more complete understanding of the issue?

Part 4: What is our shared moral ground? Can we agree that:

1. In an ideal world, no one would have an unwanted pregnancy.
2. All parties to an unwanted pregnancy that results from consensual sexual activity had a role in, and have responsibility for, that pregnancy.
3. Some unwanted pregnancies are the result of sexual assault. We must do everything we can to prevent sexual assault.
4. All people should have access to health care.
5. Other moral agreements?

Based on what we discover has been found to reduce unwanted pregnancies, what can each of us do to advocate for policy changes that would reinforce that approach and make our shared goal a reality?

Finding common ground isn't easy. It requires all sides to engage in the process. And for those who see themselves as having nothing to gain, the motivation to engage may be low. Yet if we live in a system that defines itself as democratic, we have an obligation to find common ground for issues that are in service of the public good.

DISCUSSION QUESTIONS

1. Explain in your own words the difference between critical thinking and opinion.
2. What does it mean to say that knowledge is socially constructed? Give some examples.
3. What do the authors mean when they say that "what you know" is connected to "who you are"?

EXTENSION ACTIVITIES

1. Choose a newspaper article, textbook passage, novel, film, commercial, or other text. Identify which of the various forms of knowledge (personal/cultural knowledge, popular knowledge, school knowledge, mainstream academic knowledge, transformative knowledge) manifest in the text, and describe how.
2.
   a. Read Chapter 1 of Howard Zinn's *A People's History of the United States: 1492–Present* (HarperCollins, 1980/2010) or all of Bill Bigelow and Bob Peterson's *Rethinking Columbus: The Next 500 Years* (Rethinking Schools, 1998).
   b. Watch one of the following films:
      Pocahontas (Goldberg, E., & Gabriel, M. (1995). Buena Vista Pictures)
      Avatar (Cameron, J. (2009). Twentieth Century Fox)
      Moana (Clements, R., Musker, J., Williams, C., & Hall, D. (2016). Walt Disney Studios Motion Pictures)
      Pirates of the Caribbean: Dead Man's Chest (Verbinski, G. (2006). Buena Vista Pictures)
   c. Using the text and the film as windows into knowledge construction, reflect upon the following questions:
      » Which story of first contact or Indigenous/colonizer relations is most often taught in schools? How is it taught?
      » Whose interests are served by "school knowledge" about first contact?
      » How do these works illustrate the concept of knowledge as socially constructed?
3. Exercise: How do you know what you know?

About Knowledge 37

By the next class, ask three people, "How do you know something to be true?" Record their answers. Then review their responses. What words and phrases appear frequently? For example, are words like "learned" or "taught" commonly used? Do people say, "I know something is true because I've seen it with my own eyes" (i.e., knowing through observation)? Have they read or studied the topic? Compare and analyze the themes from their answers. What insight does this give you about how knowledge is validated?

4. Other issues to practice finding common ground on:

Using the 4-part process described in this chapter, practice finding common ground on the following social issues:

Issue A: Should all dogs be on-leash in all public spaces?
Issue B: Is it okay for a grandparent to use the term "Oriental"?
Issue C: Should safe drug consumption sites exist?
Issue D: Should my nation adopt a Universal Basic Income for all its citizens?
Issue E: Should this book (or books about same sex families, or the Bible, or books in languages other than English) be banned from your school's library?

PATTERNS TO PRACTICE SEEING

1. What kinds of knowledge are presented as fact and which are presented as opinion? How is this difference conveyed to us?
2. How do families tend to feel about what school their children go to? What are all of the different processes and options related to school choice? What does this say about the idea that all knowledge is equal and that anyone can succeed if they try?

CHAPTER 3

Culture and Socialization

"I don't think about people's race, class, or gender. I just see people as human."

This chapter explains the process of socialization and the interplay between our individuality and our membership in social groups. We also explain how important it is for us to understand that our ideas, views, and opinions are not simply individual, objective, and independent, but rather are the result of social messages and conditioning forces. We describe how, in addition to our families, institutions and other social forces work together to influence our worldview. Examples are provided to illustrate the power of socialization and how it works as an unconscious filter shaping our perceptions.

> **Vocabulary to practice using:** dominant culture; binary; normalized (norm, normative); gendered; racialized; minoritized

Imagine that you are in a class or workshop and your instructor makes any one of the following statements:

> "White people receive the message that they are more important and more valuable than people of Color."
> "Members of the middle and upper classes have an easier time getting into universities and getting jobs."
> "When men enter women-dominated fields, they quickly rise to the top to positions of leadership over the women."
> "Heterosexuals publicize their sexuality daily in a multitude of ways."

Several people in the class, perhaps including yourself, hear this and have an immediate defensive reaction: "Wait a minute, you can't generalize like that!" "I was taught to see everyone as equal." "You don't know me, and you definitely don't know what obstacles I faced getting into college." "I have a female boss!" "I don't talk about my sexuality in public!"

> ✓ **PERSPECTIVE CHECK:** Of course, some members of this class may be excited to hear the instructor make these statements precisely because they challenge dominant ideas and/or affirm their own experiences.

Such reactions are common when discussing politically charged issues such as race, class, gender, and sexuality. But defensiveness is triggered by more than a difference of opinion about what the instructor is saying. In order to understand the instructor's statements and why they so often cause defensiveness, we have to have a thorough understanding of culture and socialization.

WHAT IS CULTURE?

Each one of us is born into a particular time, place, and social context—into a particular *culture*. Culture refers to the characteristics of everyday life of a specific group. Some of these characteristics are visible and easily identified by the members of the culture, but many (indeed most) of them are below the surface of everyday awareness.

> 📖 **Culture:** The norms, values, practices, patterns of communication, language, laws, customs, and meanings shared by a group of people located in a given time and place.

The iceberg illustration presented in Figure 3.1 is a helpful visual representation of culture. While we may be able to identify superficial elements of culture (such as food, dress, and music), deeper levels of culture (such as notions of modesty and concepts of time) are more difficult to see. Like a fish that is immersed in water from the moment of consciousness and thus cannot know that it is separate from the water, we too are immersed from birth in the deep water of our culture.

WHAT IS SOCIALIZATION?

Socialization refers to our systematic training into the norms of our culture. Socialization is the process of learning the meanings and practices that enable us to make sense of and behave appropriately in that culture. Notice the massive depth of the iceberg under the water and how many aspects of socialization are below the surface—not consciously thought about; we just *know* when someone is "friendly," or is "acting oddly," or has "poor hygiene." We know because we have been socialized into the norms of our culture, norms that regulate these aspects of social life, and if our

Figure 3.1. The Iceberg of Culture

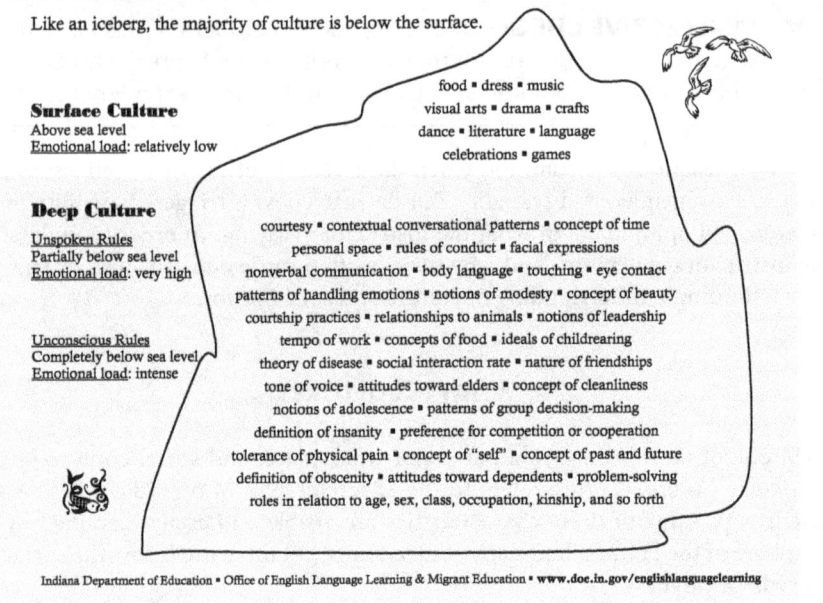

Indiana Department of Education • Office of English Language Learning & Migrant Education • www.doe.in.gov/englishlanguagelearning

Source: www.homeofbob.com/literature/esl/icebergModelCulture.html

friends have been socialized this way too, getting along is easy. Socialization begins at birth and continues throughout life. Indeed, the forces of socialization are gathering even before birth, when our families begin to project their hopes, dreams, and expectations onto our lives.

> ✓ **PERSPECTIVE CHECK:** What's below the surface is often *easier* to see when the deep culture you have been socialized into does not match the deep culture you are currently navigating; for example, if there is a difference between your home culture and your school or work culture.

One of the clearest examples of this cultural education is the process of gender socialization. Consider the first question most people ask expectant parents, "Is it a boy or a girl?" Why do we ask this question? We ask because the answer sets in motion a series of expectations and actions. For example, if parents are informed that they are having a girl, they may begin to buy clothes and decorate the room in preparation for their daughter's arrival. The colors they choose, the toys they buy, and their expectations for the baby's future will all be informed by what that culture deems appropriate for girls.

> 📖 **Cisgender:** The term for people whose sex category given at birth and subsequent gender socialization are the same as their own gender identity.
> **Transgender:** The term for people whose gender identity is different from the sex category assigned at birth.
> **Nonbinary categories:** People who do not identify in binary terms and/or whose gender identity and expression are fluid and dynamic.

But even our conception of what girls and boys are is rooted in our culture. Although *sex* and *gender* are often used interchangeably, they mean different things. *Sex* refers to the biological, genetic, or phenotypical markers that are used to categorize us into female and male bodies: genitals, body structure, hormones, and so on. These markers are related to reproduction. *Gender*, on the other hand, is what it *means* to have that body in a given culture. Gender refers to the roles, behaviors, and expectations our culture assigns to those markers: how you are supposed to act based on whether your body is seen as female or male. Males are expected to learn to "act like a man"—they are trained into *masculinity*; and females are expected to learn to "act like a woman"—they are trained into *femininity*.

> ✓ **PERSPECTIVE CHECK:** Of course this binary construct is the dominant construct in Western society. In other cultures, there are "third" or alternate gender identities that are normalized, such as *Two-Spirit* or *Muxe* in Indigenous traditions, *Hijra* from South Asian traditions, or *Kathoey* from Asian traditions (among many others). This shows that societies around the world have grappled with the complexity of gender and sex identity and expression for millennia.

When we fit neatly into these binary categories, scholars sometimes use the prefix "cis" to describe us. *Cis* is Latin for *same* and indicates that one's sex assignment and gender identity are the same or in alignment. People who are transgender have a gender identity that is different from their assigned sex at birth. A transgender woman is someone who was categorized as male at birth but whose gender identity is female and lives (or desires to live) her life as a woman. A transgender man is someone who was identified as female at birth but whose gender identity is male and lives (or desires to live) his life as a man. Nonbinary people are those whose gender identities are not fixed to either of these categories. One thing we all have in common, regardless of our gender identity, is that we live in a society that imposes gender roles from birth. We all have this in common, though we will undoubtedly have different experiences and feelings about these roles. At minimum we are all expected to follow a prescribed script throughout adolescence about what it means to achieve manhood or womanhood.

The terms—"man," "woman," "male," "female"—are neither natural nor unchanging. Still, we use them here to indicate what it means to be a man or a woman, a boy or a girl, male or female in mainstream society. That we have no other widely understood terms to use is itself an example of how entrenched the gender binary is. Thus, we use the terms men and women to refer to the current sides of the gender binary within Western societies. In Chapter 7, we will explore the roots and consequences of this binary in more depth.

> 📖 **Binary, binaries:** Either/or categories that have rigid boundaries and are set up as mutually exclusive; e.g., good/bad, right/wrong, Black/White, boy/girl.

More often than many people realize, babies are born with ambiguous sex characteristics that are not easily understood as being female or male, or with a combination of both female and male characteristics (Bergvall et al., 1996; Fausto-Sterling, 2000). Because gender in many cultures is a binary system that insists on male/female opposites, doctors routinely opt to surgically and/or hormonally "correct" any variations and impose one or the other category on the child, even though many of these babies are healthy at birth. Through medical intervention, the bodies of sex-variant babies are reshaped into what is considered normal for a male or female and therefore understandable in terms of gender *binaries* (either/or categories).

> ✔ **PERSPECTIVE CHECK:** Some may say that being a male or female is an indisputable matter of science; XX chromosomes make a female and XY chromosomes make a male. While these DNA distributions seem clear-cut, there are two important factors they ignore. First, biological diversity around sex in humans is not limited solely to chromosomes. Hormone distribution is also involved and varies widely across sex categories; some females have more testosterone than some males. Second, what it *means* to have a body with XX or XY chromosomes is a socially constructed matter of culture (Bhargava et al., 2021; Heller, 2019; Van Anders et al., 2015).

Because we are taught that sex and gender differences are based in biology, we rarely notice how much culture informs those differences. In fact, while there are actually few differences between male and female bodies biologically, society amplifies the cultural differences between men and women (Cilveti-Lapeira et al., 2024; Fausto-Sterling, 1992, 2019; Schmader & Block, 2025). We might rightly ask why society would be invested in amplifying the differences.

CULTURAL NORMS AND CONFORMITY

Like gender, many other aspects of our socialization are also invisible to us. For example, how close do we stand when talking to someone? How do we know when someone is standing too close? And how do aspects of socialization (such as age, social class, religion) and context (such as at a party, in the office, or at home) influence our assessments of whether or not someone is standing too close? The norms of our culture are most often invisible until they are violated.

Let's consider the example of grooming norms to illustrate the power of cultural socialization. Imagine it is a hot summer day and you are having lunch in an outdoor café. You notice an attractive man and woman sitting at the table next to you. Just like many others, they are wearing shorts and tank tops, enjoying the warm weather. At some point, the man raises his arm to flag down the waiter. The café's busy, and the waiter doesn't notice. After a few minutes of being ignored, the woman raises her arm in an attempt to get the waiter's attention, and you see that she does not shave under her arms and has a thick patch of black underarm hair.

> ✔ **PERSPECTIVE CHECK:** You may be thinking, times have changed. Underarm hair on women is no longer shocking and most people wouldn't care, they might even find it attractive. Besides, some men do "manscaping" and shave the hair on their bodies too. The norms around body hair have always been impacted by the times (Fernandez et al., 2013), illustrating how they are socially constructed.

Many people would feel a sense of shock; some might even lose their appetite. You might point it out to your lunch mate and tell your friends about it later that day. However, thinking back to when the man raised his arm, you didn't have any reaction at all to his unshaved armpits. In fact, they didn't even register. Yet underarm hair is completely natural to the adult human body—male *and* female. Why would the woman's hair disgust many of us, but not the man's? It is because we have been socialized to see underarm hair as inappropriate for women. This socialization is so effective that we actually have a physical reaction when the norm is violated. Further, this norm is specific to dominant culture in Canada and the United States. In a different social context (or place or time), underarm hair on women would appear natural, perhaps even sexy, to most people.

This leads to another key aspect of socialization—our beliefs need not be inherently true to have very real consequences. For example, it is not inherently true that underarm hair on women is disgusting. But if that is the norm in our culture, it will be true in its impact; we will still *feel* disgusted and this disgust will seem natural and appropriate. Similarly, while the colors blue and pink are simply colors that occur in nature and are not naturally male or female, once we assign gender to them, that meaning becomes real in its consequences. Any man who has worn pink (in the wrong shade, the wrong amount, or to the wrong place) will know this firsthand; young men in particular actually risk physical harm if this norm is violated in certain spaces. Why then, you might ask, can a girl wear blue without risking violence? To understand why, you must understand social power, which we address in Chapter 5.

> ✔ **PERSPECTIVE CHECK:** People who challenge expected norms of gender presentation face especially high levels of violence (Daigle et al., 2025; Katz et al., 2025). These additional risks are amplified if they are people of Color.

On an abstract level, most people grasp the concept of socialization. However, applying it personally to our *own* lives is more challenging. We live in a culture that teaches us that human objectivity (or independence from socialization) is not only possible, but that it can be readily attained through simple choice. In other words, if I *want* to be an individual who is not influenced by the forces of socialization around me, then I can just decide that I *am* an individual who is not influenced by those forces; it is presumed that this is a choice I can make and is all it takes to break from the forces of socialization. Yet breaking from socialization is much more challenging than it may appear. There are social, psychological, and material rewards for following society's rules, such as acceptance, being treated as "normal" by family, peers, and superiors, and even opportunities for career progression.

Conversely, there are penalties for not following society's rules. Returning to our example of the woman with underarm hair, while she has the right to not shave under her arms, she also has to deal with the consequences of that choice. For example, she will face looks of disgust, pressure from family and friends, and questions about her sexuality and her hygiene; this choice may result in penalties in the workplace. That is, by not playing by the rules, she jeopardizes her status as a "normal" member of that society. And the penalties do not necessarily go away if the woman has greater social power. For instance, while female celebrities who do not shave their armpits have their fans, their choice is also routinely discussed in the media.

Studies reveal that we do indeed see the world through socialized filters. If we deny that these filters exist, we can't put protections in place to help minimize acting on them, when those actions lead to unaware and unintentional discrimination. Understanding how bias shapes our "ways of seeing" is crucial to addressing how we perceive and make or block opportunities for others.

IMPLICIT BIAS

The Harvard Implicit Association Test (IAT) was developed in 1995 by psychologists Tony Greenwald and Mahzarin Banaji in order to access aspects of bias that a person is either unaware of or cannot admit to. These aspects are termed *implicit* because they are not held at the conscious, or *explicit*, level of awareness. The test measures implicit bias toward a wide range of social groups. It is accessible to anyone online via Project Implicit (at https://implicit.harvard.edu) and guides the reader through a series of rapid associations. For example, test-takers are asked which of the two terms "male" and "female" is more strongly associated with the term "logical." The more rapid your response, the more closely the terms are associated in your memory. The test has been highly researched and has consistently demonstrated validity (Greenwald et al., 2009). The test has now been used for over 25 years and many scholars have studied the results. The following conclusions are widely accepted (from the Project Implicit website https://www.projectimplicit.net/):

- **Implicit Biases Are Pervasive and Well Established**
  As of 2023, more than 80 million study sessions have been launched and more than 40 million IATs completed at the Project Implicit website—an IAT is taken every 21 seconds. Greenwald and colleagues' paper introducing the IAT in 1998 has been cited more than 16,000 times (Ratliff & Smith, 2024). Between 1998 and 2006, more than 250 IAT-related studies were published (Bower, 2006; Leboeuf, 2020).
- **Most People Are Unaware of Their Implicit Biases**
  People have been found to hold negative biases in relation to various social groups even while reporting that they regard themselves as not holding these biases. Implicit bias is found equally across all groups. No one group of people is any more or less biased than another (Chin et al., 2020; Lewis & Lupyan, 2019).
- **Implicit Bias Predicts Behavior**
  The published scientific evidence of the relationship between bias and behavior is vast (Czopp et al., 2014; Fishbein, 2002; Kite et al., 2022). Everyone has socially learned prejudice based on the culture they are immersed in, and everyone acts on (discriminates based on) that prejudice. From simple acts such as friendliness and inclusion to more consequential acts such as the evaluation of work quality, those who display greater implicit bias have been shown to display greater discrimination.
- **People Differ in Their Levels of Implicit Bias**
  Although implicit bias is universal, levels vary from person to person (Aberson, 2019; Jiang et al., 2019). Certain experiences can make a person more aware of bias and thus able to challenge it in themselves. The level of bias existing in the immediate environment can also impact individual levels. The groups we have bias towards can change over time and across cultures (for example, there was a time when tattoos in mainstream society were associated with criminality, and tattoos on women were shocking and virtually unheard of). In other words, the bias

we hold is socially constructed and therefore can be deconstructed. We can minimize bias by taking steps to interrogate the misinformation bias is based on and the segregation that keeps that misinformation alive. This is why media literacy, critical thinking, and exposure to social differences are so crucial.

Much of our socialization is so internalized and taken for granted that we don't even see it as a choice—we just believe that it's natural to feel and act the way we do. Consider one of many studies of its kind (J. Eberhardt, 2019) regarding discrimination in hiring that reveals how much of our socialization is hidden from our conscious minds (Bertrand & Mullainathan, 2004). Seeking to understand the well-documented patterns of inequality between White and Black applicants in the U.S. job market in terms of rates of employment and pay, researchers at the University of Chicago conducted a large study. These researchers responded to over 1,300 Help Wanted ads in Boston and Chicago newspapers by sending out close to 5,000 resumes. While the qualifications on the resumes were consistent, they randomly assigned stereotypically White-sounding names, such as Emily Walsh or Greg Baker, to half of the resumes, and stereotypically Black-sounding names, such as Lakisha Washington or Jamal Jones, to the other half. Resumes with White-sounding names received 50% more callbacks than the resumes with stereotypically Black-sounding names, regardless of the employer, occupation, industry, or size of the company.

The researchers also investigated how improvements in credentials affected the callback rate. While the resumes with White-sounding names received 30% more callbacks when the credentials improved, there was no significant improvement in callback rates for the applicants with Black-sounding names. In other words, there were no benefits to Black applicants for improving their credentials. Despite popular perceptions that racial minority candidates have an advantage when applying for jobs, this research showed that not only is there no advantage, but in fact they faced consistent discrimination. This disadvantage did not vary across occupation, region, or industry; even when applicants perceived as Black were *more* qualified, they were still discriminated against.

While this study along with others of its kind (M. Eberhardt et al., 2023; Pedulla et al., 2023; Quillian & Lee, 2023; Quillian et al., 2020) provides clear evidence that racial discrimination is alive and well, it raises an important question: What happened when the human resource workers screened these resumes? They were likely not aware that they were discriminating and would probably have vigorously (and sincerely) denied any suggestion to the contrary. They would not be intentionally lying when they denied discriminating, and herein lies the power of socialization: We often have no idea that we are acting on bias. What we see appears to be just the truth; that is, *this* batch of applicants appears to us as more qualified than *that* batch. But we have interpreted these resumes through racial filters. When we read the resume and see, for example, the name Lakisha Washington, a name traditionally associated in culture with Black people, those racial filters are

Culture and Socialization

activated. We are now subconsciously reading her resume with the assumptions and expectations about her qualifications that we have absorbed from the culture at large. Because studies of this kind have provided powerful evidence of racial discrimination in hiring, many organizations now block out names when possible before sending resumes out for review in order to protect against unconscious bias.

> ✋ **STOP:** While many of us believe that we treat everyone the same, this is not actually possible. Countless studies show that humans are not and cannot be objective (independent from our socialization) about one another. This socialization drives us to discriminate. Most of our discrimination is not at the conscious level and therefore not intentional, but can be harmful in its impact nonetheless. There are strategies to help us minimize our discrimination, but we can't use them if we refuse to accept that we don't in fact treat everyone equally.

Ongoing studies have shown this type of racial discrimination across multiple fields. Among them are a handful of important studies about higher education itself. For example, in 2015, Katherine Milkman, Modupe Akinola, and Dolly Chugh set out to explore how the biases in hiring at the levels of organizations manifest in the steps before hiring—when people were applying to universities, and to doctoral programs in particular. In their experiment, they contacted over 6,500 professors working in 89 different disciplines at 259 top universities throughout the United States, presenting (fictional) prospective students who were seeking mentorship in the form of research opportunities and entry into a doctoral program. The researchers randomly assigned gender and race (White, Black, Hispanic, Indian, Chinese) signals to otherwise identical messages. Their findings revealed that faculty were significantly more responsive to White males than to all other categories of students, particularly in higher-paying disciplines and at private universities. In 2024, a similar study was published on research conducted in Australia with an audit of prospective student emails seeking a meeting with faculty, in order to examine systemic bias via informal pathways into academia. The researchers (Goldsmith et al., 2024) sent over 7,000 emails to professors at eight Australian universities. Their findings confirm that women and non-White racialized groups are substantially underrepresented as faculty at the universities studied. MacKenzie and her colleagues found that there were differences in the rates and positivity of responses to prospective students depending on the implied racial identity of students' names. "While emails from *Thomas* or *Melissa Smith* received positive replies in 47–49 percent of cases after 24 hours, those from *Rahul* or *Priyanka Kumar* received only 34–35 percent positive responses over the same period" (MacKenzie et al., 2023, p. 8). While admission to academic programs may seem like a simple matter of good grades and access to opportunities, these studies show that even when some people get all the way to the door of desired programs, implicit bias is at play, creating barriers at every step in the process.

Entry into the institution is not the full story of inclusion. Social psychologist Dr. Dolly Chugh and her colleague professor of business ethics Dr. Arthur Brief offer a helpful way to understand the complexity of the impacts of our implicit biases. The authors distinguish between "gateways" and "pathways" to inclusion. "*Gateways* are the entry points into valued organizations, communities, or institutions, whereas *pathways* describe the more fluid processes that influence one's ability to access an entry point and succeed after entry" (Milkman et al., 2015, p. 1680). In other words, while attention to the "gateway" or "the way in" is important, it certainly isn't the end of the story. How we perceive others also directly impacts their ability to succeed in the institution once they are in the door.

> **Implicit Bias:** The largely unconscious and automatic prejudice that operates below conscious awareness and without intentional control. Implicit bias is absorbed from the messages surrounding us. These aspects are termed *implicit* because they are not held at the conscious, or *explicit*, level of awareness. Because implicit bias is below awareness and often in conflict with what a person consciously believes, the person is unaware that they hold this bias. In turn, they are unaware that they are acting—or discriminating—based on their bias.

To develop critical social justice literacy, we must be able to see how our ideas, views, and opinions are not solely independent and unique to us, but rather derive from social messages circulating around us. The first layer of socialization we might easily identify is our family. While our families do indeed form the first unit through which we learn language, values, and behaviors, our parents and families are not the sole or dominant source of our beliefs about the world. There are many other socializing forces including schooling, media, and religion that also wield great authority. The common conception that we learn our values at home is also incomplete because our families themselves are products of socialization. In order to critically reflect on all the forces that shape us, we must understand the power of society at large.

YOU IN RELATION TO THE GROUPS TO WHICH YOU BELONG

We have discussed bias and socialization; now let's connect these concepts to group membership. Humans are social beings who depend on the humans around us to make sense of our world. While this may be universal to all humans, socialization tells us that the sense we make of the world, including what we learn about

Figure 3.2. Frame of Reference Glasses

"us" and "them," is culturally dependent. In other words, it changes from place to place, people to people, and time to time. As we explained in the discussion of bias, the chosen target of our bias is not natural and seldom unique to us; it is taught to and learned by everyone else in our society.

A useful metaphor for understanding how we are socialized into our bias is to think of culture as a pair of glasses that we wear at all times (see Figure 3.2). Just like a fish is always immersed in water, we too are always immersed in culture, wearing cultural glasses that cannot ever truly be taken off. There are two significant parts to these glasses: the frame and the lenses. The frame consists of the *macro* or group-level norms—what everyone in that culture must learn in order to function effectively in society. The lenses represent the individual (*micro* level) perspective—ways of seeing that develop based on one's unique experiences and life history.

At the frame (macro) level, for example, in the culture of mainstream United States and Canada, we are all taught that a young woman's wedding day should make her feel like a princess, that democracy and free market capitalism are the best forms of government and economic policy, and that we should strive to be independent from others. Regardless of whether or not we personally agree with these teachings, we all receive them through social institutions like schools, government, and the mass media.

For example, even if as parents we want to challenge traditional gender roles and intentionally avoid dressing our daughters in pink or sons in blue, or even go so far as to not tell friends and family the sex of the baby, we still receive the message in mainstream culture whenever we watch TV, walk through the toy aisles in stores, or go clothes shopping and need to choose between the clearly delineated girl or boy sections. In fact, many parents who try to avoid traditional gender teachings find it to be a losing battle, given the relentless messages children receive from everything else around them; we are constantly being pressured to follow the norms of society.

Ideas about social *groups* make up the frames of our glasses. We are socialized according to the norms of these groups. The primary groups that we address here are race, class, gender, sexuality, ability, religion, and nationality. While these divisions are not in reality this clear-cut, society organizes us into simple either/or categories. For every social group, there is an opposite. Indeed, one cannot learn what a social group *is*, without also learning what the group *is not*.

Figure 3.3 is intended to help readers begin the process of identifying their social group memberships. Readers can use this table to explore the relevance of social groups in society at large and their impact on us as individuals.

We develop our ideas about people in terms of their race, class, gender, sexuality, ethnicity, religion, ability, and citizenship from the culture that surrounds us, and many of these ideas are "below the surface" or below the conscious level. We hold shared understandings about these social groups because we receive messages collectively about them from our culture. This means that the frameworks we use to make sense of race, class, or gender are shared, taken for granted, and often invisible to us.

✓ **PERSPECTIVE CHECK:** We have based the list in Figure 3.3 on categories of identification that are collected by the Canadian and U.S. governments. However, these categorizations do not reflect the complexities of race and ethnicity as experienced in society. For example, in Figure 3.3 we have included Latino/Hispanic under the category of race despite the fact that this is not technically a singular racial group; it includes many racial groups. We have included it because of the very real racialized experiences that occur for people who are identified as Latino/Hispanic.

Race and ethnicity are examples of how complex and interrelated these categories can be. While race and ethnicity are connected in important ways and often used interchangeably, they are not interchangeable. *Race* is a socially constructed, pseudo-scientific system of classifying humans based on particular phenotypical characteristics (e.g., skin color, hair texture, and bone structure). *Ethnicity* refers to a group of people bound by a common language, culture, spiritual tradition, and/or ancestry. Ethnic groups can bridge national borders and still be one group (such as the Cree community, which straddles the United States and Canada). At the same time, ethnic groups can live within the same national borders and not share the same ethnic identity. For example, "British" refers to people of English, Scottish, and Welsh ancestry who live in the United Kingdom of Great Britain. However, the English, Scottish, and Welsh are distinct ethnic groups. As well, British can refer to citizens of Great Britain who may have racial and ethnic heritages other than English, Scottish, or Welsh—such as African, Asian, or Arab.

As these examples show, race and ethnicity interact in complex ways with language and citizenship. For those new to the study of critical social justice, mastering these complexities is of secondary importance. Of primary importance is the ability

Figure 3.3. Group Identities

Group	Group identities
	It is unavoidable that some groups have not been listed. If your group has been left out, please write it in.
Race	Perceived as person of Color, racialized, Indigenous, BIPOC
	Perceived as White
Race detailed	Asian (e.g., Chinese, Japanese, Korean, Hmong, Vietnamese ancestry)
	South Asian (e.g., Indian, Sri Lankan, Nepalese ancestry)
	Black (e.g., African, Caribbean ancestry)
	Bi- or multiracial (parents and/or grandparents of mixed racial ancestry)
	Indigenous (e.g., Cherokee, Inuit, Dakota ancestry)
	Native Hawaiian/Pacific Islander (e.g., Samoan, Guamanian, Fijian ancestry)
	White (e.g., Irish, Italian, French, Ashkenazi/European Jewish ancestry)
	Hispanic or Latino/a (e.g., Puerto Rican, Cuban, Mexican ancestry)
Class	E.g., poor, working poor, working class, lower middle class, middle class, professional class, upper class, owning/ruling class
Gender	E.g., cis woman, cis man, transgender, nonbinary
Sexuality	E.g., lesbian, bisexual, gay, Two-Spirit, heterosexual, asexual
Religion	E.g., Hindu, Buddhist, Jew, Christian, Muslim, Atheist
Ability	E.g., people without disability, people with physical or cognitive disabilities, visible or nonvisible disabilities
Nationality	E.g., Canadian, French, Japanese, Indigenous or Tribal Nation, immigrant, people perceived to not be citizens, people perceived to be citizens

to understand these categories as reflective of a particular sociopolitical context. Their instability does not mean that we can dismiss categories of race, ethnicity, and nationality; rather, we must understand their context and the impact of that context on our lives (this will be discussed in more depth in Chapter 8).

While they are distinct, there are important interactions between race and ethnicity. We also must recognize internal and external dynamics of identity: how one personally *identifies* versus how one *is identified* by others—how I see myself versus how others perceive me. While how we see ourselves and how others see us may not be the same, they are inseparable. How our identities develop is shaped by how others see and respond to us. Sociologist Charles Cooley (1922) called this interconnection the "looking-glass self" to capture the idea that we come to know who we are in large part through the process of what others reflect back to us, as well as ideas about which groups we belong to and which we do not.

If we are resisting the very notion of having to identify ourselves in terms of social groups, such as our race or gender, this too provides insight into our collective socialization. In Western society we are socialized to prioritize our individuality. Yet, although we *are* individuals, we are *also*—and perhaps fundamentally—members of social groups. These group memberships shape us as profoundly, if not more so, than any unique characteristic we may claim to possess.

Consider how one of the key aspects of individuality is one's preference for certain food, music, and dress styles. However, these preferences are never simply one's internally driven likes or dislikes. It is no coincidence that popular shows of the day (e.g., *Bridgerton* or *Stranger Things*) influence which names rise to the top of "most popular baby name" lists. Think back to when other iconic figures from popular culture influenced hairstyles of the time (Amy Winehouse, Jennifer Aniston, Justin Bieber, Angela Davis). Conversely, seeking names or hairstyles that are "different" is also a function of culture—you are still reacting to the culture at large. Without the popular name or hairstyle, your different one (different from what?) would not have the same meaning.

The point is, while parents may have preferences for particular names, and any individual may have a preference for a particular hairstyle, it is not *simply* a matter of preference. There are predictable patterns of group behavior we can observe and study. And we can make predictions about your preferences based on your class, race, gender, and so on.

Returning to our opening vignette, hopefully you now have a better idea of what was meant by the instructor's statements when she said for example that, "Members of the middle and upper classes have an easier time getting into universities and getting jobs." The instructor was not making claims about each *individual person* in these groups, but about *patterns among social groups*. These patterns are long-standing, measurable, and well documented. The fact that these kinds of statements often cause defensiveness speaks to the way they challenge the cherished Western ideology of individualism. We have been taught that social group memberships such as race, class, and gender do not and should not matter, and thus must be minimized and denied.

Specifically, the instructor is challenging a societal norm by moving past individual difference and instead focusing on shared patterns between members of social groups. She is also challenging a norm connected to our elevation of the individual—the idea that people should be seen as unique, and thus it is inappropriate to generalize. And finally, she is naming the dominant group in each of these examples, which violates assumptions that dominant groups are neutral and that difference lies with the "other."

DISCUSSION QUESTIONS

1. While there are always exceptions, key careers tend to be organized in ways that are gendered (police and firefighters tend to be men, while elementary teachers and nurses tend to be women). How would the authors explain this pattern?
2. According to the authors, why do so many people feel immune to the forces of socialization?
3. How does the concept of *socialization* challenge the idea of *individualism*?
4. Many sociologists say that in part how we come to know ourselves is by knowing who we are not. Sociologist Charles Cooley described this process as the "looking-glass self" to capture the idea that it is what others reflect back to us that teaches us who we are—that is, our ideas about ourselves are based on how we see ourselves (people like us) in relation to others (people not like us). What kind of people did you learn were different from you? How were they different? How were you taught about this difference? If you were told that everyone is equal, did your connections match this message? For example, think about whether there were key groups (rather than individuals) such as the elderly, people with disabilities, people of different social classes, people from different religious groups, or people from different racial groups that were not integrated into your schools and neighborhoods. As you reflect on this question, consider implicit (unspoken) messages as well as explicit (direct) messages about your value in relation to those who were not like you.

EXTENSION ACTIVITIES

1. "Act like a boy or girl." This is a popular diversity exercise intended to draw out the forces of gender socialization.

    Divide into small groups of 4–6.

    Now, imagine that an alien has landed in your group. This alien comes from a planet where gender is not organized as binaries. The job of this alien is to get by, blend in, and learn about human society. The alien has already received treatments to look human but has no idea how to either "act like a boy" or "act like a girl" in order to pass. Generate a list of instructions for your alien about how to "act like a boy" and how to "act like a girl" in public settings like school, work, family gatherings. Your list should include verbs. Remember, the goal of your alien friend is to blend into mainstream society and understand its basic customs, not to challenge them.

    Write your list of instructions on the board or chart paper, then draw a box around it. As the groups share their lists, ask the following questions:

- » How do we know these rules? (Even if we personally reject them or think they are silly, notice that we must still know what they are in order to refuse them.)
- » What are the costs of stepping outside of your gender script? That is, what happens when you don't "act like a boy"? Are there some areas (settings? places? with certain company?) where there is more permission to act in ways outside the script? In what settings is it less okay?
- » It should be obvious that many of the things on the list are rather absurd and limiting to our lives. What keeps us in line? In other words, what are the penalties for stepping too far out of these boxes? What do we get called or seen as? What risks are there for those humans who do not conform to these instructions?

As a large group, discuss: What doors would be open to you that are not open to you now, if we were truly free of gender roles? Notice if there is any hesitation about eliminating gender roles. What are the reasons given for this hesitation? Think about these reasons through the lens of key concepts discussed so far, such as socialization, looking-glass self, group membership, normalization, and iceberg of culture.

2. a. Read Simon Wiesenthal's (1976) *The Sunflower: On the Possibilities and Limits of Forgiveness* (Schocken, 1976). Summary: *During the Holocaust, a Nazi soldier calls the author, Simon Wiesenthal, a Jewish concentration camp prisoner at the time, to his deathbed and confesses his crimes against Jews. The soldier asks Simon to forgive him. Should Simon offer forgiveness? The author never reveals his decision. Instead, he asks 53 distinguished theologians, political leaders, writers, jurists, psychiatrists, human rights activists, Holocaust survivors, and victims of attempted genocides in Bosnia, Cambodia, China, and Tibet to respond to this question. Their responses are as varied as their experiences of the world.*
    b. Watch the film *The Question of God: Sigmund Freud & C. S. Lewis* (C. Tatge & D. Lasseur, Producers; C. Tatge, Director; Tatge-Lasseur Productions, 2004). *Does God exist? How does your answer to that question frame how you think about and act in the world? This documentary is a roundtable discussion among scientists, theologians, and atheists on these questions. They explore the question of God in relation to the human condition, morality, and how we treat one another.*
    c. Using the text and the film as windows into finding common ground, reflect upon the following questions:

    - » How would you answer Wiesenthal's question on forgiveness?
    - » What framework are you using to address the question?
    - » How did you acquire this framework?

Culture and Socialization

» Why might so many others answer such a question very differently?
» How can excavating our shared values help us work toward common ground, when our answers to questions such as those above seem so fundamentally different?

PATTERNS TO PRACTICE SEEING

1. Practice identifying patterns at the *group* (rather than individual) level. For example, in school, in workplace meetings or media, practice seeing which groups are represented and which are less so. Who do you see and not see? Do you notice any patterns in which group members are likely to participate more?
2. Practice naming people by their key social groups. For example, "Tina, a White nondisabled cis woman, went to the store." Notice your own as well as others' levels of comfort in naming these identities.

CHAPTER 4

Prejudice and Discrimination

"I was taught never to judge a book by its cover."

This chapter explains two key interrelated terms: prejudice and discrimination. We explain that prejudice and discrimination cannot be avoided; we all hold prejudices and we all discriminate based on our prejudices. We argue that the first step in minimizing discrimination is to be able to identify (rather than deny) our prejudices.

> **Vocabulary to practice using:** prejudice; discrimination; bias; stereotypes

Imagine that you are on a hiring committee to identify the best candidate to join your elementary school faculty. Ms. Hardy, the principal who chairs the committee, reports that there are too many applicants for the position and that the committee needs to thin out the applicant pool. As she is distributing the files for review, she says, "Oh, here's a male applicant. We definitely want to consider this one, since we have so few male teachers at our school." As she says this, she is thinking, *I really want to get some male teachers in here; just the other day a parent was complaining that there weren't any male role models for the boys*.

Liz, a teacher on the committee, thinks, *Oh great, a man. That's all we need. He'll probably be the vice principal by next year*, and says, "Yes, but there are many other characteristics associated with what a candidate brings."

Wendy, another teacher, thinks, *I hope he's gay; men teaching at the elementary level usually are. He'll probably be a blast to work with*, and says, "Yeah, we should look closely at his application. And it would be so great to have more diversity around sexual orientation too."

Mary, another teacher, thinks, *Uh-oh, he's probably gay . . . that's going to be an issue for a lot of the parents*, and says, "Yes, but we should consider how the candidate fits the culture of our students' families. In the past, we've had problems around gay teachers."

Liz exclaims, "Whoa, this is prejudice!"

Everyone is stunned by this charge. Wendy retorts, "That's a terrible accusation! We have a process here, and policies that we will follow to ensure that every candidate is evaluated fairly. And I can assure you that Mary and I are not prejudiced in any way and evaluate all candidates objectively and equally!"

WHAT IS PREJUDICE?

This vignette illustrates the importance of understanding the relationship between our socialization and the prejudices we have and act upon. While most people want to be fair, we can't help but have preconceived notions about other people based on our socialization about their social groups (in this case, the candidate's gender). At the same time, we often feel offended when someone suggests that we have prejudices, let alone that they are showing. To understand the dynamics in the above vignette, we must first learn about two interrelated concepts: *prejudice* and *discrimination*.

> **Prejudice:** Learned prejudgment about members of social groups to which we don't belong. Prejudice is based on limited knowledge or experience and projected onto everyone from that group.

Prejudice is learned prejudgment toward social others and refers to *internal* thoughts, feelings, attitudes, and assumptions based on the groups to which they belong. Our knowledge about prejudice comes primarily from the field of social psychology. This field can be described as both *sociology* and *psychology*; social psychologists study how our internal thoughts and attitudes drive interactions with the external social world, as well as how individuals and groups interact with one another (Lindesmith et al., 1999). While prejudice in particular has been studied since the 1920s, it was not until Gordon Allport's classic book *The Nature of Prejudice* in 1954 that this substantial body of work came together and solidified. After the Second World War, social scientists felt the need to explain how social prejudices and their consequences (such as intolerance and intergroup conflict) occur and how to interrupt them. Researchers approach prejudice as a type of *attitude*. And while our lay understanding of the word attitude might make you think about a person's *confidence* or *spunk*, social psychologists think about attitudes as *evaluations* involving degrees of positivity or negativity, such as like or dislike (Jackson, 2020). Attitudes can be about people, issues, or objects. The important part about attitudes is that they are subjective and are our internal thoughts and feelings, not necessarily connected to any truth about the thing we make an evaluation about (Olson & Maio, 2003).

Our evaluations can be complicated and include making assumptions without knowledge (stereotyping), and also *feelings* or emotional responses such as disgust or anger (Duckitt, 1992; Jackson, 2020). Thus, a key concern for psychologists is the emotionality of prejudice and its ability to persist and fuel strong action (Allport, 1954; Jackson, 2020). Stereotypes are an aspect of prejudice in that they primarily constitute qualities ascribed to a group. For example: *Swedish people are blond*. The result is an exaggerated impression of the group. Prejudice makes use of stereotypes, but produces a negative, unsubstantiated attitude about the group; for example, *blondes are dumb*.

While everyone has prejudices based on distinctive experiences that are unique to them—for example, someone got into a legal dispute with a cashier and now doesn't trust cashiers—here we are concerned with the collective prejudices we learn from the culture at large about our own and other social groups. These prejudices are always unfair, because they are not earned by the individual but granted or imposed based on ideas about the group that the individual belongs to. For example, *I prefer to teach math to Chinese students because I assume they will do well on the math test, and I don't like to teach math to White female students because I assume they will do poorly*. While the prejudice I have toward the Chinese heritage students appears to be positive, it is still unfair in that it isn't earned, will interfere with my ability to make valid assessments, and sets one racial group up against others.

Prejudice manifests in attitudes about an individual, but it is based on our ideas about the group to which that individual belongs. Prejudice is part of how we learn to sort people into categories that make sense to us (boy/girl, old/young, rich/poor). Although this is a process necessary for learning, our categorizations are not neutral. We are socialized to perceive and value these categories differently.

For example, take the categories of "attractive" and "unattractive." While there is some variation in opinion between people, on the level of collective socialization, there are sanctioned norms of beauty constantly communicated to us through major institutions such as the entertainment industry. Media-based representations present a consistent image of who the attractive people are, what they look like, and what we can do to look more like them (if you doubt this, just scan the magazine rack at your local grocery store).

Most of us are acutely aware that there are social benefits that go with being in the "attractive" group and social penalties for being in the "unattractive" group. These benefits and penalties are communicated to us *explicitly*—effusive praise for a celebrity's beauty, magazine covers featuring the "100 Most Beautiful People," the "20 Hottest Bodies," the open ridicule of unattractive people, more praise for us when we "dress up"—and *implicitly* through larger salaries, career advancement, better evaluations, and other research-documented benefits that accrue to those considered attractive (Hamermesh & Parker, 2005; Rhode, 2010).

These definitions are not natural but are specific to a given cultural context. They change over time and our perceptions change with them, indicating the learned nature of our prejudices. For example, in the United States Marilyn Monroe was once considered one of the most beautiful women in the world. However, while she might still epitomize the White, blonde ideal of feminine beauty, she would be considered overweight today and therefore would not have the beauty status that she held over 70 years ago.

Prejudices begin as stereotypes. While many use these terms interchangeably, there are important nuances. *Stereotypes* refer to reduced or simplified characteristics attributed to a group. For example, if we ask someone to describe Americans and Canadians, they may answer that Americans are industrious, independent, and like fast food, while Canadians are polite, love hockey, and end their sentences with "eh." When we ask what elementary school teachers are like, we may have ideas that they are nurturing and loving. These kinds of simplifications are either a set of characteristics *attributed to* a group (elementary school teachers are nurturing), or a feature of some members of a group that *stands out* (Canadian speech, American eating habits).

People often say that there is always a kernel of truth to stereotypes, but this belief has more to do with the ways in which stereotypes work and less to do with their validity. For example, although some Canadians end some of their sentences with "eh," most Canadians do not. Yet this distinction is what helps us make sense of the category "Canadian" as distinct from the category "American." This is especially easy to see in the realm of media, where having, for example, a character say "eh" establishes that character as Canadian. For an American watching these movies, this stereotype is reinforced again and again. Because many Americans may not know many Canadians, we don't have much else to draw on and over time come to believe this is how Canadians talk. The stereotype is now formed in our minds and will appear to be true because we are drawing on the fixed representation we have seen so consistently. When we encounter people who don't fit the stereotype, we either don't notice or we view these people as exceptions. On the other hand, when we encounter people who do fit the stereotype, even if we encounter them very rarely, they stand out to us and reinforce the stereotype as true. Therefore, if we hold this stereotype and visit Canada, we will notice any Canadian we hear say "eh" and disregard the countless Canadians we meet who don't, thus reinforcing our belief.

Prejudice comes into play when we add values to our stereotypes. Let's put stereotypes together with values, using the example of "elementary school teacher." If I am a parent going to meet my son's 2nd-grade teacher for the first time, I would expect to meet a female (as the vast majority of elementary teachers are female). If instead I meet a male, I may wonder if he is gay (a common stereotype about male elementary school teachers) and worry that if he is, he will be an inappropriate role model for my son (a common prejudice about gay men). This worry develops from the interaction between stereotypes about male elementary school teachers and the values associated with those stereotypes in our culture, leading to a prejudicial attitude that my son's gay teacher will be an unsuitable role model.

✓ **PERSPECTIVE CHECK:** If I am a gay parent or have close relationships with many gay people whom I advocate for, I am more likely to be informed and educated on the issues and thus not have the same worry.

Note: While imperfect, here we are using "gay" as a stand-in for the diversity of 2SLGBTQ+ people and families.

Notice how conceptions about the teacher are interwoven in important ways with conceptions about gender roles. These conceptions are important because they are the basis of our evaluations of what is "normal"; every teacher we encounter who does not match our internal definition of "teacher" will be evaluated differently than the "normal" teachers who do match them. These evaluations don't just distinguish between who is deemed normal and who isn't, but also influence our assessments of other important social values such as character. When we assign character values, our stereotypes have moved into prejudice.

Many of us think that we don't hold prejudicial thoughts against people. Because we think this, we see ourselves as free of prejudice. But the process is much more complicated. The reality is that no one can avoid prejudice because it is built into our socialization. All humans have prejudices, but they are so normalized and taken for granted that they are often very difficult to identify. This is one of the challenges of critical social justice literacy: developing the critical thinking that would enable us to bring our prejudices to the surface and reflect upon and challenge them. Yet society tells us that it is bad to have prejudices, and thus we feel pressure to deny them.

Because social acceptance of prejudices varies over time, we don't feel compelled to deny all of our prejudices. In fact, when we hold prejudices against certain groups—groups that it is socially acceptable to hold prejudices against—we often don't see them as prejudices at all, but as facts. For example, not too long ago it was socially acceptable for White people to openly admit holding prejudicial beliefs about Black people, which they saw as justified because most White people believed that Black racial inferiority was simply *true*. Today this belief is understood to be untrue, and to admit to holding such a belief is no longer considered acceptable in most circles. However, admitting to prejudices against people considered overweight (especially women) *is* currently acceptable. Not only are these prejudices acceptable, but many magazines, for example, openly ridicule women perceived as overweight.

While there are health risks to obesity, not all people who are overweight are unhealthy (Lavie et al., 2015; Tomiyama et al., 2016). But the beauty and entertainment industries are invested in selling us the *idea* of fat as ugly, as undisciplined, and as worthy of contempt. These ideas allow us to rationalize our prejudice. The economic interest in maintaining these prejudices is so deep that they are marketed to all people. Consequently, girls who have not even reached puberty are socialized into a culture of dieting, and very few people feel satisfied with their bodies regardless of their size or health (Grogan, 2016; Levin & Kilbourne, 2008). These industries relentlessly present the image of the ideal body, and this ideal has become increasingly unattainable and in some contexts (such as the modeling industry) unhealthy. In fact, the image is so unrealistic that the magazine cover models themselves don't actually look like the images presented; images are routinely digitally modified to reshape their bodies, decrease their weight, enhance their breasts, remove their pores, and more. This leads to deep body dissatisfaction, which in turn translates into billions of dollars for the beauty and diet industries.

WHAT IS DISCRIMINATION?

When we *act* on our prejudices, we are *discriminating*. Acts of discrimination can include ignoring, avoidance, exclusion, ridicule, jokes, slander, threats, and violence.

> 📖 **Discrimination:** Action based on prejudice toward social others. When we act on our prejudgments, we are discriminating.

Consider this example: You are at a play and you notice that the person in the seat next to yours is fumbling with something. You feel irritated by the distraction. You turn to look at her and see that what she is fumbling with is a white cane. Once you realize that she is blind, she is placed in your mind into a new social category that triggers a new set of possible responses to her. These responses could range from ignoring (because you are not sure of the proper way to communicate with someone who is blind) or avoidance (if you find her blindness discomfiting), to an offer of help (based on an assumption that she will need it). Your irritation has suddenly shifted to compassion and concern. If you decide to offer your assistance, you may, without even realizing it, speak more slowly than you normally would to an adult stranger, reflecting a common (but unaware) assumption that a visual impairment also implies cognitive impairments.

> ✓ **PERSPECTIVE CHECK:** The example discussed in the text assumes the perspective of a person without disabilities who has not thought deeply about ableism. If you come from the perspective of a person with a disability (or have a person with a disability in your life whom you advocate for), you are more likely to be informed on the issue and thus interact more constructively.

While you might insist that you would never interact differently with a blind person than with anyone else, research supports the prediction that you would (Dovidio et al., 2005; J. Eberhardt, 2019; FitzGerald & Hurst, 2017; Greenwald & Krieger, 2006). That doesn't make you a bad person; our prejudices and the discriminatory behaviors they produce are often not consciously known to us. Nor do we have to be aware of them in order for them and their effects to be real.

The prejudice that leads to the differential treatment we name here—either ignoring/avoiding the blind woman or offering unsolicited help and speaking as if to a child—is not unique to us, and can be predicted precisely because of that fact. The messages that reinforce prejudice toward blind people are everywhere and affect all of us. This prejudice in turn informs our behavior. Consider representations of people with disabilities in media, as either inspirational heroes valorized for having "overcome" the tragedy of disability or horror movie villains whose ability to scare victims is connected to "freaky" eyes or disfigurements of the body. Add to that admonishments to children to avoid activities that could cause them to go blind (implying that this would be the worst possible condition to have).

When we add the fact that most sighted people don't know any low vision, visually impaired, or blind people (because in our society most people with visual impairments are separated out and sent to special schools and workplaces), you ensure the likelihood of problematic ideas and interactions. Notice that blind people (and people with other exceptionalities) are both highly *visible* in the ways their blindness is amplified in films and popular culture, and at the same time *invisible* in that they are often separated from the mainstream. This dynamic sets us up to rely on misinformation and starts the cycle of prejudice and discrimination. We are not saying every person will discriminate in these specific ways against the woman in the theater, but many will. In addition, given the dynamics of prejudice and discrimination, our own personal assessment of whether we will is simply not reliable.

ALL HUMANS HAVE PREJUDICE AND DISCRIMINATE

Just as all people have prejudices, learned from socialization, all people discriminate. The blind woman in our previous example may also hold prejudices against us because we are sighted. Based on her previous experiences with sighted people, she may assume that we are ignorant about people with disabilities and that we will be condescending toward her. Thus, if we attempt to speak to her, she may ignore us; she is discriminating against us based on her prejudice toward us. However, her prejudice and discrimination against us will not have the same impact as will ours against her (we will discuss why in Chapters 5 and 6).

If we all have our prejudices, can we avoid discriminating? Without conscious effort, this is highly unlikely; because prejudice informs how we view others, it necessarily informs how we act toward others. This action may be subtle—as subtle as avoidance and uninterest. But this lack of interest is not accidental or benign; it is socialized and results in not developing relationships—in this case, with people with disabilities. However, while we can't avoid prejudice, we can work to recognize our prejudices and gain new information and ways of thinking that will inform more just actions.

A key aspect to challenging our prejudices is challenging the social segregation that is built into the culture; the more educated we become about people who are different from us and the more relationships we build with them, the more likely we are to have constructive responses when interacting with other members of their group. This education requires more than knowing one or two individuals in the past and in a limited way, such as having a coworker or neighbor who is blind. If we engage in ongoing study and education, while also building wide-ranging and authentic relationships with people who are blind, we are more likely to have an informed rather than superficial response to the woman in the theater.

In order to get a sense of the power of our deep-structure, below-the-surface socialization in terms of our ideas about and actions toward others, consider this thought experiment:

You are going about your day and engaging in conversations with the following people: your friends, your romantic partner, your children, and your supervisor. You might be joking with your friends, sweet-talking with your romantic partner, speaking with formality to your supervisor, and talking irritably with your children. Now add a layer of context: your friends in the classroom before class versus on the weekend at the bar; your romantic partner while walking across campus versus alone in your dorm room; your children when they are celebrating an accomplishment versus struggling with a disappointment; and your supervisor when you are receiving positive feedback on your work versus when you are explaining a series of missed deadlines.

In each of these scenarios you are weighing the value of the social group of the other person in relation to the value of your own social group in a given context. These relational values inform how you speak—your tone, the words you use, and even your facial expressions. The navigations we make are the result of our socialization about groups and do not generally occur at the conscious level. You don't need to pause and figure out how to switch gears from your friends to your supervisor; your awareness of the value relations is so internalized that you shift gears effortlessly.

Awareness of ourselves as socialized members of a number of intersecting groups within a particular culture in a particular time and place (social location or positionality) will increase our critical social justice literacy. We need to see the general patterns of our socialization and be aware of ourselves in shifting contexts. In other words, we need to step back, become aware of ourselves shifting gears, and examine the assumptions underlying these shifts and the behaviors they set in motion. When interacting cross-culturally with members of less familiar groups, the codes we rely on are more likely to be based on stereotypical assumptions and messages. A key goal of critical social justice literacy is to raise our awareness of these patterned codes. When we are more conscious of them, we are more equipped to change them when they are based upon misinformation.

Returning to the vignette of the search committee that opens this chapter, we can see that this scenario illustrates several dynamics related to the key concepts of prejudice and discrimination. First, every person in the room had prejudices about a male elementary school teacher. These prejudices were both negative (the candidate is less suitable because he is male) and positive (the candidate is more suitable because he is male). While the members of the hiring committee necessarily also held stereotypes, assumptions, and value judgments (prejudices) about female teachers, these prejudices were invisible, unremarkable, and taken for granted because female teachers are the norm in the elementary grades. Only the male teacher stood out to them. In other words, for someone to be seen as *not* suitable for the job based on their social group membership, someone else has to be seen *as* suitable for the job, based on their social group membership.

Second, each person tried to present this prejudice in a way that she believed was more socially acceptable than simply stating it bluntly. This indicates her awareness of the belief that it is wrong to be prejudiced.

And third, when someone pointed out the prejudice, others became defensive and insisted that no one in the group had any prejudice whatsoever. This illustrates the belief that it is possible to *avoid* prejudices altogether. Mary's final statement that they had policies and procedures that would prevent any prejudicial evaluations leads us to the next chapter.

In conclusion, we all have socially learned prejudices, but because they are learned, they can be unlearned. So what might it look like to unlearn prejudicial attitudes? Of course we have to first stop denying that we have prejudices and begin to engage in an honest examination of the messages that surround us and how we have absorbed them. We can do this through readings and other forms of education, exercises, and in dialogue with others. But it's not realistic to think we can accomplish this solely on our own. We need a supportive community that understands that learned prejudices are not a reflection of someone's moral character—absorbing misinformation that circulates at all levels of society is not a choice we are given. At the same time, we are responsible for our actions and should be accountable for their impact. Acceptance and responsibility are the first step. The second step is to work with others to put protections in place in the form of policies and practices that are measurable and can be enforced.

DISCUSSION QUESTIONS

1. Decades of research has established that all people have prejudice and all people act (discriminate) based on their prejudice, even when they think they do not hold any biases, much less act in discriminatory ways. Explain how this is possible.
2. What are some steps we can take to minimize the effects of bias and safeguard against the impacts of discrimination on social others?

EXTENSION ACTIVITIES

1. Generate a list of actions (verbs) and personality attributes (characteristics) that people in various occupations perform and have. For example:

Teacher	Environmentalist
Police officer	Dentist
Soldier	Counselor
Librarian	Stay-at-home parent
Scientist	Housekeeper
Farmer	Car wash attendant

What is the picture in your mind of the person who holds that occupation? Try to be honest about your *immediate* images and expectations. What gender, race, and class is that person? Does the person have a visible disability? Is she or he someone who will observe religious/holy days? If so, which ones? *(Note: Researchers have observed that the faster subjects respond to the prompts in the Harvard Implicit Association Test, the more accurate a measure the test is of their attitudes and beliefs. This is why in this extension activity we ask for your immediate thoughts.)*

Then compare your list with others' lists. Based on these images and expectations, how might we behave toward the person?

2. Get a magazine and choose 10 photos of people, representing a range of differences and occupations. Swap your photos with others (so you are working with a different set). Sort the people in the photos according to each of the following questions:

   1. Who's the smartest?
   2. Who's the wealthiest?
   3. Who's the most religious?
   4. Who reads a lot?
   5. Who's careful with money?
   6. Who's a stay-at-home parent?
   7. Who's the most likely to feel included in society?
   8. Who's the most likely to feel isolated?
   9. Who's the most likely to be put in charge?
   10. Who's the most likely to travel freely anywhere in the world?

   Then pick one question and rank all 10 photographs for that question (for example, how would you organize the 10 people from "smartest" to "not the smartest").

   Optional assignment: Interview two people (outside your class), asking them to do what you did. Write a short essay about your findings. What patterns do you see in the responses? What do these patterns reveal about how bias works?

PATTERNS TO PRACTICE SEEING

1. How do people often respond when their prejudices are pointed out? How might an understanding of how social bias works help us respond more constructively and protect against bias?
2. What kind of person is most often depicted as prejudiced? What kinds of people are depicted as free from prejudice? Notice the details in how they are depicted (accent, manner/isms, gender, education, age, and so on).

CHAPTER 5

Oppression and Power

"The only one holding you back is you."
"Saying you're oppressed is whining. Just get over it."

This chapter introduces the concept of power, which transforms group bias into oppression. We explain the difference between concepts such as "race prejudice" (which anyone can hold) and "racism," which only the dominant racial group can impose. The chapter introduces the "ism" terms (e.g., racism, sexism, classism) and explains how these terms allow us to capture the dynamics of prejudice and discrimination, plus structural power at the group level.

> **Vocabulary to practice using:** hegemony; power; oppression; internalized dominance; internalized oppression

Let's return to the hiring committee vignette in Chapter 4. Regardless of the final choice the committee makes, it is impossible for the candidate's gender *not* to play a role in the decision. Gender would play a role even if the committee had not openly discussed it and whether or not the committee was aware that it did. We all view people through the socialized lenses of group memberships—theirs and ours.

Gender socialization influences every aspect of our perceptions and evaluations, both of ourselves and others. Returning to the glasses metaphor introduced in Chapter 3, gender is one of the key frames through which we understand the world. We are *always* wearing these glasses, and in the example of the hiring committee, always reading the resumes through them. We don't notice the frames when all of the resumes match what we expect to see. Because the position is one traditionally held by women, we automatically assume that we are reading women's resumes. As soon as we come across a resume that does not match this assumption—one that is not expected for the context—we are surprised, and become conscious of our gender expectations because they are not being met. We now begin to interpret the candidate's qualifications based on our gender expectations for *male* elementary school teachers.

If the candidate is not hired due to prejudice against him as a male, this will constitute discrimination but not oppression. However, if he is not hired because of prejudice against him based on an assumption that he is gay, this will constitute oppression. To put it another way, Mary (who is prejudiced against a *gay* candidate) is enacting oppression, but Liz (who is prejudiced against a *male* candidate) is not. Why?

Why is Mary enacting oppression but Liz is not? In order to understand the difference, we must build on the concepts of prejudice and discrimination by adding an understanding of how *power* works. But before we begin this discussion, let's revisit an important element of critical thinking introduced in Chapter 3, "Culture and Socialization." Distinguishing between the impacts of Mary's prejudice and Liz's prejudice will likely seem unfair, at least initially. Understanding the interplay between our individual identity and our social group identities is central to understanding the difference. We remind readers that the way we have been taught to think about this interplay hides its operation in society.

SOCIAL STRATIFICATION

In Chapter 3 we discussed that individuals belong to various social groups. For the purposes of understanding *socialization*, we described how important it is to recognize the significance of these social groupings. For the purposes of understanding *oppression*, we must also understand that these groups are given different value in our society. The term to describe this difference in valuation is *social stratification*.

> ✓ **PERSPECTIVE CHECK:** Figure 5.1 is not intended to imply that these are the only forms of oppression in society, or the only terms to identify groups of people. For example, we have not included oppressions such as adultism, ageism, linguicism, or sizeism, nor have we separated out the way that antisemitism is both a form of religious oppression and also ethnic oppression. This is not to deny the reality of these forms of oppression but rather to provide a starting point for those new to the recognition of group membership and social stratification. Further, while we refer to "Peoples of Color," different terms may be used, such as People of the Global Majority, IBPOC or BIPOC (Black, Indigenous, People of Color), White adjacent, or White passing. These are important nuances to know about your specific context. Treat this table as a starting point for understanding the basics of relationships of power between groups.

All major social group categories (such as gender) are organized into binary, either/or identities (e.g., men/women). These identities depend upon their dynamic relationship with one another, wherein each identity is defined by its opposite. The category "men" can have no meaning without an understanding of a category that is not-men (i.e., "women"). Not only are these groups constructed

Figure 5.1. Group Identities Across Relations of Power

Minoritized Group	Oppression	Dominant Group
Perceived as Peoples of Color	Racism	Perceived as White
Poor; Working Class; Middle Class	Classism	Owning/Ruling Class
(Cis) Women; Transgender; Nonbinary	Sexism	(cis) Men
Gay; Lesbian; Bisexual; Two-Spirit	Heterosexism	Heterosexuals
Muslims; Buddhists; Jews; Hindus; other non-Christian groups	Religious Oppression; Antisemitism	Christians
Persons with disabilities, including physical or cognitive, visible or nonvisible	Ableism	Persons without disabilities
Immigrants (or people perceived to be)	Nationalism	Citizens (or people perceived to be)
Indigenous Peoples	Colonialism	White Settlers

as opposites, but they are also ranked in a hierarchy. This means that one group (men) is granted more value than its opposite (women). The group that is positioned as more valuable—the *dominant* group—will have more access to the resources of society. The group that is positioned as less valuable—the *minoritized* group—will have less access to the resources of society. These resources include decision-making power (they have seats at the table where policies that affect others are made) and representation (their interests and experiences are visible and addressed). The dominant group's perspective is presented as normal and objective, and typically not identified as a particular perspective at all (the National Basketball Association); the relationally positioned minoritized group will be presented as "special interest" or limited, if it is represented at all (the *Women's* National Basketball Association). The terms used to describe these relationships of inequality between dominant and minoritized groups usually end in "ism." Figure 5.1 illustrates the historical and current relationships between some of these key social groups in Canada and the United States and the term for that specific form of oppression (a specific "ism").

> 📖 **Social Stratification:** The concept that social groups are ranked in a hierarchy of value. Groups that are valued more highly (dominant groups) have a greater degree of access to social, political, and economic resources. Beliefs about differences between the groups are used to justify the unequal distribution of resources.

As you read down the table, you will probably find yourself in some dominant and some minoritized group positions (i.e., falling sometimes on the left side and sometimes on the right side of the oppression column). One is not simply a man, but a cisgender man, a White man, or a man of Color; or a working-class White man, perhaps a working-class gay White man, or a heterosexual Christian man of Color without disability—and a position on one side for one identity does not cancel out another side for a different identity. Rather, these identity positions intersect in important ways.

> **Minoritized Group:** A social group that is devalued overall in society in relation to its dominant group. This devaluing is created and maintained through legal, historical, social, and institutional authority. It is sustained by how the group is represented, what degree of access to resources it is granted, and how the unequal access is rationalized. Traditionally, a group in this position has been referred to as the "minority" group. However, this language has been replaced with the term "minoritized" (making it a verb and thus active) in order to capture the dynamics that create the lower status in society. The term also signals that a group's status is not necessarily related to how many or few of them there are in the population at large. Inequality between groups is based on power, not numbers—minoritized groups can be larger in numbers than dominant groups.
>
> **Dominant Group:** The group at the top of the social hierarchy. In any relationship between groups that define each other (men/women, person without disability/person with disability), the dominant group is the group that is valued more highly. This higher value is created and maintained through legal, historical, social, and institutional authority. It is sustained by how the group is represented, their degree of access to resources, and how that access is rationalized. The dominant group sets the norms by which the minoritized group is understood and found lacking. Dominant groups have greater access to the resources of society and benefit from the existence of the inequality. Avoid referring to the minoritized group as "non" some dominant group, e.g., "non-White."

UNDERSTANDING POWER

In order to oppress, a group must hold (or uphold) institutional power in society. In this way, the dominant group's worldview is imposed on others and controls the ideas (ideologies), political rules (the technical mechanisms), and social rules for communication (discourses) that we are all taught (socialized) to see as normal, natural, and required for a functioning society. This domination is historical (long-term) and normalized.

> **Power** in the context of understanding oppression refers to the ideas, methods, and narratives with which the interests of the dominant group are imposed on everyone. Power is the ability to assert institutional control, ideological domination, and the imposition of one group's culture on others. While people who are not members of the dominant group can participate in imposing these interests, it is ultimately the dominant group who benefits.

Sometimes it can be difficult for individuals to understand power as a political and social concept because many of us do not see ourselves as having the ability to impose our personal beliefs on others. However, the choices we have and make as individuals and the barriers we may face are tied to our group memberships as well as to our positions within institutions. For example, a person without disabilities, while they may have problems and struggles, as a member of the dominant group has access and representation. In other words, there are major barriers that they simply do not face, and in fact they benefit from not having to compete with people who do face those barriers. Even if they are strong advocates for people with disabilities, society's institutions are set up in a way to advantage them and uphold ableism as a social system.

At the group level, power is maintained by imposing ideology across society. *Hegemony* is the concept that refers to a group's ability to control the systems by which this happens. Recall that ideology refers to the stories, myths, explanations, definitions, and rationalizations that are used to justify inequality between the dominant and the minoritized groups. The key element of hegemony is that it enables domination to occur with the consent of the minoritized group, rather than primarily by force. If people have been taught through the culture's ideology that they deserve their unequal positions—that these positions are fair and natural—no force is necessary. In other words, the minoritized group accepts their lower position in society because they come to accept the rationalizations for it. Hegemony, then, includes the ability to define and impose self-discipline on others in ways that serve dominant group interests.

> **Hegemony:** The imposition of dominant group ideology across society. Hegemony makes it difficult to escape or to resist "believing in" this ideology. Social control is achieved through conditioning rather than primarily by force or intimidation.

At the institutional level, power is maintained through the normalization and enforcement of rules. Sociologist Allan Johnson (2004) describes the necessary shift we must make conceptually to grasp this relationship: moving away from individualistic thinking (sexism is the outcome of "bad men"), to a systems model of thinking (sexism—or "patriarchy"—is a social system which everyone accepts because we have been socialized into it). Johnson writes, "If a society is oppressive, then people who grow up and live in it will tend to accept, identify with, and participate in it as 'normal' and unremarkable. . . . When oppression is woven into the fabric of everyday life, we don't need to go out of our way to be overly oppressive in order for an oppressive system to produce oppressive consequences" (p. 26). While acts of hatred are often easier to see, it is what is harder to see in the patterns of everyday life that most powerfully underwrites oppression.

WHAT IS OPPRESSION?

To oppress is to hold down and deny a social group full access and potential in a given society. *Oppression* refers to a set of policies, practices, traditions, norms, definitions, and explanations (discourses) that function to systematically limit access for one social group to the benefit of its opposite (dominant versus minoritized).

> **Oppression:** The prejudice of one social group against another, backed by the institutional power to infuse and normalize that prejudice across all aspects of a society. Oppression occurs when one group is able to discriminate against another group throughout society because it controls the institutions. Further, those institutions continue to uphold the ideas of their original creators (who were also members of dominant groups). Oppression describes discrimination occurring at the group level and goes beyond individuals and their intentions. In other words, oppression is built into society and has become "normal" and "natural." Sexism, racism, classism, ableism, and heterosexism are specific forms of oppression.

Oppression is different from prejudice and discrimination in that prejudice and discrimination describe dynamics that occur at the individual level and in which all individuals participate. In contrast, oppression occurs when one group's prejudice is *backed by legal authority and historical, social, and institutional power*. This backing of power is what positions the group as the *dominant group*. This differential in collective power transforms the prejudice into a far-reaching system (or form of oppression).

Common shorthand is: Prejudice + Power = Oppression.

Oppression involves institutional control, ideological domination, and the imposition of the dominant group's culture on the minoritized group. No individual member of the dominant group has to do anything specific to oppress a member of the minoritized group; the prejudice and discrimination are built into the social system as a whole and become automatic, normalized, and taken for granted.

The example of women's suffrage (gaining the right to vote) in the United States and Canada illustrates several features that distinguish oppression from discrimination alone.

> ✓ **PERSPECTIVE CHECK:** In this example of suffrage which we use to explain the concept of *oppression*, we use the categories "men" and "women" as defined in mainstream society and in law in the context of this example. These categories of identity have since been challenged and expanded. We will build our understanding of the multidimensional aspects of group identities (called *intersectionality*) in later chapters.

Women of course played a primary role in the struggle for suffrage; they had to organize and fight to gain the vote. Yet ultimately the ability to grant women suffrage rested in the hands of men; women could not grant themselves the right to vote because they did not hold *institutional power*. Only men could actually grant suffrage to women because only men held the institutional positions of power to change the laws. Hence, while both groups could be prejudiced against the other, men's prejudice took on a much more powerful and all-encompassing form, a form of oppression termed *sexism*.

Because men controlled all of the major institutions—government, media, economics, religion, medicine, education, police, and military—the collective effect of men's prejudice was radically different. Indeed, men had set up these institutions and made the rules that excluded women in the first place. In this way, men's prejudices were infused into the very fabric of society. Prejudice is often implicit, so this would happen whether or not any individual man agreed that men's attitudes should be infused in these ways. Because men made the rules, the rules reflected their prejudices and served their interests. For example, because scientists began with the premise of female inferiority, their research questions and the interpretation of their findings were informed by that assumption (Caleb, 2022; Holdcroft, 2007; Tsakiropoulou-Summers & Kitsi-Mitakou, 2018). Because they were in the position to disseminate their findings, they further reinforced and rationalized their superior positions. All other institutions (also controlled by men) were constructed in ways that normalized male superiority (Tuana, 1989): The clergy preached male superiority from the pulpit and rationalized it through the holy books; doctors used the male body as the reference point for health; psychiatrists based definitions of mental health on male norms for emotions and their beliefs about who was capable of rational thought; and male professors taught men's history, ideas, and concerns.

The term for male centrality is *androcentrism*. Androcentrism is not simply the idea that men are superior to women, but a deeper premise that supports this idea: the definition of males and male experience as the standard for *human*, and females and female experience as a deviation from that standard.

> **Androcentric:** Male-centered. The centering of society on the interests, needs, norms, patterns, and perspectives of men.

Androcentrism remains invisible in all contexts except when we are specifically referring to women, for example: women's literature, women's movies (or "chick flicks"), women scientists, and women's rights. "Men" (as a group) are the invisible reference point that women are measured against, and because women do not fit the norms of men, they appear inferior. Male superiority is rationalized, normalized, disseminated, and reinforced through every social institution. As a result of its invisibility, male superiority becomes the unnoticed water we all swim in. Returning to our suffrage example, because oppression is one group's prejudice plus the power to enforce that prejudice throughout society, even if individual men believed women should have the right to vote, as men they still benefited from women's exclusion from voting (for example, they did not have to speak to women's interests as voters, they didn't have to compete with over half of the population for how to use society's resources, and so on). Thus oppression need not be personal, and intentions are irrelevant in terms of benefiting from oppression when you are in the dominant group.

In the case of women's suffrage, we can see how intersecting group identities add more layers of complexity. Women's suffrage is a more complicated story when we add the dimensions of class and race. White women of the upper classes led the initial movement for women's suffrage in both Canada and the United States (A. Y. Davis, 1981; Devereux, 2005; Newman, 1999). In Canada, racial exclusion in suffrage was not removed until the 1940s and the right to vote freely was not extended to Indigenous peoples until the 1960s. In the United States, Black women did not have full access to the right to vote until the Voting Rights Act of 1965. So while the women we commonly refer to as suffragists were oppressed *as women*, they were privileged as *White* women: Their race was made neutral and natural to the exclusion and marginalization of women of Color, as

Figure 5.2. Dolores Huerta (b. 1930)

Huerta is a pioneering labor and civil rights leader, and the cofounder (with Cesar Chávez) of the United Farmworkers of America. In 1955 she became involved with a grassroots organization (the Community Service Organization) that was fighting police brutality in the community and pushing for improved public services. It was at CSO that she met Cesar Chávez. Together they became involved in supporting farm workers, and she played a central role as cofounder, organizer, and leader for the movement. She led some of the most important peaceful demonstrations and public boycotts, spoke out against the harmful effects of pesticides, organized field strikes, and lobbied for changes to policies to support workers. All of her efforts helped win recognition for farm workers' rights. She was also significantly involved in the feminist movement and challenged gender discrimination within the farm workers movement.

Today, the Dolores Huerta Foundation pursues its mandate to motivate and organize sustainable communities in order to attain social justice.

Note. Photo available at https://feminismandreligion.com/2012/11/02/delores-huerta-si-se-puede/

they were held up as representing *all* women. For example, one of the key issues of suffragists was entry into the workforce. But of course women of Color had long been working outside the home. Their interests may have been better served by calls for economic justice. The life and work of Dolores Huerta (Figure 5.2) embodies the concept of intersecting group identities.

UNDERSTANDING THE "ISMS"

In order to understand how oppression works and why it is different from discrimination, we must understand that oppression involves pervasive, historical, and political relationships of unequal power among social groups. It is more than an individual, situational, or momentary interaction. Scholars capture this large-scale, historical, political, and pervasive relationship through the "ism" words, such as racism, sexism, heterosexism, classism, ableism. When scholars use the "ism" words, we are not referring primarily to individual acts of discrimination, which all people can commit. Rather, we are referring to specific forms of oppression.

The "ism" words give us the language to discuss specific forms of oppression and include in the discussion the reality of unequal social and institutional power between dominant and minoritized groups. In this way, we avoid denying power dynamics by reducing oppression to individual acts of discrimination and claiming that these acts are comparable, regardless of who commits them. From this perspective, "reverse racism" or "reverse sexism" are misnomers and do not exist, because racism and sexism (or any form of oppression) refer to power relations that are historic, embedded, and pervasive—they are not fluid and do not flip back and forth; the same groups who have historically held institutional power in the United States and Canada continue to do so.

> **STOP:** Discrimination and the "isms" (e.g., sexism and racism) are not the same thing. All people have prejudice and discriminate, but only the dominant group has the social, historical, and institutional power to back their prejudice and infuse it throughout the entire society. Thus these terms cannot be used interchangeably.

For example, despite suffrage and women's numerical majority, in 2025 women in the United States hold only 26% of 100 Senate seats and 29% of 435 House seats (women hold 28% of the 535 seats in Congress). Statewide elected executives are 30% women; 12 of the 50 governors are women (11 are White, one is Latina); of the 1,686 mayors of large cities in the United States, 25% are women. Four of the 9 members of the Supreme Court are women (44%). Out of the 59 presidential elections since the founding of the United States, only one woman has ever held the position of vice president, and a woman has never been elected president (Center for American Women and Politics, 2025).

In 2025, Canada appointed a slightly less than gender-balanced cabinet with 46% of cabinet positions held by women (18 of the 39 members are women). Furthermore, women remain underelected to the federal government, making up only 30% of members of Parliament (MPs) in the House of Commons (out of 343 seats in the House, 104 are held by women MPs). Many of the cabinet positions, such as Treasury, National Defence, Justice, Public Safety, Energy and Natural

Resources, and Finance and National Revenue, are held by men. Cabinet positions such as Jobs and Families, Health, Emergency Management and Community Resilience, and three Secretary of State positions related to children and youth, seniors, and nature are held by women (House of Commons of Canada, 2025). Fewer women MPs will result in fewer women representatives available to serve and be a voice on the dozens of standing House committees. In 2023, across Canada women represented 33% of city councillors and 22% of mayors (Federation of Canadian Municipalities, 2023).

In 2025, women's representation in federal government is 28% (for United States) and 31% (for Canada) (Inter-Parliamentary Union, 2025). The number one country in terms of women holding office is Rwanda (with women holding 64% of seats in 2025). Only one country in the top 10 for share of women in parliament in 1995 is still there in 2025 (Iceland at #9). In 2025, the parliaments with the most women representatives are: Rwanda, Cuba, Nicaragua, Mexico, Andorra, United Arab Emirates, Costa Rica, Bolivia, Iceland, and Monaco (Inter-Parliamentary Union, 2025). Women parliamentarians most frequently hold portfolios such as: Women and gender equality, Family and children affairs, Social inclusion and development, Social protection and social security, and Culture—reinforcing in their political roles their presumed greatest competence as in the familiar social roles as caretakers (UN Women, n.d.). While numbers do matter, oppression is not simply the result of a numerical majority (e.g., women are the majority of the world, as are poor and working-class people, yet they don't hold institutional power).

Oppression is a multidimensional imbalance of social, political, and institutional power that builds over time and then becomes normal and acceptable to most people in the society. There are four key elements of oppression:

Oppression is historical. The underrepresentation of women in government is not simply the result of the last federal election in a given country. Women's exclusion from government in the United States and Canada well into the 21st century illustrates their long-term overall exclusion as citizens, guaranteeing that they would have no role in deciding how society would be organized or governed. The cumulative effect of this exclusion cannot be corrected in a single election nor within one generation. The institution of government itself—its processes and practices—has been established by men. If tomorrow only women were appointed to government, they could not govern outside the rules that men had established. To reshape the institution and its norms and practices would take generations of effort (and be solidly resisted all along the way). (White) women received the right to vote in the early 20th century in Canada and the United States, but injustice between men and women did not end the day suffrage was granted. In fact, victories enacted through law, while important, often work to slow progress because they mislead people into believing that a single change has solved the issue. In 2025, many key protections in the U.S. Voting Rights Act have been struck down, illustrating the tenuous nature of civil rights advancements in the face of deeply embedded systems of oppression.

Oppression is ideological. Ideology, as the dominant ideas of a society, plays a powerful role in the perpetuation of oppression. Ideology is disseminated throughout all institutions and rationalizes social inequality. Via ideology, oppression is embedded within individual consciousness and rationalized as normal; once people are socialized into their place in the hierarchy, injustice is assured. Oppressive beliefs and misinformation are internalized by both the dominant and the minoritized groups, guaranteeing that overall each group will play its assigned role in relation to the other, and that these roles will be justified as natural. Thus oppression cannot be remedied through law alone. When we believe the social hierarchy is natural, it is difficult to see our positions within it as unequal at all. Not all women were invested in gaining suffrage or saw themselves as oppressed without it. The suffrage movement had to convince other women, as well as men, that it was an issue of rights (although only men had the institutional power to actually grant suffrage to women).

> **Ideology:** The big, shared ideas of a society that are reinforced throughout all of the institutions and thus are very hard to avoid encountering and believing. These ideas include the stories, myths, representations, explanations, definitions, and rationalizations that are used to justify inequality in the society. *Individualism* and *meritocracy* are examples of specific ideologies.

Oppression is institutional. Government is only one of many institutions that men dominate. Men also dominate all other major institutions of society (military, medicine, media, criminal justice, law, policing, sports, art, finance, industry, higher education, religion, and science). These institutions are interconnected and function together to uphold male dominance across the whole of society. Using our suffrage example, while male government officials denied women the right to vote, all the other institutions of society which are dominated by men worked simultaneously with government to block suffrage. Male doctors claimed that women did not have the capacity to engage in politics, male psychiatrists claimed that women did not have the capacity for rational thought necessary for suffrage, male clergy preached that a woman's place was in the home and ordained by God *him*self—a male God who only spoke to men and whom only men could speak for, male journalists published editorials critiquing suffrage, male police officers shut down demonstrations and made arrests, and male judges determined punishments (Bem, 2004; E. C. Green, 1997). Women were not in a position to use any institution in service of suffrage and could only rely on a few sympathetic men who could present their case for them or allow them limited opportunities to present it for themselves.

Oppression is cultural. Oppression is embedded in all dimensions of culture. Referring to the iceberg diagram from Chapter 3, consider how the norms of what constitute deep culture (the unspoken and unconscious rules) are gendered and manifest in government processes and policies. These norms privilege men. Women who do enter politics are most successful when they are able to demonstrate their ability to fit into the androcentric (male-centered) culture (by either being ultra-feminine and nonthreatening or being "one of the boys" and nonthreatening). Demonstrating their fluency with the norms of androcentric culture demands that women conform with the deep structure rules of masculinity (e.g., don't show emotions, don't be distracted by family responsibilities, don't name sexism). While demonstrating this fluency, women simultaneously enact the deep structure rules of "their own" culture. Thus minoritized group members carry the extra burden of duality. W.E.B. Du Bois (1903/1989), speaking about race, coined the term "double consciousness" to capture this burden of having to perform the dominant culture's norms as well as your own. Because none of these conditions of oppression apply to men, there is no oppression against men *as men* and therefore no "reverse" sexism (although there *is* oppression against men where they also inhabit oppressed positions, e.g., *working class* White men or *gay Asian* men or *elderly Sikh* men).

> **STOP:** There is no such thing as reverse racism or reverse sexism (or the reverse of any form of oppression). While women can be just as prejudiced as men, women cannot be "just as sexist as men" because they do not hold political, economic, and institutional power. Social justice scholars reserve the "isms" terms exclusively to capture the essential difference in power that transforms the dominant group's prejudice into a system of oppression.

Men may be a numerical minority in a given context and experience short-term and contextual discrimination. For example, male teachers in elementary education are the minority in number and may experience feelings of isolation and disconnection from cultural norms in elementary school, and they may experience discrimination and exclusion from the women with whom they work. However, this is not oppression, because while these feelings and experiences may be painful, they are individual, temporary, and situational, and do not have the necessary elements to constitute oppression. The historical, ideological, and cultural aspects of schooling are still androcentric and will reward and advance men over women. Men are most often in positions of authority, advance faster than women—even in female-dominated fields such as K–8 education—and are consistently paid more for the same work across multiple sectors (Bishu & Alkadry, 2016; Budig, 2002; McMurry, 2011).

Precisely because the care of children is associated with women, early childhood education is naturally seen to be the responsibility of women and perceived as little more than advanced babysitting with very low status. As children grow older, more male teachers and masculine approaches to schooling appear. For example, values associated with primary education such as play, community, cooperation, and sharing virtually disappear in the higher grades, as values such as rationality, independence, and competition take over. As well, the status of teaching increases in the higher grades because more men are present, and subject areas increase in status when they are associated with men: mathematics, science, and philosophy over literature, drama, and art (Charlesworth & Banaji, 2019; Llorens et al., 2021; Ortiz-Martínez et al., 2023).

American philosopher Marilyn Frye (1983) illustrates the interlocking forces of oppression through the metaphor of a birdcage. If you come up close and press your face against the bars of a birdcage, you will have a close view of the bird inside, but your perception of the bars will be limited. If you turn to look closely at just one bar in the cage, you cannot see the other bars. If your conception of what is before you is determined by this limited view, you could look at that one bar and be unable to see why the bird could not escape by simply flying around it. Even if you slowly moved around the cage and closely inspected each bar, one at a time, you still would not understand why the bird would have trouble going past any particular bar and flying away. But if instead of the close-up view, you step back and take a wider view, you begin to see how the bars come together in an interlocking pattern, a pattern that works to hold the bird in place. It now becomes clear that the bird is surrounded by a network of systematically related barriers. In isolation, none of these barriers would be that difficult for the bird to get around, but because of their connections to one another, they can be as confining as solid walls.

It is now possible to grasp one of the reasons why oppression can be hard to recognize: We have been socialized into this close-up view, focusing on single situations, exceptions, and anecdotal evidence, rather than on broader, interlocking patterns. Although there are always exceptions, the patterns are consistent and well documented; the experience of oppressed people is that their lives are confined and shaped by forces and barriers that are not accidental, occasional, or avoidable, but are systematically related to each other in such a way as to consistently restrict and penalize their movement.

Dominant groups have the most narrow or limited view of society because they do not have to understand the experiences of the minoritized group in order to survive; because they control the institutions, they have the means to legitimize their perspective ("I worked hard for what I have, why can't they?"). Minoritized groups often have the widest view of society, in that they must understand both their own and the dominant group's perspective—develop a double consciousness—to succeed. But because they are on the margins, the view of minoritized groups is seen as the least legitimate in society, dismissed via phrases such as "they just have a victim mentality," are "woke snowflakes," want "special rights and pronouns," and "play identity politics."

In order to understand the power of dismissive phrases we must understand language as political. Language is not a neutral transmitter of a universal, objective, or fixed reality. Rather, language is the way we *construct* reality, the framework we use to give meaning to our experiences and perceptions within a given society. The scholarly term for language in all of its dimensions is *discourse*. One dimension of language is cultural, making it dependent on the historical and social moment in which it is used (e.g., colorblindness as a means to end racism is a discourse, and one that would not have made sense before the Civil Rights movement). Furthermore, discourse is not just words; it includes all of the ways we communicate with others, including body language, pauses, and emotions. Discourses include not only what we say, but also what we *don't* say (how we learn what lies under the surface of the iceberg).

> **Discourse:** The academic term for meaning that is communicated through language in all of its forms. Discourses include myths, narratives, explanations, words, concepts, and ideology. Discourses are not universally shared among humans; they represent a particular cultural worldview and are shared among members of a given culture at a given time. Discourse is different from ideology because it refers to all of the ways in which we communicate ideology, including verbal and nonverbal aspects of communication, symbols, and representations.

Take the word "tree," a seemingly neutral term. Yet notice that how we *see* the tree is connected to our frame of reference. A tree that looks big to someone who grew up on the East Coast might not look big to someone who grew up on the West Coast. A logger might see employment, an environmentalist might see a limited resource, and a member of the Coast Salish nation might see a sacred symbol of life. Each of these "ways of seeing" is a discourse and connects to other discourses (consider the politics between the logger and the environmentalist, and the environmentalist and the Coast Salish member). These politics are rooted in the meaning the tree has for each group, and the investments that result from those meanings.

Discourses, because they shape how we think about and relate to one another, shape relations of power. For example, the discourses of the dominant group about the minoritized group will always represent the dominant group's interests and thereby reinforce their meaning-making framework. Dominant discourses socialize us into seeing our positions in the hierarchy as natural. Scholars use the terms *internalized dominance* and *internalized oppression* to refer to this acceptance of our unequal positions (Adams et al., 2016; Freire, 1970; Nieto et al., 2010; Tappan, 2006).

INTERNALIZED DOMINANCE

Internalized dominance refers to those in the dominant group believing in and acting out (often unintentionally) the constant messages circulating in the culture that you and your group are superior to the minoritized group and thus entitled to your higher position.

Examples include:

- Rationalizing advantage as natural ("It's just human nature—someone has to be on top.")
- Rationalizing advantage as earned ("I worked hard to get where I am.")
- Perceiving you and your group as the most qualified for and entitled to the best jobs ("She only got the position over me because she's Black.")
- Living one's life segregated from the minoritized group yet feeling no loss or desire for connections with them ("I want my kids to grow up in a good neighborhood and go to good schools.")
- Lacking an interest in the perspectives of the minoritized group except in limited and controlled doses (e.g., during cultural film festivals, or holidays such as Chinese New Year) or when it appears to benefit the dominant group ("I want my child to experience diversity.")
- Feeling qualified to debate or explain away the experiences of minoritized groups ("I think you are taking this too personally, I don't think that's what he meant.")

> **Microaggressions:** The everyday slights and insults that minoritized people endure and dominant people don't notice or concern themselves with.

Internalized dominance manifests in our daily actions through what psychologist Derald Wing Sue (2010) termed *microaggressions*. By definition, microaggressions are everyday slights, insults, and insensitivities from dominant group members to minoritized members. These messages are expressed through statements and actions that remind the minoritized person of their lesser status. Examples of microaggressions are asking a multiracial person, "What are you?", telling an older woman, "I bet you were beautiful when you were young," and telling a Black person, "I don't see you as Black."

INTERNALIZED OPPRESSION

Internalized oppression refers to those in the minoritized group believing in and acting out (often unintentionally) the constant messages that you and your group are inferior to the dominant group and thus deserving of your lower position.

Examples include:

- Believing that dominant group members are more qualified for and deserving of their positions ("I understand. I'm glad he got the position. He's a natural.")
- Seeking the approval of and spending most of your time with members of the dominant group ("I'm the Whitest Chinese guy you'll ever meet!")
- Behaving in ways that please the dominant group and do not challenge the legitimacy of its position ("The company has said it's struggling, we can renegotiate our salaries another time, we don't want to risk job cuts.")
- Silently enduring microaggressions from the dominant group in order to avoid penalty ("Oh, it's okay. I didn't mind him hugging me.")
- Having low expectations for yourself and others associated with your group ("What do you expect when we dress like that? You have to have respect for yourself before expecting it from society.")
- Believing that your struggles with social institutions (such as education, employment, health care) are the result of your (or your group's) inadequacy, rather than the result of unequally distributed resources between dominant and minoritized groups ("Medication is expensive. If I had a better job I could have better care.")
- Harshly criticizing members of your group who do not assimilate to dominant norms ("Speak English!" "Come on. If you don't know how to use self-checkout, stay at home!")

Internalized dominance and internalized oppression create observable social group patterns in members of dominant and minoritized groups. While there will always be exceptions, these patterns are well documented, recognizable, and predictable (Adair & Howell, 2007). Figure 5.3 illustrates common patterns of each group as a result of their group's overall position in society. It illustrates the common patterns for each side of the social hierarchy, as well as how they fit perfectly together to hold each group in place.

Returning to the concept of *power*, in the context of understanding social justice, power refers to the ideological, technical, and discursive elements by which those in authority impose their ideas and interests. And further, it encompasses the role of internalized oppression in how these ideas are accepted. Michel Foucault's (1977/1995) analysis of a 19th-century prison structure may be helpful for understanding how power is institutionalized and how it sets up what historian Timothy Snyder (2017) calls "obeying in advance." The panopticon shown in Figure 5.4 is a design unveiled in 1843 in which the cells of a prison were located

Figure 5.3. Patterns of Internalized Dominance and Internalized Oppression

An individual from the DOMINANT GROUP	An individual from the MINORITIZED GROUP
Defines rules, judges what is appropriate, patronizes	Feels inappropriate, awkward, doesn't trust perception, looks to expert for definition
Is seen as, and feels, capable of making constructive changes	Is seen as, and feels, disruptive
Assumes responsibility for keeping system on course; acts without checking in with others	Blames self for not having capacity to change situation
Self-image of superiority, competence, in control, entitled, correct	Self-image of inferiority, incompetent, being controlled, not entitled, low self-esteem
Presumptuous, does not listen, interrupts, raises voice, bullies, threatens violence, becomes violent	Finds it difficult to speak up, timid, tries to please; holds back anger, resentment, and rage
Seeks to stand out as special	Feels secure staying in the background, feels vulnerable when singled out
Assumes anything is possible, can do whatever one wants, assumes everyone else can too	Feels confined by circumstances, limits aspirations, sees current situations in terms of past limits
Initiates, manages, plans, projects	Lacks initiative, responds, deals, copes, survives
Sees problems and situations in personal terms	Sees problems in social context, results of system
Sees experiences and feelings as unique, feels disconnected, often needs to verbalize feelings	Sees experiences and feelings as collectively understood and shared, no point in talking about them
Sees solutions to problems as promoting better feelings	Sees solutions to problems in actions that change conditions
Thinks own view of reality is the only one, obvious to all, assumes everyone agrees with this view; disagreements are result of lack of information, misunderstandings, and/or personalities	Always aware of at least two views of reality, their own and that of the dominant group
Views self as logical, rational; sees others as too emotional, out of control	Often thinks own feelings are inappropriate, a sign of inadequacy
Believes certain kinds of work below their dignity	Believes certain kinds of work beyond their ability
Does not believe or trust ability of others to provide leadership	Does not believe has capacity for leading

(continued)

Figure 5.3. (continued)

An individual from the DOMINANT GROUP	An individual from the MINORITIZED GROUP
Unaware of hypocrisy, contradictions	Sees contradictions, irony, hypocrisy
Fears losing control, public embarrassment	Laughs at self and others; sees humor as way of dealing with hypocrisy
Regards own culture as civilized, regards others' as underdeveloped, disadvantaged; turns to other culture to enrich humanity while invalidating them by calling them exotic	Feels own culture devalued; uses cultural forms to influence situation; humor, music, poetry, etc. to celebrate collective experience and community; sees these as being stolen

Source: Adapted from Adair & Howell (2007), with permission.

around the circumference of a circle with a tower in the center and a guard located in the tower. The key to the panopticon design is the funneling of light in ways that create strategic darkness and blindness. Much like the effects of being on stage with the lights shining in your eyes, the prisoners in the cells could not see the tower guard watching them. The prisoners were constantly visible to the central tower while they themselves were blinded—never knowing when they were being watched. Thus the guard could monitor the prisoners without the prisoners knowing when, or even *if*, they were being observed.

This model produced a type of *self*-policing, a self-imposed mechanism for control and supervision. In other words, the prisoner becomes fearful of the threat of the ever-watching eye of authority. Not knowing when that eye will be turned on him, he begins to monitor himself in order to avoid penalty. This structure of surveillance produces a conforming and passive prisoner.

Foucault argued that the panopticon was a metaphor for how power is transmitted and normalized through social institutions such as prisons, the military, hospitals, and schools; a metaphor for how these institutions socialize us into compliance with norms that serve controlling group interests. Those who have the motivation, authority, and resources to design, institute, and enforce the panopticon are those who hold institutional power in a society. These power relations are in place well before our birth, and we might think of ourselves as born into a cell that already exists and is waiting for us.

However, Foucault did not see these relations as fixed and unchangeable but rather as constantly reproduced and negotiated in society. This means that we have the ability to challenge power, but first we must see and understand how power works.

Consider the example of schools. Schools train students to conform to a set of self-disciplining measures by structuring students' time and handing out rewards and punishments such as grades, honors, tracked placements, detentions, and expulsions. While this seems normal to us, the organization of the school is not

Figure 5.4. The Panopticon

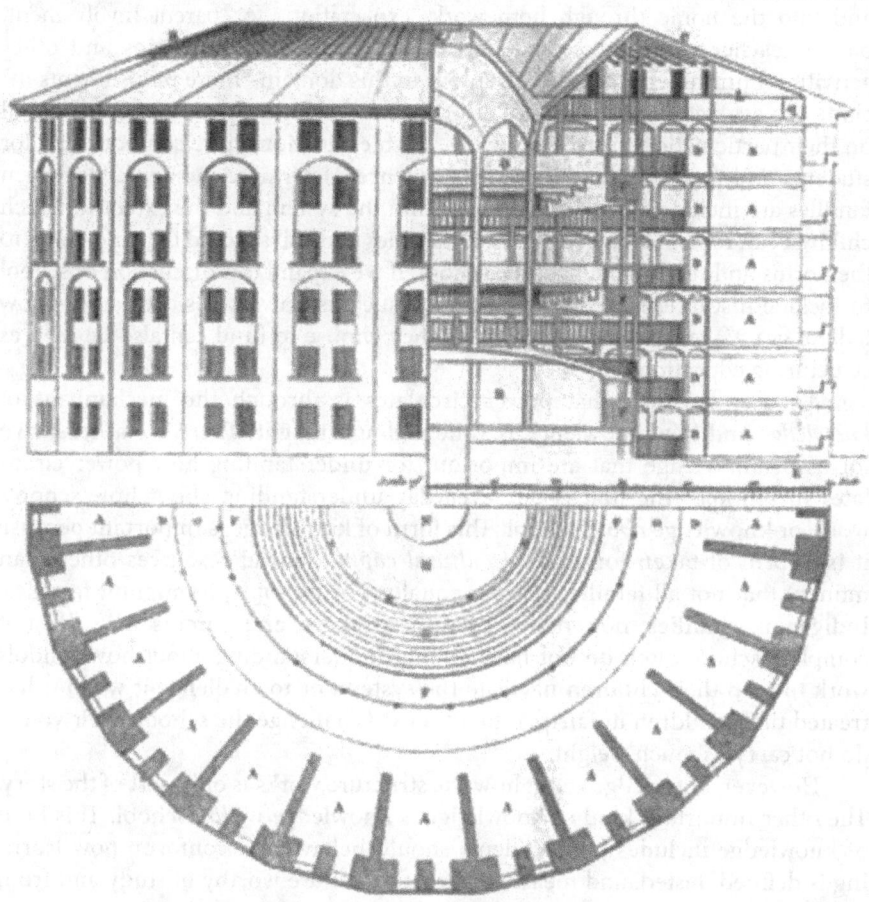

Source: https://www.moyak.com/papers/Panopticon.jpg

natural. Through its structures, the school regiments and monitors all activities, such as what will be studied; when, how, and for how long it will be studied; how proficiency will be demonstrated; how intelligence will be defined and measured; when (and often what) students will eat; when they will rest; when they will play; when they may use the bathroom; and when they will go home. The structures that regulate schools are also regimented and monitored. The principal oversees the activities within the school, while the school trustees or district officials monitor and regulate the schools in the district, and the relevant government bodies (state, provincial, federal, ministry of education) monitor and regulate the institution of schooling at large.

The school also mandates the continuation of this regimen beyond its walls and into the home through homework, expectations for parent involvement, parent–teacher conferences, and parent participation in field trips and other activities. Punishments are also given out in this domain. These punishments include the evaluation and assessment of parents as either "good" or "bad" based on their participation in these activities. Such evaluations have consequences for students and their families. These consequences determine the degree to which families are included or marginalized within the system and the extent to which children can remain connected to their families and still succeed in conforming to the norms and requirements of the school. If we expand our discussion of school to include institutions of higher education such as universities, we can see how federal grant agencies and the research they choose to fund can also be seen as structuring education.

Another key way that power circulates is through the mechanisms of *knowledge* and how knowledge is validated and taught. There are at least two forms of knowledge that are important for understanding how power circulates in schools. The first is our everyday understanding about how schools work, or knowledge *about* school. This form of knowledge is important because it is a form of taken-for-granted *cultural capital* (social resources other than money) that not all families possess equally. For example, immigrant families, Indigenous families, non–native English speakers, and parents who did not complete school often do not have enough understanding about how schools work to help their children navigate the system, or to challenge it when it has treated their children unfairly. When they do challenge the school, their voices do not carry as much weight.

However, knowledge about how the structure works is only part of the story. The other important kind of knowledge is knowledge *within* school. This kind of knowledge includes how students should behave and conform; how learning is defined, tested, and measured; what topics are worthy of study and from whose perspective; what topics and perspectives will be rendered nonexistent; and how the creation and justification of "tracks" label and separate students into categories such as "advanced" and "special." These categories dictate the kind of knowledge that students will have access to, which in turn translates into the kinds of opportunities they will have in later life. This knowledge also shapes their sense of place in society, for example, as either those who *manage* others or those who are *managed by* others. Thus knowledge within the school benefits some students at the expense of others, while being presented as neutral, logical, and normal.

To illustrate that school knowledge is not neutral, revisit the study by Jean Anyon that was described in Chapter 2 (Anyon, 1981). Anyon asked children from three different kinds of schools—working-class, middle-class, and affluent-professional—to define knowledge. Their responses, summarized in Figure 2.1, reveal the differences in what kind of education the children receive, and how this education will direct their future and the kinds of work—or place in society—for which they are being prepared. The structures in place between groups of people limit mobility in very significant ways. While there is always the possibility of an individual working-class child moving beyond the limited education she's been given, clearly this will take a great deal of effort. Conversely, because this system benefits the affluent child, she will be less invested in removing these barriers for others. In fact, she (and those who advocate for her) will most often resist removing them, believing them to be neutral and fairly applied to all.

Returning to the hiring committee in the beginning of Chapter 4, we may now understand why Mary (who is prejudiced against a gay candidate) is demonstrating oppression but Liz (who is prejudiced against a male candidate) is not. Mary's discrimination against gay people is backed by historical, ideological, cultural, and institutional power in all major institutions in society. Indeed, the United States did not have federal protection from discriminating against a gay candidate until 2020 (Valenti, 2021). Just 5 years later, in 2025, the Trump administration removed that protection (White House, 2025a). In other words, this hiring committee could openly state that they are not hiring this candidate because he is gay. In Canada, while federal protections do exist, they cannot be taken for granted because they are regularly challenged and must continually and actively be defended.

On the other hand, Liz's discrimination against men is not backed by historical, ideological, cultural, or institutional power. Indeed, if the man gets hired, he will be more likely to rise to a position of leadership over the very women who hired him. Why, we might ask, are men who enter women's fields more likely to rise to positions of leadership in the organization, while women who enter male-dominated fields are unlikely to rise to positions of leadership in the organization? To understand this we must understand internalized dominance and internalized oppression. The forces of socialization are powerful. Once the message of our superiority or inferiority is internalized, very little outside force is needed in order to ensure that we will play our social roles. Of course the messages about where our group belongs continue to circulate in the culture all around us and reinforce what we have internalized, but the fundamental acceptance is complete by an early age. Men will tend to see themselves in positions of leadership and expect to be in these positions, and women will support this tendency because they will also tend to see and expect men to be in these positions.

STOP: Remember that both groups in a social relationship receive the same messages about their positions; the minoritized group is also taught to see the dominant group as more deserving of, or suitable for, leadership.

Women will also tend to be more comfortable with men in positions of leadership (recall the common patterns from Figure 5.3). For example, as instructors, we often see these dynamics play out in class. Even when there is one male in a group of women for a small-group discussion, he will invariably be the spokesperson for the group when it comes time to report out. When this pattern is pointed out, the women often say, "But we wanted him to be our spokesperson" or "We asked him to be our spokesperson." We would argue that this perfectly illustrates the power of internalization. Wanting a man to speak for you as a woman does not negate the impact of this pattern; it demonstrates both prescribed roles. Most often, the male as spokesperson happens automatically; in other words, there is no discussion of who will actually report out, it is just assumed that it will be the male. The women see themselves as choosing this, even in cases where no explicit decision was made. This is how both groups play their roles in keeping oppression in place. We may choose members of the dominant group to lead, but that does not negate that this choice reinforces relationships of power. These patterns play a foundational role in moving men up in female-dominated fields, while limiting women's movement up in male-dominated fields.

We must also remember that we are never solely members of one group; we occupy multiple and intersecting groups. The disadvantages of one membership do not cancel out the advantages of another. In other words, if our candidate is in fact a gay man, the disadvantages of being gay would not cancel out the advantages of being male (although it certainly impacts how we see his masculinity). A key project of critical social justice is to help untangle the complex ways these locations work together to hold oppression in place.

DISCUSSION QUESTIONS

1. The authors argued that Mary (who was prejudiced against a presumed gay candidate) was enacting oppression, but Liz (who was prejudiced against a male candidate) was not. What are the reasons for this distinction? Why was Mary enacting oppression but Liz not?
2. In your own words, explain the authors' argument that there is no such thing as a reverse form of oppression (i.e., no "reverse racism" and no "reverse sexism").
3. Review the four elements of oppression. What are some contemporary examples of sexism across all four elements?

EXTENSION ACTIVITIES

1. Case Study on Power Dynamics
    Consider well-publicized cases where people did not receive resources (e.g., grants, admissions, civil rights) based on their race,

class, or gender (they were not of the racial, class, or gender group the resources were reserved for). For example, from the United States, look at *Regents of University of Southern California v. Bakke* (1978) or *Students for Fair Admissions v. Harvard* (2023), and from Canada, *R. v. Kapp* (2008 SCC 41), *Lovelace v. Ontario* (2000 SCC 37), or *Gibraltar Mines v. Harvey* (2022 BCSC 385).

Avoiding agree/disagree or right/wrong responses, consider:

» How is power functioning in these cases?
» Why were these programs formed in the first place? What are their goals? What problems were they created to remedy?
» How will eliminating oppressed group–based considerations impact the achievement of goals related to why they were formed in the first place?

2. Research the life of Dolores Huerta (see Figure 5.2). Write an essay that describes how her life and work exemplify resistance to power relations.
3. Choose five other countries in which women currently have the right to vote and research what year they gained it, who the key players in their struggle were, and whether some women were excluded. How long did the struggle take? What pushback or barriers did they face? Did they face any barriers that were different from those faced by women in your nation?

PATTERNS TO PRACTICE SEEING

1. When are people's group identities most often named (e.g., their race, gender, sexuality, ability)? Consider movie directors, teachers, celebrities, writers, etc. Which group identities are most likely to be named or not, and in which context?
2. Pay attention to participation patterns in class discussions and other group settings. Which group members tend to speak first and most often? How do these patterns change depending on the topic under discussion?

CHAPTER 6

Understanding Privilege Through Ableism

"No one's ever handed me anything. I've worked hard for what I have."

This chapter explains the privileges automatically received by being a member of the dominant group. From a critical social justice perspective, privilege is defined as systemically conferred status and the institutional processes by which the beliefs, values, and advantages of the dominant group are made "normal" and universal. While, in some cases, the privileged group is also the numerical majority, the key is social and institutional power, not numbers. This chapter also extends our discussion of related concepts such as internalized oppression and internalized dominance, and offers examples of how they work to hold existing relations of power in place.

> **Vocabulary to practice using:** internalized dominance; internalized oppression; privilege; normalize

A female prime minister was strategizing with her all-male cabinet about how to address a string of recent sexual assaults on women throughout the city. Someone suggested a 9:00 p.m. curfew, which the cabinet thought was a good idea. The prime minister also nodded her head in agreement. "Yes. No men will be allowed out after 9:00 p.m." Her cabinet was shocked and said that was unfair; it was women who should stay in after 9:00 in order to ensure their safety. They only had the best interest of women in mind, they insisted, and the curfew was for women's own good. The prime minister replied, "It is men who are committing these assaults, not women. Why should women's movements be restricted?"

Imagine from a woman's perspective what it would be like to walk freely throughout a city at night with no fear of sexual assault from men. But also notice whose movements are assumed to need restricting and who would be blamed for being in the wrong place at the wrong time were an assault to occur. In Chapter 5 we discussed the relationship between dominant and minoritized groups. In this chapter, we examine a key aspect of that relationship for the dominant group: privilege.

WHAT IS PRIVILEGE?

The academic definition of *privilege* used in critical social justice contexts may be different from how our readers know the word in everyday usage. Consider, by way of analogy, how most people use the word *average* to mean "ordinary." In contrast, mathematicians would use the term average to specifically describe the mean, median, or mode of a series of numbers. In mathematical usage the average is the sum of all the numbers divided by the total number of items (the mean), the number in the middle when a series of numbers is ranked lowest to highest (median), or the number that occurs the most frequently in a series (mode). As you can see, while the everyday—or lay—usage may be loosely related, the mathematical usage has much greater specificity.

Similarly, the lay usage of *privilege* means to be *lucky,* to have opportunity, and to benefit from this luck and opportunity. These definitions suggest that privilege is a positive outcome of happenstance ("she was just born with a silver spoon in her mouth"). However, when academics use the term in describing how society works, they refer to the rights, advantages, and protections enjoyed by some at the expense of and beyond the rights, advantages, and protections available to others (Ahmed, 2007; A. G. Johnson, 2006; Pailey, 2020). In this context, privilege is not the product of fortune, luck, or happenstance, but the outcome of systemic advantages some have and others do not. Because dominant groups occupy the positions of power, their members receive social and institutional advantages; thus one automatically receives privilege by being a member of a dominant group (e.g., cis men, White people, heterosexuals, persons without disabilities, Christians, upper classes).

In Chapter 3 we described our immersion in our cultural socialization as similar to a fish immersed in water. Now let's extend that metaphor: While the fish is moving through the water, the water is also moving around the fish. Even when the fish is simply floating without expending effort, currents still affect its movement. When you are swimming in open water, your outcome (where you end up and how long it takes you to get there) is not determined solely by the effort you expend, but in large part by the particular current you are in.

If the water is moving *against* you rather than with you, the amount of effort it takes to move forward is enormous. Yet this effort results in only the smallest increments of advancement. On the other hand, if the current is *with* you, swimming is almost effortless. With minimal effort, you can quickly travel a great distance and are seldom aware of the current at all (we are much more likely to be aware of the current when we have to swim against it). Privilege is like having this powerful current propelling you forward throughout your life.

While this metaphor may be useful for understanding privilege, we do not want to reinforce the idea of privilege as natural or an outcome of luck and happenstance; privilege is neither. Privilege is socially constructed to benefit members of the dominant group. Further, structures of privilege are not just artifacts of a racist, sexist, or classist past; privilege is an ongoing dynamic that is continually reproduced, negotiated, and enacted. Consider *The Bell Curve* (Herrnstein & Murray), a bestselling book published in 1994 that argued that there were genetic differences in intelligence among racial groups, a perspective that is in line with the scientific racism (called eugenics) that legitimized the enslavement, extermination, genocide, and colonization of racialized groups around the world. Geneticists have debunked this "fact," yet books such as these continue to be published and widely read (Gould, 1981/1996; Nisbett, 1998).

Another example of the ongoing maintenance of privilege is the work, well known among educators, of Ruby Payne (2005), who promotes the idea of a "culture of poverty." She argues that those who are at the bottom of society are there because they are socialized within their family into a culture of poverty rather than into the culture of the middle class—that is, they lack the attitudes or work ethic necessary to "get ahead" in society (Hambacher & Thompson, 2015; Pearl & Valencia, 1997; Solorzano, 1992). Perspectives such as these are sometimes referred to as *cultural deficit theory*.

> **Cultural Deficit Theory:** The explanation that minoritized groups do not achieve in society because they lack the appropriate cultural values (e.g., "They just don't value education") or because their culture is deficient in some other way.

In this chapter we want to unravel two interrelated dynamics that are central to understanding social and institutional privilege: the *external and structural* dimensions and the *internal and attitudinal* dimensions. We will use the example of ableism to examine how these dimensions of privilege play out.

EXTERNAL AND STRUCTURAL DIMENSIONS OF PRIVILEGE

Are you left-handed? If so, you may notice how left-handed people are excluded by social norms: the desks in classrooms, the shape of scissors, the positioning of shirt pockets, and even the standard way one is taught to strum a guitar or swing a hockey stick. It is possible that you may not have noticed these things, or perhaps they don't seem significant to you, even if you are left-handed. It may even be the case that left-handed people prefer to use the "normal" tools, having become used to doing things "backwards." And perhaps there are some right-handed folks who, just for fun, like to use lefty tools to see how it feels for a while. Yet it is still the case that only right-handed people have automatic *structural privilege* (i.e., unearned advantages)—because they were born right-handed in a social world that was designed for people like them.

Moving on from left-handedness to consider a case with higher stakes, think about how ableism operates (*ableism:* the oppression of peoples with disabilities). Those of us whose bodies fit the fluid social category termed "normal" can go through entire days, weeks, and months never having to consider the barriers that limit access to our environment. How we will get to a certain event, whether we can enter a building, or how we will be seated at the coffee shop, can all be taken for granted. Even if a building is considered (or required by law to be) accessible, there is often only a single entrance providing access to a limited part of the space, such as the top of a large lecture hall. Such limits segregate people who use wheelchairs or other tools for mobility. They will likely have the most limited view and find it difficult to hear the questions posed to the speaker, and would have difficulty being heard or seen were they to pose questions. Those of us who are persons without disabilities can take access for granted because the social and physical environment was set up to accommodate the ways our bodies work, giving us social privilege and enabling us to not have to think about life without such "rights."

"But," you may wonder, "aren't there more people *without* disabilities than people *with* disabilities? Shouldn't social institutions accommodate the majority?" While in some cases the privileged group is also the numerical majority, that is not the key criterion. For example, the following dominant groups do not constitute a numerical majority: men in the United States and Canada, the upper classes, and White South Africans under apartheid. The key criterion is institutional power; a focus on numbers hides this reality.

As the example of ableism illustrates, privilege has the following external and structural dimensions:

- The integration of dominant group norms into the way society is set up
- The definition of normality set by the standards of the dominant group
- The invisibility of privilege to the dominant group

The integration of group-based norms into the way society is set up. As we explained in Chapter 5, oppression is a deeply embedded system that operates on multiple levels at all times. The result of this system is consistent unearned advantages for the dominant group, regardless of any one individual member's intentions. As with our male who sympathized with suffragists but still benefited from an androcentric system that granted him the vote, intentions are irrelevant to receiving privilege. Even if a male disagreed with denying women the right to vote, and even if a male worked for women's suffrage, he still lived in a society that had systems in place which automatically granted him privileges that were denied to women.

Similarly, in the example of ableism, because many of the things taken for granted for persons without disabilities (such as access to buildings and transportation) cannot be taken for granted by people with disabilities, they become privileges for nondisabled persons. It is not necessary to do anything in order to receive these privileges; it isn't even necessary to agree that we should receive them. Simply as a result of living in a society that defines some bodies as normal and some as abnormal, and then devalues the latter while accommodating the former, those defined as normal (the dominant group) gain unearned benefits. Having always had these benefits, we come to see them as natural, inevitable, and something to which we are entitled (if we see them at all).

As an example of the structural integration of dominant norms, consider how cities and towns are designed. Prior to the 1990s, curb cuts (the place where the sidewalk slopes to the street), or tactile paving (textured surface to assist the visually impaired) did not exist. For persons without disabilities, the need for curb cuts would not cross our minds—we can simply step onto or off the curb. But for people with limited mobility, or who use wheelchairs or other technology, the absence of curb cuts severely limits access. Because a basic component of oppression is segregation between the dominant and minoritized groups, people with disabilities were not "at the table" and therefore their perspectives and interests were missing from the city planning decisions that profoundly affect their lives. For many cities in the United States, the incorporation of curb cuts into city planning became law only with the enactment of the Americans With Disabilities Act (ADA) of 1990. This simple change in structure opened the physical environment to people with disabilities in life-changing ways. Yet it took decades of activism from people with disabilities and their allies to get the ADA passed. Since then, cities have come to see that curb cuts are beneficial not only to people with disabilities, but to the elderly, the very young, people pushing strollers, bicyclists, and many others. Despite this, the ADA is not consistently enforced and many buildings remain inaccessible.

The definition of what's normal and abnormal by the dominant group. In Chapter 3 we introduced the concept of social construction using the example of sex and gender. In the context of ability, there is a similar process of social construction. For example, while it is true that biological variance among humans exists, the *meanings* of particular biological differences are socially constructed. Consider this question if you wear glasses: At what point in the spectrum does your weak vision move from being perceived as a relatively insignificant variance that requires the socially accepted technology of eyeglasses, to being a significant variance (a disability) that requires your segregation from other children in schools and legal policies to protect you from discrimination?

Now take a moment to imagine what you consider a normal body. Perhaps you could sketch it out on a piece of paper. Try to describe that body in detail:

- What gender is that body?
- What race?
- What is its age?

Understanding Privilege Through Ableism

- How tall is it?
- What does it weigh in relation to its height?
- Can that body walk? Can that body swim? How does it walk or swim? And for how long, or for what distance?
- Can it see? To what degree? Does it use technology to see (glasses, or intraocular implants)?
- To what extent can it hear? Does it use technology to hear?
- What emotions does that body have? Under what conditions does it show these emotions? How does its presumed gender impact what emotions are considered for that body? Does its race impact what emotions you attribute to it? What about its age?

As you think about these questions, decide at what point this body would no longer be normal. Where in its range of doing and being and feeling does this body cross the line from being a "normal" body to being an "abnormal" or disabled body? If the body can do all of the above, but does them differently than most people, do you still consider the body normal? If not, why not?

If you are having trouble pinning this point down, it is because "normal" itself is socially constructed. Normal is the line drawn around an arbitrary set of ideas a group determines as acceptable in a given place and time. For example, in the early part of the 20th century in many parts of the United States and Canada some people were categorized as "feeble-minded." This was a broad category that included many people considered "other," including women who had children out of wedlock, "vagrants," and immigrants. Those with this classification were in some cases forcibly (and in many cases without their knowledge or consent) sterilized to prevent them from passing on their feeble-mindedness (Grekul et al., 2004; Kline, 2005). A range of learning disabilities that are seen as common today (such as dyslexia) would have been included in the early-20th-century classification of abnormal (feeble-minded). Based on the socially constructed idea of what constituted normal, people's lived experiences became radically different.

As you can see, these constructions are significant, because depending on whether we fall into the normal or abnormal social category, very real privileges are either granted or denied. These privileges are embedded in *definitions* (at what point does a characteristic move from normal to abnormal?), *language* (classifications such as feeble-minded versus dyslexic), *structures* (the way cities and buildings are built), and *systems* of society (legal policies such as forced sterilization or educational segregation).

A powerful yet subtle way dominant group members have received the message that people with disabilities are not important is through the ways these groups have been segregated in major social institutions like schooling, housing, and the workplace. For example, in schools this segregation has been rationalized as necessary because were students with disabilities to be in the main classroom, "normal" students would be slowed down and limited. This rationalization conveys the problematic idea that persons without disabilities have nothing to gain or learn from people with disabilities.

> **STOP:** Many teachers believe that they evaluate each child as a unique individual and that their assessments are independent of race, class, and gender. However, as explained in Chapters 3 and 4, it is not possible to assess anyone outside of our preconceived and often unconscious beliefs about them based upon the groups that they and we belong to. This does not mean that it is impossible to make fair assessments, but that we must not deny that these group relations play a powerful role in what we "see."

Consider the way classrooms are organized. A single teacher might have to meet the needs of up to 40 students, often without supports such as classroom aides. This organization makes it virtually impossible to meet the needs of individual students. Therefore, the more alike and conforming students are, the easier it becomes to efficiently teach the group. With schooling organized in this way (out of the myriad ways it is possible to organize schooling), it becomes logical to remove children with disabilities from "regular" classrooms.

Even people who support mixed classes often do so in order to help children with disabilities, assuming that the flow of knowledge and benefit is always *from* persons without disabilities *to* the disabled. This reveals one of the ironies of privilege: Because the dominant group does not see the minoritized group as valuable, the dominant group loses meaningful experiences and relationships. These rationalizations reinforce the idea that the "regular" classroom is a neutral space of equal opportunity, and that the students in this classroom are normal—obscuring the fact that schooling is constructed to accommodate the ways that certain children learn. Labels such as "regular," "normal," "gifted," and "special" shape the policies that social institutions (like schools and medicine) create that maintain this privilege and segregation.

Categories of special education referred to as nonjudgmental include children who are deaf or blind, or who have significant physical or mental disabilities and who come to school with their status identified by medical professionals. Unlike nonjudgmental categories, judgmental categories are based on an individual teacher's assessments, such as "learning disabled" or "emotionally disturbed." Consider the subjective nature of the assessment to place students in Special Education versus Advanced Placement or Gifted Education programs. Figure 6.1 illustrates how a particular characteristic (such as activity level) can be interpreted in very different ways with profoundly different consequences.

In the chart, notice how being perceived as hyperactive is aligned with negative characteristics that are poorly tolerated by the school, whereas being perceived

Figure 6.1. Common Subjective Evaluations of Child Behavior

Negative and Abnormal	Positive and Normal
Hyperactive	Energetic
Impulsive	Spontaneous
Distractible	Creative
Daydreamer	Imaginative
Inattentive	Global thinker with a wide focus
Unpredictable	Flexible
Argumentative	Independent
Stubborn, irritable	Committed, sensitive
Aggressive	Assertive
Attention deficit disorder	Unique

Source: Thomas Armstrong as cited in Jawanza Kunjufu, *Keeping Black Boys Out of Special Education* (2005), p. 10. See also Bonilla-Silva, 2019; R. Watson & De Gelder, 2017.

as energetic is aligned with positive characteristics that are welcomed by the school. These subjective categories are consistently found to have overrepresentation of minoritized students—most significantly Black, Latino, and Indigenous students (Adjei, 2016; Connor et al., 2016; Gregory et al., 2010; Love & Beneke, 2021; Owens, 2022; Pearman et al., 2019).

Notice how one's preconceived attitudes toward the child shape which characteristics are attributed to the child, and in turn, that child's schooling experiences and outcomes. Black, Brown, and Indigenous students are much more likely to be assessed by teachers as exhibiting problematic rather than desirable character traits (Diamond & Gomez, 2023; Gregory et al., 2010; Kunjufu, 2005; Owens & McLanahan, 2020). When you add the demographic of the teachers who make these assessments (the overwhelming majority of whom are White middle-class females) you can see how dominant culture determines what constitutes normal behavior.

The invisibility of privilege for the dominant group. Like the invisible current of water that is carrying us effortlessly forward, privilege is something we do not need to think about when we have it. Because those in dominant groups are not disadvantaged by the oppression, but in fact benefit from it, they find it fairly easy to dismiss the accounts of members of minoritized groups. Living lives that are segregated (in schools, neighborhoods, workplaces, and social circles), it's also easy to avoid seeing what minoritized group members experience. Further, we are not taught in schools and mainstream culture about the experiences of minoritized groups. This makes it difficult for dominant group members to see oppression, or to believe accounts of it happening to others. In addition to the structural barriers, there are psychological and social investments in not seeing oppression. To see and validate oppression requires that we question a system that benefits us. These investments cause us to resist pressures to acknowledge oppression; where we are dominant, we generally don't like to have our privilege pointed out (and many of us actively deny having any benefits beyond those equally available to others). Thus simply naming privilege typically causes defensiveness and avoidance. This, of course, is another way that oppression stays in place: dominant group resistance to acknowledging it, and the social penalties meted to those who try to bring it up (DiAngelo, 2011; Eddo-Lodge, 2017; A. G. Johnson, 2006).

The following are examples of ability privileges that we can take for granted on a daily basis if we are persons without disabilities:

- There are thousands of recreation leagues specifically set up for us and rarely, if ever, any for people with disabilities. When they are, they are often separated from the "regular" events.
- We can choose courses by their academic appeal rather than by the building they might be located in.
- We do not have to make extensive travel plans just to get groceries, attend an event at a colleague's home, or go out to dinner with friends. We don't need to consider whether a building has ramps, handrails, or adequate lighting.
- We aren't labeled and segregated into "special" classes, schools, and buses.
- The social paradigm rewards values associated with "normal" bodies, such as competition, individualism, and speed, over collaboration, patience, and diversity—elevating persons without disabilities.

Those of us who are defined as persons without disabilities will likely not recognize advantages as privileges at all but as simply normal aspects of life. We have been socialized into our superior position since birth and have internalized this position as natural.

Now let's consider how the external and structural dimensions of privilege interact with internal and attitudinal elements.

INTERNAL AND ATTITUDINAL DIMENSIONS OF PRIVILEGE

Imagine that you have lived your life in a small, gated community. You are surrounded by family and friends and overall live a happy and healthy life. One day the gates open and you are told that you must venture out and make your way in the larger society. You are excited about the adventure that awaits you and all that you will see and discover.

On the way into the nearest city you stop at a café for lunch and notice people staring at you and whispering. A child points at your head while

Understanding Privilege Through Ableism

her mother shushes her, and another child begins to cry and hide behind his mother's legs. Some people smile at you kindly and offer to help you sit down, while others turn away and ignore you. You ask for a menu and the waitress points it out on the wall behind you, and with an irritated sigh asks you if you need her to read it to you. You turn around and tell her no, you can see it just fine. When you turn your body, people look away in pity and disgust. As the waitress walks away, you notice that she has a third eye on the back of her head. You are shocked and quickly look around to realize that everyone in the café has an "extra" eye on the back of their heads. Feeling very uncomfortable, you rush through your meal and pay your check. When the waitress returns your change, you hold out your hand but she places it on the counter to avoid touching you.

As you enter the city, the same dynamics occur. Although you occasionally see other two-eyed people, they are usually in service positions, working with their heads down. You begin to feel shame and dread as throughout the day it becomes clear that the three-eyed people see you as abnormal and beneath them. A doctor approaches you and offers to "fix" you. He adds that although the technology to implant a third eye is expensive and dangerous, you might be a good candidate to participate in a university study he is directing on two-eyed people post-implants. You don't want a third eye; you have done just fine throughout your life and are not interested in becoming "normal" on their terms. You try to explain this to the doctor, but he insists that you would find more social acceptance, which would help you have a better quality of life. "Don't you want to be normal?" he asks. "We have the technology, why suffer unnecessarily?"

You quickly leave the doctor and enter a sunglasses store in the mall. Three teenagers are having fun trying on a range of trendy styles. Although the extra lens at the back isn't necessary for you, you can still wear them like everyone else does, wrapped fully around your head. You smile, momentarily excited by what you see, but as you pick up a stylish "trio," a saleswoman approaches, takes the glasses out of your hand, and offers you a choice between two "modified trios" while gently patting your arm.

The modified glasses are bulky and unattractive and you don't want them. The girls stop talking and watch your interaction with the saleswoman. You overhear one of them say, "Oh my god, can you imagine being born like that? How sad." Then one of them calls out across the store, "What happened to you?" At this point you have had enough, so you tell her that nothing happened to you and that she is being rude. Shocked, she replies, "Whatever. I was just asking." And she says loudly to her friends, "Two-eyed people are always so angry." Her friends nod along in agreement. The saleswoman steps in and says, "Dear, maybe you should go," as one of the teens snaps a picture of the back of your head with her phone, and says to her friends, "Oh my god, this is going to be my costume this Halloween!" Frustrated and near tears, you walk out. The last thing you hear is the saleswoman say, "What on earth was she doing in here anyway?"

To avoid further interactions, you decide to take in a play at the theater, looking forward to the relief of sitting in the darkness. As you purchase your ticket an usher hands you a white cane and tells you that you need the cane to get to your seat. You realize that although you don't actually need the cane, it does serve the purpose of alerting others to your difference. You sit down and try to read the program but it's written in a way that assumes a third eye; folded in order to be visible simultaneously to you and the person sitting in front of you. As you fumble, trying to figure out the sequence of the text, a three-eyed person sitting next to you glances over and speaking very loudly and slowly asks, "Do you need help?" Feeling insulted, you ignore her.

The play starts and you realize that it is a biographical drama. It takes place in a special community much like the one you grew up in. But although you loved your neighborhood, it is clear that from the perspective of the three-eyed people it is a sad and depressing place. The main actor is depicting a character who has lost his third eye in a tragic accident. The play tells the story of his struggle to come to terms with his "disfigurement." Once considered a handsome and talented young man with his whole life ahead of him, it is obvious to you that the three-eyed people now see him as ugly and his life as wasted. The sense of shame you felt earlier returns and you sink lower in your seat, hoping others don't notice you only have two eyes. You see that the main actor is actually a three-eyed person concealing his third eye (you later learn that this actor wins an award for his "courageous and inspiring" portrayal of a two-eyed person).

When the play ends, you feel very self-conscious about what the three-eyed people who are the majority of the audience might be thinking about you, and quickly exit the theater. You walk home with your head down, feeling ugly, and begin to wonder if you are losing your mind.

While there is no "three-eyed society" that enacts its privileges in this way, we use this imaginary scenario to illustrate many very real dynamics minoritized groups must navigate every day. These dynamics include both the structural and institutional dimensions discussed earlier, as well as internal and attitudinal dimensions we will discuss below.

Privilege has the following invisible *internal and attitudinal* effects:

- The belief that your group has the right to its position
- The internalization of messages of your group's superiority
- The lack of humility that results from your limited knowledge of the minoritized group
- The invisibility of your privilege to you

Many educators use Peggy McIntosh's (1989) classic "invisible knapsack" article to explain privilege. In this article, McIntosh lists 46 privileges she takes for granted on a daily basis because she is White. McIntosh's privilege inventory is useful for revealing the invisibility of White privilege for many White people and captures some of the important layers of internal and attitudinal effects of privilege. In the story of the three-eyed society above, we can see the following internal and attitudinal elements of privilege playing out:

- The privileged group feels comfortable invading the space of minoritized persons.
- The privileged group feels qualified to represent the experiences of minoritized persons.
- Members of the privileged group see themselves as superior and believe that the minoritized person could and should be "fixed" or otherwise assimilate to be like them.
- The privileged group prefers to live segregated from the minoritized group.

The belief that your group has the right to its position. Ideology is a powerful way to support the dominant group's position. There are several key interrelated ideologies that rationalize the concentration of dominant group members at the top of society and their right to rule.

One is the ideology of meritocracy. *Meritocracy* is the belief that people's achievements are based solely on their own efforts, abilities, or merits. Meritocracy posits that social positionality doesn't matter and that the son of a day laborer has as much chance of "making it" as the son of Mark Zuckerberg or the daughter of a Kardashian, as long as they work hard. Canada and the United States are presented in dominant culture as meritocratic systems. From this perspective, those who do not succeed are simply not as capable or don't try as hard as those who do.

A second related ideology is that of *equal opportunity*. This is the idea that in today's world, people are no longer prejudiced, social injustice is in the past, and everyone has the same opportunities. In fact, many dominant group members believe that society has swung the needle past center to the opposite end and now unfairly privileges minoritized groups through "special" rights and programs that are denied dominant group members. From this perspective, there may occasionally be isolated cases of injustices, but these are explained away with the "bootstraps" myth—that anyone can pull themselves up by their bootstraps or improve their lot in life by working harder and having the right attitude.

A third related ideology supporting the dominant group's right to its position is *individualism*—the belief that we are each unique and outside the forces of socialization. Under individualism, group memberships are irrelevant and the social groups to which we belong don't provide us with any more or less benefits. The ideology of individualism explains gaps between dominant and minoritized groups (in education, health, income, and net worth) as the result of individual strength or weakness. Therefore, those at the top are there because they are the best, brightest, and hardest working.

A fourth related ideology is the ideology of *human nature*. This ideology rationalizes privilege as natural—"it's just human nature; *someone* has to be on top"—and underpins ideas about civilized versus uncivilized societies. Through this ideology, some societies are seen as more "advanced" due to genetic superiority, cultural superiority (holding values and characteristics such as innovation and tenacity), and/or divine forces (such as Manifest Destiny or the Protestant work ethic). Because they are "advanced" societies, they often "help" less advanced societies. Concepts such as "First World versus Third World" illustrate how human societies are ranked and how these rankings are rationalized. Science and religion have historically been used to support this ideology. For example, science has been used to argue that it is biologically natural for women to be second to men, while religion has been used to argue that it is "God's will."

Ideologies such as "Someone has to be on top" further support these hierarchies—consider who is more likely to believe that someone has to be on top, those on the bottom or those on the top? Thus for scholars of critical social justice, because it is so difficult to separate ideas about nature from culture, the question moves from "Is this true?" to "Whom does this belief serve?" With privilege rationalized through ideology, it follows that dominant groups are socialized to see their dominance as normal and/or earned.

The internalization of messages of superiority. In the story, it was clear that the three-eyed people believed that their bodies were better, more attractive, and more *normal* than yours. As was evident in the interactions, they set every aspect of what was considered normal in that society. These norms not only included the layout and organization of physical space but also included *values* such as which kind of bodies were beautiful and preferable.

As members of the dominant group—in this case persons without disabilities—seeing how our privileges manifest can be extremely challenging because everything in our environment is constructed to enable us to take our privileges for granted. The story illustrates the following manifestations of internalized superiority:

- There is no value in the experiences of people with disabilities and nothing to gain or learn from their experiences. (The three-eyed people believed that it was better to be three-eyed and wanted to "fix" you as a two-eyed person. Even though you told them you liked yourself the way you were, they felt entitled to tell you that it was better to be like them.)
- Persons without disabilities are capable of understanding the experiences, representing, and speaking on behalf of people with disabilities. (The play's writers and producers were the ones to represent two-eyed people and believed that all a three-eyed person had to do was "pretend" to be two-eyed in order to understand and represent their experiences. This was reinforced through the award granted to the actor by other three-eyed people, even though the script reinforced negative stereotypes.)

In ways such as these, those in dominant positions tend to see themselves as superior and tell stories that affirm and support that superiority. They tend to lack interest in the perspectives of the minoritized group except in limited and controlled situations—for example, writing and producing inspirational stories from the dominant perspective on how brave people with disabilities are and how much they have overcome, or conversely, how fundamentally damaged or frightening they are.

In popular culture, people with disabilities are either presented as bodies to be feared or as inspiration. Consider how frequently a horror movie villain's badness comes directly from either a physical or cognitive characteristic, or, on the other end, the character with a disability is tragic and has a story that is presented as inspiring because despite the tragedy, the person lives on or, in some cases, dies as a fortunate release. It's worth asking why stories about people with disabilities are so inspirational or scary to persons without disabilities. Notice how they can only be inspirational if the person is presented as overcoming the tragedy and suffering that persons without disabilities believe to be inherent to having a disability. If we are telling a story of someone who cannot overcome their disability, then we draw our inspiration from their determination and courage to simply live. These narratives communicate and reinforce the idea that body diversity (anything beyond what is socially constructed as normal) is undesirable; a terrible and tragic medical condition that no one would ever choose and that, if possible, must at all costs be fixed. If the condition cannot be fixed, then it is perceived as a terrible waste of life. Thus the only way to "overcome" the condition is to "put a positive face on it" and struggle to be pleasant. If you have ever thought (or been reminded by others) how "fortunate" you were not to have a disability, consider what ideas about people with disabilities are being conveyed.

These discourses of overcoming disability obscure the nature of disability itself. Disability isn't a condition external to a person that can be discarded with a cure and left behind. People with disabilities must navigate structures of privilege, definitions of normalcy, and the internalized superiority of persons without disabilities every day. Their development is profoundly shaped by this navigation. Thus disability is a central (although certainly not the only) part of the experience and identity of a person with a disability. Many people with disabilities appreciate aspects of the experience, such as having an outsider's vantage point and gaining innovative perspectives and insights they wouldn't otherwise have.

In addition to how inspiration stories position people with disabilities, notice what the story of inspiration does for the storyteller, for example, when we glorify people who are "willing" to work with children with disabilities. For persons without disabilities, the telling and retelling of the inspiration story affirms *our* goodness, benevolence, and superiority. Unfortunately, this sense of superiority results in an arrogance and ignorance that limits our understanding of ourselves and others.

The lack of humility that results from your limited view of others. The dominant group, while the least likely to understand oppression and the most likely to be invested in holding it in place, is the group in the position to write the rules. Thus the rules will continue to benefit them. In addition, the minoritized group is rarely at the table in any numbers significant enough to challenge the dominant group or provide another perspective, even when the intentions of the rules are to prevent oppression. One of the outcomes of unearned privilege—arrogance—causes the dominant group to feel capable of representing the interests of the minoritized group (if they consider them at all), regardless of whether they have consulted with them. In fact, the dominant group members may be seen as more legitimate to represent minoritized group interests since they will see themselves as "objective" and not furthering a "special interest agenda."

In Chapter 3's discussion of socialization, we introduced the concept of switching effortlessly between contexts, explaining how our relationships to others are so deeply internalized that we shift effortlessly back and forth between them. For example, we know that when we are talking to our supervisor we need a level of deference that is not necessary when we are talking to our friends. We may also reveal secrets to a significant other that we would never share with coworkers. Adding the dimension of social power, we can think about internalized dominance as the default mode for engaging with the minoritized group. Because we have internalized our position in relation to theirs, we automatically interact with them from a position of unconscious superiority. We are seldom aware of this, because the messages of superiority have been circulated and reinforced since birth. Further, because at the same time, we have been taught that it is wrong to treat others differently, we would likely deny our sense of superiority.

Yet research shows that dominant group interactions with minoritized groups are based in a sense of internalized superiority and are different from interactions with other dominant group members (Bonilla-Silva, 2006; Myers, 2003; Picca & Feagin, 2007). Again and again, studies have shown that *actual* behavior toward minoritized groups does not line up with dominant group beliefs about these interactions—recall the resume study described in Chapter 3 (Dovidio et al., 2005; Greenwald & Krieger, 2006; MacKenzie et al., 2023; Milkman et al., 2015). Our lack of awareness or denial of our behavior does not lessen the reality of its impact. In fact, our unawareness and denial make it more likely that we will continue. Figure 6.2 offers guidance on disability inclusive language.

The invisibility of privilege for the dominant group member. While many of the dynamics discussed above make privilege invisible to the dominant group, there is also a phenomenon that scholars describe as "sanctioned not-knowing," "willful ignorance," and "willful hermeneutical ignorance" (Applebaum, 2022; Dei et al., 2004). These terms attempt to describe dynamics that allow dominant group members to remain ignorant of the overwhelming evidence of injustice in society, especially evidence brought forth by minoritized groups. While many dominant group members claim that they simply don't know about the minoritized group, invoking a sense of innocence, the information is easily available. Thus we use the phrase "willful ignorance" because minoritized groups have always tried to get dominant groups to see and understand their experiences, but dominant group

Understanding Privilege Through Ableism

Figure 6.2. Disability-Inclusive Language

Recommended	To be Avoided
Person(s) with disability(ies), person with [type of impairment], people with disabilities	Disabled person, handicapped, person with special needs, handicapable, atypical, person living with a disability, differently abled, people of all abilities, people of determination, those with disabilities
Person(s) without disability, person(s) without impairment, nondisabled, the rest of the population	Normal, healthy, able-bodied, typical, whole, of sound body/mind
Have [disability/impairment/condition]	Suffer from, afflicted by, stricken by, troubled with
Person with a psychosocial disability	The deaf, hearing impaired, deaf and dumb, deaf and mute
Blind person, deafblind person, person who is blind, person with a vision/visual disability, person with a vision/visual impairment, person with low vision	The blind, partially sighted
Person with a physical disability, person with a physical impairment	Crippled, invalid, deformed, lame, handicapped, physically challenged, person with physical limitations, limp
Wheelchair user, person who uses a wheelchair, person with a mobility disability, person with a mobility impairment, person using a mobility device	Confined/restricted to a wheelchair, wheelchair-bound
Accessible parking, parking reserved for persons with disabilities, accessible bathroom	Disabled/handicapped parking, handicapped bathroom

Source: Integrated Health and Social Services University Network for West-Central Montreal (CIUSSS West-Central Montreal), Government of Quebec (n.d.)

https://cdn.ciussscentreouest.ca/documents/ciusss-coim/A_propos_de_nous/Diversite_equite_inclusion_et_appartenance/Nouvelles_et_evenements/Disability_inclusive_language.pdf

members often aggressively resist this information. These forms of denial and resistance include:

- Demanding more data to prove the injustice ("When were these statistics published? I think things have changed in the last 10 years.")
- Feeling qualified, without any study of the issue, to argue with people who experience the oppression and with experts in the field ("I disagree that disability is socially constructed.")

- Giving counterexamples or exceptions to the rule ("But Roosevelt had a disability and he was president!")
- Channel switching ("The true oppression is class. If you eliminate classism all other oppressions will disappear.")
- Intimidation ("You might advance more if you were a team player.")
- Defensiveness ("Are you calling me ableist? I have an aunt with a disability!")
- Negating research and explaining away injustice by giving personal and anecdotal stories ("There was a kid in a wheelchair in our class. Everybody loved him and no one even noticed his wheelchair or treated him differently.")
- Emotional fragility ("It hurts my feelings that you think I would say something ableist.")

The ideologies of meritocracy, equal opportunity, individualism, and human nature we described earlier play a powerful role in denying the current of privilege and insisting that society is just.

Perhaps the most subtle yet powerful way we resist knowing is by simply being uninterested. Internalized superiority makes us indifferent to learning about the minoritized group because we don't see them as valuable. If we did see them as valuable, we would seek them out. For example, we might not know much about what it means to be rich and famous, but many of us spend a lot of time reading about rich and famous peoples' lives because they are important to us. The life and work of Leroy Moore (Figure 6.3) illustrate the intersections of oppression.

COMMON DOMINANT GROUP MISCONCEPTIONS ABOUT PRIVILEGE

As you read through these common misconceptions, it might be helpful to identify a group that you are dominant in and through which you experience privilege. Apply the dynamics discussed here to your experience as a member of that group.

"If we haven't personally discriminated, we are not benefiting from privilege." Some dominant group members can admit that the minoritized group is oppressed, but still have a limited view of oppression. We look at the minoritized group from our specific position—one that is elevated—yet see ourselves as *neutral*; perhaps we recognize that *they* are below us, but assume that our own position is merely level ground. It follows that if we could just pull them up to where we are, their lot would improve. What we don't recognize is that their oppression *lifts us up*; we have more *because* the minoritized group is granted less. The concept of privilege challenges the perceived-neutral reference point by revealing how the dominant group is actually elevated by virtue of the oppression of the minoritized group. Language helps illustrate this point: While we refer to the minoritized group as *underprivileged* or *disadvantaged*, we rarely talk about the dominant group as *overprivileged* or *overadvantaged*.

Figure 6.3. Leroy F. Moore Jr. (b. 1967)

Writer, poet, and activist Leroy F. Moore lectures throughout the United States and Canada, as well as other parts of the world, on topics including the intersections of disability, race, and sexuality, as well as police brutality against people with disabilities. He has written extensively on the history of Black artists and musicians with disabilities in popular culture. His book *Black Disabled Art History 101* was published in 2017. Moore was the founder of Disability Advocates of Minorities Organization and a member of the U.S. National Minorities with Disabilities Coalition. He is a regular contributor to *Poor* Magazine, a webzine for community activism. He is also the cofounder of an arts performance series in San Francisco called *Sins Invalid: An Unshamed Claim to Beauty in the Face of Invisibility*. The project serves as a dialogue space where artists with disabilities examine and challenge normative conceptions of beauty and sexuality. Moore was also a founding member of the disability radio collective Pushing Limits at KPFA 94.1 FM in Berkeley, CA and is the founder of Krip-Hop Nation, an international project bringing together and disseminating the work of hip-hop artists from around the world.

Source: https://en.wikipedia.org/wiki/Leroy_F._Moore_Jr.
https://www.poetryfoundation.org/poets/leroy-f-moore

"*If we can't feel our social and institutional power, we don't have it.*" Dominant group members do not have to feel powerful in order to have privilege. The social and institutional power and privilege of dominant groups is normalized and outside of conscious awareness. Yet we often expect that power is something that one can feel, rather than something one takes for granted. For example, in the case of race privilege, a struggle in one aspect of a White person's life often becomes confused with a lack of racial privilege. In discussions on race we often hear White working-class men protest that they don't have any social power. They work long and grueling hours, often at jobs with no long-term security, and come home feeling beaten and quite disempowered. These men often cannot relate to the concept of holding social power. The key to recognizing group-level power is recognizing *normalcy*—what can be taken for granted. These men are indeed struggling against classism, but they are not also struggling against racism. A man of Color in the same job would be dealing with both classism and racism. Indeed, men (and women) of Color have traditionally been kept out of working-class jobs when White men were available. Thus, our own sense of power is not necessarily aligned with how others perceive or respond to us, nor our relationship to social and institutional networks.

"If a minoritized person is in charge, there is no oppression." In our work we are often asked questions such as, "But our boss is a woman, so how can there be sexism in our department?" In thinking about numbers, there is an important distinction between *rank* and *status* (Nieto et al., 2010). *Rank* refers to social membership (such as race, class, gender, sexual orientation, ability, age), and thus rank is not temporary and impacts all aspects of one's life. *Status* refers to a temporary position/job and is contextual. Your boss may be a woman but she will have to enact male norms and values to keep her position and will still deal with unaware sexism from the men she supervises.

A Latino manager, while holding status over a White person he supervises, will still have to deal with the racism of his employees. Research shows that women and people of Color in positions of leadership are scrutinized more closely and judged more harshly than White men (Elsass & Graves, 1997). People of Color are often assumed to be the recipients of special programs rather than to have earned their positions, and are often perceived as being biased, having special interests, and being "troublemakers" (Bonilla-Silva, 2006; Calliste, 1996; Duncan, 2014). Conversely, one of the privileges of being in the dominant group is that you are perceived to be "just human" and thus neutral and unbiased in your viewpoint.

"If we are oppressed in one social group membership, we can't be privileged in another." Remember that we occupy multiple social groups. One may be oppressed as a female but elevated as White; oppressed as a person with a disability but elevated as male; and so on. Consider the oppression of sexism. While all women experience sexism, they experience it differently based on its interaction with their other social group identities.

The experiences of a woman will vary greatly depending on whether she is heterosexual or a lesbian. Further, imagine this woman is heterosexual and has a disability. Perhaps she is living with a disability and is Muslim; or living with a disability and is Asian, Muslim, and a nonnative English speaker. In these ways, her experiences are determined not simply by her gender, but also by her ability status and racial, religious, and sexual identity. We can be oppressed in one axis of life and still experience privilege in another. Intersectional analysis requires that we consider how these various social group identities interact.

Forms of oppression can overlap and compound the experience of minoritized groups. Notice how in the examples below, adapted from the work of Zeus Leonardo (2004, 2009), racism intersects with ableism to produce the following manifestations of oppression:

- Women of Color, Indigenous women, and women with disabilities have been forcibly sterilized, denying them agency over their own bodies.

- Intelligence testing and eugenics (selective breeding of humans) construct the idea of the genetic inferiority of Black, Latino, and Indigenous peoples.
- Beliefs that Asian-heritage people are smarter than other groups of Color sets up a competitive hierarchy and reinforces racist concepts of intelligence as genetic.

Dynamics of privilege are deeply embedded into our socialization and thus into our psyches. Ending a system of privilege is not as simple as identifying its external manifestations and "stopping them" or "giving them away." We may be able to do this with some types of privileges, such as changing the way we design buildings in order to make them more accessible or challenging our assumptions about who is more or less likely to engage in criminal activity (i.e., reduce racial profiling). But many aspects of our privilege are intertwined into our very identities and personalities—how we see ourselves in relation to those around us and thus how we interact with one another.

Returning to our opening vignette concerning the prime minister and her cabinet, we can see some of these deeply internalized manifestations. The men assume that it is women whose movements will be restricted. They also assume it is their right to walk freely wherever and whenever they choose. They take offense at the suggestion that their rights should be restricted, even though it is their group that is causing the problem. They appear to be unaware that women must monitor and restrict their movements on a daily basis. Ironically, women as a group must do this monitoring because of the patterns of men as a group. In this situation, it isn't as simple as suggesting that the men "give away" their privilege to women so that women can move more freely. There are many complex dynamics involved that make this not only challenging, but also highly unlikely. The very idea of men giving up their privilege will likely be foreign to them, even though it makes sense—or is rational—that it should be *their* movements that are restricted under these conditions, not the women's. Due to internalized dominance, we can be confident that they will vigorously resist the prime minister's proposal. The prime minister also now risks being seen as seeking "special rights" for women and of having a biased perspective. In other words, she now becomes a *woman* prime minister who is no longer seen as representing everyone or playing by the rules. Deep-level ideological, institutional, and behavioral shifts would need to occur in order to challenge the male cabinet members' privileges.

DISCUSSION QUESTIONS

1. The authors argue that privilege is not the product of luck, happenstance, or natural occurrence. If it is not these things, then what is it?
2. What are the "external and structural" dimensions of ableism? Identify some specific examples beyond those the authors provide. What are the "internal and attitudinal" dimensions of ableism? Identify some specific examples.

3. Identify the external/structural and internal/attitudinal dimensions of another form of oppression (such as sexism, heterosexism, classism, or racism).

EXTENSION ACTIVITIES

1. Identify an aspect of privilege that makes you uncomfortable to think about. Write a short letter to yourself explaining why you are uncomfortable thinking about this privilege. Write back to yourself from a social justice perspective.
2. Watch the video *Examined Life—Judith Butler & Sunaura Taylor* (https://www.youtube.com/watch?v=k0HZaPkF6qE).
    » What is the difference between impairment and disability?
    » How is disability "political"?
    » How does the discussion illustrate the concept of "socially constructed"?
3. Research the writing, poetry, and performance art of Leroy F. Moore Jr. (see Figure 6.3). Watch the 37-minute lecture by Moore titled *Black Disabled Art History 101*, where he reads from his children's book, *Black Disabled Art History 101* (https://www.youtube.com/watch?v=9lSdblDv34o). What feelings and reactions did you have as you watched this video? How do these feelings relate to your own ability status in relation to his? What did you learn about Black disabled art history that was new to you?

PATTERNS TO PRACTICE SEEING

1. Practice identifying the physical accessibility of your work or school environment (the external dimensions of ability privilege). Think about the places you go, how you get there, the layout of the rooms. What do you notice about the space? What do you notice about how much effort it takes to remember to think about these details as you practice this prompt?
2. How many people who have clearly identifiable physical or cognitive disabilities (and who are not family members) have come to your home? If few or none, why do you think that is?

CHAPTER 7

Understanding the Invisibility of Oppression Through Sexism

"I believe women should be equal, but I am not a feminist."

This chapter traces a specific form of oppression—sexism—in order to illustrate how our ideas, views, and opinions are shaped by interlocking and ongoing social messages. We describe how such messages serve as barriers to seeing oppression and as such are central to how oppression is normalized.

> **Vocabulary to practice using:** feminism; commodification; internalized oppression; misogyny; androcentrism; patriarchy

Imagine: A prominent businessman is running for office. He has been married three times and has five children by two different women. He owns several Las Vegas nightclubs that are famous for their servers who work while wearing lingerie. This businessman is on record for making sexist comments about women, including his own daughters. He has run on a platform that would deny women access to all forms of reproductive healthcare, including birth control. Just before the election a recording emerges that shows him bragging about having extramarital affairs and sexually assaulting women. When his behavior is made public and critiqued, several women you know say that they don't think it was very nice behavior, but he was only joking. And besides, these women add, it's only the radical feminists who are complaining. They don't see why feminists are making such a big deal about it. The businessman goes on to win the election, with a majority of women voting for him. Within the first week in office, he removes all mention of women's rights, civil rights, and LGBTQ+ rights from the official state website, ends global funding for women's health, and issues an executive order banning women's access to birth control. Many women who voted for him are in shock and don't understand how rights they took for granted were so quickly lost.

Women today have the right to vote and a multitude of other rights that may be taken for granted. However, sexism is a cogent example of how the cultural "water" makes oppression difficult to see while we are swimming in it. Further, oppression relies on our complacency. We must not forget that any rights granted to minoritized groups are always the result of years of their activism and can be taken back if the dominant group chooses to do so. One example is the reversal of rights and opportunities previously gained for LGBTQ+ people (T. Jones, 2024; Lyonga, 2021; Quinan, 2025).

> **Feminism:** The belief that women are equal to men; advocacy for the social, economic, and political equality of all sexes. Sometimes heard as *feminisms*, to capture the plurality of ways that feminist theorizing and critique have occurred (e.g., Marxist feminism, transnational feminism, Black feminist thought, and so on).

Feminism is defined as advocacy for women's rights, based on the idea that men and women are equal. Yet many women (as well as men) distance themselves from feminism. In this chapter, we examine how oppression is made invisible and even normal for both the dominant and minoritized groups through the example of sexism.

WHAT IS AN INSTITUTION?

The term *institution* refers to a large-scale and established set of laws, customs, practices, and organizations that govern the political or social life of a people. Institutions make and enforce a society's rules and norms. Examples of institutions include marriage and family, religion, schooling, military, prisons, government, law, mass media, and corporations.

From a critical theory perspective, institutions serve as primary socializing forces in society. Institutions are the systems that guide and enforce our practices in daily life. For example, consider again how schools regulate students. Schools establish the hours of attendance, decide what will be studied and how, define good and bad behavior and how that behavior will be rewarded or punished, determine which holidays will be celebrated and how, establish dress codes, define play, cooperation, and competition, establish the norms and language with which to speak to authority, and so on. Thus there is much more going on within schools than intentional instruction of subject matter.

Institutions produce, circulate, and maintain the dominant culture's norms, values, definitions, language, policies, and ideologies—and do so in ways that are above as well as below the surface of the cultural water. Institutions are directly connected to (and reflective of) the larger dynamics (interests, power relations, definitions of "others") of a given society. The overarching ideology that has shaped all institutions is *patriarchy*. Patriarchy is the organization of society based on the belief in the inherent superiority of men and their right to rule, and the creation of institutions, norms, policies, and practices based on and enforcing that belief. Examples of patriarchal ideology worldwide are: a male god; the father (or another male) as the head of the household; men as the authority in the institutions of society, such as law, government, religion, and culture, which they established in their image and representative of their interests; the belief of women as inherently inferior to men and the assumed property of men, supported in the holy books written by men; and the erasure of women's experience in history. We might think of patriarchy as the macro-level system from which sexism flows.

> **Patriarchy:** The system based on the belief in the inherent superiority of men and the male right to rule, and the organization of society based on this belief.

To think critically about institutions and how patriarchy and related oppressions are embedded within them requires us to move beyond our personal experiences and see the big picture; we must consider the interlocking outcomes institutions produce collectively and the impact of these outcomes in society. This understanding moves us well beyond the simplistic idea that equality is simply a matter of what each individual believes.

SEX/GENDER AND SCIENCE

There is a lot of new and challenging information related to sex and gender that can be confusing for many of us. You may be thinking:

> *I'm confused*... The only way we can reproduce is with one male and one female. So isn't it a biological fact that there are only two sexes?
> *I'm confused*... Is it wrong to call a transgender woman a "trans woman"? Or should I just refer to her as a woman?
> *I'm confused*... How am I supposed to know which pronouns to use?
> *I'm confused*... These issues are much more appropriate to adults. Shouldn't we leave it to the parents to teach their kids about sex and gender?

Sex and gender have been written about and studied in disciplines ranging from sociology and psychology, to biology and medicine, to theology. Given this range of disciplines, research on sex differences is typically organized under three categories: social/cultural, biological/evolutionary, and religious/theological (Ellis et al., 2024). Still, for many of us who haven't spent time studying how humans come to be, the difference between boys and girls or men and women seems obvious: you either have a penis or a vagina because biology dictates one of each as necessary for reproduction of the species. So we may ask, "Aren't the differences between XX and XY bodies hardwired?" The view of sex differences as wired into our bodies and directed by our brains to circulate the hormones that make us masculine or feminine is called "brain organization theory" (Jordan-Young, 2010). The scientists who study this theory believe that in species that are dependent on sexual reproduction, as humans are, the brain is a key organ directing how our bodies develop and respond to hormonal messaging intended to facilitate reproduction.

> ✓ **PERSPECTIVE CHECK:** A note on the trend of "gender reveal" parties: We don't know the gender a child will come to identify with as they develop, mature, and are socialized. Nor are ultrasounds done to "find out the gender of the baby." At best, the ultrasonographer will read the genital development at a given point. Based on this reading of genitalia, doctors will assign the child as "male" or "female." This is the same information a "gender" party is revealing—the sex category—"male" or "female" ("boy" or "girl"). Thus, the use of the term "gender" in these two instances is a misnomer.

In her extensive review of hundreds of scientific studies about human sex and gender, Dr. Rebecca Jordan-Young (2010, 2014) finds that today's brain theory science is not too far advanced from the 17th century. At that time, the theory was "preformationism"—the belief that organisms develop from a pre-formed essence (or mini version) of themselves embedded in the sperm or egg. "Spermists" believed the essence of a human could be found in sperm, and "ovists" believed that the pre-human was in the egg. While mainstream science today may no longer see mini men and mini women inside either sperm or ovum, they often remain locked in newer scientific versions of the same model for understanding sex differences. In this new model it is theorized that hormones such as testosterone and estrogen (instead of the old-fashioned "mini" men or women) direct a predecided male or female body (Jordan-Young, 2014). What Jordan-Young's studies reveal is that the science upon which we come to know who we are as humans contains so many gaps and contradictions that it cannot be considered a coherent body of evidence about how sex differences work.

The 1960s and 1970s gave rise to a new conceptual distinction between *sex* and *gender*, in which sex (male or female) came to signify the *biological* differences, and gender (masculine or feminine) came to signify the *social and cultural* responses to difference (Conte, 2018). A baseline for understanding these terms is that when we refer to the *sex* of humans, we are referring to biological differences (bodies that are female or male). When we refer to the *gender* of humans, we are referring to social and cultural differences (bodies that are women or men). But even these reference points are not as settled as they seem.

There are common expectations about how sex development proceeds. As Laura Erickson-Schroth and Benjamin Davis (2021) explain, people with XX chromosomes are typically born with ovaries, a vagina, a vulva, and a clitoris. At puberty, we assume they will develop breasts and start to menstruate. People with XY chromosomes are typically born with testicles and a penis. At puberty, we assume they will gain height, develop facial and body hair, and produce sperm. Yet even for those who match these trajectories, there can be a wide range of variation. There are women who are tall and have lots of body hair, and men who are short with very little body hair. Further, intersex people can differ from these expectations; they may have XY chromosomes and a vagina, or XX chromosomes and an enlarged clitoris. Sex can be as complicated as gender, and certainly more complicated than expectations suggest (Erickson-Schroth & Davis, 2021).

While there are many scientists who are in favor of preserving the distinction between sex and gender, others argue that distinguishing between biological and social variables is problematic because *learning* (or culture) is always a complex interaction between internal biology (the brain) and the external cultural setting (the environment) (Ellis et al., 2024; Erickson-Schroth & Davis, 2021). In fact, scientists are still trying to determine the variables that cause male/female sex differences (e.g., genitalia, hormones, chromosomes) and, given how intertwined they are, asking whether it is useful to try to separate biological sex from sociocultural gender at all (Ellis et al., 2024). Our study of sex and gender has been impacted by what is called *a priori thinking* (when our assumptions predetermine the questions we ask and the evidence we look for). We must remember that scientists themselves are embedded in a social context that sees clear differences between bodies that are male or female, men or women. When we look at genetics, however, the differences between, say, male and female cognitive and behavioral traits are not as significant as we may at first believe (Ellis et al., 2024).

Taken as a whole, what the range of research reveals is that our cultural feelings and beliefs about sex differences are stronger than the scientific evidence we have to date. So in this landscape, how do we thoughtfully study and critically think about sex and gender, and sexism in particular? The fact that the science is not settled does not mean that sex/gender is not real in our lives. So for now, we will proceed with the most settled interpretations to date:

Human *sex* as we currently understand it is determined by chromosomes and hormones. Human bodies are typically male, female, or in some cases intersex (having chromosomes, hormones, and physiology that varies from the male/female binary or is a combination).

Our *gender* as we currently know it is determined by our social environment. Gender is a combination of our inner sense of who we are (our gender *identity*) and our external social behaviors (our gender *expression*). Human cultures typically have two ways of understanding and expressing gender: masculine or feminine. While boys and men are expected to act the way their culture defines masculine, and girls and women expected to act as their culture defines feminine, both genders are capable of behaving in masculine or feminine ways and might do so in different contexts.

When a person's gender identity and expression match their sex, they are *cisgender*. When a person's gender identity and expression do not match their sex, they are *transgender*. Some transgender people have gender identities that fit the "opposite" sex. Others have gender identities that do not match either sex or are a combination.

While Western cultures have two, binary, genders, this is not the only way humans have described genders. For example, many Indigenous cultures express a multiplicity of gender and sexuality, as was noted by colonizers as early as the 16th century (Roscoe, 2020). European explorers and anthropologists often used terms like "hermaphrodite" or "sodomite" or "berdache" to describe Native people they encountered who appeared to be crossing or mixing genders. Europeans had no framework for understanding the multidimensional diversity of identities and social roles across Native American and Pacific Island cultures. Unlike the Western framework of their colonizers, these cultures were not limited to an opposite-gender framework (Roscoe, 2020). It wasn't until the 1990s that these colonialist terms were officially recognized for their inappropriateness, and at a gathering of First Nations and Native American peoples, the term "Two-Spirit" was coined (Roscoe, 2020). While specific tribes have their own languages and terminologies, in 1993 the term Two-Spirit was formalized, referring to both male and female Native people who mix, cross, or combine the standardized roles of men and women (Roscoe, 2020).

One's *sexuality* or *sexual orientation* is different from their sex. Sexual orientation describes which sex or gender of people someone is attracted to. Because mainstream culture is invested in sexual attraction existing primarily for the purpose of reproduction, our cultural ideas about gender expression and sexuality are hard to question. For example, do women naturally want to mate with one man who is her "true love" for life? Are men naturally more sexually aggressive and promiscuous? And are these traits necessary for reproduction? Despite our strong cultural stories about these questions, the science is not conclusive.

There are other terms related to sex and gender identity and expression that may be new to you, such as *queer*, *nonbinary*, and *gender diverse*. To illustrate how insiders' language can seem complicated to outsiders, consider the lexicon of Inuit terminology for sea ice, which has 93 different terms listed (Canadian Encyclopedia, 2015). Because it has historically been such a defining aspect of their world, Inuit people have multiple ways to describe variations in snow and ice. This allows them to recognize and speak in much greater detail about the nuances of weather that dictate their daily lives. In other words, their language enables them to see and communicate with much more precision than those of us outside their cultural context. Unless snow and its variations concern us on a daily basis or beyond one annual season, we have just a few simplistic descriptors. This means our language literally limits our ability to comprehend a full range of variations; we simply don't see anything much more complex than "snow." What is important for our purposes is that when people use terms to describe an experience we don't share, those terms may appear alien to us. This lack of understanding does not mean the terms should be rejected. Rather, we should consider whether the limitation lies with those of us whose lived experience hasn't depended on our understanding.

Attitudes about sex and gender and the actions that result from them are not just theoretical. The following exchange—and the legislation it is regarding—is a real-world example of how our attitudes and actions play out in practice. The National Center for Lesbian Rights and GLAAD Law (Gay & Lesbian Alliance Against Defamation) filed a suit on behalf of six active-duty transgender U.S. military personnel and two trans Americans seeking to enlist, as a response to Executive Order (EO) No. 14183 (2025). The exchange below is from the Memorandum Opinion written by U.S. District Court Judge Ana C. Reyes about the court case *Talbott v. Trump* (2025). In reference to EO 14183, President Donald J. Trump's "Prioritizing Military Excellence and Readiness," 90 Fed. Reg. 8757 (January 27, 2025), and Secretary of Defense Peter B. Hegseth's policy implementing EO 14183's directives, Dkt. 63-1 (February 26, 2025), she writes:

> They [these two policies] pronounce that transgender persons are not honorable, truthful, or disciplined—but Defense counsel concedes that these assertions are pure conjecture.
> THE COURT: Is [EO 14183] saying that transgender people or people with gender dysphoria, [that] their inherent identity is inconsistent with a commitment to an honorable, truthful, and disciplined lifestyle, is that demeaning to them?
> DEFENSE COUNSEL: I don't have a characterization for that, Your Honor.
> THE COURT: Okay. And if I asked you about all the other words in [the Military Ban], with respect to the characterization of transgender people or people with gender dysphoria, you would have the same answer?
> DEFENSE COUNSEL: Yes, Your Honor.
> THE COURT: There's nothing [supporting these assertions] in the studies; right?
> DEFENSE COUNSEL: That says those same things, no, Your Honor, not that I know of.
> THE COURT: [No study] says anything close to those things; correct?
> DEFENSE COUNSEL: Not that I know of, Your Honor.
>
> (pp. 3–4)

As we can see from this exchange, these legal policies are not based on research or other forms of evidence, yet have very real consequences for people's lives.

Returning to the common points of confusion that opened this section, we offer the following guidance:

- Start with a sense of humility. Given the complexity of human sex and gender, what you think you know is not yet settled in the science.

- Notice and question your emotional reactions when people express their gender differently than you do. What do you fear is at risk or under threat?
- Allow people to define themselves. It's okay to ask people how they identify, but be respectful and don't ask people you don't have a relationship with personal and invasive questions about their bodies.
- Remember that how we describe ourselves is shaped by (and limited to) our cultural scripts and vocabulary.

> **STOP:** We may have heard some version of the dismissive, "So now if someone says they identify as a cat I have to act like it's true?" It is highly unlikely that the person asking this question will encounter people who identify as animals, but let's take the question seriously for a moment, as it may be masking more vulnerable fears. At its heart, this is an expression of discomfort about the disconnect between gender identity—which is subjective—and sex—which is believed to be objective. When discomfort about someone's gender identity arises, we suggest you use that as an opportunity to expand your understanding of the world. Trans people have existed across all cultures and eras in some form—this is an established historical reality. A more constructive use of your efforts is to move your focus to working through your own discomfort and seeking further education.

AN EXAMPLE: SEXISM TODAY

A key challenge in understanding current manifestations of oppression is that oppression is often much easier to see in the past (or in another context) than in the present (or in our own context). For example, it is easy for most people to see and accept that denying women the right to vote, enslaving Africans, or forcing Indigenous children to attend residential schools are all examples of oppression. We may also believe that since those things have ended, so has oppression. Because our attention is directed to events from the past that appear isolated and disconnected from the present, current patterns of oppression become harder for us to see. We are led to believe that once women got the right to vote, or enslaved people were freed, or residential schools closed, the people affected all became fully equal. However, it is important to understand that oppression can adapt and change over time while still maintaining inequitable outcomes overall. And the culture we live in today was shaped by events of the past and the systems we inherited and cannot be fully separated from that history.

Let's trace a specific example of oppression, sexism, and learn how it can be pervasive while also difficult to see. The following statistics demonstrate the pervasiveness of sexism and the connections between isolated incidences and the overall system.

In the global context:

- Assault and violence based on trafficking (the illegal trade in human beings that constitutes a modern form of slavery) of women and girls for forced labor and sex is widespread (Watts & Zimmerman, 2002; World Health Organization, 2024). Since the COVID-19 pandemic, there has been a 25% increase in trafficking, particularly among women and children (United Nations, 2025).
- 7 in 10 human trafficking victims globally are women or girls (Novotney, 2023).
- The majority of victims of trafficking for sexual exploitation are women and girls at 61% (United Nations, 2024a).
- One woman or girl is killed every 10 minutes by their partner or family member (United Nations, 2024b).
- Women and girls account for more than 95% of victims of conflict-related sexual violence (CRSV), which includes rape, sexual slavery, forced prostitution and trafficking, and other forms of sexual violence (UNRIC, 2024).
- Most violence against women is committed by current or former husbands or intimate partners. More than 640 million women aged 15 and older have been subjected to intimate partner violence (IPV) (World Health Organization, 2021).
- In 2023, around 51,100 women and girls worldwide were killed by their family member or intimate partner. On average 140 women or girls are killed daily by someone in their family (UN Women, 2024).
- 60% of female homicides (as compared to 12% of male homicides) are committed by intimate partners or family members (UN Women, 2024).
- By the time they are 19, 1 in 4 (24%) girls who have been in a relationship have already been physically, sexually, or psychologically abused by a partner (Sardinha et al., 2024).
- Over 230 million women and girls have been subjected to female genital mutilation, representing a 15% increase since 2015 (UNICEF, 2024).
- Women with disabilities, and those who are also low income, are at an increased risk of violence and IPV than women without disabilities (García-Cuéllar et al., 2023).

While war rape is considered a crime against humanity and trafficking affects women in developing nations at higher rates than women in the United States or

Canada, violent crimes and other forms of exploitation against women are not restricted to developing nations. Sexism affects U.S. and Canadian women's lives, producing many kinds of violence:

- One woman or girl is killed every 48 hours (Canadian Femicide Observatory for Justice and Accountability, 2022).
- More than 4 in 10 women have experienced intimate partner violence (IPV) in their lifetimes (Statistics Canada, 2021). The most severe forms of IPV involve being sexually assaulted, choked, or threatened with a weapon (Cotter, 2021).
- Indigenous girls and women are 12 times more likely to be missing or murdered than other groups of girls or women in Canada, and 16 times more likely than White women (National Inquiry into Missing and Murdered Indigenous Women and Girls, 2019).
- In the United States, transgender people experience victimization at a rate of 86 per 1,000 (as compared to cisgender people at 22 per 1,000) (Flores et al., 2021).
- 1 in 4 women in the United States will experience physical violence by their intimate partner at some point during their lifetimes (Huecker et al., 2023).
- About 1 in 3 women experience some form of sexual violence during their lifetimes (Huecker et al., 2023).
- 1 in 6 women have experienced stalking during their lifetimes. The majority are stalked by someone they know (Huecker et al., 2023).
- At least 5 million acts of domestic violence occur annually to women aged 18 and older (Huecker et al., 2023).
- Approximately 1.5 million intimate partner rapes and physical assaults are perpetrated annually (Huecker et al., 2023).
- About 1 in 4 women have experienced completed or attempted rape at some point in their lives (Leemis et al., 2022).
- More than 4 in 5 female rape survivors reported that they were first raped before age 25 and almost half were first raped before age 18 (Leemis et al., 2022).
- Annually, domestic violence is responsible for over 1,500 deaths in the United States (Huecker et al., 2023; Zeppegno et al., 2019).

What these statistics reveal is that rape, sexual assault, and violence against women (perpetrated primarily by men) occur at extraordinary rates and many of us are unaware of the severity and pervasiveness of this violence. This violence is both direct and indirect. For example, Canada and the United States are primary consumers of clothing, accessories, and household goods produced by sweatshop labor, which is labor primarily performed by women and girls.

> 📖 **"Sweatshop"** refers to labor that is subcontracted in order to evade labor laws that require safe working conditions and fair wages. A typical sweatshop factory employs female workers in developing countries at subminimum wages to work in unsanitary, unsafe, and other extreme conditions in order to increase profits for multinational corporations. Apparel, toy, and electronics manufacturing are examples of industries that extensively use sweatshop labor (Warner, 2011).

WHAT MAKES SEXISM DIFFICULT TO SEE?

Given the pervasiveness of violence against women globally as well as locally, how are so many of us able to deny its existence? Why does mainstream culture position sexism as a problem of marginalized societies (developing nations or people living in poverty) rather than as a pervasive system that affects all women throughout the world, mediated by their additional social positions of race, class, sexuality, and other identities? The pervasiveness of violence against women, and violence against women of Color, Indigenous women, trans women, poor women, and women with disabilities in particular, is so normalized as to be virtually invisible. In order to see it, one must pay attention to the relationship between history, socialization, institutions, and culture, and especially how we tell stories about ourselves through these relationships.

> ✔ **PERSPECTIVE CHECK:** In the context of understanding sexism as a particular system of oppression that maintains patriarchy, we use the term "men" to refer to the dominant group and "women" to refer to the minoritized group. While we use these two terms for brevity, we want to be clear that the term "women" is a placeholder that includes cis women, trans women, nonbinary people, intersex people, non-cis men, and gender nonconforming people.

First, sexism is difficult to see because it is naturalized very early on in children's culture and is reinforced across our life spans. Corporate-produced popular culture has become a pervasive institution in our lives through multiple points of entry, such as advertising, sponsored curriculum in schools, and social media. Consider children's toys and how they amplify rigid gender roles, socializing girls into femininity (pleasing, child care, homemaking, beauty play) and boys into masculinity (aggression, violence, competition, physical play). Walk through any major toy department and peruse the aisles and you will see that rather than expanding, gender roles have become increasingly narrow and rigid. Male musculature in toys and media representations has become more exaggerated, the emotional range has become more limited—usually to some variation of rage—and violent play for boys has become more realistic through AI-generated video games and weapons (Bailey & Burkell, 2021; Morrison & Halton, 2009). At the same time, girls' toys and imagery remain more passive as girls' play is focused primarily on beauty and clothing, self-grooming and fitness, friendship, and preparing for their wedding day.

Corporate-produced messaging reinforces masculinity as dominance, disconnection from feelings, invulnerability, and immunity from emotional attachment, and femininity as passive, pleasing, and above all else attractive to men. At the same time, advertising promotes the idea of individualism and free choice. It is through products (and the lifestyles advertisers associate with them) that we can demonstrate our uniqueness. These scripts, introduced in childhood, are continuously sold to us as what we already desire. In this way sexism is naturalized very early on by creating an explanation of real-world inequities between men and women (such as in income and status) as the inevitable outcome of biology and natural choice, rather than the outcome of systemic forces.

> ✓ **PERSPECTIVE CHECK:** Some people may say that they can name several shows that are counter to these narratives. That is good news, but does not alone undo the foundation of the characters we have been repeatedly exposed to, how early we were exposed to them, and for how long. There will always be exceptions, but they don't unmake the rule.

Because we are all exposed to gender messaging through the wider culture, film and TV directors (overwhelmingly men) rely on familiar characters and plots in films and shows as an effective way to quickly communicate an emotion, story element, or plot tension. For example, if a director wants to convey ideas about a "studious female," he can signal this idea by visually coding the character as someone who wears glasses, has brown hair, and dresses conservatively. Conversely, in a slasher film, we know from the start which females will be murdered and which won't. The women who will be murdered are sexually promiscuous and often unintelligent and thus "deserve" to die. This is signaled through cues in dress, behavior, and music. The audience, because it has seen these signifiers repeatedly, immediately understands the character types. This process normalizes these outcomes for women and what they deserve. What women deserve is always tied to their relationships to men, whether she will be killed by a man if she is bad, or get the man if she is good. Further, because the women who die in slasher films are highly sexualized, the violence toward them is also sexualized. The repetitiveness of these storylines makes these roles and outcomes for women seem normal and unremarkable, while reinforcing these concepts under the surface of our conscious awareness.

> **📖 Signifier:** A sign or symbol that conveys specific cultural meaning. Signifiers connect to larger discourses that work together to construct that meaning.

Another typical character and plot sequence is in the subgenre of romance movies (often called "chick flicks"). The script usually follows the fairy-tale storyline: The main character is a young woman who is a selfless caretaker or ultra career-oriented, or she is too involved in her work or school to realize how wonderful she is "inside and out" and doesn't "fix herself up" or "accept herself for how special she is." Perhaps it is *she* who does not realize that *he* is really a prince in beast's clothing, a beast that she will tame with her love or risk her life trying. She is often encouraged by her friends (or sister or gay best friend) to get out more, try something new, take a chance, and/or get a makeover. Despite her career success, family commitments, and fulfilling friendships, this state of being without Prince Charming is presented as problematic. She is not as beautiful, desirable, or fulfilled as she could be were she to also have that perfect man in her life. When she meets Prince Charming through a serendipitous encounter, she often does not realize at first that he is "the one." He must break her coma in order to complete her life. After Prince Charming breaks her coma, she becomes more beautiful, which is signaled to the audience through improvements in hair, makeup, clothes, and softer lighting, and in her behavior as she is now relaxed and smiling.

Mainstream movies, as well as many reality makeover shows, normalize the idea that it is important for women to transcend their race and class status and align with traditional notions of femininity. Prince Charming facilitates her transformation, as through him, she acquires access to an improved lifestyle, self-esteem, and a better wardrobe. These movies reinforce the ideology that women are fundamentally incomplete without a man. This man brings not only personal fulfillment and definition but also increased social status through heterosexual marriage and a middle- or upper-class consumer lifestyle, and kinship with other women who have done the same.

We may very well—and likely often do—enjoy a film or show that reproduces sexism. Indeed, it's likely that due to how normalized these narratives are, we won't see them as sexist at all. Yet the more a narrative appeals to us (especially if we are women), the more important it is for us to be able to think critically about it so that we can resist its effects. Recall the concept of internalized oppression and that minoritized groups often collude with dominant ideology. Thus, no socially constructed text can or should be off-limits to a critical analysis, regardless of how popular or enjoyable it is. There is no need to feel defensive about enjoying a film or show that is embedded with problematic storylines. Films are designed to manipulate our emotions in enjoyable ways. The point is to be able to think critically about those storylines. Thinking critically can also be an enjoyable part of the process, working to uncover the clues and hidden messages.

Second, sexism is difficult to see because our attention is drawn to individual cases rather than to connecting the dots between these cases and revealing the consistent group-level patterns. If we view oppression as isolated historical events that have been remedied (such as suffrage or reproductive rights in Canada), or as an extreme example of violence against a single woman, the broader patterns are hidden. It is harder to see everyday and ongoing sexism when placed alongside the sensationalized "true crime" examples (e.g., a woman sexually mutilated and strangled, or a woman drugged and raped by multiple men). When we define oppression solely as individual acts that individual bad people do, we conceal the ways that social institutions organize and normalize everyday violence against women. Further, women who live through an assault and have the courage to speak out about it will have to endure public shaming and disbelief—being "taken apart in court" by defense lawyers. This sends the powerful message to women that seeking justice is not worth the additional emotional trauma, leading many women to remain silent about sexual assault (Caron & Mitchell, 2022; Wieberneit et al., 2024).

A third way that sexism is difficult to see is because the West is presented as civilized and liberated, in contrast to places that are uncivilized and backwards. For example, the Muslim woman is the archetype of an oppressed woman, standing in stark contrast to our own perceived liberation in the United States and Canada (places that are presumed to be free of Muslim women). Indeed, many of our female students frequently deny that sexism is a socializing force in their own lives and support this denial by giving the example of the Muslim woman as the woman who is *truly* oppressed (Fairbairn et al., 2023; Jiwani, 2006; Olwan, 2019, 2021; Sensoy & DiAngelo, 2006). When people look to the Muslim woman in this way, they see the opposite of themselves. Think about the following list and consider which side is associated with Western women and which side is stereotypically associated with women seen as non-Western:

Modern—Primitive
Active—Passive
Individual—Group
Industrious—Idle
Pretty—Ugly
Open—Covered
Free—Restricted

Through this binary organization of desirable or undesirable opposites, we come to understand forms of social oppression such as sexism through the most simplistic explanations and examples. Such simplification cannot account for the ways that other social positions such as race and class also limit women's lives. Even while corporate interests are amplifying rather than reducing rigid gender roles, we are socialized to believe that in the United States and Canada, we are liberated and free; the way we "do" gender just seems normal, even healthy, and certainly better than the way *they* do it (for example, we can wear whatever body-revealing clothes we choose from chain stores in the local mall, where our heavily marketed brand choices are believed to demonstrate our individuality, while *they* "have to" wear clothes that cover their bodies and all look the same). While our attention is continually drawn to examples of sexism that occur "over there"—in non-White, non-Western contexts—examples of sexism "over here" are usually situated in the past. Yet patriarchy is a global system and the fact that it manifests differently in different cultures does not render it nonoperative in our own.

Sexism is also difficult to see because it is often presented as a personal *choice*. This is the idea marketed to us through ubiquitous media messaging that our choices are freely made and unique to our individual personalities or styles. While kids may spend 6 hours a day for 180 days per year in school receiving instruction, they interact with media—especially social media—almost constantly (as reported by nearly half of teens responding to a 2023 survey [M. Anderson et al., 2023]). A 2024 Pew Research Center study reports that when teens (13–17) were asked how often they visited the top five social media platforms (YouTube, TikTok, Snapchat, Instagram, and Facebook), a third of the teens reported using at least one of the five sites "almost constantly" (Faverio & Sidoti, 2024, p. 5). Further, according to Pew's research as of 2024, 95% of U.S. teens aged 13–17 have a smartphone, 88% have a laptop or desktop computer, 96% go online daily, and 46% report being online "almost constantly" (p. 3). These platforms go hand in hand with carefully curated advertising, algorithms that track and direct them to curated content, and armies of kid-influencers ("kidfluencers") impacting youth consumption activities in real life (Rasmussen et al., 2022). A kidfluencer unboxes, plays with, and comments on a new toy or game while being recorded. Kidfluencing is one of many covert marketing strategies that have grown in the new era of VSPs (video sharing platforms).

The continual sophistication and innovation of new technologies have dramatically changed the landscape of marketing. Overt advertising methods have been replaced by immersive tactics that are deliberately designed to blend into everyday life. In this way they have become harder to see, especially for children (Smith et al., 2024). To understand the scale of the genre, kidfluencer Ryan has nearly 39 million subscribers to his YouTube channel *Ryan's World*. He is among the most popular of kidfluencers on the platform, and it is reported that in 2020 alone he earned nearly $30 million reviewing branded toys and products (Rahali, 2021). Other top kidfluencers include 16-year-old Charli D'Amelio with over 40 million Instagram followers and brand partnerships with beauty and makeup corporations; 8-year-old Everleigh Rose with nearly 5 million Instagram followers on her kid fashion and toy reviews; and 7-year-old Elle, who began kidfluencing at age 4 and has 4 million Instagram followers (Amra & Elma, 2023). It is clear that the scope of kids' consumption of social media and the marketing activities directed at them make influencer-generated advertising (compared to overt ads such as those at the start of YouTube videos) harder for younger children to recognize as advertising (Smith et al., 2024).

There is no doubt that kids are plugged in. Yet when discussing the power of advertising with our students, we often hear, "I don't pay any attention to the ads. They don't affect me at all." Advertising is a multibillion-dollar industry based on copious research (Radesky et al., 2020; Statista, 2025). There are no accidents in ads—every aspect of an ad is designed to affect us, even if we only glance at it for a moment. This is important to understand because one of the ways that media and popular culture work to perpetuate sexism is by normalizing particular kinds of people and relationships. Over and over, as we see *these* kinds of women and girls (and not others) playing out certain scripts of behavior (and not others), those roles and relations become normal (and ideal) to us. The same, of course, goes for the scripts reinforced for boys.

> **Androcentrism:** "Male-centered." A worldview that presents men's experience, bodies, and associated traits as universal and the standard for human. Via androcentrism, male norms are the reference point by which women are judged and inevitably found deficient.

Virtually everything in advertising is gendered, furthering the strict division between the roles of men and women and thereby shaping our seemingly neutral and individual consumer choices. Food is a cogent example of gender divisions reinforced through marketing. According to advertisers, women drink iced tea and eat yogurt, salads, chocolate, and cake, while men drink beer and eat pizza, hamburgers, bacon, and other red meat. Even smell is gendered. While there is no biological difference in hair between women and men, shampoo is marketed to us as if there were. What makes a shampoo masculine or feminine? Smell. The smell of fruit or flowers is for women, while smells associated with the "rugged" outdoors, such as pine and musk, are for men.

The gender associated with a product and how that association impacts our behavior indicates the direction of power. The minoritized group can emulate the dominant group because in doing so they are emulating the higher status group and thus gain status; but the dominant group does not emulate the minoritized group because they are emulating the lower status group and thus lose status. This is why women wear pants as well as dresses, but men in mainstream society do not wear dresses as well as pants (there has been a small resurgence of kilts for men in alternative subculture, but these kilts are acceptable because they are masculinized by their association with ancestry and battle). Men who order cosmopolitans or other fruity drinks risk ridicule (because fruit is gendered female). These examples show how powerful the interplay of gender roles, unequal power, and marketing is in shaping what we think of as our everyday preferences and choices.

DOMINANT DISCOURSES OF SEXISM AS EMPOWERMENT

Sexism today relies on the discourse that women are not only equal, but *empowered*. In fact, the claim goes, women are not just empowered—they actually hold all of the power because sexism has "reversed." This discourse rests on two key ideas. One is the false equivalence between numbers and power—e.g., "There are so many more women in X today than there were in the past." The other is the idea that if we choose something, it is chosen freely and therefore can't be problematic—e.g., "A woman chooses to do X and so it isn't sexism." In these ways empowerment discourse is in large part tied to numbers and choice. Let's examine three aspects of empowerment discourse that hide sexism.

Women are equal now. This discourse presents the idea that the status of women today is equal to the status of men and that women are no longer disadvantaged. Social measures such as voting rights, representation in media, visibility in politics, and participation in leadership are cited as examples. While this story of women's equality is cherished, we must ask, in which ways are women equal? And to what extent can equality be a taken-for-granted reality for women?

Consider these hugely powerful multinational corporations that shape our everyday lives and that are regularly at the top of the Nasdaq trading lists. Every CEO is male, as is the majority of every executive leadership team:

- Apple Inc. (Tim Cook, CEO; executive leadership team 84% men)
- Microsoft (Satya Nadella, CEO; executive team 60% men)
- Nvidia (AI, gaming, etc.; Jensen Huang, CEO; executive team 70% men)
- Alphabet (Google; Sundar Pichai, CEO; executive team 80% men)
- Amazon (E-commerce, streaming, AI; Andy Jassy, CEO; executive team 86% men)
- Meta (Facebook, Instagram, WhatsApp; Mark Zuckerberg, CEO; executive team 80% men)
- Tesla (Elon Musk, CEO; executive team 90% men)
- Broadcom (semiconductors, software; Hock E. Tan, CEO; executive team 66% men)
- Netflix (Ted Sarandos and Greg Peters, co-CEOs; executive team 65% men)

While even those corporations on the above list with only 10% female representation have more women than in the past, men still overwhelmingly control these and all other major institutions and organizations in society, including religious, scientific, policing, military, health, and economic institutions. Keep in mind that women are slightly more than 50% of the U.S. and Canadian populations. Also remember that these institutions and organizations were all founded by and led by men. This means that women who succeed at the top of these organizations do so on terms established by men.

Now let's consider women's presence in some of the other major halls of economic, governmental, and political power:

- Fortune 500 CEOs: 89% men (Ajemian, 2025)
- The 10 richest Americans: 100% men (Peterson-Withorn, 2024)
- Forty-seven U.S. presidents: 100% men
- Fifty U.S. vice presidents: 98% men

- U.S. Congress: 82% men
- U.S. mayors: 75% men
- U.S. governors: 86% men
- The 40 richest Canadians: 100% men
- Canada's elected prime ministers: 100% men
- Canadian members of Parliament: 70% men
- Canadian provincial/territorial premiers: 85% men

These numbers illustrate how oppression is a one-way historical imbalance of legal and institutional power; there is no reverse sexism or the reverse of any other form of oppression. If men as a group chose to deny women's civil rights, *they could*; if women as a group wanted to deny men their civil rights, they *could not*. Women are not, in fact, equal now. Men control all major institutions, as they have since the founding of our countries.

Women are empowered now. This discourse presents the idea that the status of women today is not just *equal* to the status of men, but that women are forceful and have taken charge of their lives, as evidenced in depictions of women bosses, business owners, and entrepreneurs. While there are no doubt many examples of powerful women, let's consider the question of empowerment through two institutional contexts: sports and sex work.

Many people cite sports as an example of female empowerment. Today, a strong emphasis on sports for girls often begins in schools. But what is emphasized between boys and girls varies greatly, as does the status. There is often a lack of funding for girls' sports in school, and when there is funding for girls, it is not typically equal. This is in part because the broader culture reinforces the idea that girls' sports are not as important since girls in sports don't "go" anywhere in terms of professional leagues. The results of games between women's teams are not announced daily on local and national radio and television as they are for men's teams (men's teams of course are not identified as "men's" teams at all, but just as "teams").

Neither girls' and women's sports teams nor girl and women athletes are taken seriously in mainstream culture. In fact, they are barely visible except in contexts such as the diet/fitness industry or as male-oriented entertainment such as the X League (formerly called the Legends Football League, and Lingerie Football League). While society's interest in women athletes increases during the Olympics, the final matches that end the games (and most other competitions, such as the U.S. Open or Wimbledon) are between men.

In both salaries and individual prize money from competitions, professional male athletes in basketball, golf, soccer, baseball, and tennis earn from 15% to nearly 100% more than professional female athletes (Baker, 2024; Knight et al., 2024; J. Lawson, 2024; UN Women, 2025). In terms of visibility, peruse the daily news in either print or streaming and notice who is covered in the Sports sections. Close to 100% of the coverage is of male athletes.

Sex work is another area often cited as an example of women "taking back" their stories as well as their resources. Sex work includes street prostitution, brothels, escorts, massage parlors, pornography, and other forms of online sexual services. The term *sex work* was adopted to be "sex positive" and to convey that this type of work was like any other and should be respected as such. Scholars such as Robert Jensen (2024) reject the term and have argued that the buying and selling of objectified female bodies for male sexual pleasure makes it different from other forms of work, and proceeding as if it isn't different only protects sexism, not women. He argues that "sexual-exploitation industries" is a more accurate description given the higher rates of assault, rape, murder, and sexually transmitted diseases. Risks of prostitution also include posttraumatic stress disorder (PTSD), dissociative disorders, depression, eating disorders, suicide attempts and successful suicides, substance abuse, sexual assaults, and murder. Childhood abuse is such a common precursor to prostitution that it is considered by most experts to be a necessary if not sufficient risk factor for prostitution (Farley, 2018; Farley & Donevan, 2021). Some women find sex work valuable but there is not agreement on the question of sex work as a fully elected choice (Benoit et al., 2019; Bettio et al., 2017; Cantillon & O'Connor, 2021), much less a form of empowerment within the context of patriarchy and capitalism.

OnlyFans, a subscription-based media platform where people pay to access pictures, videos, and livestreams posted by content creators, has been profitable for many women and may be a safer form of sex work. A major part of what has been called the "platformization of sex work" (Franco & Webber, 2024), since 2020 the streaming platform has grown by over 553% (Ever Accountable, 2024) and continues to grow. Women purportedly can control their own sites and illegal content such as child exploitation, nonconsensual sexual acts, violence, and abuse is not allowed (Social Rise, 2024). OnlyFans offers a safer way to make a living selling one's body, and some women have made millions doing so. We have no objections to these aspects of the platform. Our concern is twofold: First, with what is required of women in order to be successful on OnlyFans. Performing for the male gaze, catering to narrowly defined male desires, and abiding by mainstream beauty standards are just as reinforced here as they are elsewhere. Second, with the very real and well-documented risks to content creators, including promoter scams, copyright infringement, identity theft, and stalking. Youth are especially at risk of these dangers, being susceptible to exploitation and pressure to post explicit content. Nude photos posted online exemplify content that is very hard to retract and can impact the rest of a poster's life (Finkelhor et al., 2022; O'Malley & Holt, 2020; Patchin & Hinduja, 2018). The people we are talking about as "empowered" by sex work and platforms such as OnlyFans are girls and women. The primary consumers of sex work and platforms like OnlyFans are men who have been socialized to dehumanize girls and women in these same contexts. Given the direction of power, for women to take charge of their lives still depends on terms defined by men.

> 📖 **The Equal Rights Amendment (ERA) in full:** Equality of rights under the law shall not be denied or abridged by the United States or by any state on account of sex. (The ERA first proposed in 1923 has still not passed.)

Women have all the power now. It is not uncommon to hear men say that the direction of power between men and women has "reversed" and it is women who have all the power now. A cogent example is a speech given by Vice President JD Vance at the Conservative Political Action Committee Conference in February of 2025 (Fiallo, 2025). Vance claimed that American men are under attack for simply being who they are: "My message to young men is don't allow this broken culture to send you a message that you're a bad person because you're a man, because you like to tell a joke, because you like to have a beer with your friends, or because you're competitive." Equating masculinity with the ability to drink beer and tell jokes—presumably racist and sexist jokes—Vance echoed a familiar complaint: Apparently men can't say anything anymore. (Note that the list of things that Vance and other men complain have been taken from them does not include freedom from being stalked, drugged, assaulted, raped, murdered, or having their reproductive rights taken away.) So let's compare the narrative that women have taken so much power away from men as to emasculate them and compare it to the gendered facts of daily life.

Overt sexism occurs in U.S. and Canadian women's lives in these ways:

- 47.3% (59 million) women in the United States report sexual violence, physical violence, and or stalking at some point in their lifetime (Leemis et al., 2022).
- The number of American troops killed in Afghanistan and Iraq between 2001 and 2012 was 6,488. The number of American women who were murdered by current or former male partners during that time was 11,766 (HOPE, n.d.).
- Girls and women account for 90% of victims of sexual assault incidents reported to police in 2022; only 6% of cases are reported (Conroy, 2024); sexual assault is the least reported crime, with 6% of assaults coming to the attention to police as compared to 36% of physical assaults and 47% of robberies (Conroy, 2024).
- In Canada, 11% of women students experience sexual assault in a postsecondary setting (Burczycka, 2020).
- 83% of women with disabilities will be sexually assaulted in their lives (Disability Justice, 2023).
- 80% of women with developmental disabilities have been sexually assaulted, half of them more than 10 times (Weiss, 2012).
- More than 6 in 10 Indigenous women have been physically or sexually assaulted during their lifetime (Statistics Canada, 2021).
- In the United States, Native women and girls experience a murder rate 10 times higher than the national average (House Appropriations Committee, 2024).

While the real and everyday violence against women is so common as to be unremarkable, imagined violence against women as a form of entertainment surrounds us. Women's power is often linked to their sex appeal to men, at the same time that the victimization of women most commonly comes at the hands of men. Thus women are simultaneously taught to appeal to men and also to protect themselves from men. The 2024 viral TikTok "Man or Bear" debate asks women: If you were hiking alone in the woods, would you rather come across a man or a bear. Overwhelmingly, women say they would rather encounter a random bear than a random man. In fact, when the question is flipped and men are asked if they would rather have their daughter or wife encounter a random bear or a random man, they too choose the bear. In fact, the threat of men's violence is so taken for granted that there are social media user channels devoted to sharing tips for women on how to stay safe when on a date (e.g., don't give out your address, don't share too much personal information, tell a friend or family member where you are going). Many women carry a whistle, or a glass cover or drug detector to prevent their drink being tampered with, or carry a knife or sharp-toothed keys as they walk to their car or front door. Women create decoy strategies when camping, at home, or in taxis. Examples include having a male voice recording to play and pretend to be responding to in case of threat; leaving large men's boots by their front door as decoys to indicate a man also lives there; not meeting a first date at their favorite coffee shop (because if it's a bad date he might go back and try to find her there again); knowing where the closest police station or fire hall is in case she needs to drive there first on the chance she is being followed; not turning the apartment lights on as soon as she enters her home (in case he followed her home and now will know from outside which floor and unit she lives in). The list goes on and on.

Let's consider a key domain of culture that is both ubiquitous and seldom openly talked about, a domain steeped in deep messaging not only normalizing violence against women, but also normalizing the idea that women actually desire physical pain and find it pleasurable. That domain is the world of pornography. Before we continue however, we want to be clear: Our concern is not with sex or sexual imagery. Our concern is with the narrow scripts and relentless dehumanizing of women in mainstream pornography that distort and actually limit sexual expression.

Scholars such as Diane Levin and Jean Kilbourne (2008), Sut Jhally (2007, 2009), Chyng Sun and Miguel Picker (2008), Robert Jensen (2021), and Gail Dines and Mandy Sanchez (2023) have established compelling evidence that the line between popular and porn culture has blurred. Images and films that were once taboo and hidden behind paper-wrapped magazines have, since the rise of the Internet era, become easily accessible and circulated. It is now not uncommon for young women to remove all of their pubic hair (giving them a prepubescent look) and expect to have and enjoy anal sex. These practices were not remotely mainstream in the '70s, '80s, or '90s but have been normalized through the widespread circulation of Internet pornography, illustrating how powerful the forces of media are in shaping what we come to see as normal and "naturally" desirable.

Pornography increasingly amplifies the most violent aspects of the rigid gender divisions between men and women. The physical brutalization and emotional degradation of women in porn, particularly in gonzo or "raw" unscripted porn shot from the male perspective (one of the biggest moneymaking genres of online porn, which depicts painful penetration, gang rape, and men slapping, choking, gagging, and spitting on women while they penetrate them orally, anally, and vaginally), has become more normalized as men become desensitized and need ever more intense images to feel stimulated (Binnie & Reavey, 2020; Daneback et al., 2018; DeKeseredy, 2015). The misogyny of these discourses has been amplified in involuntary celibate (or "incel") online fora, and research has shown how both incels and mainstream porn reinforce the storyline of sex as women's punishment and connected to women's submission to men (Tranchese & Sugiura, 2021).

To some, it may seem an exaggeration to say that pornography shapes our everyday lives. However, consider that within a few decades, pornography has moved from an underground business with ties to organized crime to a huge corporate industry (Altman & Watson, 2018; Cookney, 2019; DeKeseredy, 2015). The worldwide porn industry is estimated to be worth over 97 billion dollars (Nocella, 2024). In 2022, three of the top 10 most visited websites worldwide were porn sites, with PornHub and XVideos in the top 5 after Google, YouTube, and Facebook (Hammond, 2024). Many of us regularly receive unsolicited pornographic spam in our workplace and other email accounts. Porn is ubiquitous in popular culture and an increasing presence in young people's lives. In fact, one of the most popular forms of pornography is called *hentai* (sexualized anime), which depicts children and childlike characters engaged in sexual violence. This violence almost exclusively targets female characters and normalizes seeing sexual violence towards minors (Dines & Sanchez, 2023). In fact, in one of the most popular porn sites, review of search terms reveals children's animation and characters in pornographic contexts are among the most common. These include kids' characters such as Wonder Woman, Pokémon, Dora the Explorer, the Little Mermaid, Elsa from *Frozen*, Harry Potter, and many others (Dines & Sanchez, 2023). This normalization of childhood within porn culture is termed *the pornification of childhood* (Dines & Sanchez, 2023). By embedding their sites with children's characters, many porn sites target children as tomorrow's paying users by luring and tricking them into early exposure (Dines & Sanchez, 2023; R. A. Gomez, 2007).

The tactics for early exposure to pornography are effective, as evidenced by a 2025 UK report that surveyed 1,020 youth aged 16–21 (Children's Commissioner, 2025). Despite policies intended to protect children, the report found that 70% of respondents had seen pornography online, with the average age of first exposure being 13. Twenty-seven percent first saw pornography online at age 11, with some respondents reporting having seen online pornography by age 6 or younger. Eight out of 10 main sources for exposure were social media or networking sites with X (formerly Twitter) being the most common source, exposing more children to pornography than dedicated porn sites. Among other acts of violence, 58% of respondents had seen porn depicting strangulation and 44% reported seeing a depiction of rape. A sobering 44% of respondents agreed with the statement that "Girls may say no at first but then can be persuaded to have sex." The report concludes that it is normal for children to be exposed to online pornography at very young ages; children are most likely to see pornography by accident; it is normal for the pornography children see to be violent; and pornography impacts children's attitudes toward women and girls.

The representation of men as dominant, aggressive, and in control of women's bodies depends upon the representation of women as submissive, pleasing, and available for every aspect of *men's* desire. If the narratives of pornography were to acknowledge women as human beings with thoughts, feelings, and desires of their own, the viewer could not tolerate the pain, physical damage, and humiliation inflicted upon women that are a basic feature of gonzo porn (Dines, 2010; Navarro-Mantas & Sáez-Lumbreras, 2025; Thorneycroft et al., 2025; Westlake et al., 2025). Yet over time, even as we are looking directly at men brutalizing women, the ideology of sexism rationalizes it as a natural outcome of biological roles, personal choice, and mutual desire. The imagery of porn, repeated over and over, constructs an ideal female who is always available for and seeking sex with any, every, and multiple partners; who wants to be watched, touched by strangers, and objectified; who enjoys humiliation and abuse; and who has no real power, other than the illusory and temporary power of sexual attractiveness. Through repetition, the rigid gender roles presented in movies, videos, pornography, and ads come to seem normal and natural and make it difficult to conceptualize any other reality (Di Gironimo, 2025; Gavey & Brewster, 2025). In addition to the misogyny (hatred of women) in gonzo porn, the racist discourses are extreme and unparalleled in their degradation of women of Color. What was shocking in the past no longer moves us and needs to be intensified to achieve a similar impact. As elements of porn cross over into the mainstream, our sexuality is ever more rigidly defined and we become less free, not more.

We may see these images as a matter of choice—the women choose to perform and we can choose to watch them or not. But at what cost could they make different choices, in an industry dominated by men? As for our choice to watch them or not, we would first have to be able to avoid them, which is difficult given how ubiquitous they are. Pornography is simultaneously everywhere and nowhere, as few people talk openly about their porn consumption. We may insist that while we do watch porn, we don't take it seriously. But, as the research on children's exposure to pornography makes clear, engaging with porn is not merely a matter of choice (Children's Commissioner, 2025). Porn cannot be avoided, and its impacts cannot be dismissed.

How might corporate forces depend on our not taking these dynamics seriously? Corporations like OnlyFans, PornHub, etc. rake in billions of dollars annually (Happ et al., 2024; OnlyFans Annual Report, 2023). Clearly, we *are* influenced by these images and corporations depend on our capacity to be thus influenced. No one is outside of socialization, and marketers spend billions on research to find ever more effective techniques for infiltrating our subconscious. The insistence that the women in these images can just choose not to participate, or that we can just choose not to watch them, or if we do watch them that we can just choose to be unaffected by them, is naïve. It is critical that we set aside whatever discomfort about our attachment to porn we may personally feel and think deeply about the power of porn to shape our sexuality and normalize misogyny, racism, and classism. The life and work of Rachel Lloyd (Figure 7.1) illustrate the impact of prostitution on the lives of women and girls, as well as the possibility to challenge it.

Of course sexism doesn't stand in isolation from other forms of oppression. Women are not *just* women with one shared experience under sexism. Our race, class, ability status, and sexuality profoundly shape how we will experience our gender under patriarchy. Further, the gains women have made thus far have been fought for long and hard and can be revoked at any time, as demonstrated in the United States with the 2022 *Dobbs v. Jackson Women's Health Organization* (597 U.S. 215) decision that overruled *Roe v. Wade* and allowed states to outlaw abortion. *Roe v. Wade* had granted access to abortion for over 50 years and the right to abortion was assumed to be settled. As we write this 3rd edition, we expect there will soon be a federal ban.

Returning to the vignette that opens this chapter, consider our candidate's platform. This platform—as well as his success running on it—illustrates how tenuous women's gains are and how critical it is that we not take them for granted. The presence of women on his leadership team or in his political campaign does

Figure 7.1. Rachel Lloyd (b. 1975)

Lloyd is the founder and executive director of Girls Educational and Mentoring Services (GEMS). She is an activist, international speaker, and nationally recognized expert on child sex trafficking in the United States. She played a foundational role in the passage of the 2010 Safe Harbor Act for Sexually Exploited Youth, which puts into effect protections from prosecution for youth victims of sexual exploitation.

Lloyd's organization serves young women and girls who have experienced commercial sexual exploitation. Her advocacy is important because she examines the ways in which misogyny and violence are normalized in popular culture. She has won countless awards for her activism and is featured in the 2007 documentary *Very Young Girls*.

Source: https://www.gems-girls.org/about/our-team/our-founder

not in and of itself guarantee that issues of concern to women will be valued or taken seriously. In fact, it is often the women who deny sexism (or are the least threatening to it) who are seen as "team players" and allowed to enter androcentric spaces of power. Our institutions have been set up by men, for men. This means that women who want to participate will have to conform to the culture of the institution or risk being seen as incompetent, or too aggressive, or too sensitive, or too demanding, and so on, reinforcing the belief that women don't belong at the table in the first place. She certainly must dare not utter the word "sexism." As feminist scholar Sara Ahmed (2017) says, "When you expose a problem you pose a problem. It might then be assumed that the problem would go away if you would just stop talking about it or if you went away" (p. 37). Provisionally including some women does not fundamentally change the direction of power, nor does it mean that women will find the environment hospitable. Of course this presumes that the current culture is blank or neutral, and that it is minoritized people bringing a form of difference who create problems in an otherwise stable environment.

On the other hand, institutions that acknowledge the value of diversity tend to focus on increasing the numbers of "different" people, rather than addressing the culture of the institution. Basic inclusion is, of course, important. But if your inclusion is resented and seen as something "we were forced to do," you are being inserted into a hostile environment; you may survive there but are not likely to thrive. The current backlash against DEI and the assumption that any effort to be more inclusive automatically means that incompetent people are taking a White male's "rightful place" illustrates that hostility. Initiatives to increase workplace diversity were not put in place to make sure that less qualified minoritized people were hired instead of more qualified White men. *They were put in place to ensure that White men were not consistently hired over qualified or even more-qualified minoritized people.* While these programs have had some impact, they have not brought most workplaces even close to parity. But the enduring resentment about them *has* had a profound impact. The speed with which so many major corporations backed away from even appearing to value diversity, much less to take action to address historic and current underrepresentation, illustrates how deep the resentment runs and how shallow the professed commitment was. As milestones of women's progress, such as reproductive rights and suffrage—fought so long and hard for—are back on the table as legitimate questions, we repeat: We can never be complacent.

In 2024 a rape case in France was brought to trial and the details were so shocking they reverberated around the world and were reported on by a wide range of international news outlets (Wires, 2024). Dominique Pelicot was arrested for taking upskirt photos of women in a grocery store. When police searched his home, they found a folder on a USB drive connected to his computer, titled "abuses," that contained over 20,000 images and videos of men raping his wife Gisèle Pelicot while she was unconscious. Over the course of 9 years, he had systematically drugged Gisèle's food and invited at least 82 men he contacted through a website—all strangers—to come to his home and rape Gisèle while she was unconscious and he recorded the assaults. Gisèle was unaware of the assaults but had repeated health issues including hair and weight loss, four sexually transmitted diseases, and memory loss. She had been concerned about her health but Dominique accompanied her to doctor's appointments and insisted she was just exhausted from taking care of their seven grandchildren.

Over the course of two years police were able to identify 51 of the recorded men. They were aged 21–68 and included a firefighter, IT worker, journalist, nurse, plumber, prison guard, and truck driver. Many had partners and children. Twenty-three had previous convictions, including domestic violence and sexual assault. Some of the men admitted guilt, but others claimed the acts were consensual and Gisèle was just pretending to be asleep or agreeing to be drugged. Some of the men claimed that Dominique's permission, as Gisèle's husband, was all they needed.

As a rape victim, Gisèle had the right to anonymity and a private trial, but she insisted on a public trial in order to raise awareness and encourage other victims of sexual crimes to speak out. While she recognized that it was her husband who orchestrated the abuse, when she took the stand she faced the men and asked why not one of them reported Dominique to the police when they clearly saw the situation. She allowed the videos to be shown in court when the public was present, claiming, "The shame is theirs." Soon seen as a heroine, she received support from around the world. An organization that raises awareness of assault against older women, The Australian Older Women's Network, sent Gisèle a scarf made by Aboriginal women, which she often wore to court (McGuirk, 2024). She left the courthouse each day to applause from the crowds waiting outside and chants such as "The shame has changed sides." Her image appeared in street art, and words of support were pasted around the courthouse. Speaking through her lawyer, she said that she had been touched by the connection uniting women across the world in standing up to violence against them. All 51 men were found guilty and received sentences.

We conclude this chapter with the story of Gisèle Pelicot because it illustrates so many aspects of sexism. There was nothing particularly remarkable about the men involved. While 51 men were identified, a total of 82 were documented raping Gisèle. This was not a group of "monsters" lurking in an alleyway. The sheer number of men, the wide range in their ages and backgrounds, and the denials of and excuses for their crime illustrate the depth of patriarchy and misogynist conditioning. This case makes clear that the ability of men to dehumanize women is not an anomaly. These men are the product of a conditioning process that crosses boundaries of age and class, a conditioning so endemic as to be banal. Yet it is highly unlikely that this story would have been believed on Gisèle's word alone (had she become aware of what was happening). Even though Gisèle Pelicot was a wife, a mother, and a grandmother and could not be dismissed based on what she did for a living, how she dressed, or where she went in the evening, it is still unusual that she was believed. In her case, unlike the cases of countless women before her, police had indisputable video evidence. The fact that all 51 of the men who were brought to trial were convicted is also atypical. But perhaps what is most remarkable about this case is that Gisèle Pelicot was able to move the shame off herself as the victim and onto the perpetrators. And while we draw inspiration from Gisèle's courage, we want our readers to recognize that sexism hurts all of us, albeit in different ways. Our hope is that men as well as women will see that their own humanity also rests on challenging sexism.

DISCUSSION QUESTIONS

1. According to the authors, oppression is difficult to see. Discuss some of the reasons why this is so. How does sexism as the oppression of women impact men?
2. Pick a social group and describe how that group is represented in advertising, music videos, movies, magazines, and wider popular culture. As an extension activity, you might collect some data on how that group is represented in various institutions besides media (remember, a group's absence is also significant).
3. The authors argue that there are at least four reasons why sexism is difficult to see. Explain in your own words what each of these are and how they work.

EXTENSION ACTIVITIES

1. Watch the lecture by Rebecca Jordan-Young titled *Testosterone*, available on the YouTube channel *Radboud Reflects Lectures* (https://www.youtube.com/watch?v=yTvg2pvEnXA). Write a 2-page summary of Dr. Jordan-Young's challenge to our beliefs about testosterone. Include at least two things about testosterone that were new to you.
2. The authors identify several female archetypes and plot lines that reinforce sexism in children's and adult films and shows intended for a female audience. Generate a list of examples of these types of films and shows over the last 20 years. Try to focus on those that have been very popular and financially successful. What do you notice in your findings? What, if anything, has changed over time? What hasn't? Do any challenge these scripts? If so, in what ways?
3. Spend an evening recording information contained in network media (commercials, ads, shows) depicting the "average family." What is the composition of the average family? What do they do? What kinds of activities does each member of the family engage in? Record all the places you have seen this "average family" in mainstream culture. How do they communicate to us what is normal in terms of race, class, gender, ability, and sexuality? How does their presence function as a kind of "looking-glass self"?

4. Watch the documentary film *Very Young Girls* (2007) by David Schisgall and Nina Alvarez, an exposé on the sex trafficking of adolescent girls (https://www.gems-girls.org). Imagine that you are a journalist investigating this issue. Research at least two other anti-sex-trafficking activists/organizations in addition to Rachel Lloyd and GEMS (see Figure 7.1). Based on what you learn, convey the issue to the broader public or your peers, in ways such as (but not limited to) the following: a poster, stencil art, article, graph, or short public service announcement video (3–5 minutes long).
5. Research some of the ways that Canadian and U.S. consumers can influence the working conditions of women and girls worldwide.

PATTERNS TO PRACTICE SEEING

1. Think about all of the most popular television shows about friendship between women.
   » What race and class are most of the women?
   » What activities organize these women's days?
   » What seems to be the most important aspect of life to them?
2. How often do you hear women speak out publicly against sexism? How often do you hear men speak up publicly against sexism? What response do they most often receive when they do speak up? How do these responses differ based on the gender of the person speaking up? Identify examples of the range of responses, with silence on one end and violence on the other.

CHAPTER 8

Understanding the Structural Nature of Oppression Through Racism

> "I was really lucky. I grew up in a good neighborhood and went to good schools. There were no problems with racism. I didn't learn anything negative about different races. My family taught me that everyone is equal."

This chapter traces a specific form of oppression—racism—in depth. Racism within the U.S. and Canadian contexts is defined as White/settler racial and cultural prejudice and discrimination, supported intentionally or unintentionally by institutional power and authority, and used to the advantage of White people and the disadvantage of peoples of Color. We illustrate aspects of racism through an examination of economic, political, social, and cultural structures, actions, and beliefs. We take a closer look at the concept of intersectionality and describe how building an in-depth understanding of racism allows an entry point into building an in-depth understanding of other forms of oppression.

> **Vocabulary to practice using:** racism; structural; institutional; peoples of Color

In this chapter we examine racism. One note before we begin: Race is a deeply complex sociopolitical system whose boundaries shift and adapt over time. As such, "White" and "peoples of Color" are not fully discrete categories, and within these groupings are other levels of complexity and difference based on the various roles assigned by dominant society at various times. For example, Asian and Black people, while both identified as peoples of Color, have very different experiences under racism based on the roles dominant society imposes on each of these groups, as do Indigenous and multiracial peoples. When we use the term "peoples of Color," we realize that not everyone will accept this term because (a) it conflates very complex dynamics among and between groups and (b) it does not deal adequately with the experiences of Indigenous and multiracial peoples. However, at the introductory level, we use this terminology because it is most widely understood as capturing the overall dynamics of White–settler dominance over Indigenous groups and groups of Color, and people perceived as belonging to those groups. The term "peoples" is used (rather than "people") to signal the heterogeneity of groups' experiences under this umbrella term. Sometimes you may hear IBPOC or BIPOC as another way to recognize the diversity of the groups under this umbrella. These terms indicate the two broad, socially recognized divisions of the racial hierarchy in the United States and Canada. Thus, when we use the terms *White* and *peoples of Color*, we are speaking in general terms about dynamics that occur at the group level and are pervasive throughout U.S. and Canadian societies. When we use the pronouns "we" and "us," we are speaking specifically as White authors about ourselves and other White people.

Racism is among the most charged issues in society and is challenging to discuss for many reasons: pervasive miseducation about what racism is and how it works; a lack of productive language with which to discuss racism; institutional and economic interests in upholding racism; ideologies such as individualism and colorblindness; and an emotional attachment to commonsense opinions that protect (rather than expand) our worldviews. In order to meet these challenges, we offer the following reminders:

- A strong opinion is not the same as informed knowledge, and minoritized people have insight into oppression that people in the dominant group do not.
- There is a difference between agreement and understanding. When discussing complex institutional dynamics such as racism, consider that "I don't agree" may actually mean, "I don't understand."
- We have a deep interest in denying forms of oppression which benefit us.
- We may also have an interest in denying forms of oppression that harm us. For example, peoples of Color can deny the existence of racism and even support its structures. However, this still benefits White people at the group level, not peoples of Color.
- Racism goes beyond individual intentions to collective group patterns.
- We don't have to be aware of oppression in order for it to exist.
- Our racial position (whether we are perceived as White, a person of Color, Indigenous, or multiracial) will greatly affect our ability to see racism. For example if we swim against the current of racial privilege, it's often easier to recognize, while harder to recognize if we swim with it.
- Putting our effort into protecting rather than expanding our current worldview prevents our intellectual and emotional growth.

Many of the dynamics of racism that we explain here will be familiar to peoples of Color. However, they may find this discussion useful in that it provides language and a theoretical framework for everyday experiences that often go unacknowledged by dominant culture.

WHAT IS RACE?

In order to understand racism, we first need to address our ideas about race itself. Many of us believe that race is biological; in other words, that there are distinct genetic differences between races that account for differences in traits such as sexuality, athleticism, or mathematical ability. This idea of *race as biology* makes it easy to believe that many of the divisions we see in society are natural. But race, like gender and disability, is socially constructed (Du Bois, 1903/1989; López, 2000; Omi & Winant, 2014). The differences we see with our eyes, such as hair texture and eye color or shape, are superficial and emerged over time as humans adapted to geography (Cavalli-Sforza et al., 1994). However, *race as a social idea* has profound significance and impacts every aspect of our lives. This impact includes where we are most likely to live, which schools we will attend, who our friends and partners will be, what careers we will have, and even how long we can expect to live (Durou et al., 2023; Hill & Artiga, 2023; Schachner, 2022).

Race as we commonly understand it is a relatively modern concept (Battalora, 2013). Humans have not been here long enough to evolve into separate species and we are, in fact, among the most genetically similar species on Earth (Graves, 2015). External characteristics we attribute to race, such as skin color, are not a reliable indicator of internal variation between any two people (Cooper et al., 2003). To challenge deep-seated ideas about racial difference and genetics, we need to understand the early social investment in race science that was used to organize society and its resources along racial lines.

A BRIEF HISTORY OF THE SOCIAL CONSTRUCTION OF RACE IN THE UNITED STATES

Ancient societies did not divide people into racial categories, although other categories of organization (such as religious affiliation or class status) were common. When the United States was formed, freedom and equality—regardless of religion or class status—were radical new ideas. At the same time, the United States' economy was based on the enslavement of African peoples and the displacement and genocide of Indigenous peoples and the theft of land. There were enormous economic interests in justifying these practices. To reconcile the tension between the noble ideology of equality and the cruel reality of genocide and enslavement, Thomas Jefferson (who owned hundreds of enslaved Africans) and others turned to science. Jefferson suggested that there were natural differences between the races and set science on the path to find them (Jefferson, 1787/2002). These social and political interests shaped race science (for example, in the early to mid-1800s, skulls were measured in an attempt to prove the existence of a natural racial hierarchy). In less than a century these studies enabled Jefferson's suggestion of racial difference to become commonly accepted scientific "fact" (Stepan, 1982).

This "scientific" basis for racism is called *eugenics* and it has influenced all domains of society including schooling.

But while race has no biological foundation, it has developed as a social idea with very real consequences. In the late 1600s the term *White* first appeared in colonial law. By 1790 people were asked to claim their race on the census, and by 1825 the degree of blood determined who would be classified as "Indian." In the late 1800s through the early 20th century, as waves of immigrants entered the United States, the idea of Whiteness became more and more concrete (Gossett, 1997; Ignatiev, 1995; Jacobson, 1998).

While slavery was abolished overall in 1865, Whiteness remained profoundly important as legal racist exclusion and violence continued. To gain citizenship and other rights, one had to be legally classified as White. Individuals seeking these rights began to challenge their classifications and petitioned the courts to be reclassified as White. These legal challenges put the courts in the position of deciding who was White and who was not. In fact, in 1923 the U.S. Supreme Court stated that Whiteness was based on the common understanding of the White man (*United States v. Bhagat Singh Thind*, 1923). In other words, people already seen as White got to decide who was White (Tehranian, 2000), and by extension, a citizen. We can see this playing out in the present in the anti-immigrant propaganda that circulates widely and is a cornerstone of many political campaigns, as well as the acceleration of U.S. Immigration and Customs Enforcement (ICE) deportations (Campani et al., 2022), often with no regard to people's actual legal status. The focus of this rhetoric is not on immigrants from Western (or mainly White) cultures; it is always focused on Black and Brown immigrants—or people perceived to be immigrants because they are Black or Brown. The consistent message is that peoples of Color are perpetually foreign and do not or could not belong (Campani et al., 2022; Restifo & Bostic, 2024).

While they may have initially been divided in terms of ethnic or class status, over time European immigrants were united in Whiteness. For example, early Irish, Italian, and Jewish immigrants were not considered White, but they "became" White as they assimilated into the dominant culture (Brodkin, 1998; Ignatiev, 1995; Jacobson, 1998; Roediger, 1991). Reflecting on the social and economic advantages of Whiteness, critical race scholar Cheryl Harris (1993) coined the phrase "Whiteness as property." This phrase captures the reality that being perceived as White carries more than a mere racial classification. It is a social and institutional status and identity imbued with legal, political, economic, and social rights and privileges that are denied to others.

A BRIEF HISTORY OF THE SOCIAL CONSTRUCTION OF RACE IN CANADA

Like the United States, Canada is a nation that was built on the genocide and forced removal of Indigenous peoples who had been living on the territory for several thousands of years before the arrival of Europeans (Dickason, 2002; Thobani, 2007). The Indigenous peoples of Canada (also referred to as Aboriginal) were living in all regions of the territory when first contact occurred in the 15th century, and had very well-developed social, political, and economic structures. Today, Canada recognizes three main groups of Indigenous peoples: First Nations, Inuit, and Métis. In the 2021 Census, 1.8 million people self-identified as Aboriginal—approximately 5% of Canada's total population (Statistics Canada, 2023).

There was a very complex relationship among French and English colonial powers and the various Indigenous communities during the process of colonization. In some cases the colonizers forced relocation and even genocide, while in other cases colonizers pursued strategies to coexist. These strategies included "civilizing" initiatives whereby the government and Christian religious organizations set out to reform the "savage Indian" and help him assimilate into colonial society (Milloy, 2000). A major part of this strategy was the Gradual Civilization Act of 1857, and one of its mechanisms was the system of residential schools (Haig-Brown, 1998; Hare, 2007). The mission of these schools was primarily to "civilize" Indigenous children. By the late 1800s, attendance in residential schools for Indigenous children aged 7–15 was compulsory. These children were forcibly removed from their homes, taken to residential schools, forbidden to speak (and punished for speaking) their native languages, forced to convert to Christianity, and prevented from seeing their families for long periods; in many cases they were physically, sexually, and emotionally abused. Over 150,000 Indigenous children went through the mandatory residential school system (Milloy, 1999). The formal curriculum at the schools was the bare minimum, focused mostly on reading and writing in English or French and on manual labor skills. By the 1930s, the goal of education was described simply as "Christian citizenship," achieved through "mingling with Canadians" (Milloy, 1999).

The harsh punishments in residential schools combined with long periods of isolation from their families, recorded in historical accounts as well as in oral testimonies, have had an irreparable impact on Indigenous communities and on Canada as a whole. Thousands of children died while in school and the mortality rate at some schools was over 50% (Milloy, 1999). Recordkeeping was woefully inadequate and the extent of the crimes within the schools and churches and the political leaders involved is only slowly being revealed. For example, unmarked graves are still being discovered through ground-penetrating LiDAR (light detection and ranging) technology used on the grounds of former residential schools. As recently as January 2023, an estimated 2,000 graves were discovered on the Qu'Appelle Indian Residential School site on the Star Blanket Cree Nation in Saskatchewan. Also in January 2023, 171 suspected graves were discovered by the Wauzhushk Onigum Nation at St. Mary's Indian Residential School in Ontario. In February 2023, 17 suspected graves were found with dozens more suspected at the Alberni Indian Residential School by the Tseshaht First Nation in British Columbia. In April 2023, 40 suspected graves were found by the Shíshálh Nation at the St. Augustine's Indian Residential School site in British Columbia.

In June 2023, Sucker Creek First Nation reported that 88 suspected graves were discovered at St. Bruno's Indian Residential School in northern Alberta (APTN National News, 2023; Canadian Press, 2023; CBC News, 2023a, 2023b; Connors, 2023; Dubey, 2023).

Most of the schools were closed by the 1960s, but the last school didn't close until 1996. Some living residential school survivors still recount the atrocities they experienced and witnessed. The psychic trauma is still a part of the Indigenous community's collective memory and has resulted in a generational gap within communities (Federer et al., 2025; Supernant, 2025). Scholars who study the history and legacy of residential schools contend that this trauma is deeply connected to the higher rates of alcoholism, drug abuse, and suicide among Indigenous people (Haskell & Randall, 2009; Kirmayer & Valaskakis, 2009).

The race science that was conducted and disseminated in the United States was adopted into government programs and policies in Canada as well. Black and Indigenous peoples were enslaved (Winks, 1971/1997), Chinese workers were excluded from citizenship (Li, 1988; Mar, 2010), and extremist hate groups have long flourished in Canada (Lund, 2006). But since the 1970s one of the key strategies for managing racial diversity has been the policy of multiculturalism. The "melting pot" ideology of the United States was not useful in Canada, in part because it pressures the so-called two founding, colonizing nations (France and England) to assimilate. It would have meant an end to official bilingualism, on which Quebec would not compromise. The ongoing challenges to sustain the Canadian federation (and prevent Quebec from seceding) required an ideology that represented Canada as a tolerant, pluralistic, multicultural society. For these reasons, the "mosaic" (rather than "melting pot") became the dominant image used to describe Canadian racial and ethnic diversity (Joshee, 1995, 2004). In 1985 the government passed the Act for the Preservation and Enhancement of Multiculturalism in Canada. These policies promote the idea that all groups are positioned equally in Canadian society (the colonizer nations of England and France and their respective languages, people of Aboriginal heritage, and the multitude of immigrant communities in the nation) while leaving structural inequality unaddressed.

WHAT IS RACISM?

Racism is a form of oppression in which one racial group dominates over others. In the United States and Canada, White people are the dominant group and peoples of Color are the minoritized group; therefore, racism in this context is White racial and cultural prejudice and discrimination, supported intentionally or unintentionally by institutional power and authority, used to the advantage of White people and the disadvantage of peoples of Color (Hilliard, 1992). In other nations the dominant and minoritized racial groups will not be the same because of the difference in their social and political histories. From here forward, we will be speaking of racism as it plays out in the United States, Canada, and other Western-oriented societies such as Australia, New Zealand, Europe, and South Africa.

> **STOP:** Remember, we are addressing racism at the group, not individual, level. At the group level, all of us navigate the current of dominant culture. In the United States and Canada, if we are perceived or defined as White, we swim with that current, and if we are a person of Color, we must swim against it. While this is the racial reality at the group level, how we respond individually may vary.

Racism is not fluid in that it does not move back and forth, one day benefiting White people and another day (or even era) benefiting peoples of Color. The direction of power between White people and peoples of Color is historic, traditional, normalized, and deeply embedded in the fabric of U.S. and Canadian societies (F. Henry & Tator, 2006; James, 2007; Kendi, 2016). The critical element that differentiates *racism* from *racial prejudice* and *discrimination* is the historical accumulation and ongoing use of institutional power and authority that supports discriminatory behaviors in systemic and far-reaching ways. Peoples of Color may hold prejudices and discriminate against individual White people, but do not have the social and institutional power backing their prejudice and discrimination that transforms it into racism; the impact of their prejudice on White people is temporary and contextual. Peoples of Color do not hold the institutional power and legal authority to impact White people collectively. They may also hold prejudices and discriminate against their own and other groups of Color, but the impact of their prejudice and discrimination ultimately serves to hold their groups down. From a critical social justice perspective, the term *racism* refers to this system of collective social and institutional White power and privilege.

TWO KEY CHALLENGES TO UNDERSTANDING RACISM

Dominant society teaches us that racism consists of individual acts of meanness or violence committed by a few bad people. The people who commit these acts are considered racists; the rest of us are not racist. These ideas construct racism as an individual binary: racist/not-racist (Trepagnier, 2010). As we have discussed, a binary is an either/or construct that positions a social dynamic into two distinct and mutually exclusive categories. As with the gender binary, virtually all people know how to fill in the two sides of the race binary: If you *are* a racist, the discourse goes, you are ignorant, prejudiced, mean-spirited, and most likely old, Southern, and drive a pickup truck (working class). If you are *not* a racist, you are nice, well-intentioned, open-minded, progressive. Most of us understand, at this moment in our cultural history, which is the right side of this binary to be on. But these categories are false, for all people hold prejudices, especially across racial lines in a society deeply divided by race.

> **Racism:** White racial and cultural prejudice and discrimination, supported by institutional power and authority, used to the advantage of people perceived and defined as White and to the disadvantage of peoples perceived and defined as of Color. Racism encompasses economic, political, social, and institutional actions and beliefs that systematize and perpetuate an unequal distribution of privileges, resources, and power between White people and peoples of Color.

So the first problem with the binary is that it is a false division. It reinforces the idea that racism only occurs in specific incidences and is only done by specific (bad) people. Of course, racism can certainly manifest as individual acts of meanness, ignorance, and violence. However, the focus on individual *incidents*, rather than on racism as an all-encompassing *system*, prevents the personal, interpersonal, cultural, historical, and structural analysis that is necessary in order to challenge it. As spoken word poet Kyle "Guante" Tran Myhre captures in his 2014 poem, "How to Explain White Supremacy to a White Supremacist," *racism is not a shark, it is the water* (Myhre, 2020).

The second problem with the binary concerns the impact of such a worldview on our actions. If, as a White person, I conceptualize racism as a binary and I see myself on the "not racist" end, what further action is required of me? No action is required at all, *because I am not a racist*. Therefore racism is not my problem; it doesn't concern me and there is nothing further I need to do. This guarantees that as a member of the dominant group, I will not build my skills in thinking critically about racism, or use my position to challenge racial inequality, while I continue to accumulate its rewards. Further, if I conceptualize racism as an either/or proposition, then any suggestion that I have racist thoughts or feelings places me on the wrong side of the binary. As a result, all of my energy will go to denying and negating this possibility rather than toward trying to understand what these thoughts and feelings are and how they are manifesting. If you are White and have ever been challenged to look at an aspect of yourself related to racism—perhaps you told a joke or made an assumption that someone pointed out to you was racially problematic—it is common to feel very defensive. This defensiveness reveals the binary that informs our understanding of racism; we interpret the feedback to mean that we have done something bad and are thus being told that we are bad people. This binary, which is the foundation of how most White people conceptualize racism (Trepagnier, 2010), and the defensiveness it triggers are primary obstacles preventing us from moving forward in our understanding. As historian Ibram X. Kendi (2021) says, "The opposite of racist isn't 'not racist.' It is 'anti-racist.' There is no in-between safe space of 'not racist'" (p. 9). There is no neutral position on an uneven playing field (Bonilla-Silva & Peoples, 2022; Rutter, 2024; Tatum, 1997; Zinn, 2018).

Along with White people, peoples of Color may also be invested in denying racism for a range of complex reasons including: they have also been socialized to see racism in binary terms; they have been socialized to see peoples of Color as "just as racist" as White people; denying racism helps them to cope with its overwhelming dynamics; they have had some measure of success in mainstream society and rationalize that members of minoritized racial groups just need to work harder; they have an immigrant experience that is different from that of some other racial groups; they do not carry the weight of internalized racial oppression because they have not grown up in the U.S. or Canadian contexts; or White people are more comfortable with their racial group, skin tone, social class expression, or other aspects of their identity. Yet there are costs for this denial, including a disconnection from one's cultural roots and separation from other minoritized racial groups.

The racist/not-racist binary illustrates the role that ideology plays in holding oppression in place, and the ideology of individualism in particular. Individualism is a storyline or narrative that creates, communicates, reproduces, and reinforces the concept that each of us is a unique individual and that our group memberships, such as our race, class, or gender, are not important or relevant to opportunities available to us. This narrative causes a problematic tension because the legitimacy of our institutions depends upon the concept that all citizens are equal. At the same time, we each occupy distinct race, gender, class, and other positions that profoundly shape our life chances in ways that are not natural, voluntary, or random; opportunity is not equally distributed across race, class, and gender (Keister & Southgate, 2022). Individualism helps manage this tension by claiming that there are no intrinsic barriers to individual success, and that failure is a consequence not of social structures but of individual character. According to the ideology of individualism, race is irrelevant. Specifically, individualism obscures racism because it does the following (DiAngelo, 2016):

- Denies the significance of race and the advantages of being White
- Hides the collective accumulation of wealth over generations
- Denies the historical context of our current positions
- Prevents a macroanalysis of the institutions and structures of social life
- Denies collective socialization and the power of dominant culture (such as media, education, and religion) to shape our perspectives and ideology
- Maintains a false sense of colorblindness
- Reproduces the myth of meritocracy, the idea that success is the result of hard work alone

Let us be clear—we are not arguing against individualism *in general*. Rather, we are arguing that White insistence on individualism *in regard to the significance of race* prevents cross-racial understanding and denies the salience of race and racism in White people's lives. Further, being viewed as an individual is a privilege only available to the dominant group. In other words, peoples of Color are almost always seen as "having a race" and described in racial terms (e.g., "a *Black* man," "an *Aboriginal* director"), whereas White people are rarely defined by race (e.g., "a man," "a director"). This allows White people to move through society as "just people," while peoples of Color are seen as part of a racial group (DiAngelo, 2016; Dyer, 1997). This dynamic also allows White people to see themselves as objective and peoples of Color as having "special" or biased interests and agendas.

Of course to see oneself as an individual is a very different dynamic for peoples of Color. While for White people insisting that one is an individual is often a strategy for *denying* that their race has meaning, for peoples of Color it can be a strategy for *coping* with always being seen in racial terms. Since peoples of Color are denied individuality by dominant society, individualism can actually be a way to challenge racism and an important counter to the relentless imposition of racial identity on them. Because the social and institutional positions are not the same between White people and peoples of Color, the dynamics of how ideologies are used are not the same.

Thus to challenge a particular form of oppression requires different tasks based on one's position. If we fall into the dominant group, one of our tasks is to look past our sense of ourselves as individuals and examine our group history and socialization. If we fall into the minoritized group, one of our tasks is to claim individual complexity; that is, to challenge how society has focused solely on our minoritized identity and denied us a sense of individuality.

RACISM TODAY

Racial disparity between White people and peoples of Color exists in every institution across both Canadian and U.S. society.

> **STOP:** While they may be difficult to see and thus are often denied, racial disparities and their effects on overall quality of life have been extensively documented by a wide range of agencies, including: federal (such as Statistics Canada, U.S. Census Bureau, United Nations), university (such as UCLA Civil Rights Project, Metropolis Project), and nonprofit (such as the Canadian Centre for Policy Alternatives, Canadian Anti-Racism Education and Research Society, NAACP, and Anti-Defamation League, among others).

Disparities are an important reminder about the role of theory in explaining data. Readers may recall from the discussion in Chapter 2 that theory is the way we make sense of what we see. Reflect for a moment on how you explain racial disparities, for example, in encounters with the criminal justice system. This is an important exercise because our explanations reveal our meaning-making frameworks and thus are a great entry point into deeper racial self-knowledge. We can explain these disparities with cultural deficit theory (in other words, there is something wrong with the culture of communities of Color that results in these disparities) (Fox, 2016; Kendi, 2021). However, cultural deficit theory blames peoples of Color for their struggles within a racist society while obscuring larger structural barriers. Cultural deficit theory also exempts dominant culture from the need to play any role in the eradication of racism.

If we consider historical, institutional, and cultural racism, the explanation looks very different. Many incarcerated peoples of Color have attended underfunded and deteriorating schools, have had poor access to health care, have historically been denied mortgages and other wealth-building programs, and have received inequitable treatment in every other major institution that would have given them and their children an equal starting point in life (Alexander, 2010; Shanks & McLoyd, 2024). These are examples of institutional racism, not a personal lack of responsibility or a cultural flaw.

The way that we explain (or theorize) a problem determines how we respond to the problem. If we perceive the problem as one of violent and criminal people, we might build more prisons and create more sophisticated mechanisms to monitor them. And in fact, although crime has actually *decreased* over the last 30 years, this is the view we have taken, and in response the United States has built more and more prisons and incarcerated more and more peoples of Color. The United States has the highest number of people incarcerated in the world, and the vast majority of them are Black and Latino, a rate that is way out of proportion with their numbers in the wider population (Alexander, 2010; Conyers et al., 2023). But if we perceive the problem as one of structural racism, we might change the way we fund schools, ensure that every family has affordable access to health care and social services, work to decrease racial profiling, and change the policies that allow wealth to be ever more concentrated into fewer hands.

Both Canada and the United States are nations that were built on the labor of peoples of Color: the labor of Indigenous peoples who were enslaved, served in military capacities, and helped early colonizers navigate the land; the labor of enslaved Africans who fueled high-value agricultural industries such as cotton, tobacco, sugar, and coffee; and the labor of Chinese and Japanese workers who did the backbreaking work of building the railways that formed the major transportation lines for the nation state. All of this labor was given for very little if any financial remuneration, authority, or ownership of the national infrastructure and wealth it built.

While we might acknowledge that these were unfair practices of the past, consider the division of labor along race lines in the United States and in Canada today. Who are the people picking the fruit we buy, cleaning our homes, hotels, and workplaces, providing at-home child care or elder care, and sewing the clothes that come to our local department and box stores at remarkably cheap prices? Backbreaking, low-wage, low-reward work is still performed primarily by peoples of Color (Nair & Hofman, 2022; Ross & Bateman, 2019; Shook et al., 2020).

There have been some protections put in place to guard against the most blatant and intentional manifestations of racism from the past, but racism still operates in new and modified ways. Colorblind racism is a cogent example of this adaptation. This is the belief that pretending that we don't notice race will end (or has already ended) racism. This idea comes out of the Civil Rights movement of the 1960s and Martin Luther King's 1963 "I Have a Dream" speech. King's speech marked a turning point in the adaptation of racism in dominant culture. Before his speech, many White people felt quite comfortable admitting to their racial prejudices and sense of racial superiority. But once the Civil Rights movement took root and civil rights legislation was passed, there was a significant change in mainstream culture; it was no longer as acceptable for White people to admit to racial prejudice.

White racism didn't disappear, of course; White people just became somewhat more careful in public space (Picca & Feagin, 2007). Seizing on one part of King's speech—that one day his children might be judged by the content of their character and not the color of their skin—dominant culture began promoting the idea of "colorblindness" as a remedy for racism. King's speech (King, 1998) was given at a march for economic justice—the March on Washington for Jobs and Freedom—and he was there to advocate for the elimination of poverty, but few people today know the breadth of King's advocacy.

While colorblindness sounds good in theory, in practice it is highly problematic. We *do* see the race of other people, and that race has meaning for us. Everyone receives racist messages that circulate in society; they are all around us. As Ibram X. Kendi (2021) explains, we might not be the producers of racist ideology, but we have all been the consumers. While some of these messages are blatant (racist jokes, for example), we must understand that most of the messages we receive are subtler and are often invisible. Drawing on what we discussed in Chapter 3 on socialization, we know that while we learn very early about race, much of what we learn is below the level of our conscious awareness (as with the iceberg). The ideology of colorblindness makes it difficult for us to address these unconscious beliefs. While the idea started out as a well-intended strategy for interrupting racism, in practice it has served to deny the reality of racism and thus hold it in place.

To get a sense of what might be below the surface of our conscious racial awareness, try the following thought experiment:

At what point in your life were you aware that people from racial groups other than your own existed (most peoples of Color recall a sense of "always having been" aware, while most White people recall being aware by at least age 5). If you were aware of the existence of people from racial groups other than your own, where did they live? If they did not live in your neighborhood, what kind of neighborhood did they live in? Were their neighborhoods considered "good" or "bad"? What images did you associate with these other neighborhoods? What about sights and smells? What kind of activities did you think went on there? Where did your ideas come from? Were you encouraged to visit their neighborhoods? Or were you discouraged from visiting their neighborhoods? If you attended a school considered "good," what made it good? Conversely, what made a school "bad"? Who went to "bad" schools? If the schools in your area were racially segregated, were their schools considered equal to, better, or worse than yours? Why didn't you attend school together? If this is because you lived in different neighborhoods, why did you live in different neighborhoods? If you were told by your parents and teachers that "all people are equal regardless of the color of their skin," yet you lived separately from people who had a different skin color, what message did that contradiction send? If you lived and went to school in racial segregation you had to make sense of this incongruity. In other words, what does it mean to say that all people are equal but live separately from them?

Our lived separation is a more powerful message than our words of inclusion because the separation is manifested in action, while inclusion is not.

✓ **PERSPECTIVE CHECK:** If some of these questions do not apply to the cultural context you grew up in, try the following: Adjust the questions to capture how you learned about racial difference, for example, how you saw people from racial groups residing outside of your nation-state or perhaps people from ethnic groups different from your own residing within your nation-state. Use socioeconomic class to think through the questions, for example, how did class differences shape where you lived and how you learned your "place" in society? Consider the impact of Whiteness as a global phenomenon. What did you learn it meant to be White? What did you learn it meant to be a member of a racial group that is not White?

DYNAMICS OF WHITE RACIAL SUPERIORITY

If we are White we receive constant messages that we are better and more important than peoples of Color, regardless of our personal intentions or beliefs (Abaied et al., 2022; Fine, 1997; Howard, 2018; Nieri et al., 2023; Skinner-Dorkenoo et al., 2023). These messages operate on multiple levels and are conveyed in a range of ways, for example: our centrality in history textbooks and other historical representations; our centrality in media and advertising; our teachers, role models, heroes, and heroines all reflecting *us*; everyday discussions about "good" neighborhoods and schools and the racial makeup of these favored locations; popular TV shows centered around friendship circles that are all White, even when they take place in racially diverse cities such as New York; religious iconography that depicts Adam and Eve, other key Christian figures, and even God as White; newscasters referring to any crime that occurs in a White neighborhood as "shocking"; and the lack of a sense of loss about the absence of peoples of Color in most White people's lives. These are examples of implicit (indirect) rather than explicit (direct) messages, all telling us that it's better to be White. Although we can attempt to notice and block out each one, they come at us collectively and so relentlessly that this is virtually impossible to do. While we may explicitly reject the notion that we are inherently better than peoples of Color, we cannot avoid internalizing the message of White superiority below the surface of our consciousness because it is ubiquitous in mainstream culture.

> ✔ **PERSPECTIVE CHECK:** You may be wondering why it is okay to have a Chinatown or Koreatown but not a "White-town." In other words, why do marginalized groups sometimes self-segregate? As Beverly Tatum explains in her classic book *"Why are all the Black kids sitting together in the cafeteria?" And other conversations about race* (1997), we are not in a neutral landscape. In an ocean of Whiteness, White people don't need to build an island of refuge. In this case, the ocean is a metaphor representing the Whiteness built into mainstream society.

Let's look a little more closely at the increase in racial segregation as an example. White people are the racial group that lives the most racially segregated lives (Banaji et al., 2021; H. B. Johnson & Shapiro, 2003; Roberts & Rizzo, 2021), and White people are most likely to be in the economic position to choose this segregation (rather than have it imposed on them). In the United States we are actually returning to pre-integration levels of racial segregation; schools and neighborhoods are becoming *more* racially separated, not less (Monarrez et al., 2022). In fact, racial segregation is often what defines schools and neighborhoods as "good" for White people; we come to understand that a "good school" or "good neighborhood" is often coded language for "White," while "urban" is code for "not-White" and therefore less desirable (H. B. Johnson & Shapiro, 2003; D. Watson, 2011). At the same time, although we prefer segregation, most White people profess to be colorblind and claim that race does not matter (Bonilla-Silva, 2006; DiAngelo, 2018; Feagin, 2020). Even when White people live in physical proximity to peoples of Color (and this is exceptional outside of a lower-class urban neighborhood or one in the process of gentrification), segregation is occurring on many other levels in the culture (and often in schools themselves), including images in media and the formal school curriculum. Because most White people choose to live primarily segregated lives within a White-dominated society, we receive little or no authentic information about racism and are thus unprepared to think about it critically.

> ✋ **STOP:** Not all our messages are as implicit as de facto segregation. We are also surrounded by friends, family, and media that make direct comments and jokes about people of other races.

Stereotypical media representations compound the impact of racial segregation. Most people recognize that movies have a profound effect on our ideas about the world. Concepts of desire, adventure, romance, family, love, danger, crime, good and evil, and conflict are all conveyed to us through the stories told in films. Anyone who is around children will see the power of movies to shape children's interests, fantasies, and play. Now consider that the vast majority of mainstream films are written and directed by White men, most often from the middle and upper classes. In fact, of the top 50 highest grossing films of all time worldwide, 49 were directed by men (with two women as codirectors). Of the top 100 films worldwide, 98 were directed wholly by men. Of these top 100 films, 95 were directed by White people (2 had a codirector of Color) and 88 were directed by White men (Box Office Mojo, n.d.). Because of the racial segregation that is ubiquitous throughout society, these men are very unlikely to have gone to school with, lived nearby, been taught by/about, or been employed by or with peoples of Color. Therefore they are very unlikely to have meaningful or egalitarian cross-racial relationships. Yet these men are society's "cultural authors"; their dreams, desires, and fears, their conceptions of "the other" become ours. Consider the implications of this very privileged and homogeneous group essentially telling all of our stories. They may not be the only people making movies but they are certainly those who are in the position to disseminate their films widely. The life and work of Jay Silverheels (Figure 8.1) illustrates the challenges peoples of Color face when dealing with racism in Hollywood.

In addition to a wide range of films, White people see their own images reflected back in virtually any situation or location deemed valuable in dominant society (e.g., academia, politics, management, art events, popular magazines, the sciences). Indeed, it is a rare event for most White people to experience a sense of *not* belonging racially, and these situations are usually temporary and avoidable. Thus racial belonging becomes deeply internalized, along with a comfort with separation from peoples of Color.

A key dynamic of the relationship between dominant and minoritized groups is to name the minoritized group as different, while the dominant group remains unnamed. For example, when we say "Americans" we do not mean "any and all Americans," we mean White Americans, but don't name White because it is assumed unless otherwise noted. Just as when we say "soccer game" we do not mean "any and all soccer games," we mean a men's soccer game but are not naming men because it is already assumed unless otherwise noted. We would have to make the point that it was a Chinese American person, or a women's soccer game. We are

Figure 8.1. Jay Silverheels (1919–1980)

Silverheels was an elite athlete competing in high level wrestling, lacrosse, and boxing events, playing on Canada's national lacrosse team before he developed an interest in acting. Like many Indigenous actors, early in his career he was credited in bit parts simply as "Indian" [sic]. But many remember him in the role that made him famous, playing the Lone Ranger's companion, Tonto. Silverheels himself recognized the difficulty of portraying a character that was described by some as the Uncle Tom of Indigenous peoples. However, with this role, Silverheels would be the first Native American actor to star in a leading role on a television show.

Like many actors who belong to minoritized communities, Silverheels found it difficult to break out of the stereotypical characters he was asked to play. He was also an activist for improving the portrayal of Native American peoples in media. He was very aware of the problems of Hollywood's representation of Indigenous peoples but felt that working Indigenous actors could influence the films and shows in which they appeared. In 1966 he helped found the Indian Actors Workshop to offer free classes to aspiring Native American actors to work in film, theater, and television.

Source: http://www.poorwilliam.net/pix/silverheels-jay.jpg

comfortable with this pattern because we are socialized to name the minoritized groups (*Chinese* American, *women's* soccer) and assign a universal neutrality to dominant groups.

This naming/not-naming dynamic sets race up as something *they* have, not *us*. White people tend to see race only when peoples of Color are present, but see all-White spaces as neutral and nonracial. Because racial segregation for most White people is normal and unremarkable, we rarely, if ever, have to think about race and racism. Conversely, peoples of Color must navigate racism as they move about their daily lives in dominant culture. White people are free from this psychic burden. Race becomes something for peoples of Color to think about. Not thinking about race allows White people much more energy to devote to other issues and prevents us from developing the stamina to sustain attention on an issue as charged and uncomfortable for us as race.

DYNAMICS OF INTERNALIZED RACIAL OPPRESSION

All of the messages that White people receive about their value, both explicitly and implicitly, are also received by peoples of Color (Mullaly, 2002; Tatum, 1997). In other words, peoples of Color are also confronted with the myriad messages that to be White is "better" than to be a person of Color. And similar to the mixed messages that White parents send to their children by saying that everyone is equal while simultaneously living in segregation, children of Color also get mixed messages. Their parents may tell them that they are good, strong, and beautiful, but society around them is conveying that they are of lesser value.

Internalized racial oppression occurs when a person of Color, consciously or subconsciously, internalizes the negative representation or invisibility of their racial group in media, education, medicine, science, and all other aspects of society. Over time, the person may come to believe that they are less valuable and may act this out through self-defeating behaviors and sometimes by distancing themselves from others of their own or other racialized groups (Chopra, 2021; David et al., 2019; Fanon, 1961/2001; Willis et al., 2021). Although there are important differences in how various racialized groups experience internalized racial oppression, groups of Color are collectively shaped by the following:

- Historical violence and the ongoing threat of violence
- Destruction, colonization, dilution, and exoticization of their cultures
- Division, separation, and isolation from one another and from dominant culture
- Changing behaviors to ensure psychological and physical safety and to gain access to resources
- Having individual behaviors redefined as group norms, or remarked upon if they don't align with stereotypical expectations
- Being denied individuality and held up as representative of (or occasionally as exceptions to) their group
- Being blamed for the effects of long-term oppression by the dominant group, and having those effects used to rationalize further oppression

Internalized racism can cause a self-defeating cycle. Carter Woodson, writing in 1933, powerfully captures the dynamics of internalized racial oppression when he writes:

> If you can control a man's thinking, you don't have to worry about his actions. If you can determine what a man thinks, you do not have to worry about what he will do. If

you can make a man believe that he is inferior, you don't have to compel him to seek an inferior status, he will do so without being told, and if you can make a man believe that he is justly an outcast, you don't have to order him to the back door, he will go to the back door on his own, and if there is no back door, the very nature of the man will demand that you build one. (p. xiii)

Woodson is speaking to one of the more profound and painful dynamics of internalized oppression: Once people believe that they deserve their position in society, external force is not needed. As can be seen in several important studies discussed below, this internalization begins at a very early age. It is important to note that peoples of Color have always resisted internalized racial oppression, but this resistance has costs and can be very dangerous; resistance has historically been used to further rationalize violence against them (Menakem, 2017; Oluo, 2018).

Social psychologist Claude Steele's (1997) work on stereotype threat demonstrates one of the impacts of internalized racial oppression. *Stereotype threat* occurs when you are concerned that you will be evaluated negatively due to stereotypes about your racial group, and that concern causes you to perform poorly, thereby reinforcing the stereotype. Because there is a powerful stereotype in mainstream culture that Black people are less intelligent than White people and other racial groups, Steele and his research team examined the effects of this stereotype on test performance. They found that the mere threat of the stereotype diminished the performance of Black students. Their research shows that when Black students are told that their racial group tends to do poorly on a test, they score lower when taking that test. When the stereotype is not mentioned, students perform better.

In light of Steele's work, consider how much attention is given in schools to the so-called achievement gap and other disparities in outcome between White students and some groups of Color (Black, Latino, and Indigenous students in particular), and how often these disparities are formally and informally rationalized as a function of genetics or inferior cultural morals that do not value education. Concerns and assumptions about their abilities constantly surround students of Color. It is important to remember that these stereotypes are not just "in their heads"—White people do hold these stereotypes and they do affect the way White people evaluate peoples of Color (Bertrand & Mullainathan, 2004; Childs & Wooten, 2022; Gillies, 2023; Picca & Feagin, 2007). White teachers, who comprise 80% of K–12 teachers (Schaeffer, 2024), are in a particularly powerful position to evaluate students of Color. A report about the educational experiences of Black students in Ontario, Canada, shows that the racism of "low expectations" impacts many aspects of students' school experience, including grades (James & Turner, 2017). For example, Black students reported that their teachers would often attribute their good work on assignments and tests to plagiarism or cheating. Another powerful illustration of internalized racial oppression was demonstrated through the work of psychologists Kenneth Clark and Mamie Clark (1950). The Clarks used dolls to study children's attitudes about race. The Clarks testified as expert witnesses in *Briggs v. Elliott*, one of the cases connected to the 1954 *Brown v. Board of Education* case in the United States, which ruled that enforced racial segregation in schools was illegal. The Clarks found that Black children often preferred to play with White dolls over Black dolls and that when asked to fill in a human figure with the color of their own skin, they frequently chose a shade lighter than their skin actually was. Black children also described the White doll as good and pretty, but the Black doll as bad and ugly. The Clarks offered their results as evidence that the children had internalized racism. Chief Justice Earl Warren delivered the opinion of the Court: "To separate [some children] from others of similar age and qualifications solely because of their race generates a feeling of inferiority as to their status in the community that may affect their hearts and minds in a way unlikely ever to be undone" (*Brown v. Board of Education*, 1954). This is an important quote to remember as we think about the racial segregation and income inequality so common to U.S. and Canadian schools (Perry et al., 2024; Ukanwa, 2022).

In 2005 Kiri Davis, an African American teen, repeated the Clarks' experiment to see what had changed in Black children's attitudes over the past 50 years. In her documentary film *A Girl Like Me* (K. Davis, 2005) 15 out of the 21 children she interviewed (or 71%) preferred the White dolls for the same reasons as children cited in the 1940s; the White doll was "good" and the Black doll was "bad." While many people believe that children are innocent and unaware of racial messages, research has shown that children of all races and as young as 3 have internalized the societal message that White is superior to Black (Seltzer & O'Brien, 2024; Van Ausdale & Feagin, 2001). The effect of this on White children is internalized racial superiority; the effect on children of Color is internalized racial inferiority. Internalized racial inferiority has devastating impacts on all aspects of a person's life.

This brief discussion of some of the dynamics of internalized racial oppression is not to be understood as blaming the victim for the effects of racism. Rather, it is meant to highlight the damaging effects of systemic racism on peoples of Color.

RACISM AND INTERSECTIONALITY

While we have discussed racism in general terms, our other social group memberships, such as class, gender, sexuality, and ability, greatly affect how we will experience race. For example, one of the key limitations of feminism of the 1960s (called "Second Wave Feminism") was that the movement addressed women's issues as though women were a united group and assumed they had shared experiences and interests. In reality, the women we think of as at the forefront of the women's movement of the 1960s were White middle-class women (Frankenberg, 1993; Moraga & Anzaldúa, 1981). In many key areas, their interests were not the same as those of other groups of women. For example, while White middle-class women may have been eager to break their domestic confinement and enter the workplace, women of Color had long been in the workplace. Women of Color's interests may have been better served by fighting for the economic and social conditions that would allow them to stay home to raise their children without being seen as lazy or bad mothers.

Intersectionality is the term scholars use to acknowledge and study the reality that we simultaneously occupy both oppressed and privileged positions and that these positions intersect in complex ways (Collins, 2000; Crenshaw, 1991). For example, poor Whites, while oppressed through classism, are also elevated by race privilege; so to be poor and White is not the same as to be, for example, poor and Asian. Further, because of sexism, to be a poor White female will create barriers that a poor White male will not face due to gender privilege. However, while the poor White female *will* have to deal with sexism, she will not also be dealing with the racism that a poor Asian female will face. Indeed, race privilege will help a poor White female cope with poverty when, for example, looking for work or navigating social services such as welfare and health care. Facing oppression in one area of social life does not cancel out your privilege in another; these identities will be more or less salient in different situations. The challenge is to identify how our intersecting identities play out in shifting social contexts.

We return now to the student quotation that opened this chapter: "I was really lucky. I grew up in a good neighborhood and went to good schools. There were no problems with racism. I didn't learn anything negative about different races. My family taught me that everyone is equal." This sentiment is a familiar illustration of how White people make sense of race and of the invisibility of racism to us.

First, the term "good neighborhood" is usually code for "predominantly White." To believe that one learned nothing about racism and that there were "no problems" with racism in a White environment positions White people as outside of race; White people are "just human," with no racial experience of their own. Race becomes what peoples of Color have. If peoples of Color are not present, race is not present. Further, if peoples of Color are not present, not only is race absent, so is *racism*. Ironically, this positions racism as something peoples of Color bring to White people, rather than a system that White people control and impose on peoples of Color. To place race and racism on peoples of Color and to see race and racism as absent in an all-White space is to construct Whiteness as neutral and innocent.

Second, a predominantly White neighborhood is not the product of luck, a natural preference to be with "one's own," or a fluke. All-White neighborhoods are the end result of centuries of racist policies, practices, and attitudes that have systematically denied peoples of Color entrance into White neighborhoods (Conley, 1999). In the past this was done through laws. Today this is accomplished through mechanisms such as discrimination in lending, real estate practices that steer homebuyers into specific neighborhoods, funding roads but not public transportation that could make suburbs more accessible, and White flight. All-White neighborhoods and schools don't just happen (Castrillon, 2024; Rothstein, 2018; Shkembi et al., 2024).

Contrary to her claims, this student learned quite a bit about race in her White neighborhood and schools. As we noted earlier, there is a contradiction in saying to children, "Everyone is the same," while raising them in segregated spaces termed "good" precisely because peoples of Color are absent overall. Conveying to White children that living in a White neighborhood makes them lucky, rather than conveying to them that they have lost something valuable by not having cross-racial relationships, is to teach them a great deal about race.

As we write this 3rd edition, many of the gains for racial equity that were taken for granted in the United States are being systematically dismantled. The Voting Rights Act of 1965 has been gutted (C. Anderson, 2018; Page, 2022). Equity departments have been banned at the federal and state levels, along with the ability to track racial disparities. Nonprofits and scientific and academic institutions have been threatened with the loss of federal funding if they engage in equity work. Many private corporations have voluntarily ended any engagement. The history and accomplishments of marginalized groups have been erased from many public records. Highly accomplished White women and men and women of Color have been termed "diversity hires" regardless of performance and fired. Arlington National Cemetery has removed content information about Black and female veterans from its website. White South Africans have been offered asylum status at the same time that U.S.-born children of immigrants have had their constitutional right to birthright citizenship revoked and are being deported. Asylum seekers have been termed terrorists and deported without due process or indeed any evidence of criminal behavior. The president has signed an executive order creating a task force to identify "anti-Christian" bias (White House, 2025b). Universities are also being targeted, threatened with the termination of federal funding unless they shut down all DEI offices and programs, punish student protestors, and obey other demands aligned with the administration's objectives. In a 2021 speech titled "The Universities Are the Enemy," now-Vice President JD Vance said that professors are also the enemy. The Department of Education is being abolished and any teaching or programming intended to inform about or support minoritized groups has been threatened with an end to federal funding if it continues. Executive Order 14190, titled "Ending Radical Indoctrination in K–12 Schooling." (Exec. Order No. 14190, 90 FR 8853), includes dissolution of the Employee Engagement Diversity Equity Inclusion Accessibility Council (EEDIAC) within the Office for Civil Rights (OCR); cancellation of ongoing DEI training and service contracts; withdrawal of the department's Equity Action Plan; placement of career department staff tasked with implementing the previous administration's DEI initiatives on paid administrative leave; and identification for removal of over 200 webpages from the department's website that housed DEI resources. The following is *only a partial list* of words that have been flagged to avoid in government agency documents, including at NASA, the National Science Foundation, the Centers for Disease Control & Prevention, and the Department of Transportation (Yourish et al., 2025):

Accessible; activism; advocacy; affirming care; all-inclusive; allyship; anti-racism; anti-racist; assigned at birth; assigned female at birth; assigned male at birth; at risk; barrier; barriers; belong; bias; biased; biased toward; biases; biases towards; biologically female; biologically male; BIPOC; Black; clean energy; climate crisis; climate science; commercial sex worker; community diversity; community equity; confirmation bias; cultural competence; cultural differences; cultural heritage; cultural sensitivity; culturally appropriate; culturally responsive; DEI; DEIA; DEIAB; DEIJ; disabilities; disability; discriminated; discrimination; discriminatory; disparity; diverse; diverse backgrounds; diverse communities; diverse community; diverse group; diverse groups; diversified; diversify; diversifying; diversity; enhance the diversity; environmental quality; equal opportunity; equality; equitable; equitableness; equity; ethnicity; excluded; exclusion; expression; female; females; feminism; fostering; inclusivity; GBV; gender; gender based; gender based violence; gender diversity; gender identity; gender ideology; gender-affirming care; genders; Gulf of Mexico; hate speech; health disparity; health equity; hispanic minority; historically; identity; immigrants; implicit bias; implicit biases; inclusion; inclusive; inclusive leadership; inclusiveness; inclusivity; increase diversity; increase the diversity; indigenous community; inequalities; inequality; inequitable; inequities; inequity; injustice; institutional; intersectional; Intersectionality; key groups; key people; key populations; Latinx; LGBT; LGBTQ; marginalize; marginalized; men who have sex with men; mental health; minorities; minority; most risk; MSM; multicultural; Mx; Native American; non-binary; nonbinary; oppression; oppressive; orientation; people+uterus; people-centered care; person-centered; person-centered care; polarization; political; pollution; pregnant people; pregnant person; pregnant persons; prejudice; privilege; privileges; promote diversity; promoting diversity; pronoun; pronouns; prostitute; race; race and ethnicity; racial; racial diversity; racial identity; racial inequality; racial justice; racially; racism; segregation; sense of belonging; sex; sexual preferences; sexuality; social justice; sociocultural; socioeconomic; status; stereotype; stereotypes; systemic; systemically; they/them; trans; transgender; transsexual; trauma; traumatic; tribal; unconscious bias; underappreciated; underprivileged; underrepresentation; underrepresented; underserved; undervalued; victim; victims; vulnerable populations; women; women and underrepresented.

We imagine many more erasures will have occurred since this writing. This underscores a point we have made repeatedly through this text: We can never be complacent. Any hard-won gains can be taken away, as we have watched happen since 2020. First, CRT (critical race theory) was presented as the real threat (CRT is the academic study of racism as not merely individual bias or prejudice, but a force embedded in legal systems and institutional policies). Now "woke" DEI policies (Diversity, Equity, and Inclusion) are presented as the threat—*woke* being a vague stand-in for anything in support of the conscious pursuit of social justice (Cammaerts, 2022; Hernández-Truyol, 2023). The U.S. administration is imposing its agenda on non-U.S. sovereign countries' research activities and ideological views about the United States. For example, in March 2025, the U.S.

administration sent a questionnaire to Canadian researchers who receive funding or partial funding from U.S. agencies (this would include collaborative research with U.S. researchers) asking that they confirm that their research "does not include a climate or 'environmental justice' component; does not contain diversity, equity and inclusion (DEI) elements; does not ascribe to 'gender ideology,' and increases American influence globally" (Canadian Press, 2025).

We must address the deeply embedded racist conditioning we all receive or we will continue to be susceptible to racial manipulation. There is a long history of racial bogeymen used to stimulate White racial resentment among the masses and competition between racialized groups for resources we are told are scarce (Jayakumar, 2022; Matias, 2023; Sciullo, 2015). All of these narratives are also circulating internationally, impacting cultures and climates, including in Canada. We can never think, "It couldn't happen here." If we truly believe that all people are equal and entitled to basic human rights, it is imperative that we improve our capacity to find common ground. This includes seeking multiple perspectives and information sources, moving beyond sensationalized stories and doing our research to ascertain factual, real-world (not social media–circulated) information, gaining agreement on what we are actually trying to solve, and proceeding with evidence-based strategies. Working in solidarity with others to build coalitions is essential for both personal support and collective action.

COMMON WHITE MISCONCEPTIONS ABOUT RACISM

We have worked to address many misconceptions about racism. However, given their tenacity, we end by revisiting many of the most common arguments we hear. Regardless of intentions, these arguments serve dominant interests and ultimately function to protect rather than to challenge racism. In this way they can be conceptualized as ideologies of White supremacy.

"Why can't we all just be human? Isn't it this focus on race that divides us?" We have discussed the discourse of individualism and how it functions to obscure the reality of racism. While individualism asks, "Why can't we all just be different?" the "just human" discourse asks, "Why can't we all just be the same (after all, everyone's blood is red under the skin)?" Remember that a key dimension of White socialization is a sense of oneself as existing outside of race, as being "just human." Of course on the biological level we *are* all humans, but when applied to the social level, insisting that we just see each other as human has similar effects as individualism. Once again, the significance of race and the advantages of being White are denied. Further, this discourse assumes that White people and peoples of Color have the same reality, the same experiences in the same context, and that the same doors are open. White people invoke these seemingly contradictory discourses—we are either all unique or we are all the same—interchangeably. Further, on the cultural level, being an individual or being a human outside of a

racial group is a social position afforded only to White people. Someday, if and when racism is overcome, this discourse will make sense, but to pretend that day has already arrived is a form of willful ignorance.

As for the claim that focusing on race divides us, evidence shows that we are already divided by race on every measure of demographics and outcomes. We would argue that it is the refusal to take an honest account of the power of race as a social construct that keeps us divided.

"My best friend is a person of Color." First, keep in mind that we are not defining racism as something that only some people have, but as a system that impacts everyone. All White people who swim in the cultural water of Canada and the United States are socialized into psychological, institutional, and economic investments in upholding the racial system that advantages them. This socialization is not something we had a choice about nor is it something we can avoid. Nor does it depend on our awareness of it. At the same time, this does not mean that we can't challenge our socialization and work to overcome it, although this takes an ongoing commitment. Having peoples of Color in your life is of profound importance but does not in and of itself end racism in the wider culture that shapes you, them, and your relationship.

Friendships alone are not enough to overcome all of our socialization; White people still experience White advantage and maintain institutional control at the group level. Having a friend of Color does not, in and of itself, mean that you are educated about the complexities of racism, that you have worked to address your internalized dominance, or that you consistently treat your friend with cross-racial sensitivity and awareness. In addition, how much knowledge you have about the history of your friend's racial group and your receptivity to hearing about their personal experiences of racism will also impact how much you understand about racism and your role in it.

"I went to school with a lot of people of Color. In fact, I was the minority at my school." What often seems like a racially diverse environment for White people does not always appear diverse for peoples of Color. But if you are White and went to school with a lot of peoples of Color, you probably grew up in an urban environment, and possibly urban poor. Even so, most schools with a racially diverse student population are still segregated *within* the school, mirroring the racial segregation of wider society. In addition, as you progress through life, upward mobility will likely move you away from these schools, neighborhoods, and friends. White people who had a lot of childhood friends of Color rarely keep them in adulthood because our schools, workplaces, and other environments channel us in separate directions.

Some White people experience being a minority when they travel to another country. These experiences are important because they can provide some understanding of what peoples of Color experience here in Canada and the United States. However, being a minority in these contexts is not the same, because for most White people, this is a temporary situation. While you can experience prejudice and can be discriminated against as a White person in the minority—and that can of course be hurtful—it is *not* racism. First, to be in the minority as a White person is usually a situation a White person has chosen to be in and can easily escape. Second, in the larger society we are still affirmed as more valuable than peoples of Color and we still receive White advantage.

In the context of another country, keep in mind that most of the countries in which a White person would be a minority have a history of being colonized by White people and of the local Indigenous majority being forced to defer to White people. Further, our movies and media have been exported globally and Whiteness has worldwide currency. For example, blepharoplasty, a surgical technique to make the eyes appear more "Caucasian," is the most popular cosmetic surgery in Asia and the third most frequently requested procedure among Asian Americans (Kwon et al., 2021); light skin is advertised in countries such as India as the most beautiful, and skin-lightening cream is a huge industry around the world (Mady et al., 2023). While White people might feel like outsiders when traveling or temporarily working in non-White countries, they are still elevated in myriad ways and often bring a sense of entitlement with them.

"People of Color are too sensitive. They play the race card." "Playing the race card" is a common accusation White people make when peoples of Color bring up racism. To accuse a person of Color of playing the race card is to assert that the person's claim of racism is false. This is insulting to peoples of Color because it suggests that they are dishonest and that they lie about racism. This expression also reveals the lack of knowledge most White people have about racism and our arrogance that we could adjudicate whether or not peoples of Color's experiences are legitimate.

Because of the factors we have discussed, there is much about racism that most White people simply don't understand. Yet in our racial arrogance, we don't hesitate to debate the experiences of BIPOC peoples or the knowledge of those who have studied these issues. We feel free to dismiss these informed perspectives rather than to acknowledge that they are unfamiliar to us, reflect further on them, or seek more understanding. Our social, economic, and political power puts White people in the position to either legitimize or reject peoples of Color's accounts of racism. Yet we are the least likely to see, understand, or be invested in validating those accounts, and the least likely to be honest about their consequences.

Because most White people construct racism as specific acts that individuals either do or don't do, we think we can simply look at an incident and decide if "it" happened. But racism is infused in every part of society and in our perspectives. It is reinforced every day in countless and often subliminal ways. Our inability to think with complexity about racism, as well as our direct and indirect benefits from it, makes White people the least qualified to assess its manifestations. Our investment in denying racism also ensures that we will most often determine that "it" did *not* happen. The very concept of a "race card" at all, in a society so deeply divided by race, is a cogent example of White denial. It's not much of a card to play since naming racism rarely gets peoples of Color anywhere productive with White people. Very few White people believe that structural racism is real or have the humility to engage with peoples of Color about it in an open and thoughtful way.

"This is just wokeness." Charges of wokeness (or political correctness) often surface when White people are being challenged to acknowledge racism. Like other terms that originate as a challenge to unequal power, the concept of "wokeness" has been mocked and weaponized by dominant interests. Wokeness originated as a term from the Black activist community to mean awareness about historical exclusion and injustice, to describe language, ideas, policies, and behaviors that seek to minimize social and institutional oppression (Hernández-Truyol, 2023). It has been redefined by critics of social justice efforts to dismiss these efforts as cultural sensitivity brought to absurd levels, ones that stifle free speech and are in themselves discriminatory. This negative redefinition has been intentional, strategic, and effective. As soon as the term is evoked, discussion ends, for no one wants to be accused of being "woke." Indeed, this negative redefinition has been so reinforced that it has been written into presidential executive orders that ban "woke ideology." A similar example from a previous generation is the word *feminism*, which is simply the idea that women should have equal status and opportunity, but became a derogatory term with insulting variations such as "feminazi." Consider how hostile interests have managed to take the idea of equality for women and equate it with Nazism, and how such absurd perversions of the term have been so normalized that many young people don't want to be associated with feminism. We might reflect on whose interests are served by this strategy that perverts words intended to bring attention to injustice by turning those words into insults.

"People of Color are just as racist as we are. In fact, now there is reverse racism and White people can't get into college or get good jobs." If you think that racism is simply racial prejudice, then yes, anyone across any race can have just as much racial prejudice as anyone else. But racism is not merely racial prejudice. Racism is racial prejudice backed by institutional power. Only White people at the group level have the power to infuse, enforce, and benefit from their prejudices throughout the culture and transform it into racism. If you understand what racism is, then you understand that there is no such thing as reverse racism. The term reverse racism implies that power relations move back and forth, one day benefiting one group and the next day the other. But as we can see, from the founding of Canada and the United States to the present time, White legal and institutional power remain deeply rooted and intact.

For example, while the United States did elect a biracial president in 2008—and this was significant—focusing our attention on isolated exceptions allows us to overlook the wider patterns. During his presidency, Obama faced unrelenting racism, including claims that he wasn't American at all but actually African, and was persistently harassed to produce his birth certificate. What followed the end of President Obama's terms has been the most open and explicit resurgence of racism since the Civil Rights movement of the 1960s. For example, a key provision in the Voting Rights Act of 1965 that protected minority voters in jurisdictions with a history of racial discrimination in voting was removed by the Supreme Court in

2013, laws prohibiting racial segregation have been dropped (E. L. Green, 2025), programs intended to address systemic racial inequality have been banned (Office of Government-wide Policy, 2025), and White nationalism is flourishing (Mirrlees, 2022; Reyna et al., 2022). The world's richest person—a White man—performed two Nazi-style salutes at a 2025 presidential inauguration event with no censure from the administration. Clearly, racism does not go both ways. Sociologist Carol Anderson (2017) argues that every inch of Black progress has been met with a backlash of White rage, and we see that White rage following Obama's presidency, and again following the 2020 murder of George Floyd; far-right commentator Ben Shapiro has recently called for the president to pardon Floyd's convicted murderer. Seething White resentment has erupted to the surface and what was once taboo to openly express has been unleashed. Black people and other peoples of Color are not and have never been in the position to enact systems-level policies such as these. The vast majority of CEOs, Fortune 500 executives, managers, professors, doctors, lawyers, scientists, and holders of other prestigious positions of leadership and decision-making are White people. White people's overrepresentation in leadership does not match their numbers in society and isn't simply because they earned these positions.

Programs such as affirmative action in the United States and employment equity in Canada are often cited as examples of reverse racism or special privileges that peoples of Color and Indigenous peoples have over White people. These programs were developed in order to redress the reality and pervasiveness of White discrimination against peoples of Color. Still, commonsense understanding of these programs is very limited; for example, no employer is required to hire an unqualified person of Color, but they *are* required to be able to articulate why—if asked—they didn't hire a *qualified* person of Color.

Federal protections are important because although many White people claim they would "hire the best person for the job," they do not understand that because of the constant messages that peoples of Color are inferior, who we *perceive* as the best person for the job will likely be someone White. White men with a criminal record are slightly more likely to be called back for a job interview than Black men with no criminal record, even when they are equally qualified (Decker et al., 2015; Pager, 2007). In addition to unconscious preference for White applicants, another way racism manifests in the workplace is through the concept of "fit." This is the tendency to prefer people whose cultural style matches the workplace culture. Unfortunately, the culture of the workplace, unless the organization is owned by peoples of Color, will likely be White. This plays out in industries such as fashion, wherein there is a very specific and limited ideal of female beauty (such as narrow noses and slim hips), and in schooling, when teacher candidates are evaluated based on whether the staff will be able to relate to them.

Affirmative action was not designed with the stated goal of benefiting White people, and yet White women have numerically been the program's greatest beneficiaries. Affirmative action and other programs have made an impact on increasing the numbers of underrepresented groups in employment, but these programs have not come close to reaching their goals. Still, states such as California and Washington have ended affirmative action, and the Supreme Court ruled that points based on race could not be used in college admissions (*Students for Fair Admissions v. Harvard*, 2023).

When thinking about programs such as affirmative action, it's important to remember the dynamics of race. Because White people see themselves as "just people" rather than as *White* people, when they are hired it is assumed to be because they are qualified. When peoples of Color are hired (regardless of whether an employment equity program had anything to do with their hire), White people often assume that they were hired due to a special program. This assumption reveals that White people see peoples of Color as *inherently* unqualified; we have difficulty imagining they could have gotten the job on their qualifications alone. Further, this assumption reveals the sense of entitlement White people have to all desirable positions ("they got *my* place in law school" or "they got *my* job"). This also suggests that we are not quite as colorblind as we often claim. However, as of 2025, affirmative action has been overturned in the United States and people have been fired simply because they are Black or female, the argument being that they must have gained their positions via affirmative action "quotas" and could not possibly be qualified. For example, the U.S. president fired the chairman of the Joint Chiefs of Staff, U.S. Air Force General Charles Q. Brown Jr., because he was perceived as "a diversity hire." General Brown's qualifications included that he had served more than 3,000 hours as a fighter pilot, including 130 hours in combat, and commanded the Pacific Air Forces, which provides air power for U.S. interests in the Asia-Pacific region; the U.S. Air Forces Central Command, responsible for protecting U.S. security interests in Africa through the Persian Gulf; the 31st Fighter Wing, covering the southern region of the North Atlantic Treaty Organization (NATO); the 8th Fighter Wing, covering Southeast Asia; the U.S. Air Force Weapons School for advanced training in weapons and tactics for officers; and the 78th Fighter Squadron (U.S. Air Force, 2025). Pete Hegseth, the current U.S. secretary of defense, a former weekend Fox News host and former National Guard officer, publicly suggested that General Brown had been appointed because he is Black. "Was it because of his skin color? Or his skill? We'll never know, but always doubt," Hegseth wrote (Stewart & Ali, 2024). Even when minoritized peoples are not just qualified but in fact exceptional, their legitimacy will always be conditional and open to doubt.

"*Racism is a thing of the past. Besides, I didn't own slaves; I wasn't around when Indians were put in residential schools.*" Many White people are woefully uninformed when it comes to the continuing presence of racism. Seeing ourselves as individuals, with no connection to our nations' pasts, erases history and hides the way in which wealth and social capital have accumulated over generations and benefit us as a group today. Canada and the United States were founded on the exploits of slavery as well as genocide, and racism did not end when slavery or the residential school systems ended (Zinn, 1980/2010). Legal and institutional exclusion of peoples of Color, in addition to illegal acts ranging from lynching to racial profiling to police execution, continue today. Between 2000 and 2024, 622 unarmed African Americans (that there is a record of) were killed by police or while in police custody ("List of Unarmed African Americans . . . ," 2025). The following is a very brief list of some of their names: Eugene Pitchford (2000), Charmene Pickering (2001), Corey Ward (2002), Kendra James (2003), Christopher Hicks (2004), Henry Glover (2005), James Sims (2006), Kathryn Johnston (2006), Robert Harper (2007), Baron Pikes (2008), Oscar Grant (2009), Aaron Campbell (2007), Trayvon Martin (2012), Andy Lopez (2013), Sammy Yatim (2013), Michael Brown (2014), Tamir Rice (2014), Akai Gurley (2014), Tanisha Anderson (2014), Eric Garner (2014), Freddie Gray (2015), Andrew Loku (2015), Walter Scott (2015), Jacqueline Salyers (2016), Alton Sterling (2016), Philando Castille (2016), Keita O'Neil (2017), Terence Crutcher (2017), Jose Nieves (2017), Charleena Lyles (2017), Corey Mobly (2018), Crystalline Barnes (2018), George Robinson (2019), George Floyd (2020), Carl Dorsey (2021), Patrick Warren (2021), Jason Walker (2022), Tyre Nichols (2023), Alonzo Bagley (2023), Clifford Brooks (2024), Terrell Miller (2024), and hundreds of others. While we might think that racial disparities in arrest-related deaths would be decreasing over time, because we believe that there is less racism in society than in the past (Office of Justice Programs, 2024).

In spite of the increased public awareness of systemic racism following the murder of George Floyd in 2020 and the rise of the Black Lives Matter–led racial justice movement, data shows that the number of Black people killed by police has not improved in over a decade (*Washington Post*, 2024), but has *actually increased* since 2020 (Bunn, 2022). This at a time when racial justice efforts are federally banned and those who fight for racial justice are positioned as the problem, not racism itself.

Peoples of Color were denied Federal Housing Act (FHA) loans as recently as the 1950s. These loans allowed a generation of White people to attain middle-class status through homeownership. Homeownership is critical in the United States because it is the means by which the average person builds and passes down wealth, providing the starting point for the next generation. Peoples of Color were systematically denied this opportunity, and today the average White family has 10 times the wealth of the average Black or Latino family (Bhutta et al., 2020; Derenoncourt et al., 2024). Further, Black and Latinx borrowers were disproportionately targeted for the subprime mortgages that fueled the financial crisis in the late 1990s. Excluding peoples of Color from the mechanisms of society that allow wealth building continues today. Among the most common of these mechanisms are banks' setting higher mortgage rates and more stringent qualifications for home loan approval; and real estate agents reinforcing neighborhood segregation, denying racialized families access to intergenerational wealth building.

Racial group membership is consistently traced to inequitable outcomes on every indicator of quality of life, and these outcomes are well documented and predictable (Pryce, 2025; Wilson, 2011). Considering criminal justice as an example, in the United States the incarceration rate for all girls aged 10–17 is 21 per 100,000. But for Black girls it is 46 per 100,000; and for Native American girls it is 76 per

100,000 (Budd, 2024). One in five Black men born in 2001 is likely to be imprisoned at some point in his life (Robey et al., 2023). In 48 states, felony convictions can result in the loss of voting rights. Given that Black adults are disproportionately convicted of felonies, losing the right to vote further disenfranchises African Americans (Uggen et al., 2020). Black males receive sentences 13.4% longer and Hispanic males receive sentences 11.2% longer than White males. Hispanic females receive sentences 27.8% longer than White females. Black males (at 23.4%) and Hispanic males (at 26.6%) are less likely to receive probationary sentences compared to White males. Black (at 11%) and Hispanic females (at 29.7%) are less likely to receive a probation sentence than White females (U.S. Sentencing Commission, 2023). In Canada, Indigenous men account for 32% and Indigenous women were 49% of inmates in federal custody (Department of Justice Canada, 2024).

Limiting our analysis to the *micro* or individual level prevents a macro or big picture understanding. At the micro level ("*I* didn't own slaves"), we cannot see and address the macro dimensions of society that help hold racism in place, such as practices, policies, norms, rules, laws, traditions, and regulations. Consider, for example, how schools are funded in the United States through the property tax base of the community in which they are situated. Since youth of Color disproportionately live in poor communities and their families rent rather than own, youth of Color are penalized through this policy, which ensures that poor communities will have inferior schools. In turn, this practice ensures that middle- and upper-class students, who are more likely to be White, will get a superior education and have less future competition in the workplace.

Other examples of institutional racism that serve to reinforce how schools reproduce inequality include: mandatory culturally biased testing; ability tracking; a primarily White teaching force with the power to determine and place students in advanced or remedial academic tracks; cultural definitions of intelligence, what constitutes it, and how it is measured; and standards of what constitutes good behavior as determined by White teachers and administration. Rather than serving as the great equalizer, schools more often function to reproduce racial inequality. Insisting that we could not have benefited from racism because we personally didn't own slaves is extremely superficial and hides the reality of White advantage at every level of our past and present society.

DISCUSSION QUESTIONS

1. The authors argue that racism is more than the acts of individual bad people. What, then, is racism? What is problematic about reducing racism to simply the bad things some people think and do?
2. The authors argue that for White people, to grow up in racially segregated communities is to learn a great deal about race. How? What kinds of things do White people learn?

3. What is intersectionality? Choose a few of your other social group memberships (class, gender, sexuality, religion) and describe how they influence how you experience race.
4. Discuss some of the common misconceptions about racism. How would you counter these misconceptions from an antiracist perspective? In pairs or small groups, practice articulating your counterarguments.

EXTENSION ACTIVITIES

1. If you are not Indigenous, write an essay explaining the top three facts you learned about Indigenous peoples in Canada and the United States. Include where you learned this information, as well as your general attitude or feelings about this information. If you are Indigenous, write an essay about what you think most of your non-Indigenous classmates will write. After your essays are written and submitted, watch the multiple award-winning documentary film *Sugarcane* (2024), directed by Julian Brave NoiseCat and Emily Kassie. Write a one-page response to your previous essay, integrating new insights from the film.
2. Go to your school library and work with your librarian to identify 10 authors of Color who write about issues of interest to you. Create a schedule to read one book per month for each month of the 10-month school year.

PATTERNS TO PRACTICE SEEING

1. Think about the primary places you live, work/learn, and take leisure. How racially diverse are these environments? Where there is racial diversity, which groups are most represented? Which groups are least represented? Do people tend to have close relationships across groups?
2. How racially diverse are the people in leadership positions in your environment? How informed and concerned do they seem to be about racial inequity? How is this concern or lack thereof conveyed? Were they required to demonstrate any knowledge or skills in addressing systemic racism before they were considered qualified to lead? If so, how was this assessed?

CHAPTER 9

Understanding the Global Organization of Racism Through White Supremacy

"Why can't we all just be human? Isn't it this focus on race that divides us?"

This chapter explores White supremacy in the global context by tracing the history of imperialism and colonialism and how that history formed the divisions between the Global North and the Global South. The chapter connects imperialism and colonialism to industrialization, resource extraction, and labor exploitation globally.

> **Vocabulary to practice using:** Whiteness; White supremacy; colonialism; imperialism; White Man's Burden

As with other forms of oppression, one of the most tenacious elements of racism is its ability to adapt to and co-opt efforts to challenge it. Let's take an historical overview of efforts to advance social justice within the context of schooling and the continual obstruction these efforts have faced. Following the Civil Rights movement of the 1960s, an educational research approach emerged called *multicultural education*. Multicultural education offered a more accurate representation of history, one that included the contributions of all those who had been omitted from standard stories about who built the nation (J. A. Banks, 2006a, 2006b, 2008; Gay, 1983; Sleeter, 1989); it challenged the traditional notions of intelligence and how it was defined and assessed (Au, 2021; Chinn, 1979); it created classroom environments that were diverse and inclusive of all children, including those with disabilities (J. A. Banks & C.A.M. Banks, 2004); and it advocated for the idea that people who had diverse life experiences in childhood would be informed and engaged citizens (C.A.M. Banks, 2005; J. A. Banks, 2003; Sleeter, 1994).

Proponents of multicultural education recognized that schools were not set up to meet the needs of minoritized groups. While there are variations in approaches to multicultural education, J. A. Banks and C.A.M. Banks (1995) define it as:

a field of study... whose major aim is to create equal educational opportunities for students from diverse racial, ethnic, social-class, and cultural groups. One of its important goals is to help all students to acquire the knowledge, attitudes, and skills needed to function effectively in a pluralistic democratic society and to interact, negotiate, and communicate with peoples from diverse groups in order to create a civic and moral community that works for the common good. (p. xi)

However, although it started as a movement to challenge the dominant norms, definitions, practices, and policies in education, multicultural education today all too often manifests simply as "celebrating diversity." This sanitized approach to multicultural education is often done through activities such as sharing food from different cultures and celebrating holidays such as Hanukkah and Kwanzaa along with the traditional celebration of Christmas. Yet this does not acknowledge the history and politics of difference. Celebrating diversity is important, but because it tends to occur without a study of power, this celebration actually reinforces structural inequality. Contrast celebrating diversity as it is commonly practiced in schools with the Banks and Banks definition above. Clearly, much complexity is missing from the former practices.

While antiracism education and multicultural education have shared commitments, antiracism education focuses on the inequitable distribution of power—and racial power in particular. Antiracism education centers its analysis on race and the social, cultural, and institutional power that so profoundly shapes the meaning and outcome of racial difference (Dei, 2008; Dei & Vickers, 1997). Antiracism education recognizes racism as embedded in all aspects of society and the socialization process; no one who is born into and raised in Western culture can escape being socialized to participate in racist relations. Antiracism education seeks to interrupt these relations by educating people to identify, name, and challenge the norms, patterns, traditions, ideologies, structures, and institutions that keep racism in place. A key aspect of this education process is to raise the consciousness of White people about what racism is and how it works (Gillborn, 2006; Sleeter, 2017). To accomplish this, we must challenge the dominant conceptualization of racism as individual acts that only some bad individuals do, rather than as a system in which we are all implicated. Using a structural definition allows us to explore our own relationship to racism as a system and to move beyond isolated incidents and/or intentions.

WHITENESS AND WHITE SUPREMACY

White supremacy refers to the ideology of White superiority and the institutions, norms, policies, practices, and values built upon that ideology. Slavery, genocide, colonialism, and Orientalism are examples of White supremacy in practice (Brown, 2024).

Whiteness refers to the specific dimensions of White supremacy that elevate White people over peoples of Color (Applebaum, 2016; Delgado & Stefancic, 1997; Frankenberg, 1993). This elevation occurs through ideology, unearned advantages, and lack of systemic barriers. Basic rights, resources, and experiences that are assumed to be shared by all, are actually only available to White people. Although many White people feel that being White has no meaning, this feeling is unique to White people and is a key part of what it means to *be* White (DiAngelo, 2016; Frankenberg, 1993; Matias, 2016). To claim to be "just human" and thus outside of race in a society inequitably organized by race is one of the most powerful and pervasive manifestations of Whiteness.

> **STOP:** Racism is about a relationship of unequal power. As we recall from Chapter 5, relationships of unequal power do not flip back and forth; they are deeply and historically embedded in one direction.

Peoples of Color, the most prominent among them African American sociologist W.E.B. Du Bois (1868–1963), wrote extensively about Whiteness in the United States and globally in the early 1900s (Du Bois, 1903/1989; cf. Sundquist, 1996). These writers urged White people to stop studying racial Others and turn their attention onto themselves to explore what it means to be White in a society that is so divided by race. Finally, by the 1990s, White scholars began to rise to this challenge (Dyer, 1997; Frankenberg, 1993; Giroux, 1997; Kincheloe, 1999; McLaren, 1997; Roediger, 1991; Weis & Fine, 1996). These scholars examine the cultural, historical, and sociological aspects of being White and how they are tied to power and privilege.

When we use the term White supremacy, we do not mean it in its lay usage to indicate extreme hate groups such as the Ku Klux Klan, Proud Boys, Atomwaffen Division, Canadian Heritage Alliance, and other White nationalist groups. While it certainly can refer to those groups, we use the term in its academic sense to capture the pervasiveness, magnitude, and normalcy of White privilege, dominance, and assumed superiority.

> **STOP:** When we use the term *White supremacy*, we are not referring to extreme hate groups or "bad racists." We use the term to capture the all-encompassing dimensions of White privilege, dominance, and assumed superiority in mainstream society.

The life and activism of Fred Korematsu (Figure 9.1) illustrate the power of institutional racism.

Figure 9.1. Fred Korematsu (1919–2005)

Fred Korematsu was one of the many U.S.- and Canadian-born citizens of Japanese descent who were identified for relocation and internment during World War II. After being denied entry to serve in the U.S. military, Korematsu worked as a welder. In 1942, President Roosevelt signed the executive order authorizing the detention and relocation to holding camps of Americans of Japanese heritage. Korematsu refused detainment. His case was the first to challenge the constitutionality of the federal government's internment of Japanese Americans. He was convicted in 1944 when the U.S. Supreme Court decided that Japanese American incarceration was justified due to military necessity and was not motivated by racism.

In 1983 his conviction was overturned, and in addressing the court, Mr. Korematsu said, "According to the Supreme Court decision regarding my case, being an American citizen was not enough. They say you have to look like one, otherwise they say you can't tell a difference between a loyal and a disloyal American. I thought that this decision was wrong and I still feel that way. As long as my record stands in federal court, any American citizen can be held in prison or concentration camps without a trial or a hearing. That is if they look like the enemy of our country. Therefore, I would like to see the government admit that they were wrong and do something about it so this will never happen again to any American citizen of any race, creed, or color." While Mr. Korematsu made this statement 42 years ago, his words are tragically prophetic today. Throughout his life, Korematsu continued his social justice work on behalf of others. He received numerous awards for his advocacy, including the U.S. Presidential Medal of Freedom in 1998.

Source: https://www.peoplesworld.org/calif-assembly-honors-japanese-american-civil-liberties-fighter/

WHITE SUPREMACY IN THE GLOBAL CONTEXT

Although commonsense understandings about social power often have us thinking in terms of numbers, as we have argued, power is not dependent on numbers but on *position*. In other words, power is dependent on what position a group holds and their ability to affect other groups from that position. Through movies and mass media, advertising, multinational corporations, banking, political control, and Christian missionary work, White supremacy is able to circulate in the global context. In addition to specific political practices, policies, and military control, White supremacy is also a powerful ideology that promotes the idea of Whiteness as the standard for humanity.

Consider how White supremacy (invisible and universalized White cultural practices and structural privileges) circulates globally in each of these instances:

- European (most notably English, French, and Spanish) discovery myths of Africa, Middle East, North/Central/South Americas
- Colonizing geographical territories (and renaming them in colonial languages, and in relation to colonial powers—New York, New Brunswick)
- Redrawing or establishing borders in colonized territories according to the interests of colonial powers
- Impositions of colonial languages onto Indigenous peoples
- The promotion of a consumer lifestyle and the values of consumption, profit, and competition
- The exploitation of global labor for increasing Western corporations' profits and primarily for the West's consumption
- Environmental polluting, extraction of resources, and ravaging of the natural world in the global south (and rural or non-White–dominant areas of Canada and the United States)
- Multinational corporations increasing profits for shareholders through practices such as those listed above, resulting in the concentration of wealth into fewer and fewer (White and male) hands
- Christian missionary work that endeavors to bring Christianity to "Third World" and Indigenous peoples and simultaneously brings White supremacy

> **STOP:** Remember, White supremacy does not refer to individual White people per se and their individual intentions, but to a political-economic social order based on the historical and current accumulation of structural power that privileges White people as a group.

While there are many characteristics of White supremacy that scholars have studied (Ahmed, 2007; DiAngelo, 2016; Frankenberg, 1993; hooks, 2014; Razack, 2022), one of the most foundational among them is the force—and even enthusiasm—with which Whiteness defines humanity. As Resmaa Menakem (2017) explains, in a world organized by White supremacy, the White body becomes the standard against which all other bodies are measured. When the White body is the standard or ideal representation of "human," then every hue away from the White standard is deemed less than human.

If White supremacy is not simply the White nationalist or White supremacist hate group, but the standard for humanity, how is this ideology and the practices that issue from it, perpetuated? To begin to understand this, especially in its global circulation, the foundation of White supremacy has to be understood in relation to the history of colonialism and imperialism.

In their essay reviewing how historic ideologies of colonialism and imperialism structure a great part of the world we know today, sociologists Ramón Grosfoguel and Eric Mielants (2006) describe how the power of the modern world system is constituted globally through a division of North versus South. In this schema, *North*, sometimes called the *Global North* or (before the dissolution of the Soviet Union and other communist states which were deemed the Second World) the *First World*, refers to Europeans and European Americans. People of the Global North have been and continue to be the acquirers of resources and capital. The other end of this schema referring to non-Europeans is the *South*, sometimes called the *Global South* (and formerly, the *Third World*). People of the Global South were/are those whose labor, bodies, and/or lands have been exploited and ravaged for the extraction and accumulation of resources and capital (Anker, 2020; Mentan, 2018; van der Linden, 2022).

The 15th century is key to understanding how this schema was set up, and its legacies today. Among the most relevant developments for that era was sugar's arrival in the North. Sugar came from conquered Pacific Islands and the Middle East to Western Europe. At first, sugar was a rare and precious product only accessible to the ruling elite. However, by the 17th century, through European colonization of the Caribbean and advancement of plantation slavery, sugar had become a commodity the world over (Anker, 2020).

By the 1500s, Portuguese and Spanish colonial powers, and by the 1600s the English, had killed, dispersed, and enslaved Indigenous populations across the Americas, stolen the lands, and all but decimated the Caribbean islands to pursue the fortunes brought by sugar crops. Sugar is notoriously difficult to grow (more difficult than tobacco or cotton) and required that the native vegetation and crops be slashed and burned to clear land for mass sugar plantings. Tropical rainforests and fragile ecologies were transformed. By the 18th century, sugar from the tropical Americas was the most profitable industry in the world (Anker, 2020). And it wasn't just sugar that was acquired: While Portugal extracted sugar from Brazil, the Spanish extracted gold and silver from the Andes, France extracted fossil fuels and minerals from Africa, Belgium extracted rubber and ivory from the Congo, and England extracted cotton, timber, tea, and countless other resources from its exploited colonies around the world (Hickel et al., 2022; Weisbord, 2003).

> ✋ **STOP:** "There has always been slavery, it's as old as time" and "The Africans themselves sold slaves to the Europeans" are common justifications for the transatlantic slave trade. While there was slavery before that era, there was a profound difference. Prior to this time, people were enslaved as a result of being captured during local warfare, to pay debts, or as a form of punishment. They typically served a period of time and were released. Further, these captives were not seen as an inferior animal-like species who deserved wholesale subjugation. While all forms of slavery are abhorrent, the transatlantic slave trade was a form never before seen, one on a massive industrial scale, churning out kidnapped, sold, and enslaved Africans by the millions. Their captivity was not a result of warfare or debt, but as a form of profit for distant nations. This new form of slavery is termed *chattel slavery*, wherein the enslaved had no rights or legal standing; could be raped, tortured, and murdered without recourse; could be bought, sold, and traded along with their children and family members; and were enslaved for life along with their children, their children's children, and on across all subsequent generations. Thus, the transatlantic slave trade differed in scale, in the ideologies of inhumanity projected onto the racialized bodies of the enslaved, and in its cruelty, its permanence, and its very purpose: Western imperial expansion and wealth building (M'baye, 2006; Smallwood, 2019; Williams, 2014).

Alongside the colonizing of the Americas, Asia and Africa were being "discovered," colonized, and exploited by multiple Christian European monarchs in the 15th to 19th centuries, among them rulers of England, France, Spain, the Netherlands, and Portugal. In Congo alone, the regime of Belgium's King Leopold II cannot be described as anything short of barbaric. As historian Robert Weisbord (2003) describes it, harvesting ivory and rubber required conscription of Indigenous populations. If quotas for harvesting were unmet, villages would be burned by King Leopold's armies and Indigenous Congolese shot or maimed (removal of the right hand of Congolese was common practice). Vast areas were depopulated by flight, enslavement, starvation, disease, murder, or massacres. While precise mortality statistics are difficult to confirm, historians estimate the toll of what can only be described as genocide to be up to ten million Congolese, reducing the population by two-thirds by 1924 (Tunamsifu, 2022; Weisbord, 2003).

In Asia, the territories of present-day India, Sri Lanka, Malaysia, Myanmar, Singapore, the Philippines, Cambodia, and Indonesia were among the lands colonized by the English, Spanish, Dutch, French, and Portuguese. The colonizers introduced invasive plantations of cash crops such as rubber, tea, coffee, and sugar. From beeswax to sea turtles, little escaped colonial looting. Massive mining operations to extract coal, tin, and gold were established. Deforestation and degradation of people, land, native plants, and waterways were commonplace in order to harvest timber for shipbuilding, clear land for crops, and divert waterways for mass agriculture (Hägerdal, 2024). In addition to resource and capital extraction, colonial powers imposed their systems of government, bureaucracy, currency, language, and other "civilizing" projects via missionary activity (Awaya & Tsuboi, 2024; Grosfoguel & Mielants, 2006; Pomeranz, 2005).

In the 15th and 16th centuries, Christian Spain's monarchy reconquered Islamic Spain, expelling Jews and Arabs from the Spanish peninsula. This era of conquest of both internal others (the Jews and Muslims of Spain) and external others (the Indigenous peoples of the Americas) was among the first steps in establishing the modern world system. The justification for the expulsion of Jews and Muslims from Spain and the forced removal of Indigenous peoples from their territories in the Americas relied on arguments about purity of blood. In other words, *they* were inferior to the colonizing powers—below human, subhuman, closer to animals; they were people with either the wrong god (in the case of Jews and Muslims), or no god at all (in the case of Africans and Indigenous peoples of the Americas). Language referring to displaced and conquered peoples as godless, without souls, or nonhuman was common in the written records of this time. To justify the European slave trade, Christian clergy engaged in debates about the extent to which Africans were people without souls and thus could be enslaved (Grosfoguel & Mielants, 2006).

Over time, the Christian theological arguments for slavery and conquest were replaced by more secularized justifications. Scientific racism reproduced the same "findings"—who was more or less human, civilized, godly, and worthy of life and freedom, and who was not—based on criteria such as skull size and other physical features. As Ta-Nehisi Coates (2015) captures so well:

> But race is the child of racism, not the father. And the process of naming "the people" has never been a matter of genealogy and physiognomy so much as one of hierarchy. Difference in hue and hair is old. But the belief in the preeminence of hue and hair, the notion that these factors can correctly organize a society and that they signify deeper attributes, which are indelible—this is the new idea at the heart of these new people who have been brought up hopelessly, tragically, deceitfully, to believe that they are White. (p. 7)

Many of us believe that racism begins with our response to difference. In other words, difference makes us uncomfortable, and prejudice follows. In this case, that difference would be racial difference such as skin color and hair texture. So we start with race (difference) and we end up with racism (dislike of difference).

This belief is often conveyed through the common platitude, "People just like to be with their own." The point Coates is making is that the process moves in the other direction; it begins with the exploitation of resources that one group wants and has the means to take (racism), *and then they make up a justification for that exploitation* (race).

The 19th century, with the rise of industrial capitalism in the Global North fueled by the power relations and exploited labor and resources that began in the 16th century, saw rapid advancement and technical innovation. This gave more widespread access to material comforts such as running water, sanitation, refrigeration, electricity, and transportation infrastructures. These material comforts along with advances in medicine increased the global population, living standards, and leisure time, fueling consumerism (Yazdani & Castro, 2023). The Western colonial states developed an insatiable appetite for the raw materials they pillaged from Africa, Asia, and the Americas (Weisbord, 2003). These were actually rich lands *made poor* through Western exploitation of their resources.

The relationship between colonization, capitalism, and White supremacy is foundational to understanding the world today. The logic of slavery and Indigenous displacement did not go away when those practices ended. Other mechanisms of exploitation emerged. In the case of post-abolition, these mechanisms included sharecropping, debt peonage, convict leasing, lynching, and segregation; and in the case of Indigenous displacement, mechanisms for access to land and title, child abduction/removal, language/cultural genocide, and religious conversion (Gonzalez, 2021; Matheson et al., 2022; McNeil & Enns, 2022; Young, 2021). Climate change and the environmental devastation we see today are also deeply rooted in the colonial past. The phrase *environmental racism* captures this history, as well as the current reality that the peoples most impacted by the environmental damage inflicted by colonial powers are the peoples of the Global South. Today's politics of immigration are another connection (Gonzales, 2021). As climate change and the legacies of centuries of colonization force people from their homelands to seek refuge in the colonizing nations of the Global North, the North responds with increasing protectionism, escalating racial tension.

The entrenchment of colonialism established a set of twin discourses that continued to rationalize both the activities of colonialism itself and the resulting capital and wealth accumulated in Europe and the United States. These discourses are that Europe "naturally" modernizes and advances in large part due to its cultural, spiritual, intellectual, and otherwise "superior" characteristics as the cradle of knowledge and civilization, while non-Europe remains stagnant and backwards. The only way this can be remedied is via the diffusion of European institutions, ideas, and people who are willing and able to bring their progress to the regressed areas of the world (Blaut, 1989). We see White supremacist ideology across a range of social institutions during this era, and the fingerprints of this ideology still mark Western institutions today (Elaref, 2023; Mathieu, 2018).

Edward Said termed this phenomenon *Orientalism* (1978). For example, 1883 was the start of the eugenics movement of scientific racism (devoted to proving the natural superiority of "White" genes); *National Geographic* was established in 1888 as a popular social science magazine (normalizing the "White male gaze"—a way of looking at the non-White woman's body, as anthropologist Linda Steet [2000] describes it, serving as a form of soft core pornography for a White male gaze); the arts, during the 19th century, elevated to fame the works of scores of painters such as Félix Auguste Clément and Jean-Léon Gérôme, whose fetishized depictions of racialized and Indigenous people and places are still displayed in museums and studied in universities today. Another cogent example of the ideology of European superiority in this era is English journalist and essayist Rudyard Kipling's poem "The White Man's Burden," which was published in *McClure's Magazine* in 1899, excerpted here:

> Take up the White Man's burden, send forth the best ye breed
> Go bind your sons to exile to serve your captives' need;
> To wait, in heavy harness, on fluttered folk and wild—
> Your new-caught, sullen peoples, half devil and half child.
>
> Take up the White Man's burden, in patience to abide,
> To veil the threat of terror and check the show of pride.
> By open speech and simple an hundred times made plain.
> To seek another's profit, and work another's gain.
>
> Take up the White Man's burden, the savage wars of peace—
> Fill full the mouth of Famine and bid the sickness cease;
> And when your goal is nearest (the end for others sought),
> Watch sloth and heathen folly bring all your hope to nought.
> [. . .]
>
> Take up the White Man's burden, ye dare not stoop to less
> Nor call too loud on Freedom to cloak your weariness;
> By all ye will or whisper, by all ye leave or do,
> The silent sullen peoples shall weigh your God and you.
> [. . .]

The same narratives circulate today—that peoples of the Global South are lazy, ungrateful, sullen, exhausting, and ultimately irredeemable, but still look to the West as the model of superior culture. Note in the editorial cartoon on the next page (Figure 9.2) the racist depictions, as well as the titles of the various "mountains" to be overcome in order for the White man to bring the "savages" to the mountaintop of civilization that only he knows how to reach. References to "shit-hole countries" are a modern example of these same discourses circulating today (Osei-Tutu & Osei-Tutu, 2023).

Figure 9.2. "The White Man's Burden" Editorial Cartoon by Victor Gillam (April 1899)

Source: https://en.wikipedia.org/wiki/The_White_Man%27s_Burden#/media/File:%22The_White_Man's_Burden%22_Judge_1899_(cropped).png

This period before World War I saw the continued entrenchment of capitalism as resource extraction from the Global South fueled the Industrial Revolution of the North in the 19th and early 20th centuries. These systems—imperialism, industrialization, and capitalism—developed hand-in-hand, each needing, fueling, and sustaining the other.

While the causes of World War I are complex, among them was the increasing competition in global empire building. As British and French expansion continued, fueled by the industrialization that increased the need for more and more raw materials, tensions rose between regimes including Germany, Austria-Hungary, and the Ottoman Empire (Kumari & Tiwari, 2022). There was also the ongoing need to justify colonial exploitation via discourses of scientific "facts," superior culture, and civilization since *We are exploiting them* was not as palatable a justification as *We are helping them advance their society*.

The most familiar understandings of global conflicts today are rooted in this two-part story of modern versus primitive societies: *Western* societies (and people) are modern, developed, civilized, have stable and fair institutions, and either by necessity or benevolence bring this expertise to solving the problems of *primitive* societies (and people), functioning as an objective referee or peacekeeper. Yet the problems in faraway lands we read about in the morning papers or watch on the evening news may be more effectively approached when analyzed in the context of

> 📖 While there are nuances in meaning within disciplines of study (such as literary criticism, political science, or international law), **colonialism** describes the practice of dominating a territory and its people and imposing administration by a foreign power. The features of colonialism include resource extraction, labor exploitation, and civilizing missions wherein the justification for the colonial authority relies on its claim to bring modernity and improvement to the land, culture, and people (Fourchard et al., 2011). While nuanced differences are debated by political theorists, *imperialism* is often used interchangeably with colonialism to refer to the same dynamics (Arneil, 2024). **Capitalism** refers to a form of economic and social organization that emerged in Europe and expanded through the 20th century. Capitalism prioritizes profit through control of the means of production, private ownership, and control of supply and demand. Capitalism is not simply an economic system but also influences social structures, political institutions, and cultural norms (Fourchard et al., 2011; Palmowski & Riches, 2021).

colonialism and imperialism; the West's role is far from objective. For example, a familiar framing of the Palestine/Israel conflict is that it is a simple matter of two hostile religious groups competing for the same limited space. But how does our understanding deepen when we place Israel and Palestine in the wider historical context of the colonial era's machinations for control over land and resources?

The mainstream understanding of the conflict between Israel and Palestine is that it is a result of the need to create a Jewish homeland after the Holocaust (1933–1945) and World War II (1939–1945). The Holocaust was justified by the belief circulating throughout Europe that the Jewish people were a specific race which was inferior to the so-called Aryan race. European Jews were contending with antisemitism well before World War II.

In the late 19th century antisemitism was increasing across Europe. The philosophy of Zionism emerged as a Jewish response. Zionism's core tenet is that Jewish security depends upon the principle of self-determination, as a discrete entity of people with a shared identity as Jews. Prior to Zionism, Jewish peoples of Europe had identities as members of nations (such as German, French, English, and Russian). But the principles of the Enlightenment, of egalitarianism and equality, that were foundational to emergent national democracies, were dependent on the bonds of national identities. Jews did not have a national identity *as Jews* and were denied access to full inclusion in public life. Thus the road to Jewish recognition, sovereignty, and security was believed to lie in the creation of their own nation state (Halperin, 2015; Taub, 2013).

> ✓ **PERSPECTIVE CHECK:** Notice if you feel uninterested in history other than that of your own nation state and believe that this history is irrelevant to you. In the global context, Whiteness reduces our cultural tolerance for (and thus understanding of) alternative historical accounts. Understanding these accounts that may be unfamiliar to you is necessary for challenging White supremacy. In particular, it is critical to understand the history of Palestine and Israel in the wider context of White supremacy. Without this historical context, we cannot recognize solutions that may be simplistic and naïve, nor contextualize the interests of who's at the table proposing those solutions (and who's been left out).

In 1897, the first Zionist Congress to discuss the creation of a Jewish state was held in the Swiss city of Basel. In the early years of the movement, there were many debates about cultural and territorial details. What began as an ethnic nationalist movement soon developed a strong territorial dimension (Conforti, 2014). Theodor Herzl, Zionism's chief architect, believed that the only way to protect Jewish people from the widespread antisemitism in Europe was for the Jews to have their own country (White, 2014). Between 1897 and 1902, the Zionist Congress considered many options for a new homeland, including Argentina, Cyprus, the Sinai Peninsula, and East Africa (Conforti, 2014). The early leaders of the movement did not specifically define a place for a new Jewish settlement, and when talks with the Ottoman Empire (who controlled Palestine/Sinai at the time) fell through, other options were explored.

The Zionists knew securing a land of their own during this era of imperial expansion would require the support of an imperial power. In part through Herzl's visits to England and interactions with officials, the movement found a willing partner in the British government and key diplomatic figures. In 1903, the British government made a formal offer of territory in East Africa (what is now Uganda). This was considered to be an incredible achievement for Herzl, but when the "Uganda plan" (as it was known) was presented to the Zionist Congress, the territory was rejected (Conforti, 2014). It was argued by those who rejected the plan that only what the Bible termed the Land of Israel (*Eretz Israel*; the Promised Land) could unite the Jewish people.

The support Zionists needed came to fruition during and after the First World War when the allied powers secured "mandate" (territorial governance) over conquered lands which were then divided up (Bassiouni, 2005). The British strategized that it would be an advantage to have a grateful ally in the former Ottoman-controlled Arab lands, and to protect their interests in the oil reserves and critical seaways there such as the Suez Canal (Wight & Yost, 2023). The result of this British support is evidenced in part by a document called the Balfour Declaration, a letter sent in 1917 from Foreign Secretary Arthur Balfour to Lord Rothschild, a leading figure of the British Jewish community. The letter announced the government's favorable view and material support for the establishment of a Jewish homeland in Palestine. At the time, Palestine was in turmoil, as it had been a territory under the weakened Ottoman Empire. By October 1917, the Ottoman Empire was defeated by the Allied powers, ending 1,400 years of Islamic rule over Palestinian territory. Between 1918 and 1919 the Allied powers established what came to be called the League of Nations, formed with the stated goal to ensure international peace. A reduction of arms, peaceful dispute resolution, and collective security were among its core principles. Their activities began in 1920 with 32 original signatories. The League established a system to put conquered territories in a trust (the mandate) to be governed by members of the League. Their mission was to bring development and civilization, entrusted with the "tutelage" of lands "inhabited by people not yet able to stand by themselves" (Article 22, as cited in Ziegerhofer, 2019; Pedersen, 2015).

In 1921 the Mandate Commission of the League of Nations held its first meeting in Geneva to review the administration of territories seized from Germany and the Ottoman Empire during World War I. The populations placed under this mandate system protested. The Samoans insisted they were as civilized as their New Zealand "tutors" and the Arabs said they had been promised independence, not "tutelage" (Pedersen, 2015). But despite the protests of the Indigenous populations and the squabbles among colonizing members competing for spoils and control, the commissioner stated the importance of their work as marking the beginning of a new epoch in colonial history (Pedersen, 2015). The British appointed Sharif Husayn—an ally during the war against the Ottoman Empire—king and ruler of Iraq in 1921 under the mandate's tutelage system. Husayn is just one example of an insider who sold out his own people in order to personally benefit from colonial exploitation. This illustrates a familiar tactic of colonizers: granting positions of power to authoritarians who are loyal to colonial interests rather than to the interests of the local populations. Such tactics play a major part in the continuing strife we see in the Middle East, Africa, Asia, and the Americas today.

The League of Nations mandate system allowed empires such as oil-poor Britain to access oil reserves in the Arab territories of the Middle East. By 1918 the modern economies of industrialized states had shifted from the "age of coal" to the "age of oil" and could not function without access to large supplies to fuel their transportation, agriculture, and heavy industries, and to fuel and move their armies (Toprani, 2019). The largest oil holdings at the time (before World War II) were the Royal Dutch/Shell company which in 1927 produced 50% more oil than its next closest competitor, the U.S.-based Standard Oil. In this era after World War I, the British sought an independent supply of their own, and the Middle East became a resource-rich foundation on which to establish British influence in the period. In brief, British interest in the Middle East rested on two key aims: the pursuit of an independent oil supply and the antisemitic desire throughout Europe to relocate Jews.

At the beginning of the 20th century, the population of Palestine was between 90 and 96% Palestinian Arab and predominantly Muslim, with some Christian and 4–10% Jewish Palestinians (R. Khalidi, 2020; Quigley, 2022). The territory was a mostly rural and patriarchal society with a small group of urban elite families who dominated formal politics. The coastal cities of Jaffa and Haifa were more modernized with professional and trade classes, and inland towns such as Jerusalem, Nablus, and Hebron more conservative. For the most part, people's identities were based on family, religious affiliation, or city or village of origin. The Jews living in Palestine at this time were culturally quite similar to Palestinian Arabs, and were a mix of ultra-Orthodox, Sephardic, and urban Middle Eastern or Mediterranean in origin, and many spoke Arabic or Turkish (R. Khalidi, 2020).

The British armies took control of the region and accelerated the removal of Jews from Europe to Palestine (for a more detailed history, we recommend Polish historian Dr. Artur Patek's 2012 book, *Jews on Route to Palestine 1934–1944*). The Zionists considered the land a barren desert and paid little attention to the local Palestinian population, which they assumed would benefit from the settlement of Jewish people. Indeed, in 1896, Herzl had written that a Jewish state in Palestine would "form a part of a wall of defense for Europe in Asia, an outpost of civilization against barbarism" (Herzl, as cited in White, 2014, p. 20). In fact, there were already fully thriving urban and rural communities of Palestinians. For example, between 1908 and 1914 there were 32 newspapers and periodicals established in Palestine. By comparison, at the same time there were approximately 50 newspapers in London. But the British government agreed with sentiments such as Herzl's: The Indigenous Palestinians were irrelevant. They compared the plight of the Palestinians to that of the Indigenous peoples of North America and Australia. As Winston Churchill once said regarding the Palestinians, no wrong had been done because "a higher race . . . a more worldly-wise race . . . has come in and taken their place" (Churchill, as cited in White, 2014, p. 20). Thus removing the Palestinians became a practical but not a moral problem.

Between 1920 and 1946, the Jewish settlements in Palestine increased exponentially and tensions during these decades escalated. In 1922, the population of Palestine (including Jews, Muslims, Christians, and other groups) was reported by the British as being 752,048 (Hagopian & Zahlan, 1974; Patek, 2012). Of these, 83,790 were Jews (11% of total population, 14% in relation to the Muslim population of Palestine). By 1947, the total population of Palestine was reported as 1,933,673. Of these, 614,239 were Jews (32% of the total population, 52% in relation to the Muslim population of Palestine) (Patek, 2012, p. 27). During these decades, the ratio of Arabs to Jews also changed dramatically, going from 13 to 1 in 1914 to 2 to 1 by 1947 (Hagopian & Zahlan, 1974).

The mandate system ended at the end of World War II, in 1946, when the League of Nations ceased to exist and transferred its remaining authority and assets to the newly formed United Nations. On November 29, 1947, the UN passed Resolution No. 181 (UNGA, 1947) to partition Palestine between the Palestinians and the Jews, clearing the path for the creation of the state of Israel (declared on May 14, 1948). Although Jews were still a minority in terms of population and land ownership, the plan allocated 55% of Palestine to Jews (increasing their share of Palestine from 7% during the mandate period). The Indigenous Palestinian population was not consulted and was set to lose over half of their territory to a settler population, with 42% of the Palestinian population to be under the control of the new Jewish state (Falah, 1996; White, 2014).

This declaration and creation of the state of Israel and the partition of the territory and forced relocation of Palestinian Arabs from over half of their lands is called the Naqba ("Catastrophe") and triggered the 1948 Arab-Israeli war. The short- and long-term goals of the Zionist leadership were to expel the Palestinian population and to make it impossible for any displaced Palestinians to ever return, through various mechanisms such as burning villages or renaming them so villages where Palestinians once lived no longer "existed." It took 6 months to complete the mission of removing Palestinians from the land ceded to Jews. The estimated number of Palestinian towns and villages ethnically cleansed ranges from 350 to 500 (depending in part on size classification)—and 80% of them were either destroyed totally or settled immediately by Israelis. Approximately 87% of Palestinians who lived in what was now Israel had been forcibly removed (White, 2014; Pappé, 2006). The best estimates are that approximately 750,000 Palestinians were forcibly removed from the newly formed state of Israel (Pappé, 2006). By 1952 there were approximately 850,000 Palestinian refugees, mostly in neighboring Jordan, Syria, Lebanon, Iraq, and Egypt. The previously existing political, financial, and intellectual Palestinian elite, after 1948, disappeared from the territories that were now the state of Israel; any leaders who opposed Zionism were identified and removed (Jamal, 2017). By the end of the war, Israel had taken control of 77% of the territory, and only two parts of Palestine remained in the hands of the Palestinians: the Gaza Strip and the West Bank.

After this period of first-wave colonization (from the 1890s to the 1948 Naqba/Israeli state formation), conflict in the region continued. The Cold War had Arab nations in the region seeking alliances with Moscow to balance Western support of Israel (W. Khalidi, 1991). In June 1967 the second phase of Zionist colonization of Palestine began as Israeli forces took control of the remaining Palestinian territories of the West Bank and Gaza Strip and claimed East Jerusalem (an unassigned territory under the original UN partition plan). Since 1967, the West Bank and Gaza have been under continuous and—based on UN Resolution 181—illegal Israeli occupation (W. Khalidi, 1991; Popoviciu & Masarwa, 2021; UNOHCHR, 2022).

Israel has constructed a $1.1 billion iron wall along the entire boundary between Israel and Gaza. The wall is 65 kilometers long, 6 meters high, and several meters deep, locking Gaza in, with the Mediterranean Sea to the west, Egypt to the south, and the wall between Gaza and Israel on its north and east. High-tech surveillance runs along the wall, with checkpoints that Palestinians must clear, making movement extremely limited. The wall is one in a series of fortifications and "security measures" that isolate Palestinians in the occupied territories of Gaza and the West Bank (Popoviciu & Masarwa, 2021).

In a report released in 2022, Michael Lynk, a UN Special Rapporteur, stated, "There is today in the Palestinian territory occupied by Israel since 1967 a deeply discriminatory dual legal and political system that privileges the 700,000 Israeli

Jewish settlers living in the [at the time of writing] 300 illegal Israeli settlements in East Jerusalem and the West Bank" (UNOHCHR, 2022). Two million Palestinians live in Gaza, which is consistently described as an open-air prison, with little access to electricity and water, and no ability to travel beyond the occupied territories of Palestine (Ajour, 2025; Fields, 2020; Mahomed, 2023; Pappé, 2017). The statement continued, "a political regime which so intentionally and clearly prioritizes fundamental political, legal and social rights to one group over another within the same geographic unit on the basis of one's racial-national-ethnic identity satisfies the international legal definition of apartheid."

The political arm of Hamas, an acronym for *Ḥarakat al-Muqāwama al-Islāmiyya* (Islamic Resistance Movement) has ruled the Gaza Strip since 2007. It started as an offshoot of the Muslim Brotherhood political movement in 1987. Hamas served as the first active resistance force to challenge Israeli occupation, and developed in part due to frustration about the secular nationalist Fatah/Palestine Liberation Organization (PLO)'s lack of progress in negotiating a resolution with Israel (Abu-Amr, 1993). On October 7, 2023, ongoing tensions came to a head when the military wing of Hamas attacked and killed over 1,000 Israelis attending a concert and took 251 hostages. Hamas stated that the attack was a response to the ongoing Israeli military blockade (of resources, supplies, electricity, food, and humanitarian aid) of the Gaza Strip, the expansion of illegal Israeli settlements, rising Israeli settler and military violence, and other escalations. Israel responded with a sustained ground and air campaign—backed by U.S. weapons and other aid—that has to date claimed over 50,000 Palestinian lives and countless civilian casualties, and completely decimated Gaza's infrastructure, including schools, universities, and hospitals (UNOCHA, 2025).

A July 2024 opinion issued by the International Court of Justice titled "Legal Consequences arising from the Policies and Practices of Israel in the Occupied Palestinian Territory, including East Jerusalem" stated:

> Israel's continued presence in the Occupied Palestinian Territory was unlawful under international law. The Court stated that Israel was under an obligation to: (i) bring to an end, as rapidly as possible, the unlawful occupation; (ii) cease immediately all new settlement activities and evacuate settlers from the Occupied Palestinian Territory; (iii) make reparation for damages caused to all natural or legal persons concerned in the Occupied Palestinian Territory. The Court found that Israel's internationally wrongful acts gave rise to obligations of other States, the United Nations and international organizations. (International Court of Justice, 2024, pp. 2–3)

Among the many recommendations in the report, the Commission found that all international states have an obligation to (1) not recognize the ongoing occupation, since 1967, as lawful; (2) distinguish between "Israel" and "Occupied Palestinian Territory;" (3) make these distinctions clear in their diplomatic relations, for example by not recognizing Jerusalem as the capital of Israel, placing diplomatic representatives there, or issuing travel documents to settlers living in unlawful settlements; and (4) states must engage in limited relations with Israel in relation to the occupied territories, only to the extent that those relations benefit the occupied population (p. 6).

The United States has disregarded the International Court's opinion and U.S. support of Israeli military operations in Gaza continues.

At the time of this writing, the United States has aided Israel with up to $17.9 billion between October 2023 and October 2024 alone (Bilmes et al., 2024). U.S. weapons manufacturers and the Israeli government have long-standing commercial, military, and security relations, and the U.S. government has cited these ties as one of the reasons why the United States should continue to supply the Israeli military with weapons and equipment (Bhungalia, 2024; Dana, 2024). In turn, the United States is among the global beneficiaries of Israeli private and public military developments such as its 2024 showcasing in real-world contexts of their AI-enhanced drones in Gaza. These advanced systems are marketed as "battle-tested" with Gaza functioning as a "showroom" for Israeli military companies to display their products (Dana, 2024). Cast as defense in a global war on terror, the relentless security and military apparatus directed towards occupied Palestinians in effect criminalizes the decades-long Palestinian struggle for existence and self-determination (Bhungalia, 2024).

The U.S. administration has also expressed a desire to "take over the Gaza strip," clear Palestinians out completely, and turn it into the "Riviera of the Middle East" (Da Silva & Gubash, 2025; Mackenzie, 2025; Mekay, 2025; Rettig & Spanier, 2024). Whether or not this is an actual policy goal, it makes clear who the United States sees as the legitimate stakeholders in Gaza's future: not Palestinians, but the United States, Israel, and the U.S. contractors who stand to make billions from the region, including from the oil discovered off the coast of the Gaza strip in 2000 (Rettig & Spanier, 2024).

> **STOP:** You may find yourself responding to this historical overview as unnecessarily dense. If so, we remind readers that most of us have not received a formal education about this history. Despite this, we often feel ready to "take sides" and express opinions (typically strong ones) about conflicts arising from this history. Our goal is not to give a comprehensive summary of the conflict (which would be impossible in a handful of pages) but rather to hint at its depth and complexity.

So why would we include this relatively brief overview of the very complex history of Israel and Palestine in a chapter on how White supremacy organizes the world? To answer this question, consider concepts such as *colonialism*, who is seen as *civilized* and who is not, what actions are *legitimized* based on those perceptions, and the competition among nations in the Global North for resources in the Global South. How does our understanding of where we are now change when we expand the story of Israel to include the decades prior to the Holocaust? Whose complicity in current conflicts is revealed by knowing even a small part of this history? How might our ideas about who should be at the table deciding what peaceful resolution looks like and how it should be achieved be changed by this expanded contextualization? Think about these questions as we close this chapter with an exploration of how White supremacy orients our perspective on the world.

White supremacy's foundational definitions of who qualifies as *human* versus *nonhuman* were mapped globally into the Western/Global North/First World/Colonizer on the one hand, and Eastern/Global South/Third World/Colonized on the other. This core binary is still with us today and organizes our world, shaping how we think about other people, civilization, competence, emotionality, godliness/godlessness, who is deserving of life and freedom, and who is not. As Sara Ahmed (2007) explains, White supremacy is an *orientation* to the world we perceive. Drawing on philosopher Edmund Husserl's writings about orientations, Ahmed invites her readers to consider perceiving your known world as a room; let's call this room your study. Think about this room that is familiar to you as the starting point from which your world unfolds. As you turn to parts of the room, for example to what is *behind* you, notice that what you saw initially upon entering that room was dependent on which way you were facing to begin with—after all, what is *behind* is only so because of how you are oriented within the room, and what you see in the first place depends on how you entered that room (or were directed to enter the room by those who constructed it). While upon entry you are aware of the general room in front of you, your attention may be focused more specifically, for example, on the desk you are headed for to do your writing. Moving towards the desk to do the task of writing is as much about your innate intention to write, as it is about how this room (this "world") is available to you as a space with certain things which are in particular places, within reach or out of reach.

Extending the metaphor to the notion of Whiteness, Ahmed explains how Whiteness can be understood not as just the "race" (or "body") that enters that room, but rather as the general orientation of the room that directs us to face and notice some objects, while turning away from others. In this metaphor of a "body within a room," where the room in question is Whiteness, bodies enter into that room (a world) that is oriented by Whiteness. This includes the history of colonialism and imperialism that has shaped the modern world, our "room," in such a way as to make some objects and practices easy, within view, and within reach for some bodies entering that space. How we enter and move through that space, what we focus on in that space, what our habits are in there, are all predetermined by history. We each inherit history within our bodies, and these inheritances determine what is within reach to us. Ahmed puts it this way:

Such an inheritance can be re-thought in terms of orientations: *we inherit the reachability of some objects*, those that are "given" to us, or at least made available to us, within the "what" that is around. I am not suggesting here that "whiteness" is one such "reachable object," but that whiteness is an orientation that puts certain things within reach. By objects, we would include not just physical objects, but also styles, capacities, aspirations, techniques, habits. Race becomes, in this model, a question of what is within reach, what is available to perceive and to do "things" with. The world too is inherited as a dwelling. Whiteness might be what is "here," as a point from which the world unfolds, which is also the point of inheritance. (p. 154)

In other words, Whiteness shapes what we notice and do not notice, what is within reach and beyond one's reach, what we can know and not know, and how our habits and capacities are oriented.

DISCUSSION QUESTIONS

1. What do the authors mean when they use the term *White supremacy*? How does White supremacy manifest in institutions? Now think intersectionally: How is Whiteness related to patriarchy? Provide examples from this and previous chapters.
2. What is the relationship between Whiteness and humanity? How are ideas about whose humanity is more valuable (or more visible) conveyed?
3. What aspects of the history of colonialism were new to you?
4. What is meant by the terms "the Global North" and "the Global South"? What associations do you have about the differences between these two?
5. Apply Ahmed's deconstruction of the notion of "coming to a table for a purpose" to examine how Whiteness shapes your assumptions about conflict mediation, what we imagine the conditions for such meditation would be, and who would be included. Think through a contemporary conflict or issue that is relevant to you or where you live. Identify 3–5 elements of that conflict/issue that seem objective and taken-for-granted but are informed by Whiteness. Research information in order to fill in a wider timeline and missing perspectives.

EXTENSION ACTIVITIES

1. Tracing colonialism's relationship to global White supremacy and capitalism: Solo or in small group, identify a country of the Global South and prepare a presentation on the history of that nation in relation to (a) colonialism, (b) capitalism, and (c) consumerism. Suggested nations to study include: Vietnam, the Philippines, Ecuador, Brazil, Democratic

Republic of the Congo, Sierra Leone, South Africa, Indonesia. Note if the territory has been colonized. What are the major industries and who owns them? What are the major products of those industries, where are they grown, who owns them, what is the impact of those industries on the local environment, what do the workers do and what are they paid, what are the corporation's profit margins, how does the product get to Western markets, and who are the main consumers?

Nations considered the Global South by the United Nations can be found in their 2024 report, *Forging a Global South: United Nations Day for South–South Cooperation*, available here: https://www.undp.org/sites/g/files/zskgke326/files/migration/cn/UNDP-CH-PR-Publications-UNDay-for-South-South-Cooperation.pdf

2. Watch one of the following films: *Where the Olive Trees Weep* (Benazzo & Benazzo, 2024); *No Other Land* (Abraham, Adra, Ballal, & Szor, 2024); *Israelism* (Chalfen, Saah, & Axelman, 2023).

    Explain the connections between the current situation of the conflict and the history of global White supremacy and colonization. Consider creating a historical timeline, beginning before the establishment of the Israeli state. In your analysis, include how discourses about the Global North and Global South manifest in our understanding and awareness of this history. What is the relationship between the obscuring of this history (strategies of education versus propaganda) and the ability to recognize, repair, and remedy the current conflict?

3. Collect as many different maps of the world as you can find (past and present). Compare them and offer an analysis of how they orient the viewer using Sara Ahmed's concept of the world as a room.

PATTERNS TO PRACTICE SEEING

1. Learn the history of the place names in your local community. Which have colonial roots and which have Indigenous roots? What are the most common reasons given for why place names have been changed? Practice speaking back to these arguments.
2. How is Whiteness exported globally in various domains? Consider industries such as technology, entertainment, education, beauty, sports, and health.

CHAPTER 10

Understanding Intersectionality Through Classism

"Nowadays, it's White men who are the victims."

This chapter examines class oppression. We explain current economic relations of power, address concepts such as capitalism, democratic socialism, oligarchy, kleptocracy, wealth, and income, as well as review common class terms. The chapter also returns to the concept of intersectionality as an important theoretical development for understanding the multidimensional nature of oppression, with a focus on class oppression. We identify elements of class privilege, name common misconceptions about class mobility, and speak back to dominant classist narratives.

> **Vocabulary to practice using:** classism; oligarchy; capitalism; social capital; net worth; intersectional/ality; meritocracy

MR. RICH WHITE AND MR. POOR WHITE STRIKE A BARGAIN[1]

Once upon a time there was Mr. Rich White, whose forefathers had become rich by exploiting the land and labor of others. Mr. Rich White realized that in order to stay rich, he had to maintain control over his workers. But how? He looked around and his eyes fell upon the Black man. He snapped his fingers, "I've got it!" he whispered. He called Mr. Poor White to his office and said, "I've been thinking a lot about you and me and how hard it is for us to keep our factory competitive and growing so we can make enough money. To keep the business going the way I want it to go, making big profits off of little capital so I can keep you on the job, I have to keep my wages low, you can see that. It's good for me and essential for you too, for any job is better than no job at all. And whatever is causing the troubles with our economy isn't my fault or your fault, but the

---

1. This parable is adapted from Lillian Smith's "Mr Rich White and Mr Poor White Strike a Bargain" in her book *Killers of the Dream* (1949).

fault of those coming here and taking your jobs. The thing we can't forget is that whatever our differences, the color of our skin makes us kin. We are made in God's image and He intends us to lead. We are the chosen and we can't let others, like the Black man, push us out of our place. And when I say 'Black man' I'm not discriminating because I also mean the Latino man, whose job is to pick our crops, and the Asian man, who builds our railroads, and the Indigenous man, whose land we will take and use properly (*he just wastes the land, letting it sit there*). As for the woman, everybody already knows that the Bible ordained her place as secondary to ours, that's just nature. Men must always rule over and take care of the women.

"The way I see it, there are two jobs that need doing. Somebody has got to tend to making the money, to jobs, credit, prices, hours, the politicians, and so on (*and you are too low class to do that or else you'd be rich like I am*), and somebody has got to tend to the Black man—keep him in his place. So how about I boss the money and you boss the Black man? Don't worry about what I do, but here's what you do: Anything to show you are the boss you can do (*as long as you don't touch my business*). You can decide where he will live, what schools he will go to and what books his children will read. If science scares you, remember that you don't have to accept it—this is God's country and a free one at that. If you get restless when you don't have a job or your children are sick, just remember your lot is a damn sight better than the Black man's. If you need to let off some steam and rough some up now and then, go right ahead. I will make sure the law overlooks it (*but don't expect to see me in the crowd*).

"Now, if some other Mr. Poor Whites are fool enough to forget that they are White men, I'm willing to put up plenty of money to keep the politicians talking, and I don't mind supporting a demagogue or two. Of course I'll ensure the media keeps everyone distracted. We'll give you the pick of whatever jobs there are and if things get too tight you can take over his jobs too, 'cause remember, any job is better than no job at all. If you keep your end of the bargain, I will make sure that you're always better off, even if only slightly, than the Black man. There is only so much to go around and if they get their share, it will come from yours. The liberals won't let us build the pipelines, work the mines, fell the forests, or use the rivers for our factory waste, and they stall our progress with regulations and racial quotas—all of which keep you from working. Since I am the only one who understands your dilemma and can give you the work you need to earn a living, vote for my politicians."

And Mr. Rich White and Mr. Poor White thought they'd made a good bargain. Of course Mr. Poor White didn't really have much choice, but no matter how hard things got for him, at least he would always be better off than the Black man. It was hard at first for Mr. Poor White's labor to keep being exploited by Mr. Rich White, but gettin' to be the boss of someone else started to feel good and helped him hold up his end. Because the Black man reminded Mr. Poor White about what he'd done, he hated and feared him. And that hatred and fear helped Mr. Poor White continue with the bargain. It never occurred to Mr. Poor

White that the Black man could help him raise his wages and make the business work fairly for both of them.

As time passed, Mr. and Ms. Middle-Class White also had a role in the bargain. They became the lawyers, social workers, teachers, professors, doctors, judges, managers, advertisers, journalists, and celebrities—the mediators of the agreement. They settled disputes, administered policies, taught the children, and tended to the social services Mr. Poor White and the Black man would need, all while keeping everyone entertained. But sometimes Mr. and Ms. Middle-Class White felt bad about their role in the bargain. "This can't go on," they'd say. They were worried about freedom and democracy, which many of them still believed in. They called their worry "multiculturalism" or "diversity" or "the achievement gap" or "social justice." They wore T-shirts and held signs to show their worries. But in truth they were more worried about getting the best for their children, securing their property values, and maintaining their position between Mr. Rich White and Mr. Poor White. They feared what integration would mean for that position. And it was certainly better to be Mr. and Ms. Middle-Class White than Mr. Poor White or the Black man. In the end, despite their worries, they always decided that separation was best. After all, wasn't it just human nature to prefer to live near your own? separation enabled them not to see the methods used to keep the Black man away from their neighborhoods and their jobs, and not to feel as badly about the bargain. But they knew not to say aloud what they didn't want to see or feel. Mr. Rich White knew what was in their hearts, and smiled.

WHAT IS CLASS?

As with all forms of social division, social class is a human construct. The division of labor that characterizes class did not emerge until the Neolithic era, approximately 8,000–10,000 years ago (Little, 2016; Rueschemeyer, 1986). This period of human history was marked by agricultural advancement and land settlements by human population, prior to which many human communities are believed to have been nomadic hunter–gatherers. This era is sometimes described as the *agricultural revolution*, and resulted not only in settlements of land, but in the organized, systematic production of crops that could be harvested, shared, traded, and sold to others. Where once resources might have been scarce or difficult to gather, they were now more plentiful, and the outcome of increasingly managed processes.

This era of collective agricultural output created the initial divisions of labor that form the basis of class division today: those who own the land (called the *bourgeoisie*) and those who own their labor (the *proletariat*). Class division today might arguably be drawn back to these same binary groups: those who own the resources of a society and create the rules of exchange and ownership, and those who trade their bodies (their minds and hands) to work, and whose opportunity for work depends on the ongoing availability of resources, which the bourgeoisie control.

> **STOP:** Remember, oppression is less about numbers and more about historical, ideological, cultural, and institutional control. The wealthiest people are a numerical minority yet wield an extreme amount of control over social institutions.

An example of owner control is the fight for minimum wage. When workers organize to raise the minimum wage, they are told by the owners that the prices of goods must then be increased, hours cut, or people laid off. What is rarely questioned is why the owners cannot tolerate making slightly less profit, or even accept a stable profit margin, but must make ever more and more. For example, according to the American Federation of Labor and Congress of Industrial Organizations, in 2023 prices that S&P 500 companies pay for goods fell by 3%, consumer prices rose 3%, while corporate profits and CEO pay increased by 6%—and worker pay remained unchanged. The average CEO was paid 268 times what the median worker in their corporation earned (AFL-CIO, 2024a). In 2022, roughly one-third of all workers earned less than $15/hour. For workers of Color, *half* made less than $15/hour. Meanwhile, the federal minimum wage in the United States has remained at $7.25 ($2.13 for employees who receive tips) since 2009, which even with a full-time (40-hour) work week would not allow a worker to afford a two-bedroom apartment in any state in the country (AFL-CIO, 2024b; USAGov, n.d.). The pay ratio between the CEO and the median worker at their company for some of the most familiar corporations for the 2023 fiscal year was:

Abercrombie & Fitch	6,076:1 (CEO pay $15,035,354; median worker pay $2,475)
Mattel Inc.	3,620:1 (CEO pay $29,948,385; median worker pay $5,234)
McDonalds Corp	1,212:1 (CEO pay $19,155,001; median worker pay $15,802)
Starbucks Corp	1,028:1 (CEO pay $14,604,531; median worker pay $14,209)
Nike Inc.	975:1 (CEO pay $23,789,885; median worker pay $33,646)
Lululemon Athletica	845:1 (CEO pay $16,494,777; median worker pay $19,518)
Apple Inc.	672:1 (CEO pay $63,209,845; median worker pay $94,118) (AFL-CIO, 2024b)

According to a report published by the Canadian Centre for Policy Alternatives, in Canada the 100 highest paid CEOs were paid 210 times more (210:1) than the average worker. This gap is increasing. In 1998 it was 104:1, and in 2009 it

Figure 10.1. The Boss (Cartoon by the United Electrical, Radio, & Machine workers of America union artist Fred Wright's collection *So Long, Partner!* [1975])

Source: https://soc331.files.wordpress.com/2012/02/420748_183792161725872_129370207168068_259071_2121981741_n1.jpg

was 150:1. The top 100 CEOs were 97% men. The report estimates that while the average minimum wage for Canadian workers is $15 an hour, the wage for Canada's highest paid CEOs was $3,255 an hour (MacDonald, 2025). When workers ask for a living wage and owners threaten to take their jobs away or lament how raising wages will "hurt the economy," the effect is to shift our focus away from the owners and back onto the workers, who are being blamed for income inequality, as Figure 10.1, by American union activist and and cartoonist Fred Wright, satirizes.

When owners threaten to take away workers' livelihoods, workers tend to back off, for as Mr. Rich White warns, *any job is better than no job at all*. Sometimes owners pacify workers by insisting on "trickle-down economics," which is the claim that cutting taxes and increasing benefits for the richest will improve the standard of living for everyone else. The basic idea is that the more money those at the very top make, the more money will trickle down to the bottom. They claim that in order to ensure that owners make more money, they need to be less regulated and less taxed than workers are, and this will result in more jobs being created, higher wages for the average worker, and an overall upturn in the economy. However, data from the past 50 years strongly refutes the argument that cutting taxes for the richest will improve the economic standing of the lower and middle classes (Hope & Limberg, 2022; United for a Fair Economy, 2020).

Until the mid-1990s, income polarization in Canada and the United States remained relatively stable (Hulchanski & Murdie, 2013). Since then, the gap between the richest and poorest has widened immensely. In other words, the rich got richer, the poor got poorer. Here are some examples:

- Since 2015, the richest 1% has owned more wealth than the rest of the planet. The richest 1% have amassed $42 trillion in new wealth over the past decade, nearly 34 times more than the entire bottom 50 percent of the world's population (OXFAM, 2024).
- In Bloomberg's daily ranking of the world's 500 richest people, as of May 2025, the world's wealthiest three people (Elon Musk, Jeff Bezos, and Mark Zuckerberg), all men and all White American citizens, have total net worths of $344 billion, $215 billion, and $210 billion U.S. dollars, respectively (Bloomberg, n.d.). By comparison, the 2024 GDP of Portugal was $308 billion, Sri Lanka was $99 billion, and Iceland was $33 billion (World Bank, n.d.).
- The world's 10 richest people are all White men. The first woman to appear in the list at #14 is Alice Walton. Of the top 50 billionaires in the world, there are no women of Color (Bloomberg, n.d.).
- In some U.S. states, more than 26% (1 in 4) of children live in poverty, with the U.S. average being 16.3% (Benson, 2023; UNICEF, 2023).
- In Canada in 2024, the top 20% held 67.6% of Canada's total net worth, averaging $3.4 million per household; the wealth gap between the top 20% and the bottom 40% was 64.8% (Statistics Canada, 2024).

- In spite of the claim of "trickle-down economics"—the theory that the more wealth the top makes the more will flow down to the bottom—billionaire wealth surged by $2 trillion in 2024, 3 times faster than the year before, while the number of people living in poverty has barely changed since 1990 (OXFAM, 2025a).
- In 2023, the financial system extracted $30 million an hour from the Global South to the richest 1% in the Global North (OXFAM, 2025a).
- Global North countries control 69% of global wealth and 77% of billionaire wealth despite making up just 21% of the global population (OXFAM, 2025b).

> **Gross Domestic Product** is typically used as an indicator of a nation's economy and measures the value of all goods and services in a given period.

When we think about what class positions we hold, we might initially focus solely on *economics*—that is, being rich or being poor; in other words, how much money each of us has or earns. This is an important element for understanding social class, and income distribution is among the most available statistics collected. However, income is not the only element that forms our class positions. Class is also (and perhaps primarily) about political power: the ability to influence policy, control capital, and shape institutional structures. Thus, thinking about class requires that we consider together issues of *income* and issues of *power*.

As of April 2025, the world's three richest people were:

Richest people in the world	Accumulated wealth 2016	Accumulated wealth 2025
Elon Musk ($335B)	$10,700,000,000	$344,000,000,000
Chief executive of carmaker Tesla and rocket manufacturer SpaceX; owner of AI and social media company xAI		
Jeff Bezos ($210B)	$45,200,000,000	$215,000,000,000
Founder of online retailer Amazon; owner of Whole Foods grocery; cloud computing and streaming		
Mark Zuckerberg ($194B) Cofounder of Meta Platforms (Facebook, Instagram, WhatsApp).	$44,600,000,000	$210,000,000,000

It is worth noting that while we may see history as an arc of progress towards greater and greater human equality, more wealth is now concentrated into fewer hands than at any time in human history (Alfani, 2025; Sherman et al., 2024). Hold the chart above in mind as we consider the federal minimum wage in the United States. The federal poverty rate (the amount of money the average family of 4 needs to pay for basics of shelter, food, clothing) is $32,150 (Office of the Assistant Secretary for Planning and Evaluation, 2025). The federal minimum wage is currently set at $7.25 per hour. That rate has not changed since 2009—16 years at the time of this writing. States can set their own rates, but if they do not have a set rate they are required to follow the federal minimum. Working full time at $7.25 per hour is $15,080 annually (gross earnings are *before* taxes and other deductions such as Social Security, medical and dental insurance, and retirement). Twenty-one states follow the federal rate. The remaining states set their own rates, the highest being $17.50 in Washington, D.C., followed by $16.66 in Washington state. The minimum wages in the five most populated states are: California $16.50; Texas $7.25; New York $16.00; Florida $13.00; Pennsylvania $7.25 (U.S. Department of Labor, 2025). While someone working full time at minimum wage in Washington, D.C., or Washington state would earn a gross salary of $36,400 or $34,653, respectively (and thus would be above the poverty level), the majority of minimum wage workers in the United States fall below the poverty level. Efforts have been made to raise the federal rate but they have consistently been defeated in the Senate.

✓ **PERSPECTIVE CHECK:** There are many negative stereotypes about families who rely on social safety nets such as food stamps, and misinformation about how these programs work. We remind readers that (1) Most people using these supports have paid into them through their state and federal income tax contributions; all people in a democratic society are expected to contribute to these programs. (2) You can work full time at the U.S. federal minimum wage and still not rise above the poverty threshold set by the federal government and need support (Center for Poverty & Inequality Research, [2018]). (3) The segment of the population who are most likely to avoid paying into social safety nets are wealth holders who take advantage of loopholes (OXFAM, 2025b). These are the same people who pay their employees at hourly rates that keep them below the poverty level and who fight raising the federal minimum wage and unionization, which would provide a framework for collective action. This begs the question: Who is actually a "welfare cheat"? (4) Federal safety nets such as SNAP (Supplemental Nutrition Assistance Program, aka "food stamps") are difficult to qualify for and have time limits and conditions for access.

In a report released prior to the 2024 G20 Finance Ministers and Central Bank Governors meeting, OXFAM International's Head of Inequality Policy, Max Lawson, said, "Inequality has reached obscene levels, and until now governments have failed to protect people and the planet from its catastrophic effects. The richest one percent of humanity continues to fill their pockets while the rest are left to scrap for crumbs" (OXFAM, 2024). While the richest 1% have increased their wealth by $42 trillion in the past decade, globally the world's wealthiest have been paying a tax rate of less than 0.5% on that wealth (OXFAM, 2024).

We might ask how a system described as democratic allows such enormous gaps in wealth and income to exist. One familiar explanation is meritocracy—billionaires are wealthy because they have earned their wealth through hard work. Yet people working minimum wage jobs are also working hard, and most often at grueling and physically demanding jobs. Still, minimum wage workers pay tax rates that are as much as double that of billionaires. Further, in 2023, 60% of the wealth of new billionaires was inherited, not earned (Roeloffs, 2023). Clearly the difference in wealth cannot be attributed to a meritocratic system alone.

To understand the wealth gap we must understand other concepts such as *oligarchy,* which means rule by a small elite. It describes a political system where a small group of the richest people in society (called *oligarchs*) protect and expand their material wealth by influencing politics (Ramos, 2015). While it may be more visible today than ever before, rule by the wealthy is not new. Wealth has always been infused into the political process. In premodern times oligarchs engaged in wealth defense tactics such as violence (Ramos, 2015). In contemporary times, oligarchs defend their wealth within the bureaucracy of systems. They do so primarily in two ways: property defense (defending their claims to property) and income defense (avoiding taxation) (Ramos, 2015). While readers may associate the concept of an oligarchy with Russia, where open markets following the dissolution of the Soviet Union in 1991 allowed government officials and crime bosses to acquire state assets cheaply (Ramos, 2015), the United States is not immune to wealth influence in governance. In the mid-19th century, entrepreneurs who came to be known as "robber barons" built transportation, infrastructure, and industrial empires in the United States. Many are familiar with their names, such as J. P. Morgan, Carnegie, Vanderbilt, and Rockefeller, the great industrialists, philanthropists, and builders of American economic wealth. But history has revealed that these men had a great deal in common with the oligarchs of Russia (Aslund, 2005).

In more recent times the U.S. Supreme Court allowed unrestricted political donations in the 2010 *Citizens United* ruling. The Court's arguments drew on parallels from the 1857 *Dred Scott* decision that justified slavery by defining a class of people as property (Leach, 2013). In the *Citizens United* case, the Court defined a class of property as people. It determined that where a corporation is an individual, its "speech" (expressed as money) cannot be restricted—in essence designating corporate spending on elections as free speech (Leach, 2013; Weiner & Lau, 2025). After this ruling, political action committees (PACs) and super PACs were created, which enabled the wealthy to influence the political process by giving unlimited donations while remaining anonymous. In the 2024 election, billionaire-backed super PACs helped the winning candidate close a fundraising gap, and undisclosed donations (or "dark money" contributions) topped $1 billion dollars (Weiner & Lau, 2019).

Other recent examples of oligarchy rule in the United States include: exempting the products of big-oil donors from tariffs; slashing the division of the Internal Revenue Service that audits high-earning individuals and corporations; offering businesspeople a one-on-one meeting with the president at his private residence for $5 million or a group dinner for $1 million; and the richest man in the world—an unelected private citizen—handed full access to federal institutions to change policies and regulations (with no oversight) under the opaque mandate to "cut government spending" (D. Lawson, 2025). As of December 2024, 13 billionaires were tapped for top roles in the U.S. administration—making it the richest administration in U.S. history—and the president himself is a billionaire (Charalambous et al., 2024). An invitation-only Washington, D.C., club opened in April 2025, which costs more than half a million dollars to join and is designed to allow top business executives to talk privately with presidential advisors and cabinet members (Burns, 2025). The current administration is dropping federal investigations and lawsuits against 89 corporations, many of whose leaders donated to the president's inaugural fund (Public Citizen, 2025). In April 2025 the president announced that the top holders of his cryptocurrency token would be invited to a dinner with him at his private club and be offered a VIP White House tour. His meme coin jumped more than 50% upon this news, netting the president and his allies nearly $900,000 in trading fees (Almeida, 2025). To date, trading activity has generated approximately $324.5 million in trading fees for his family members. While this has been widely criticized as corruption (Chayka, 2025; Frum, 2025), there have been no consequences. A telling visual image of oligarchy is that of the three richest men in the world sitting in the front row at the presidential inauguration and regularly commanding a private audience with the president.

Kleptocracy comes from a Greek word meaning "thief" and refers to a government of corrupt leaders who expropriate the wealth of the land and people they govern, typically by embezzlement or misappropriation of government funding. It describes a state that is "controlled and run for the benefit of an individual, or a small group, who use their power to transfer a large fraction of society's resources to themselves" (Acemoglu et al., 2004, p. 162; Heathershaw et al., 2023). Kleptocracies endure today via the networks of globalization that allow authoritarian regimes and entrenched corruption within states, aided by "enablers" (Heathershaw et al., 2023). These enablers include intermediaries in banking, law, real estate, creditors, multinational corporations, and offshore tax havens that facilitate and maintain corruption. The integration of authoritarian politicians and business elites within global economic networks allows private wealth accumulation and secures corrupt regimes (Heathershaw et al., 2023). Colonial powers also relied on these networks to uphold exploitation of labor and resources in colonized territories. The post–World War II rebuilding of financial institutions, along with the opening of markets after the dissolution of the Soviet Union in the 1990s, solidified these relationships. Kleptocracies are not linked exclusively to states defined as "authoritarian" as compared to those that are "democratic." Kleptocratic governance that is influenced by corporations and the privately wealthy has been a feature of both types of nation-state.

Kleptocrats use resources they have stolen from their countries and the institutions they have subverted to maintain their power. As Alexander Cooley, John Heathershaw, and J. C. Sharman explain (2018), "state institutions are set up to allow elites and their families to systematically loot, while protecting these elites politically" (p. 39). Much of this looting happens in the light of day, as unlike terrorists and drug cartels, kleptocrats are out in the open, cultivating extensive global networks to camouflage their theft and sanitize their public image as savvy business leaders and philanthropists who attend charity balls and cultural galas (A. Cooley et al., 2018).

Examples of kleptocrats who have faced scrutiny include "Equatorial Guinea's vice-president standing trial in France for corruption, the former president of Uzbekistan's daughter facing investigations for money laundering in a half-dozen countries, or the Malaysian prime minister under suspicion in connection with the diversion of more than US $4.5 billion from his country's sovereign wealth fund into personal bank accounts around the world" (A. Cooley et al., 2018, p. 39). More often there is no public explanation or apology for the theft, nor any legal charges or punishment for the offenders, in part because the workings of kleptocracy are rationalized as "standard business practice" from which all of society will benefit.

In the United States, the Department of Government Efficiency (DOGE) has been a cogent example of this rationalization (Halperin, 2025). The richest man in the world, despite facing some resistance from citizens, is $100 billion richer now, just 5 months after he was granted access to and unelected authority over government systems by the administration. This enhanced wealth was gained by his defunding of agencies that regulate and provide public oversight over his many businesses and gaining government contracts his companies did not have to compete for. He also had access to the public diplomatic infrastructure (using relationships which have been established over generations) to pressure smaller foreign countries to accept licensing deals and other arrangements that benefit his companies (Hyatt, 2025; Warren, 2025). We might consider the Left versus Right divisions we see a distraction to keep us from seeing what is actually the *top* versus the *bottom*.

Another cogent example of modern-day kleptocracy in the United States is the president's slate of pardons for white-collar criminals. When someone is convicted of a financial crime such as fraud or embezzlement, the law requires them to pay back the money they stole from the public; this is called restitution. When a crime is pardoned, the restitution owed is also forgiven. The pardons that were granted between January and May 2025 alone have erased $1.3 billion in debts owed by wealthy Americans to victims and taxpayers (U.S. House Committee on the Judiciary, 2025). The restitution owed by one such person who was pardoned— Trevor Milton—had not yet been determined by a judge, but federal prosecutors estimated he owed more than $680 million to defrauded shareholders. Milton and his wife contributed more than $1.8 million to the president's reelection campaign before the pardon was granted (Mangan, 2025).

Oligarchies and kleptocracies are somewhat interchangeable, as the rule of an elite few goes hand-in-hand with public theft, and many examples fall in both categories (Nonini, 2005; Shelley, 2024). Worldwide examples of prominent kleptocrats include president of the Philippines Ferdinand Marcos (1965–1986), President Suharto of Indonesia (1967–1998), Haitian president Jean-Claude Duvalier (1971–1986), Zairean president Mobutu Sese Seko (1965–1997), Yugoslav president Slobodan Milošević (1989–2000), Peruvian president Alberto Fujimori (1990–2000), and former Ukrainian prime minister Pavlo Lazarenko (1996–1997). These men grossly enriched themselves personally and moved billions of dollars from their nations to their own private bank accounts (A. Cooley et al., 2018; Shin & Judah, 2023). The wealth stolen from their people is staggering in its magnitude: Marcos is estimated to have stashed away $5–10 billion, Suharto $15–35 billion, Mobutu Sese Seko $5 billion, Milošević $1 billion, Alberto Fujimori $600 million, and Lazarenko $114–250 million (Shin & Judah, 2023).

In 2016, the leak of information about the holdings of the Panamanian law firm called Mossack Fonseca (an incident known as the "Panama Papers") revealed how complex the vast networks of untraceable shell companies and their nested structures are with Western democracies. As scholars studying kleptocracies and tax havens have reported, the presumption that the most problematic settings for such systems are small exotic tax shelters is unwarranted. While the British Virgin Islands and Cayman Islands are among the busiest hosts of shell companies, the top 10 list includes the U.S. states of Delaware and Wyoming. Their research has shown that the United States and United Kingdom are rife with some of the most secretive shell company providers in the world (Aliprandi et al., 2023; Cockfield, 2021; A. Cooley et al., 2018; Findley et al., 2014).

> 📖 A **shell company** is an entity that exists only on paper and whose purpose is to hide the identity of its owner. While shell companies are legal, they are most often used for illegal purposes (Jancsics, 2018). Their activities are untraceable and because they are outside of the tax jurisdiction of the country the money comes from, allow kleptocrats to circumvent taxes and pool their illegally obtained wealth. We might think of a shell company as a "fake" company with an anonymous or secret owner. In the United States, shell companies are often registered with the sole purpose of receiving untraceable donations for political campaigns; this is another way that shell companies facilitate the rule by elite.

Returning to the understanding that power is more than wealth accumulation, consider that the ruler of a nation-state might draw a relatively modest income, but have an incredible degree of power to influence, create, and repeal policy. The prime minister of Canada's salary was $209,800 (Canadian dollars) in

2025 (Parliament of Canada, 2025). While the U.S. president's salary has remained at $400,000 since 2001, the position does include a generous pension of approximately $250,000 annually as well as personnel, equipment, office space, and other benefits upon leaving office (Brady, 2024; National Taxpayers Union Foundation, n.d.). While these are salaries and benefits that most of us will never see, there are, still, people earning much higher incomes than this. Yet these positions have access to a great deal of political power that lies in their ability to influence social and institutional policy. Very few among us will ever have access to this kind of political power.

It may be hard to envision any alternative to democracy under capitalism—or democratic capitalism—because it is the only form we are taught in school to value. If fascism, communism, and socialism are all bad, then democracy is the only good option that remains. But of course there are alternatives. Some of the politicians whose names we know in Canada and the United States represent perspectives from one of these less visible options: *democratic socialism*. Democratic socialism combines democratic principles with social welfare, aiming for a society where the economy is democratically controlled and managed for the public good and the benefit of all, rather than for private profit (Adler, 2019; A. Jackson, 2021; Sanders, 2024). Democratic socialists advocate for workers having a say in how their workplaces are run and how profits are distributed. They believe that key industries and utilities that people depend on should be owned and controlled by the public, not private for-profit companies. While advocating for a socialist society in the long term, they also fight for reforms within the existing capitalist system to unify and empower workers, fight for global justice and a more equitable world, and reduce corporate power. Examples of their goals in practice are: universal healthcare funded by the government, free public college, investing in communities rather than relying on police, and addressing climate change. Because there is no formal party structure, democratic socialists run for public office as members of the Democratic Party, Green Party, Working Families Party, or New Democratic Party of Canada, or as independents. Examples of public figures who are democratic socialists in the United States include Alexandria Ocasio-Cortez, Rashida Tlaib, Jamaal Bowman, Cori Bush, Bernie Sanders, and Zohran Mamdani. In Canada they include Niki Ashton, Henry Giroux, Joel Davison Harden, and Naomi Klein.

COMMON CLASS TERMS

Classism is the systematic oppression of poor and working people by those who control necessary resources (jobs, wages, education, housing, food, services, medicine, cultural definitions, and so on). Classism is held in place by institutional systems that reproduce hierarchies among people according to economic status, "breeding," job, and level of education. Discourses of classism present upper-class people as naturally smarter and more articulate than lower-class people. The standards of upper-class people define what's normal, acceptable, and intelligent. Their ideas, values, and culture form the canon of what is considered "high-class" culture (think opera, golf, literature), as compared to "low-class" or "popular" culture (think WWE, county fairs, reality television).

> 📖 **Class:** The system of relative social rank as measured in terms of income, wealth, status, and/or power.

> 📖 **Classism:** The institutional, cultural, and individual set of practices that assign differential value to people and access to resources according to their socioeconomic status (SES). Classism ensures inequality between classes.

While there are no universal rules about what makes someone poor versus working class versus middle class and so on, there are some common trends in the usage of class terminology that are important to understand. For example, in political discourse we frequently hear politicians talking about protecting the *middle class*, and activists referring to the *1%* or the *99%* and wanting to help *the poor*. But what do these terms mean?

As discussed above, *classism* captures the overall dominance of the owning class over all other classes. As with all forms of oppression, classism exists on binary terms (in this case, rich versus poor). Yet actual measures of class are often tied to measures of income distribution, which is a spectrum (Das et al., 2024; DeNavas-Walt & Proctor, 2015; Yassin et al., 2024). These measures of income distribution are complex but overall refer to average family incomes in a given geographical context, as well as the width of the gap between those at the very top and bottom of the range.

While these official class measures are typically organized around income distribution and shape what constitutes the middle class (often also called *average income* families), class is a more complicated landscape than the average, the highest, and the lowest on the spectrum. Depending on the framework being used, there are anywhere from two, to twelve, to dozens of class groupings. At the same time, dominant culture provides only a handful of class categories to fit ourselves into. The categories made available to us through language are sometimes referred to as *class vernacular* (Metzgar, 2010).

In Canada and the United States there are typically four broad class categories in our class vernacular: the *owning* class (the rich), the *middle* class (the middle), the *working* class, and the *poor* or *working poor*. What this class vernacular reveals is that:

- Class positions are relational. The boundaries between these categories can shift; a family designated as working class in the 1950s might be designated as working poor in the 2000s.
- Class positions exist across a spectrum. Much like gender existing as a spectrum (rather than a binary with two sides), some scholarship defines class as a spectrum. This allows us to include additional groups in order to acknowledge different lived experiences.

For our purposes, we will focus on the following four class groups. These capture the broad groups in Canada and the United States that are recognizable and in line with income distribution information and social signifiers. They are:

The owning class: Those who inherit wealth and who are not dependent on work for income. They can live off of the interest of their holdings. The owning class is sometimes referred to as the ruling class. Although the ruling class might have a lot of wealth and not much actual income, they have a great deal of political power and ability to influence government.

The middle class: Those who must use their bodies (hands and minds) to work for income; who have some advanced education beyond high school. Sometimes these are described as white-collar workers, indicating office work (primarily mind work). Generally middle-class people are able to own their homes and expect their children will go to college.

The working class: Those who must use their bodies (hands and minds) to work for income; who typically have high school education and possibly some vocational education. Sometimes these are described as blue-collar or pink-collar workers, indicating physical jobs (primarily body work) such as policing, trade labor (plumbing, carpentry), secretarial, and food services. They may only be able to rent rather than purchase a home and are often unable to help their children go to college.

The poor: Those who must rely on assistance (such as welfare or other government benefits); possibly chronic or intermittent jobless/unhoused. They may also be minimum-wage workers who fall under the federal poverty line (sometimes called the *working poor*). They seldom have any savings or safety net. Some scholars (e.g., Metzgar, 2010; Zweig, 2000) argue that the poor are not a class per se, but a *condition*. The condition of poverty is more likely to impact the working class than the middle or owning classes because the working class have less of a safety net.

These are the main recognizable groupings in the United States and Canada, and most of us would consider them a natural outcome of a merit-based democracy. But democracy is in principle antithetical to class divisions such as these. In other words, if we had a truly democratic system we would not see these kinds of divisions. Democracy means rule by the people, with each person equal in the eyes of the law and with a guarantee of civil liberty and human rights. If democracy is "rule by the people" and more specifically a form of governance that depends on—as sociologist Walter Parker notes—citizens having "knowledge about the ideals of democratic living, the ability to discern just from unjust laws and actions, the commitment to fight civic inequality, and the ability and commitment to deliberate public policy in cooperation with disagreeable others" (Parker, 2008, p. 68), then can we claim to live in a true democracy?

Capitalism, in contrast to democracy, cannot function without inherent inequality built into its system. In other words, in order to maximize profits, the owning class must continuously exploit the labor of workers (make them work more for less, and sell the outcome of their labor for more than they pay for it), and workers must in turn compete with one another for fewer and fewer resources and benefits (Anyon, 2011). Within a capitalist system, the worker who works for the least wages, benefits, and conditions is the most desirable. If owners can get 5 people to do the work that 10 people were doing last year, then company profits increase (along with workers' pressures and workloads). Thus, under capitalism, the interests of owners to maximize profits are in tension with the interests of workers to have fair wages, benefits, and a share of the product of their labor, as Figure 10.2 satirizes.

> **Wealth vs. income:** *Wealth* refers to the value of one's assets (e.g., land or stocks) that can increase in value over time. *Income* refers to the specific amount of money earned over a period of time (e.g., salary). This income can be added to assets, or used for needs (e.g., housing and transportation).

Capitalism's need to make ever more owner/shareholder profit and deny workers' rights has played a fundamental role in the current economic conditions in the United States and Canada (and elsewhere in the world). Increasing profits have driven the export of jobs and manufacturing to poorer countries where sweatshop workers can be paid pennies per day and do not have rights (including the right to take a break).

The supply chain primarily links corporations of the Global North with low-wage, low-cost resources from the Global South. Our attention in these relationships is often focused on people at either end of the chain—those who produce the goods (for low wages and in poor working conditions that might even be called sweatshops), and those who buy the goods for low cost. However, the other links in this chain also warrant attention and scrutiny. In the early days of the COVID-19 pandemic when global supply chains were severely disrupted, brands like Gap, H&M, Oscar de la Renta, and Balmain protected their bottom lines by canceling and exercising their contractual right to refuse to pay for over $400 billion in orders from suppliers, with some of these orders having already been shipped (Pham, 2022). In fact, this was not merely a COVID-era problem; corporations have long had standard clauses in their contracts for the right to withhold

Figure 10.2. Pyramid of Capitalist System, 1911

Source: en.wikipedia.org/wiki/Pyramid_of_Capitalist_System

payment, cancel orders in whole or part unilaterally, and at no cost to the corporation. These rights are legally enshrined in international trade and labor laws, many of which were written in the Global North (Deva & Anand, 2024; Pham, 2022).

While the exploitation of supply chain labor may be better known in the domain of fashion, textiles, and technology, these are not the only industries that allow the Global North to export low-wage and high-risk work to the Global South. Environmental damage is also exported. For example, shipwrecking (or ship breaking) refers to the dismantling of thousands of decommissioned ocean ships from nations such as the United States, United Kingdom, and France for scrap and salvage (Chatterjee, 2022; Deva & Anand, 2024). This industry has flourished in South Asia (Bangladesh, Pakistan, and India), where children and migrants are among the workers in the shipyards breaking apart decommissioned ships. The shipwrecking industry is labeled by the International Labour Organization as among the most dangerous occupations in the world, with significant health and safety risks (Deva & Anand, 2024). Valuable components (like steel or wood) are salvaged, but much of the remainder is toxic waste, including fluorescent light tubes, batteries, and metals like mercury, lead, and arsenic. The dismantling process produces and releases toxic chemicals such as benzene, asbestos, and thousands of liters of oils (engine oil, bilge oil, hydraulic oil, lubricant oil, and grease) into the local ecosystem (Ali et al., 2022). More than half of workers are injured via exposure to these pollutants and related carcinogens, as well as by the waste byproducts which are all dumped in the local soil and waterways, impacting the fisheries and agriculture (Ali et al., 2022; Deva & Anand, 2024).

We might believe that workers in the United States and Canada have more rights and experience less exploitation of their labor than workers in the Global South. They can certainly strategize and use their limited resources to pressure corporations for more equitable conditions (via collective action, unionization, work slowdowns), but in turn, owners strategize and use their abundant resources to stop them. They do so through union busting, dividing workers from each other via unequal bonuses and privileges, controlling messaging via networks of power such as government and media, threatening to fire workers and hire workers who will work for less, and lobbying politicians to deregulate.

There is yet another class of workers in the United States who can't pressure employers or fight for collective action at all: prison labor. The United States has the highest incarcerated population in the world (Kazemian & Galleguillos, 2025; Sawyer & Wagner, 2025). (See Figure 10.3 for a comparison with other NATO nations.) The United States accounts for 5% of the world's population, but 25% of the world's total prisoners, and has incarcerated more people than China, which has 5 times the population. Thirty-two states incarcerate at a rate higher than Turkmenistan, a country the U.S. State Department has criticized for its authoritarian government and human rights abuses (U.S. Department of State, 2023). In many states, African Americans are 5 times more likely to be incarcerated than White people, with the rate rising to 9 times in seven states: California, Connecticut, Iowa, Maine, Minnesota, New Jersey, and Wisconsin (Budd & Napal, 2022). The incarceration rate for Latino/a people is 1.4 times that of White people. In many states, more than 50% of the prison population is African American.

Federal and prison industries rely on penal labor for private sector profit, and that labor is overwhelmingly performed by racialized people. These workers are

Figure 10.3. Incarceration Rates Among Founding NATO Countries (2024)

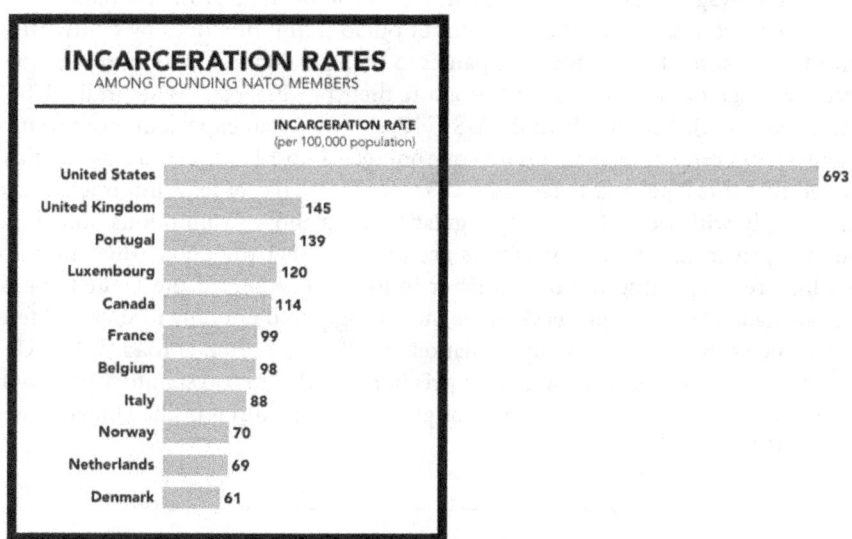

Source: https://static.prisonpolicy.org/images/NATO_US_2024-2X.webp?v=2

subject to substandard wages as well as discipline and punishment measures that include having their sentences extended if they become ill or don't make their quotas (Pham, 2022). For example, in California, prison workers sew masks for up to 14 hours daily, earning 8 cents per hour (Pham, 2022). The masks are sold to state and federal agencies (such as state hospitals and the California Highway Patrol) and help to finance the Prison Industry Authority (Pham, 2022). Scholars have described this form of prison labor as "neo-slavery," capturing its function as a new form of involuntary servitude (Appleman, 2022; Lord, 2025).

> **STOP:** While some people believe that prisoners should work for reasons such as for their health, as therapy, to learn discipline, to practice a skill, to be productive, or to repay a debt to society, when they work for private for-profit corporations who do not pay them (or who grossly underpay for their labor), their efforts are not going towards self-improvement, the good of society as a whole, their families, or even to victims/victims' families (in cases where victims exist). They are essentially enslaved laborers for corporations earning profits for shareholders. Further, if they were working for rehabilitation purposes and to become familiar with workplace culture, their working conditions would have to more closely resemble those outside prison.

The loss of jobs in the United States is often blamed on the outsourcing of jobs to low-wage workers in poor countries (Helfenbein, 2016), and many companies have responded to the criticism of outsourcing practices by contracting with U.S. prisons. This enables companies to keep production costs extremely low, access a range of tax benefits, and promote their products as "Made in the USA" (Amadeo, 2018). The "Made in the USA" label conveys an expectation of product quality and compliance with basic environmental and labor standards. It is assumed that this label guarantees that U.S. companies pay at least minimum wage and comply with workplace safety regulations, but those assumptions don't hold true for prison labor and consumers are unaware that the goods they are purchasing are supporting the prison labor industry. Further, in the United States, prison-made products and services are increasingly sold not only to state and federal agencies, but also on the open market and then exported abroad. While U.S. laws ban imports of goods made from prison labor, there is no statutory provision prohibiting U.S. exports of prison labor goods manufactured in the United States (Cao, 2019).

✓ **PERSPECTIVE CHECK:** Consider how profits for U.S. companies from the use of prison labor impact the kinds of "tough on crime" legislation and politicians that corporations support. When the prisoner is a worker who cannot demand fair wages or treatment, what then is the incentive for programs that reintegrate those who have served their time and reduce recidivism? With the increasing backlash against immigration to the United States and following mass deportations, corporations will likely turn more and more to prison labor to replace the low-paid immigrants who formerly worked, for example, in fields and slaughterhouses. This reliance will also motivate policies and practices that lead to more incarcerations and longer sentences. There is a well-established body of sociological and legal literature that connects increases and decreases in incarceration to fluctuations in the labor market (Muller & Scrage, 2021).

CLASS SOCIALIZATION

Class is about money and power, but it is also about culture. Different class groups have different cultural norms and patterns associated with them. So how do we each learn our class positions as well as the class positions of others? Or, because class is also a form of our cultural identity, we might ask how we learn to perform our class and to read and understand the class performance of others? There are two key sites where a majority of this learning occurs: school and media.

School and class messages. Scholars have explained how mass public schooling is about more than subject-matter education; it is also about ideological socialization (Apple, 1993). In Chapter 2, we reviewed Jean Anyon's classic study comparing schoolchildren from working-, middle-, and affluent-class schools, and learned how children are schooled to conceptualize knowledge and their relationship to it, based in part on the school curriculum they receive. As the histories of both Canada and the United States show, the requirement for mass schooling has always been about more than education. Through both required attendance (e.g., via a system of residential schooling) as well as denied attendance (e.g., females and racialized children) and segregated attendance (e.g., children with disabilities), mass schooling has been in large part a project of mass socialization. In fact, compulsory mass schooling is a relatively new social idea in Western nation-states (Ballantine & Spade, 2008). The architects of the compulsory mass schooling that started in the mid-19th century wanted to educate children into a common curriculum (a common language, national history, and set of values) so they would become productive and compliant citizens of the nation-state (Tyack, 1976). We may rightly ask: Whose language, history, and values made up the framework for all children's education—those who created, implemented, and monitored compulsory attendance in mass public schooling, or those who were forced to attend the schools?

Media and class messages. Media is another primary institution socializing us about what it means to be owning class, middle class, and working class (Leistyna, 2009). Two key elements of this institution in relation to class messaging are the consolidation of media ownership (control by fewer and fewer entities, and therefore more homogeneous messaging) and the class representations that circulate through media. In other words, who is in the position to control the messages, what are those messages, and how do they serve the interests of those who control the schools?

Media consolidation is an issue around the globe. As multinational corporations have bought up other companies, there are fewer and fewer corporations owning more and more of the news and entertainment that we consume. As of 2024, the world's top 10 media conglomerates were (Seth, 2024):

- Comcast (CMCSA)
- Thomson Reuters (TRI)
- Naspers (NAPRF)
- Bell Canada Enterprises (BCE)
- Rogers Communication (RCI)
- Warner Bros. Discovery (WBD)
- Fox Corp (FOXA)
- News Corp (NWS)
- The New York Times Company (NYT)
- Nexstar Media Group (NXST)

Once we understand that media consolidation necessarily limits the range of perspectives available to us, we need to examine how media represents class. To do so, try a brief thought experiment:

As you follow your favorite social media feeds, read reviews of films and shows you plan to see, and watch videos of your favorite performers and product reviews and endorsements from superstars, consider how those forms of representation are classed. For example, consider work. What work is presented? Who is doing what kinds of work (paid work as well as unpaid work) or not working at all, and how do they seem to feel about it?

How are speech and accents classed? Which accents and speech patterns are considered "low class"? Which are "sophisticated" or "romantic" or "threatening"?

Who wears business suits, high heels, and other "uniforms"? How do people move? How are various movements classed? How do race and gender inform how we understand class embodiment?

How is food classed? Who eats organic? What does farm-to-table mean? What about alcohol? Which beers are "high class" and which are associated with "low class"? What kind of leisure activities do the various classes engage in? Who goes to the symphony? Who skydives? Who goes to monster truck shows and watches the WWE?

All of these cues tell us what it means to be working, middle, or owning class. Now consider what class the people who generate these images—the writers and directors—most likely occupy. In other words, who is in the position to represent class? While media messages may not deliberately set out to teach about class, how the various class groups are represented (or absent altogether) is a critical part of our class socialization.

COMMON MISCONCEPTIONS ABOUT CLASS

"We live in a society where anyone can make it regardless of where they started." From very early on in school we receive the message that anyone can make it if they try, and that the West is the land of opportunity. We are told rags-to-riches stories—from Cinderella to Oprah—and that we live in a classless society. The myth of the American Dream is so powerful that research shows the vast majority of Americans (over 70%) overestimate class mobility and believe that personal motivation is more important to mobility than the state of the economy or the economic circumstances they are born into (Kraus & Tan, 2015; Wyatt-Nichol, 2016). In addition to strictly economic reasons for class immobility, such as net worth, class immobility is also influenced by class culture. The cultural norms we are socialized into are based on our class position, and this ensures that we will be most comfortable in our own class culture and around people who share that culture. The schools we go to, the neighborhoods we live in, the jobs we aspire to, all reinforce our class positions and who surrounds us.

While some people will change class, they will be the exception rather than the rule. The rags-to-riches story so beloved and repeated in Hollywood is unlikely in real life. Very few children born to parents with income at the very bottom rise to even the middle class, much less the very top (Connolly et al., 2021). Consider the 10 richest people in the United States in 2024 (Peterson-Withorn, 2024), most of whom were already born into the upper classes. Now imagine their children. What schools will they go to? Whose children will they be surrounded by? What opportunities will be given? Are they likely to mingle with you or your children? It is highly unlikely that we will interact across these vast class differences.

> **Social mobility:** The idea that one can easily move from one class position to another.

"A rich person can become poor as easily as a poor person can become rich." Because we tend to think of class strictly in terms of how much money we have, we assume that a rich person who loses everything will end up in the same boat as a poor person. But in reality, a rich person does not lose everything when they lose their money. They will still have an internalized sense of entitlement, contacts with other wealthy people they can call upon and network with, knowledge of systems and how to navigate them, and the language and norms of the upper class that will open doors for them. In other words, they do not lose their *cultural capital*. Further, they have much more time before they use up their material capital—real estate, antiques, artwork, cars, boats, jewelry, investments—known as *net worth*.

> **Net worth:** All of your assets combined together set against your liabilities. When you subtract your debt from what you own, you have your net worth.

"Education is the key to getting ahead." While certainly there are more opportunities open to people with more education, education itself is also stratified. As discussed in Chapter 2, the kind of education we receive is based on the kind of school we go to (public or private), where it is located, and how it is funded. Within the school are different tracks that offer different kinds of knowledge intended to prepare us for different kinds of careers. If we graduate from K–12 public schools and go on to college, we again enter a system that is stratified. Consider the difference between a 2-year college with a focus on the trades and a student population from the local community, and an Ivy League university with wealthy students from all

over the world, many of them *legacy* (i.e., students whose parents also attended and who therefore were favored for acceptance). Whether you have to work while in college and still graduate with a massive amount of debt or have everything paid for by your family will also impact the outcome of your education. Which doors your education opens is greatly impacted by the status of the school you go to. So while education clearly makes a difference in terms of life opportunities, schooling is a stratified political structure that very predictably and efficiently reproduces rather than eliminates class hierarchies. Of course education has the potential to contribute to a more equitable society, depending on the knowledge and skills it imparts. This is why authoritarian regimes target the work of schools and universities as places where how to think and what to think intersect. If they were not fundamental to a society's outcome, they would not receive so much political focus.

"*Sports and sports scholarships offer poor kids a way out.*" The idea that sports are a way out of poverty for poor youth, and youth of Color in particular, is deeply cherished and continually reinforced in films and television. Yet this is an extremely rare outcome. Consider the following: How many openings on professional teams are actually available? Take basketball as an example. There are 5 positions on a team, with 7 extra players, for a total of 12 players. There are 11 players on a football team. Baseball is played with 9 players. The degree of exceptionality required to make it onto the field for these teams is very high and limited to a very select few. The possibility of women "making it" through sports is even more unlikely, given that their teams do not have the visibility or bring in the kind of wealth that men's teams do. It is also relevant that for the few who do succeed through sports, their run is limited. The average age of retirement for a football player is 35, and they often suffer from lifelong debilitating injuries.

The people who truly get rich from sports are the owners. In 2025, all of the top 15 richest professional sports team owners were White, and 14 were men (the one woman inherited the team from her husband). Of the 32 National Hockey League governors, all are White and 31 are men. While a poor boy from the projects making it big in sports is a romantic idea reinforced through countless movies, that dream comes true for an extremely rare number of youth. Notice how the bodies of these young men are seen as worthy of scholarships that support entertainment, but not their minds. This is a key signifier of class position. The lower your class status, the more your body is seen as exploitable. Think about who decides to go to war and who actually does the fighting, who owns the coal mines and who does the mining, who writes the laws and who is on the street enforcing them. Most of the latter are not the upper class. Manual labor literally means working *with your hands*. We also have to ask ourselves what it means to see sports as a way out of poverty for young racialized men but not other fields such as law, medicine, or teaching.

"*Class is the true oppression. If we eliminate classism we will eliminate racism.*" The point of the opening parable is that class and race are deeply intertwined. Even if Mr. Rich White stopped exploiting Mr. Poor White we would still be left with racism. Indeed, racism is consistently what Mr. Rich White has used to manipulate

Mr. Poor White into voting against his own best interests, convincing him that rights for "the Black man" will come at the cost of his rights, as if there were a limited number of rights to go around.

Poverty for White people does not take away racial advantage. Peoples of Color who occupy the same class position as White people are still experiencing racism, and of course, that racism can come from poor White people as well as wealthy. DiAngelo (2006) speaks to this in her personal narrative of growing up poor and White:

> From an early age I had the sense of being an outsider; I was acutely aware that I was poor, that I was dirty, that I was not normal and that there was something "wrong" with me. But I also knew that I was not Black. We were at the lower rungs of society but there was always someone on the periphery, just below us. I knew that "colored" [sic] people existed and that they should be avoided. I can remember many occasions when I reached for candy or uneaten food laying on the street and was admonished by my grandmother not to touch it because a "colored person" may have touched it. The message was clear to me; if a colored person touched something it became dirty. The irony here is that the marks of poverty were clearly visible on me: poor hygiene, torn clothes, unhoused, hunger. Yet through comments such as my grandmother's, a racial Other was formed in my consciousness; an Other through whom I became clean. Race was the one identity which aligned me with the middle class girls in my school. As I reflect back on the early messages I received about being poor and being White, I now realize that my grandmother and I needed people of Color to cleanse and realign us with the dominant White culture that our poverty had separated us from. (pp. 51–53)

Poor White people, and especially poor White people living in urban areas, are most often in closest proximity to minoritized people (hooks, 2000). Consider the term *White trash*. It is not without significance that this is one of the few expressions in which race is named for White people. This may be because within the White collective, it is poor White people who are most likely to live in proximity to racialized people. In a society in which racism is infused, this closeness highlights and "degrades" Whiteness. Owning-class people also have racialized people near them because the latter are often their domestics and gardeners—in other words, their servants. But they do not interact with them socially in the same way that poor White people do. Middle-class White people are generally the furthest away from racialized people. They are the most likely to say that "there were no people of Color in my neighborhood or school. I didn't meet a Black person until I went to college" (often adding, "so I was lucky because I didn't learn anything about racism"). Focusing attention solely on undoing class oppression simply denies the realities of racism in the lives of racialized people, and the privileges of Whiteness for White people, regardless of their class position. Class cannot be understood outside its relationship to race, gender, ability, and other social positions.

"*People just need to work hard and stay out of trouble.*" As previously discussed, minimum wage work is among the hardest. It tends to be physical, of lower status, and exceptionally grueling (e.g., fast food, retail, factory, and agricultural work). Further, a person working at minimum wage to support a family will likely need to work more than one job. To say that these people do not work hard is unfair and inaccurate. Yet their hard work will not typically pay off in the sense of "making it." These workers are more likely to come from families with very little net worth to begin with, and without resources such as college degrees, they are less likely to advance. When middle-class people proclaim that they have achieved what they have because they were taught the value of hard work, we need to ask ourselves who we believe wasn't taught that value. Further, how are we defining hard work?

As for people "staying out of trouble," between 1970 and 2005, the U.S. prison population grew by 700%, mostly due to policy changes, such as three-strikes, mandatory minimum, and truth in sentencing laws (American Civil Liberties Union, 2011). Since 1970, the number has increased sevenfold, far outpacing population growth and crime (American Civil Liberties Union, 2022, 2024). Twenty to 25% of incarcerated people are locked up for nonviolent drug offenses, despite no change in drug use rates, with Black people incarcerated for drug offenses at 10 times the rate of White people, despite the same rates of drug use (American Civil Liberties Union, 2017). Black people make up 14% of the U.S. population and White people make up 57%, yet Black people comprise 41% of people incarcerated in jails and prisons compared to 36% of White people (Sawyer & Wagner, 2025). Further, thousands of youth are behind bars for technical violations that are not adult crimes, such as running away or truancy (Sawyer & Wagner, 2025; Wagner & Rabuy, 2017). Many youths' involvement with the criminal legal system overlaps with their involvement with other systems, such as child welfare. Nearly 40% of inmates in state prisons were first arrested at age 15 or younger, with the numbers highest for Black (43%), Indigenous (42%), and mixed race (41%) men (Sawyer & Wagner, 2025).

One in 3 people imprisoned in the United States is in a jail; there are approximately 750,000 people held in pretrial jails—these are people who have not yet been convicted of any crime and thus are legally presumed innocent but cannot afford bail (Sawyer & Wagner, 2025). This translates to 80% of the local jail population consisting of people who are imprisoned because they are unable to come up with the bail money needed (typically $10,000) to release them until their case is resolved. A 2025 report by Prison Policy shows that in 2025 bail of $10,000 represents 8 months' income for a typical person in jail who is awaiting trial (Sawyer & Wagner, 2025). Thus the detention of people who are legally innocent is in practice a form of housing the poor in public jails. Bail that is set at rates many people can't afford creates increased profits for corporations servicing jails, while in effect criminalizing poverty (Preston & Eisenberg, 2022; Rabuy & Kopf, 2016; Ziegler, 2020). The business of other forms of detention beyond jails, such as the detention of migrants, refugees, and asylum seekers, is a multibillion-dollar industry in which private corporations benefit from government contracts. For example, the private companies CoreCivic and the

> 📖 People are incarcerated in a variety of ways. **Jails** are run by local law enforcement (sheriff, police chief, city administration) and are used to confine persons usually before their trials. Some are privately operated. **Prisons** are run by state or federal authorities and are used to confine persons who have been convicted of a crime. State prisons are for offenses such as rape, murder, and robbery; some are privately operated. Federal prisons are for offenses such as drug trafficking and white-collar crimes such as fraud. While there is a great deal of variability, state prisons have less security, are less uniformly regulated, and are thus considered more dangerous than federal prisons. The U.S. Marshals, territorial prisons, and immigration detention are also forms of incarceration in the United States.
>
> In Canada, jails are commonly referred to as pretrial or remand centres where people can be confined for up to 2 years. There are corrections centres run by each province (for violations of provincial laws), and federal prisons run by Corrections Canada for federal crimes. There are no privately operated prisons in Canada. Between 2001 and 2006, the province of Ontario housed Canada's first private adult prison. Penetanguishene's "super prison," the Central North Correctional Centre, gave a 5-year trial contract to U.S.-based Management & Training Corporation (MTC). But at the end of the contract, the province took back control of the prison, with the Community Safety Minister stating the reason as: "In every single area, outcomes were better in the publicly run facilities" (CBC News, 2006).

GEO Group run 90% of detention centers (Cho, 2025; Gomez & Cataldo, 2016; Nielsen-Reagan, 2021).

The expansion and privatization of incarceration has provided enormous financial gains for the private prison corporations involved. From 2000 to 2020, the combined revenue of CoreCivic and GEO Group rose from under half a billion dollars to approximately $4.5 billion. Between a quarter and a third of that revenue comes from Immigration & Customs Enforcement (ICE) detention contracts. In 2023, CoreCivic reported that 30% of their contracts were for ICE detentions; for GEO Group the figure was 43% (Scholtens, 2025). Both companies expect exponential growth in the current era and have contracts for up to $45 billion submitted to the federal government. These contracts are to enhance existing facilities and build new detention centers throughout the United States to service the administration's agenda and to comply with the president's declaration that the southern border is experiencing a "national emergency."

A key driver of these profits is the private prison business model: prison labor. Prisoners fight wildfires, work in the kitchens of food franchises, and provide other forms of essential labor across the United States. On average, their wage is between 13 and 52 cents an hour, and many times they are unpaid. Prison laborers are excluded from the basic rights and protections afforded to most workers. Their labor brings billions of dollars in profit for the public and private sectors. Prison labor has been likened to slave labor, especially as most prison laborers are Black and the practice is most common in the South (Mast, 2025). Corporations with huge financial stakes in profiting from mass incarceration include many we are familiar with, such as Coca Cola, Pepsi, McDonald's, Burger King, Target, and Whole Foods, among many others (Zhang, 2024).

While not all prisoners are forced to work, most need to in order to afford very basic necessities, including the ability to use a phone to speak to family members, for which they are charged (in many cases by private companies). Further, prisoners who choose not to work may lose the opportunity to reduce their sentences or be otherwise disciplined and can face isolation in their cells for up to 23 hours per day. Thus, many choose to work in conditions that can be toxic. For example, prison labor is often used before, during, and after disasters. Before Hurricane Harvey in 2017, Texas prisoners filled sandbags to prevent flooding. During wildfires in states along the West Coast, prisoners were deployed to fight fires for salaries of $1–2 per day (Taylor, 2024). And in 2010, the BP oil corporation used prisoners to clean up the Deepwater Horizon oil spill resulting from an oil rig explosion in the Gulf of Mexico (Kujawinski et al., 2020). The Louisiana prisoners cleaned oil sludge, debris, and dead wildlife on Louisiana's beaches. They worked on average 72 hours per week, for little to no pay (Baker et al., 2021). They received minimal protection against the toxic chemicals and crude oil, which can damage every system in the body (Taylor, 2024; Thompson, 2012).

When thinking about the relationship between mass incarceration and corporate profits made from the prison industry, we are led back to the very definition of crime and whose crimes we are most likely to focus on, prosecute, and punish. Wall Street executives and bankers essentially defrauded and robbed millions of their homes and economic stability through illegal practices and caused a global economic crisis in 2008. Yet the government gave banks a $700 billion bailout through the Troubled Assets Relief Program (TARP) (Pontell et al., 2014). These loans came from the public purse and were repaid by the banks at a lower interest rate than those banks charged their own clients who hold loans with similar risks (Flanagan & Purnanandam, 2024). In other words, the TARP loans were repaid with an interest rate of 9%, on the type of loan the banks themselves would charge 39% for (Flanagan & Purnanandam, 2024). These reduced interest rates translate into a subsidy for the at-fault banks of up to $54 billion in reduced borrowing fees (Flanagan & Purnanandam, 2024; Lucas, 2024). Consider this bailout and who paid for it, both to lend the funds and to divert that money from public services those funds would have paid for. Now consider the U.S. Supreme Court overturning student loan forgiveness, and how many student loans the $54 billion in uncollected borrowing fees alone might have relieved. Not only does this illustrate the social construction of crime and how we perceive, name, punish, and prosecute crime, but it also illustrates how we define work, whose labor is visible and under what conditions, and who is seen as working hard and who isn't. We can't understand how these forces work together without considering class in relation to race and gender. This brings us back to the concept of intersectionality.

UNDERSTANDING INTERSECTIONALITY

As introduced in chapter 8, *intersectionality* is the idea that identity cannot be fully understood via a single lens such as gender, race, or class alone—what legal scholar Kimberlé Crenshaw (1989) called a "single axis framework" (p. 139). Rather, our identities and the social meaning attributed to them must be understood in their interdependence on one another; identity is multidimensional. For example, one is not just a woman but a *White heterosexual cisgender deaf* woman. All of these identities interact in complex ways that shape how this particular woman will experience gender. Prior to Crenshaw popularizing the term, scholars had been writing about the problematics of a single axis of analysis for many years. Many of these scholars were and are Black, transnational, and queer feminists who have problematized the idea that there is a singular female experience that feminism speaks to and under which all women can be gathered.

In the mid-19th century, at a time of struggle against slavery as well as patriarchy, abolitionist Sojourner Truth advocated for both the abolition of slavery and equal rights for women. In a famous speech she gave in 1851 at the Ohio Women's Rights convention, known as the "Ain't I a Woman" speech, Truth expressed concern that abolitionists were focused primarily on the issues of Black men to the exclusion of Black women and issues of women's political rights. Truth was also concerned with property rights, which most women did not have (Brah & Phoenix, 2004). In the 1970s, 1980s, and 1990s, many feminists of Color theorized about intersectionality (though not always using that term). Among them were the Combahee River Collective of Black feminist activist scholars such as Cathy Cohen and Angela Davis, and artist activists such as Audre Lorde and Alice Walker, who examined the intersections of gender, sexuality, and race (Brah & Phoenix, 2004; Collins & Bilge, 2016). Other Black feminists also continued the theorizing and interrogation of lived intersectionality in such institutions as justice, education, and the family (Collins, 2000; Crenshaw, 1991; hooks, 1994). Transnational feminists such as Chandra Mohanty and Inderpal Grewal challenged the notion that there was an essential experience of womanhood and examined the experiences of women living under colonialism. Among the issues they were concerned with was the fetishizing of non-Western bodies (Grewal & Kaplan, 1994; Mohanty, 1988; Shohat, 1998). Chicana feminists such as Gloria Anzaldúa and Norma Alarcón critiqued the nature of borders, nationhood, and belonging. They did so under multidimensional axes of difference including gender, sexuality, class, status, and language (Garcia, 1989). Asian feminists such as Grace Lee Boggs, Yuri Kochiyama, and Celine Parreñas Shimizu, Indigenous feminists such as Paula Gunn Allen and Lee Maracle, queer feminists such as Andrea Smith and Judith Butler, and crip feminists such as Kim Q. Hall and Nirmala Erevelles all contributed (and some continue to contribute) to our collective understanding of intersectional oppressions.

This is by no means an exhaustive list. Our intention is to illustrate how widely the issues related to intersectionality of race, gender, sexuality, ability, class, and other identities have been theoretically examined, and the role that women—and women of Color in particular—have played in this examination. This is important because much of class theorizing has been centered on the work of male scholars. Yet intersectional theorizing has informed not only academia but also contemporary activist movements.

When activists gather around a single issue, the tensions of intersectionality inevitably arise. For example, in the early AIDS crisis of the 1980s, the programs and outreach created in response did not take into account the barriers different communities faced. Peoples of Color with HIV were dealing with racism as well as homophobia, yet existing programs were based on White cultural norms and networks. Indeed, the sympathetic face of HIV/AIDS is a gay White upper-class man. Without an intersectional analysis, peoples of Color with HIV were left out of drug trials, educational campaigns, and support systems. In many major cities they were forced to start their own organizations or be left behind.

As activists who may be part of such movements there are some strategies you can consider, including some of the key tenets of intersectionality:

- Social inequality cannot be understood by examining categories such as gender, race, and socioeconomic status in isolation. For example, Sarah is a White, cis woman, heterosexual, working class, and middle-aged. To understand her experience under sexism she also has to take into account how Whiteness shapes her experience of sexism; while she is female, she is most particularly a White cis woman. Thus, her experience under sexism will be different than a Black cis woman's experience. While she is disadvantaged under sexism and will face barriers rooted in patriarchy, she still benefits from Whiteness; racism is not a form of oppression she will face. In fact, she will benefit from racism and these benefits may help her get further ahead in male-dominated environments than women of Color.
- People can experience privilege and oppression simultaneously depending on what situation or specific context they are in. So while Sarah may be paid less than a White man in her workplace, she will likely be paid more than a Black woman in that same workplace. While her clothes and toiletries cost more than a man's—even though she is likely to earn less than a man in her same occupation—she won't likely be followed around in the store under the assumption that she will steal, as her Black coworker more likely will be.
- Intersectionality is more than a theoretical standpoint. It is intended to build coalitions among diverse groups so that their actions are more

inclusive and effective. Imagine what could be accomplished if Mr. Poor White from our opening parable had joined with the Black man to challenge their exploitation by Mr. Rich White.

An intersectional analysis of oppression requires that we attend to the above complexities. When we want to address a particular oppression such as classism, we often seek out statistical data alone to inform our understanding of the issue. If we add an intersectional analysis, our understanding of classism deepens and becomes multidimensional. This gives us a much more complex and nuanced view and will drive more complex and nuanced interventions.

EXAMPLES OF EVERYDAY CLASS PRIVILEGE

You have class privilege if the following applies to you:

- You can readily find accurate (not caricatured) representations of members of your class depicted in films, television, and other media.
- Experts appearing on mass media are from your social class.
- New consumer products are designed and marketed with your social class in mind.
- If you find yourself involved in a police situation, you can easily hire an attorney to ensure your perspective is heard justly.
- You can choose to eat healthy food if you wish, and it is readily available.
- Your eyesight, smile, and general health aren't inhibited by your income.
- If you become sick in the United States, you can seek medical care immediately and not just "hope it goes away."
- As a child, you were able to participate in organized sports, clubs, music, and other extracurricular activities.
- Your decision to go to college, and the type of college you chose, wasn't based entirely on financial determinants.
- Your parents are college graduates and could help you navigate the application process, as well as pay for college and living expenses.
- An annual raise in pay at your job is measured in dollars, not cents, and discussed in terms of annual salary rather than hourly wage, and you could negotiate that salary and benefits.
- Whenever you've moved out of your home it has been voluntary, and you had another home to move into.

Class may arguably be the foundational form of oppression as it is ultimately about the distribution of resources. This does *not* mean, however, that if we eliminate class all other forms of oppression will disappear, but that we cannot understand social inequality without understanding class. How we justify the distribution of resources is shaped and rationalized by how we socially construct various groups and our ideas about what these groups do or don't deserve. Given this, we have barely scratched the surface of the complex ways that classism works. However, our goal has been to provide a basic framework for understanding classism so that we may continue the lifelong work of personal reflection, political analysis, and ultimately, action.

COMMON CLASSIST BELIEFS

Our early and continual socialization into our class positions makes it challenging to break free from the hegemony of dominant narratives. Here, we speak back to some of the most common narratives:

"Immigrants are stealing our jobs." Immigrants do not and cannot steal jobs. In fact, immigrants tend to be concentrated in jobs that locally born people don't want. These immigrants are hired by companies who choose to hire them, and who benefit from their cheap (or exploited) labor. The work they do is typically the most grueling, demeaning, and dangerous work that others have refused to do (or that unionized workers have collectively bargained against doing under unsafe conditions). If immigrant workers are undocumented, they cannot complain about working conditions or unjust practices. This benefits the corporation, not the workers. The companies who exploit immigrant labor are whom we should be concerned with, not those being exploited. The discourse of "immigrants stealing jobs" puts attention on the actions of the vulnerable, and away from the actions of the powerful.

"Poor women should stop having babies." This claim rests on the assumption that women have complete control over their bodies and receive no pressure from society to be sexual, much less pressure or even force from men to engage in unprotected sex. Further, many of the forms of birth control available to women can be dangerous, faulty, expensive, and difficult to access. Perhaps the simplest, cheapest, and safest form of birth control beyond abstinence (which again assumes women are the sole decision-makers in whether or not they have sex) is the use of condoms. While condoms are the safest, simplest, and most accessible form of birth control, condom use depends on men being willing to use them. Regardless, the claim that poor women should stop having babies is particularly interesting in the face of ever-increasing curtailment of women's reproductive rights and options. These limitations go so far as to decrease funding for organizations that give birth control or family planning information. For example, in 2025 the U.S. president reinstated the Global Gag Rule of 1984, a policy that blocks federal funding to international nongovernmental organizations that provide abortions, family planning services, or information about family planning, regardless of local laws. This expansion includes global health assistance programs across all departments and agencies. This means that the Global Gag Rule applies to organizations that receive family planning funding, but also to foreign NGOs that receive funding to work on a broad range of health programs including HIV/AIDS, the Zika virus, malaria, tuberculosis, nutrition, and

maternal and child health (Center for Reproductive Rights, 2025). It is important to note that most of the arguments for limiting women's reproductive rights are rooted in religion, despite the constitutional requirement for a separation of church and state. It is also important to notice how class is at play in who we believe should not have too many children, who is valorized for being a stay-at-home mom, and who is vilified for staying home while raising children. Social class plays a powerful role in these judgments.

"It's easy when you get a government handout every month." It is a common stereotype that Indigenous people get "free money" from the government and that peoples of Color (and African Americans in particular) are the beneficiaries of welfare and other "handout" programs, and that these groups cheat these programs. When considering this belief, we need to look at several interrelated dynamics: historical oppression, what programs are actually available, and who uses them.

When we think of historical oppression toward Indigenous peoples in Canada and the United States and African Americans in the United States, we might consider the following in terms of stolen goods. It is by no means an exhaustive list:

- African Americans: kidnapping; 246 years of enslavement and brutality; the rape of Black women; torture; separation of families; selling of children; forbidden to speak their own language or practice their religion; forced Christian conversion; medical experimentation; slave codes and Black codes; mandatory segregation; lynching, murder, and mob violence; imprisonment and forced labor; disempowering Black entrepreneurs; bans on marriage and imprisonment for interracial couples; redlining to profit banks and real estate brokers; documented discrimination in employment, biased laws, and policing practices; White flight; cultural erasures and attacks; subprime mortgages; racist media representation; mass incarceration; and educational inequality.
- Indigenous Peoples: stolen land; intentional spreading of disease; cultural and physical genocide; death marches; rape; forced onto reservations; forced into residential schools; sexual exploitation; separation of families; forbidden to speak their language or practice their ceremonies; torture; forced conversions to Christianity; racist representations in media, literature, and textbooks; broken treaties; cultural mockery through such practices as racist sports team names and Halloween costumes; cultural appropriation; omitted history; educational inequality; mass incarceration; environmental destruction; corporate pollution and resource extraction from Indigenous lands; destruction of ancestral territories and sacred burial grounds; stolen artifacts and the display of stolen bones in museums; cultural erasure; profiting from an international tourism industry on the "cowboys and Indians" White settler colonial story.

The wealth of these two countries absolutely depended—and continues to depend—upon what was stolen from these groups.

There is widespread misinformation about what government-assistance supports are actually in place and who uses them. For example, many people think that citizens who receive welfare benefits live lives of luxury and that Black people in particular abuse the welfare system. Yet, in fact, to qualify for welfare—officially known as Temporary Assistance for Needy Families (TANF)—in the United States, you need to have income below half the poverty line; in some states, the income limit is much lower. Even then, states have no legal obligation to provide TANF. While states can set their own amounts, the amount that the federal government allocates to states for TANF has not changed since 1996 (Center on Budget and Policy Priorities, 2022). In 2023, there were over 3 times more children (1.5 million) than adults (just under 500,000) receiving monthly TANF benefits (The Office of Family Assistance, 2024). The median amount of cash assistance from TANF across all states is $552 per month for a family of three. States can set their own time limits, but no state offers TANF support for an adult for more than 60 months (5 years) (Center on Budget and Policy Priorities, 2022). In addition to how temporary, meager, and difficult to get TANF support is, the percentage of people using TANF is roughly the same by race (Chatfield, 2024).

"*This is class warfare.*" The term *class warfare* is frequently raised when class inequality is raised. Traditionally the term refers to the tension and antagonism among the various classes. Today, it behooves us to notice who is in the position to disseminate widely their use of the term and to what effect. Certainly activists marching in the street have carried signs referring to class warfare. But the most common usage that circulates throughout society comes from commentators on news shows and politicians. These commentators and politicians most typically represent the upper classes and invoke the term when tax breaks, deregulation, subsidies, and other "wealth-fare" programs and loopholes are questioned. Given the negative association with the term and the lack of an understanding of how class works in society, invoking the charge of class warfare effectively silences or at least invalidates further scrutiny. Yet when we understand how classism works, we understand that the actual direction of class warfare has always been directed toward the poor and working classes. In fact, as discussed earlier, rather than ameliorating class inequality over time, class inequality has grown to a level never before seen in human history. Questioning a system that has allowed the concentration of wealth into fewer and fewer hands is not class warfare, but rather class education and awareness in the pursuit of the collective good.

"*We need to stop putting labels on everything.*" When thinking about the pressure to not name a social reality, consider the various issues that were once taboo but have now become more acceptable to discuss. A key aspect of gaining acceptance has been the ability to openly explore the issue. For example, younger readers may not be aware that it was once taboo to talk about AIDS, and before that, it was taboo to talk about cancer. Today it should be clear that not only must we talk about cancer and AIDS if we are going to be able to support those who have it, but that opening the conversation has also released resources that are critical to eliminating these diseases. When the stigma on each disease was reduced, funding for research was advanced, and as a result therapies and support flourished. Today, people living with cancer or AIDS have a radically different experience than in the past; there are myriad support programs, cutting-edge medications and therapies, and less stigma. In other words, there is a relationship between talking about issues and the ability to address them; silence has never moved treatments forward. This also applies to issues such as domestic violence, eating disorders, child abuse, and sexual exploitation and assault. We live in a society in which our class and other intersecting positions profoundly shape our access to resources in far-reaching and inequitable ways. We cannot achieve more equity if we do not understand how inequity is reproduced and our role in that reproduction. Again we must ask ourselves, *Who does it serve to not name classism?*

The opening of this chapter is based on Lillian Smith's 1949 parable titled "Mr. Rich White and Mr. Poor White Strike a Bargain." Smith used satire to name and critique how White men of the owning class used White men of the poor and working class to secure their positions. In essence, the bargain was that the owning class would continue to exploit the poor and working class of all races but reward the White people of these classes with the additional resource of Whiteness (Roediger, 1991). The African American scholar W.E.B. Du Bois posed the question as early as 1937: Why have working class Blacks and Whites not found common cause in their shared suffering at the bottom of the social ladder? (Green & Smith, 1983). Roediger argues that Whiteness is a symbolic wage that has pacified the White working class by allowing both psychological and tangible (albeit limited) rewards. This wage also directs the White working classes' resentment to those below rather than above them. Smith's parable captures this dynamic and offers us the following lessons about class and its intersections with race and gender:

- Given that class continues to be a key axis of social inequity, we must continually ask whose interests are served by particular class narratives. Had Mr. Poor White considered how his race was used against his economic interests, he might have found a way to resist Mr. Rich White's exploitation and to make common cause with the Black man. Discourses that we cherish and believe to be true (rags to riches, the myth of upward class mobility, and critiques of classism as class warfare or "socialist propaganda") prevent critical thinking and action, thereby holding class inequity in place.
- We each play a role in the class system. While Ms. Poor White, the Black woman, and others were not a part of the parable, we must not assume that they have no part to play. The exploitation of the poor by the rich requires that the middle class look away (e.g., in our consumption of cheap goods produced via exploited labor) and that Ms. Poor White exploit the Black woman rather than build coalitions with her around

their shared interests. While Ms. Poor White has been placed below Mr. Poor White, she too is still above the Black woman in the classist order.

To challenge and ultimately dismantle classism and its intersections with other forms of oppression, we must be willing to look at these issues rather than avoid them; no one is outside of these systems.

DISCUSSION QUESTIONS

1. Many people say, "My parents worked hard for what they have." Practice speaking back to this narrative from a social justice framework.
2. Pick an institution (e.g., government, prisons, policing, healthcare, schooling, media) and practice explaining how class manifests and is reproduced in that institution. That is, how are the owning class, middle class, and working class represented? What kind of influence does each class have? For example, who does what work within it, who profits from that work, who makes the rules and policies, whose work is visible and whose isn't? Who creates and benefits from the discourses that are circulating about class in this institution?
3. Examine the Capitalist Pyramid political comic published in 1911 (Figure 10.2). To what extent has the class pyramid changed in the past 100+ years? Provide specific examples.

EXTENSION ACTIVITIES

1. Look at the labels on three items you used the most today (e.g., clothes, shoes, technology, or food). Track down the corporate chain between you and the producer. Where was the product made? What are the working conditions under which the product was made? How much did you pay for it? How much does the average worker who made the product earn, under what conditions? How much did the corporation make for its shareholders in profits?
2. We have named many feminist scholars whose work is foundational to understanding intersectionality. Identify two of these scholars or other intersectional feminists and select a work from each to compare and contrast. What core tenets of intersectionality are illustrated in their writings?
3. Find and study nonprofit, activist organizations emerging since the 2000s that advocate and operate from an intersectional framework (for example Native Women's Association of Canada, CorpWatch, The African American Policy Forum, Showing Up for Racial Justice, Radical Women).

In your report explain the history of the organization, its commitments to intersectionality, and how its activism demonstrates an intersectional approach.

PATTERNS TO PRACTICE SEEING

1. Consider your friends, family, and most trusted business associates. What classes are they from? Do you notice a pattern in the class positions of those in your closer social circles?
2. Where do you and the people in your social circles absorb the most messages about people of other classes? What are these messages? What class experiences are presented as desirable and should be aspired to and how is that conveyed? How are race and gender embedded in these messages?
3. How are your buying habits shaped by capitalism? Think about the past week and make a list. What did you buy? What from that list did you *need* versus *want*? How did you learn about the goods you purchased? In other words, how did you come to desire the things you bought that you wanted but didn't need?

CHAPTER 11

"Yeah, But . . .": Common Rebuttals

"So I have to watch everything I say?"

Based on our experiences teaching critical social justice in a variety of forums, we predict that readers will raise questions, objections, and rebuttals. This chapter addresses the most common ones we hear. Drawing on all that has been discussed in previous chapters, we briefly but directly speak back to these "yeah, but" comments.

The primary goal of this book is to explain key concepts in critical social justice education in ways that deepen our readers' understanding. Deepening understanding is not dependent on agreement; the back-and-forth arguing inherent to winning or losing debates is not useful to this goal. We expect that some ideas will be new and difficult to understand. But struggling to understand versus rebutting are very different choices. Raising questions because you are working through an idea is important, and we encourage you to seek out critical social justice education well beyond this book. However, rebuttals that function to block out, cut off, and negate explanations are counter to the goals of education, be it critical social justice or any other kind. We ask our readers to reflect on whether the goal of their questions is greater clarity or greater protection of their existing worldview.

As you read this chapter, remember that our socialization is not something we could choose or avoid, and doesn't make us bad people. It does, however, make us responsible for reeducating ourselves and working to change oppressive systems. This is unquestionably very challenging but can also be personally rewarding as we gain insight, expand our perspectives, deepen our cross-group relationships, align what we *believe* and *say* with what we *do*, and increase our personal and political integrity.

Based on our experience teaching critical social justice to a wide range of people in a variety of settings, we can predict that certain rebuttals will surface. In the examples below, when we refer to "students" we are referring primarily to our students in university and college classrooms. However, the objections, as well as our responses to them, should be familiar to people outside of these contexts and easily transferable.

CLAIMING THAT SCHOOLS ARE POLITICALLY NEUTRAL

- "Politics has no place in schools."
- "It's not a school's place to teach values."
- "Students should be taught to love their country and be patriots, not hate themselves or hate their country!"

Many people believe that schools are apolitical spaces and that the knowledge taught in them is neutral. However, schools have a very long history of political struggle. Specific debates such as whether creationism and/or evolution should be taught; legal cases such as *Brown v. Board of Education* that ended segregation in schools; and residential schools for Indigenous children are all examples that demonstrate the political and value-based nature of schooling. There is no neutral space and schools are not now, nor have they ever been, politically neutral.

If we believe in a just and democratic society (as the U.S. Constitution implies and the Canadian Charter of Rights and Freedoms states), then we must recognize that politics are a central aspect of schooling. To be clear, we use *politics* to refer to ideology, programs, policies, funding, and how best to serve the public or civic good. *Politics* here does not mean political parties or teaching that one party is better than another. Citizens must be prepared to foster a healthy democracy, and preparing students for democratic citizenship is a key responsibility of public schools. To do so, schools have to educate students about the nation's social history; provide a multitude of perspectives; foster critical thinking and perspective taking; and enhance students' stamina for engaging with challenging ideas. They must enable students to conduct and evaluate research, raise critical questions, assess alternative explanations, tolerate ambiguity, and foster collaboration. Without these skills, young people are ill equipped to advance a just and democratic nation-state.

All change for a more just society has come from great struggle. Enslaved Africans were not freed because White people overall thought it would be good to free them. Emancipation required decades of struggle, sacrifice, and activism including physical violence and a death toll in the hundreds of thousands. Residential schools weren't closed, Chinese workers weren't granted citizenship, and domestic violence against women wasn't made illegal because the dominant group in each case thought it was a good idea; the system changed due to pressures that took decades to build and sustain.

As the current political landscape makes clear, we cannot take the hard work and the activism of people before us for granted. These efforts must be sustained and adapted to continual pushback. The capacity to recognize the need for and ability to engage in activism is foundational to being a patriotic citizen, and public schools play a fundamental role in fostering this kind of citizenship.

DISMISSING SOCIAL JUSTICE SCHOLARSHIP AS THE PERSONAL OPINIONS OF WOKE RADICALS

- "This is wokeism."
- "This is all so one-sided. I wish you would include the other side of the conversation."
- "Liberals are more obsessed with pronouns and land acknowledgments than with facts and truth."

The "radical scholars" objection reduces scholarship in critical social justice education to personal values and so-called "woke" ideology. But "radical" must have a referent; what knowledge is it radical *in contrast to*? When we object that social justice perspectives are radical and subjective, we are also saying that mainstream perspectives are neutral and objective.

When scholarship is reduced to biased personal opinions and dismissed, that scholarship is transformed from a studied body of peer-reviewed knowledge into the "radical ideology" of a single scholar. The effect of this is that scholarship is reduced to personal opinion, disagreed with, and dismissed. This strategy effectively positions social justice classrooms as places of ideology, anecdotal evidence, and subjectivity, while simultaneously positioning other kinds of classrooms—those in which allegedly neutral frameworks are taught—as objective spaces of real and preferred knowledge.

Critical theory challenges the claim that any knowledge is neutral or objective, and outside of humanly constructed meanings and interests. Yet it is the forms of knowledge that explicitly name their perspective that are perceived as biased and open to debate; in other words, only when someone *acknowledges* their subjectivity are they seen as having subjectivity. Accusations that professors have a liberal bias (that they are "radical" or "Marxist" or "socialist" or "Left-wing") typically emerge in courses that attempt to challenge the idea of neutral knowledge. Facts and truth do not emerge from a neutral and objective base. Facts and truth can also be radical and transformative, based on the cultural context they emerge in: for example, Galileo's radical truth that the Earth revolves around the sun, or the transformative facts of germ theory, or that mold can cure illness.

CITING EXCEPTIONS TO THE RULE

- "I have a friend who's Latina and she's the CEO of the company."
- "My professor is openly gay and he still got tenure."
- "He didn't mind the joke. He said he thought it was funny too."

There are two types of exceptions that people commonly raise. One type is citing examples of public figures from minoritized groups who have "made it." The second type is giving personal or anecdotal examples. In both cases—one that we *all* know and one that only *you* know—the goal is to prove that anyone can make it if they try and that there are no structural barriers. We are not arguing that the system is inflexible and cannot allow for exceptions. Of course there are exceptions to every rule, but the exceptions also prove the rule. Why are these examples so notable that we know them by name?

The personal example ("There was one Asian guy at my school and no one saw him as different") is problematic in that it is very difficult to engage with; we are only hearing the dominant-group member's necessarily limited perception. The personal example is almost impossible to question and thus works to cut off, rather than expand, exploration. There are always exceptions, but the patterns of oppression are consistent and well documented.

As for one member of the minoritized group not minding a racist, sexist, homophobic, or whatever joke, of course there will be individuals from minoritized groups who don't mind jokes or other forms of teasing about their identity. While they may not mind, that doesn't mean the joke or comment is not offensive and doesn't rely on and reinforce the cultural devaluing of that group. On the other hand, we need to ask ourselves whether there is any room in the situation for the person to say they minded. What are the risks of speaking up? How often might they have been dismissed, distanced, or further targeted, especially within a friendship or coworker group? Why might it be easier to just "go along to get along"?

ARGUING THAT OPPRESSION IS JUST HUMAN NATURE

- "Injustice exists in every society—it's just human nature."
- "Somebody has to be on top."

Because it's virtually impossible to separate nature (biology) from nurture (culture), claims that specific human dynamics are natural are very difficult to prove. There is no line at which we can say that some human pattern is natural and occurs before or beyond the forces of socialization. Even patterns we observe in infants can only be interpreted through our cultural lenses. The more useful question for our purposes is, *Whom does it serve to say that oppressing others is natural?* In other words, who is more likely to say that oppression is human nature: those on the top doing the oppressing, or those on the bottom being oppressed? This argument always serves to support the dominant group and not the minoritized group. A more constructive and ethical use of a human nature argument is to notice that, throughout history, humans have strived to overcome oppression and make society more just. In other words, resistance to injustice is just as natural. Each of us must ask ourselves what side of nature we want to be on.

APPEALING TO A UNIVERSALIZED HUMANITY

- "Why can't we all just be humans?"
- "We all bleed red."
- "It's focusing on difference that divides us."

Biologically we are all humans, of course. But socially we are members of hierarchically organized groups. Where we are in dominant groups, we are taught to see our perspectives as neutral, objective, and representative of a universal reality; our group is the standard for what it means to be normal or "just human." Thus dominant group members have the privilege of seeing themselves as outside of any group, and able to represent all of human experience. However, when we are in a minoritized group, our group is almost always named. Continually limited to our group identification, we are perceived as capable of speaking only for that particular group; where a "guy" can speak for all guys, a "gay guy" or "Asian guy" can't speak for *all* guys, he is seen to be able to speak only for/about others in his own group.

Further, because dominant group members are taught to see themselves as normal, we assume that people in the minoritized group share our reality. This assumption imposes our reality on them, prevents us from learning more about their perspectives, and invalidates the oppression they experience. Insisting that "we are all just human" in response to evidence of oppression is a way to deny that oppression exists at all and to end any further discussion.

As for insisting that addressing difference is what divides us, dominant and minoritized groups are already divided from one another by virtually every measure, both physically and in life outcomes. In a society in which group difference clearly matters, we suggest that *not* addressing our differences and pretending that they have no significance is what keeps us divided.

INSISTING ON IMMUNITY FROM SOCIALIZATION

- "I was taught to treat everybody the same."
- "My parents raised me to believe that it didn't matter that I was a girl, I could be anything I wanted."
- "I know there's prejudice against my group, but honestly I don't let it bother me."

In addressing the claim that one has been immune to the forces of socialization, we offer the following reminders:

- Our families are not the sole forces of our socialization.
- Our families are themselves not free from socialization.

- We consistently receive many contradictory messages from a multitude of social institutions; it is impossible not to be affected by these mixed messages.
- We cannot simply decide that these messages have no effect; it takes conscious and ongoing effort to challenge them, and they are constantly being reinforced all around us.
- Our experiences occur within a socially stratified society and must be contextualized as such.

Hopefully by this point our readers understand that they cannot be immune from the larger forces of socialization and that they couldn't avoid having been socialized into groups that are positioned hierarchically in relation to each other.

IGNORING INTERSECTIONALITY

- "I am oppressed as a lesbian, so I might be White but I have no privilege."
- "I think the true oppression is classism. If we address class, all the other oppressions will disappear."

People who raise this kind of objection have usually spent a lot of time thinking about their own oppression. This is understandable; the currents we swim *against* are often clear to us and it is much more difficult to feel and identify the currents we swim *with*. Yet identifying all of the currents we swim in is a powerful step in our growth.

Someone who is of Asian heritage, while experiencing racism, may simultaneously have several other forms of privilege if, for example, that person is heterosexual, middle class, and male. Of course racism will affect how he experiences these privileges; for example, racist stereotypes about Asian men often undercut how they experience male privilege. But while the dominant White culture may diminish Asian male masculinity, he will still experience male privilege in relation to Asian women and LGBTQ+ Asian people.

The dynamics of intersectionality are deeply significant and it is impossible to develop critical social justice literacy without an ability to grapple with their complexities. For example, in addition to other intersecting oppressions, classism and racism affect the gay community; racism and heterosexism affect people with disabilities; heterosexism and sexism affect people who are poor or working class; heterosexism and classism affect peoples of Color. Rather than rejecting the idea that we have any privilege if we experience oppression anywhere in our lives, the more constructive approach is to work to unravel these intersections to see how we may be upholding someone else's oppression.

REFUSING TO RECOGNIZE STRUCTURAL AND INSTITUTIONAL POWER

- "Women are just as sexist as men."
- "I'm the only male in my group so I am oppressed."
- "People of Color are just as racist as White people."

Given the deeply embedded patterns that develop from our group identities, simply being the only dominant-group member in a given setting will not be a reversal of oppression. Dominant-group members bring their patterns of privilege with them. For example, men in relation to women (and White men in particular) are socialized *overall* to take up more physical and social space than others. Men will tend to talk first, last, and most often; set the tone and the agenda of meetings; have a disproportionate effect on decisions; and be perceived as (and presume themselves to be) leaders in almost every context (internalized dominance).

Conversely, minoritized group members also have conditioned patterns (internalized oppression) that predispose them to defer to the dominant member. Women *overall* will talk less when men are present and allow men to lead (or risk being perceived as overbearing if they do not). These patterns and relations do not reverse or change based on the ratio of dominant to minoritized members present. Without intentionality and skills of alliance, the group members will enact the inequitable relationship. The new member will not be suddenly "oppressed" or have a "minority" experience because he is the only man in a group.

Another common objection is that of numbers. Statements such as "We don't have much racial diversity here because we don't have very many people of Color in our area" or conversely, "We are doing well because we have a lot of people of Color in our department" are often heard in response to questions of racial diversity in the workplace. There are a few important assumptions to notice underlying these statements:

- They reflect the dominant perspective; for example, a workplace that seems racially diverse to White people may not seem diverse to peoples of Color. And further, that racism is only present when peoples of Color are present.
- They assume that all that is needed to interrupt inequality is the presence of the minoritized group.
- Both of these statements defend and rationalize the status quo as either fine or unresolvable and thereby limit, rather than expand, further exploration.

As for the claim that peoples of Color are just as racist as White people, this is to confuse discrimination with racism. We are all just as prejudiced as the next person, and we all discriminate. But when we use the "ism" words, we are describing a dynamic of historical, institutional, cultural, and ideological power imbalance. Without the language to describe structural oppression, we continue to hide and deny its existence. Using the terms discrimination and racism interchangeably obscures the reality that discrimination across race is not the same in its effects, because only the discrimination by White people is backed by historical, institutional, cultural, ideological, and social power and thus has far-reaching and collective impact on the lives of peoples of Color. A more interesting and fruitful line of inquiry might be why so many people are so invested in insisting that the minoritized group is "just as" prejudiced or oppressive as the dominant group. What does this insistence and "whataboutism" rationalize or excuse? What is served by the refusal to acknowledge institutional power?

DENYING THE POLITICS OF LANGUAGE

- "What do they want us to call them now?"
- "You mean I have to watch everything I say?"

Language is a form of knowledge construction; the language we use to name a social group shapes the way we think about that group. To think critically about language is to think critically about power and ideology. Take the example of *unhoused people*. The terms we used in the past included *bums, derelicts, tramps, transients, hobos,* and *winos*. These are clearly negative terms that conjure negative images and are all typically associated with men. Over time, advocates came to realize that many women and children were also in this situation, and that women and children had different issues and needs because of their gender and age. In other words, the kinds of challenges that a single man might have are different from those that a single woman might have, and different still from those of a single woman living with children. Advocates realized that they had to change the public perception of this population in order to increase the resources available to them; few people were interested in helping "bums" and "winos" (notice how some people are perceived as worthy of resources and others are not). There was a deliberate political effort to introduce the term *homeless* in order to change the public perceptions of this diverse population. When the language changed, so did the perception; this change enabled greater access to resources.

The change from "bum" to "homeless person" and now to "unhoused person" illustrates the political power of language. As our understanding deepens, our language changes; advocates began to see the term *homeless* as problematic because "home" is associated with belonging and family, while "house" is shelter; someone unhoused could feel at home in the city and community in which they live. To shift perception about the problem from a personal failing of individuals to the structural failing of cities, proponents began to use the term *unhoused*. Doing so puts our attention on the fact that homelessness is fundamentally a housing issue and not the personal vulnerability of those living in poverty (Cheng, 2025).

The traditional names that dominant groups use for minoritized groups have their roots in history and were not chosen by the minoritized groups. Further, it really isn't that difficult to keep up with changes in language. Many of us manage to keep up with popular language of the day, whether it was slang like "groovy" and "cool" in the distant past or "OMG" and "LOL" in the more recent past. It is easy for us to adopt new language when we are invested in the social context. To choose not to be aware of changes in language regarding minoritized groups indicates that we may be living in a great deal of segregation from them. It is also an indication of a lack of interest that is not accidental. On the other hand, to be aware of changes in language yet still insist that we have the right to say anything we want is willful disrespect. Of course ultimately we have the right to say whatever we want in private space, but there are responsibilities we hold for what we say in public.

In a pluralistic society that claims to uphold the ideals of equality, speech must be chosen in ways that are cognizant of the context. We wouldn't speak to our supervisor, our grandparents, or our doctor the way we might to our friends. These are choices of context-appropriate speech, and we all conform to them on a daily basis. Rather than feeling resentful (an indicator that our internalized entitlement is being challenged), we might consider our ability to adapt to changes in language as an indicator that we are growing in our critical social justice literacy.

INVALIDATING CLAIMS OF OPPRESSION AS OVERSENSITIVITY

- "People just need to lighten up."
- "Why don't you people just get over it?"
- "I didn't mean it that way; can't you take a joke?"

This objection is a variation on the "political correctness" objection, which implies that whenever minoritized groups and their allies speak to oppression they are just being oversensitive and taking things too seriously. There are several problematic dynamics in this dismissal. First, note the arrogance of someone in the dominant group feeling qualified to determine the legitimacy of a minoritized group member's reaction to oppression. Remember that for many of us in the dominant group, our socialization is invisible, and so we often assume that others will share our frames of reference and see a situation the same way that we do. If we are committed to critical social justice, then we recognize that the responsibility for understanding should rest with the dominant group.

Another problematic dynamic is that dominant group members often do not understand the collective weight of oppression. What is "just a comment" for us is one of a thousand daily cuts for someone from the minoritized group. To be willing to let us know how oppression impacts them is risky given how freely dominant groups tend to trivialize this information. Dismissing the feedback as oversensitivity conveys that we are not open to or interested in understanding the impact of our behavior on others. A more constructive use of this feedback is as an entry point to consider what understanding *we* are lacking.

Focusing on intentions is another way we often dismiss the impact of our behavior. Common dominant group reasoning is that as long as we didn't *intend* to cause harm, then our actions don't count as harmful and we don't need to take responsibility for them. We then tend to spend a great deal of energy explaining to the minoritized group why our behavior is not problematic at all. This invalidates minoritized experiences while enabling us to deny responsibility for the impact of our behavior in both the immediate interaction and the broader historical context.

Finally, this dismissal allows dominant group members to project the problem outward while simultaneously minimizing it—the problem now belongs to the injured party and they themselves create it by taking life too seriously. According to this reasoning, it isn't really an issue at all; oppressed groups could easily solve inequality by getting over it and moving on. From a critical social justice perspective, this is the equivalent of telling peoples to accept their oppression.

The life and activism of Nora Bernard (Figure 11.1) illustrate the impact of oppression and minoritized groups' struggles for justice.

POSITIONING SOCIAL JUSTICE EDUCATION AS SOMETHING "EXTRA"

- "We have to prepare students for the test; that's just the way it is."
- "Dealing with social justice in the classroom (or workplace) takes time away from the real work we have to do."
- "I care about these issues but I am not allowed to speak about DEI-related topics."

We often hear rationales for inaction in school (or workplace) contexts wherein teachers (or leadership) explain that they wish they had time to deal with social justice but they have to deal with the curriculum (or the bottom line) first, and there just isn't time in the day to do everything. Because dominant institutions in society are positioned as being neutral, challenging social injustice within them seems to be an extra task in addition to our actual tasks. Or workplaces may no longer allow social justice issues to be named or addressed.

As we have argued, the way we act in the world is based on how we perceive the world. Our worldviews are not neutral; they are shaped by particular ideas about how society is or ought to be. For example, if you believe that we are all unique, that our group memberships are irrelevant, and that the best remedy for injustice is to attempt to see everyone as an individual, then that perspective will be visible in everything you do and how you do it.

If, on the other hand, you believe that our group memberships are important, that different groups have unequal access to resources, and that we have agency to positively influence that access for the betterment of everyone, then that too will be evident in everything you do.

Although it does take ongoing study and practice before a social justice framework will be internalized and fundamentally shape your work, to decide not

Figure 11.1. Nora Bernard (1935-2007)

Nora Bernard was a Canadian Mi'kmaq activist, member of the Millbrook First Nation, and survivor of the residential school in Shubenacadie, Nova Scotia.

She testified before a House of Commons Committee in 2005 saying, "Sexual and physical abuse was not the only abuse that the survivors experienced in these institutions. Abuses included such things as being incarcerated through no fault of their own; the introduction of child labor; the withholding of proper food, clothing, and proper education; the loss of language and culture; and no proper medical attention."

She initiated and won the largest class action lawsuit in Canadian history, on behalf of over 80,000 survivors of the Canadian residential school system. After 12 years of tireless activism on the part of Bernard and others, the federal government settled the suit, conservatively estimated at between 3 and 5 billion dollars. She received her compensation check for $14,000 in 2007.

Nora Bernard was posthumously awarded the Order of Nova Scotia in 2008.

Source: https://ammsa.com/node/7019

to take on this commitment does not mean you are being neutral. Indeed, to evade this commitment is to actively support and reproduce the status quo, which is, by default, inequitable. When we have developed a critical social justice consciousness, it is evident in all that we do and no longer requires extra effort.

BEING PARALYZED BY GUILT

- "I feel so bad and I don't know what to do."
- "This is all just a guilt trip."
- "You want me to hate myself for something I didn't do."

When we begin to realize that, contrary to what we have always believed, categories of difference (such as gender, race, class, and ability) *do* matter and significantly shape our perspectives, experiences, opportunities, and outcomes, we can feel overwhelmed. These feelings are part of the process of understanding oppression and injustice. But it's important not to get mired in these feelings or to use them as an excuse to avoid action. Consider the collective impact of wealthy people who benefit from classism claiming, "I feel so guilty about my wealth, I don't know what to do," or of men who benefit from sexism claiming, "I feel so bad that men dominate every institution, but it's not all men" or of White people who benefit from racism claiming, "I feel so ashamed about my unearned advantage, it's best not to talk about it."

It is normal to feel some shame when we realize we are implicated in social harm, and shame is a very difficult feeling to tolerate. For example, Beverly Daniel Tatum (1997) describes White racial shame as one of the hidden costs of racism. While being intentionally shamed is not useful, feeling shame does not mean one is *being* shamed. As with all feelings regarding oppression, the key is what we do with them. Do we use them as opportunities for deeper self-awareness or as excuses to disengage? Do we use them as motivators to work through the issue or to collapse in the face of their manifestations? Do we build connections that support us or do we separate ourselves in defensiveness and embarrassment? We need to build our tolerance and trust that the more authentically we internalize a critical social justice framework, the less immobilizing guilt or shame will be.

Another way that paralysis manifests is by waiting for instructions before acting. Our students often lament that they are being told about all of the problems but not given any solutions. The desire to jump to the "end" or to the answers can justify avoiding the hard work of self-reflection and skill building that is required of us. This lament can also work as a way to rationalize inaction: "If you can't tell me what to do, then I don't have to do anything." But the solutions are not simple formulas that can be applied by any person in any situation; they are dependent upon the specific context and social position of the person undertaking them. Knowing how to use your group positions strategically is the most powerful first step in evaluating how you might act. Further, it is also important that we don't focus solely on an individualistic approach; critical social justice action is already underway and we need to take the initiative to find out what is happening in our community (schools, workplaces, nonprofit organizations) and get involved.

Learning about injustice in its social, ideological, and historical context is not a process of "educating to feel patriotic and good" versus "educating to feel guilty and bad." Our communities have a history that is either known to us or unknown. We have inherited these histories and can either ignore them or act according to knowing them.

Contrary to claims that learning about systemic injustice evokes guilt and shame in dominant groups, a factual accounting of our society and its institutions, relations, and resource allocation is actually liberating; we didn't choose the systems we inherited. History offers us many positive role models, which can help to undermine guilt and shame. We didn't have a choice in our country's history or the culture that shaped our socialization, but we *do* have the choice to take responsibility for the outcome of that socialization. Taking that responsibility is the antidote to guilt and shame.

In the concluding chapter we offer some concrete suggestions for what one can do, but we encourage our readers to remember that the best antidote to guilty feelings is action.

DISCUSSION QUESTIONS

1. How would the authors respond to the rebuttal, "So, I have to watch everything I say?"
2. Which of the rebuttals have you felt yourself (or perhaps still feel)? Which is the most challenging for you and why? If you could speak back to yourself with the voice of the authors, what would you say?
3. Share some rebuttals that you have heard that are not included in this chapter. Using the concepts explained in this book, how might you respond to these rebuttals were they to be raised again in your presence? What challenges might there be in responding in a public context (such as a meeting at school or in the workplace) versus a private context (such as a family celebration or small gathering of friends), and how can you meet these challenges?

EXTENSION ACTIVITY

1.
   a. The following are common suggestions people make for achieving an equitable climate:

      » Respect people
      » Treat everyone equally
      » Don't take things personally
      » Don't judge
      » Don't make assumptions
      » Assume good intentions

      In small groups, see if you can come to consensus on describing what each of these would look like in action. Be sure that your description includes indicators that would allow anyone to recognize these when they saw them in action.
   b. What were the challenges of this activity? How might we understand these challenges from a critical social justice perspective?

PATTERNS TO PRACTICE SEEING

1. In critical social justice work, a common principle is that *listening does not require agreement*. This is important because the ability to listen to one another is foundational to finding common ground on challenging topics. Proceeding from the expectation that our readers will encounter these rebuttals in conversation about the topics this book addresses, pay attention to your own ability to listen. Then *develop* your tolerance for listening, even when rebuttals are anti–social justice. We cannot hope that reasonable people can hear a counternarrative if they themselves don't feel heard. Thus listening is foundational to advancing social justice.
2. There is a tendency for us to focus on the rebuttals that we fear receiving. Practice noticing how social justice leaders whom you admire conduct their social justice practice. What do you notice that they do? What do they say? How do they demonstrate strategy, courage, and strength? Watch their body language. See what you notice about their listening, timing, voice tone, temperament, word choice, and other moves they make when speaking back to power.

CHAPTER 12

Putting It All Together

"What am I supposed to do now?"

Understanding social justice means that we must be able to recognize that relations of unequal social power are constantly being negotiated at both the micro (individual) and macro (structural) levels. We must understand our own positions within these relations of unequal power. We must be able to think critically about knowledge. And most importantly, we must be able to act from this understanding in service of a more just society. This final chapter reviews key principles of critical social justice and offers some concrete suggestions for action.

What does it mean, then, to put critical social justice into action? In this chapter we return to the four key elements of understanding from the Preface and offer practical suggestions to guide the next phase of learning.

To review, understanding critical social justice means that an individual must be able to do the following:

- Recognize that relations of unequal social power are constantly being enacted at both the micro (individual) and macro (structural) levels.
- Understand our own positions within these relations of unequal power (positionality, intersectionality).
- Think critically about knowledge: what we know and how we know it.
- Act on all of the above in service of a more socially just society.

Below, we illustrate these elements through vignettes and organize them into two general areas: critical social justice *perspectives* (how we understand the issues) and *skills* (how we act on that understanding). We offer some questions and suggestions to guide your next steps in developing your critical social justice literacy. Keep in mind that these are only examples intended to illustrate key elements; we are not suggesting that oppression is limited to these situations, nor are our suggestions meant to be foolproof formulas. Expect to make mistakes, and consider them learning opportunities.

> **STOP:** There are a few schools specifically for minoritized groups, such as the African American Academy, women's colleges, and The Triangle Program alternative schools for LGBTQ+ youth. While these schools are segregated, their intent via the curriculum, pedagogy, staff, and faculty is to counter the oppressive forces in mainstream education. Mainstream schools are not created to counter these forces. Therefore, the reasons and effects of the segregation in these schools versus mainstream schools are not the same.

RECOGNIZE HOW RELATIONS OF UNEQUAL SOCIAL POWER ARE CONSTANTLY BEING ENACTED

Imagine ... a classroom of 20 teacher education students. In this class, there are 17 women students and 3 men. The women are early childhood or elementary education majors and the men are all secondary education majors. Seventeen of the students come from a middle-class suburban background, two from a working-class rural background, and one from a working-class urban background. The students' ages range from 19 to 25. All of them are White. Two of the students are neurodivergent; none of them has visible disabilities. English is their first language. The professor, a White woman, points out that much like the demographic of teachers and teacher educators, the class is not very diverse. Many of the students, feeling defensive, argue that there is a great deal of diversity among them. "We are very diverse, I am an introvert and Marcie is so outgoing." "Annie is a total jock! I am terrible at sports." "Have you heard Jason play the guitar? He is a really gifted musician."

Critical social justice perspective: What do you see? One of the dynamics at play in this scenario is the difference between how a person using a critical social justice lens sees diversity and how people who are using a mainstream lens see diversity. The students, looking through the lens of individualism, see diversity in terms of personality. From this lens, everyone is first and foremost a unique individual and social group memberships are unimportant. The instructor, who is looking through a critical social justice lens, sees the room in terms of key social groups. From this perspective, many major minoritized groups are missing, including: racialized peoples, people with visible disabilities, people from a range of socioeconomic classes, people in nontraditional gender career tracks, and people with a range of linguistic and cultural capital.

> **STOP:** A homogenous group can still engage with critical social justice. The key factors are the awareness and skills that those dominant group members bring to the table and how they apply those skills to address challenges such as the absence of minoritized perspectives.

The absence of these key groups is not an accident nor is it irrelevant; it is the result of long-term structural oppression. The homogeneity of the class in these terms is never neutral, benign, or "just a fluke" and the forces that have led to it are always in play. Because we are socialized to think of ourselves as individuals, especially in our dominant groups, it is often difficult to understand why it is useful to think about people in terms of their social groups. When we think in terms of groups, we can begin to see patterns of structural injustice, recognize that key perspectives are missing, and know to pursue those missing perspectives. This is not to imply that adding one or two "diverse" people corrects the issue of a missing perspective. Not only does that put an inordinate amount of pressure on that person to represent their group (sometimes called "tokenism"), it also reinforces the idea that the group being represented is a monolith and everyone within that group has the same perspective.

When we don't see our social surroundings in terms of groups, we don't notice how segregated we often are from minoritized people; segregation becomes normal and unremarkable. Thus we are not compelled to change this segregation. We will inadvertently make decisions that benefit us but may harm others if they are not at the table and can't share their needs or interests. Not seeing how structural power circulates through segregation does not mean that power is absent and no oppression is occurring. Indeed, power is reinforced in the very fact that we can look around and not see anyone of value missing. Expanding your capacity to see at the group level—where groups are and where they aren't—is critical for seeing how power is reproduced in institutions.

The more social group diversity there is in any social context, the more we increase our collective ability to consider multiple perspectives. Of course the presence of multiple perspectives (or social group diversity) is only the first step. The second is to foster an environment wherein people from minoritized groups (and their allies) can voice their perspectives and have them listened to and taken seriously; environments that are numerically diverse around key social group memberships are not necessarily prepared to support and engage with those perspectives, but it is a first step.

Critical social justice perspective: Defensiveness. Another dynamic in this scenario is the defensiveness the students feel when the instructor points out the lack of diversity. This defensiveness signals that the ideology of individualism has been challenged. In our dominant positions, we are not socialized to see ourselves as *group* members and it is common to take umbrage at the suggestion that an aspect of our identity matters. To point out the relevance of our group memberships is to challenge a privilege to which we often feel entitled: the privilege to see ourselves and be seen by others as individuals, outside of social groups.

The students' defensiveness also indicates that they are coming from a good/bad binary; the teacher has raised the issue of race, among other things, and implied that something is racially problematic about the demographics of the class. Unfortunately, their reaction indicates that they might not be as open to the discussion as they could be and this makes it harder for the instructor to broach it. This also sends an unwelcoming message to anyone else in the room who may want to engage constructively with the issue. Of course, we do not mean to imply that the defensiveness is not normal or temporary, or that the students are not open to the discussion at all. But defensiveness in this context is an indication of a dominant worldview, and it functions to protect that worldview rather than expand it. We can use our defensiveness as an entry point into deeper self-awareness, rather than blocking further engagement.

Critical social justice perspective: Additional layers of complexity. Now let's imagine that the instructor who points out the lack of diversity is a racialized person (or a member of any other minoritized group who is not represented in any significant way in that setting). In this case, there are at least two key dynamics to consider. The first dynamic is the risk it takes to bring up an issue of critical social justice to dominant group members, and particularly dominant group members who are the numerical majority in the setting. Remember, key patterns of dominance include: unawareness of injustice and/or denial of its existence; defensiveness about the suggestion that it exists; discomfort with the reminder of forms of injustice that benefit them; and lack the humility and tolerance to listen to minoritized groups. These patterns make it very difficult for minoritized people to speak out. Based on well-grounded past experience, they are likely to be acutely aware of the risks and know that they are outnumbered and unable to count on anyone else in the room to support them. Even if there is a dominant group member in the room who understands the point being made and the importance of engaging with it, if they play it safe and don't use their position to support the person who raised the issue, they are de facto supporting the unwelcoming climate in the setting.

> **STOP:** In the case that the instructor is a racialized person, while she does have a temporary position of authority in that setting, this position is of status, not of rank (see Chapter 5), and she will still be dealing with racism or other relevant forms of oppression.

A second key dynamic to consider is that dominant group members tend to dismiss the voices of minoritized group members as: representing "special" or biased interests; angry and disruptive; emotional and illogical; just an "unqualified diversity hire" and therefore, as unworthy of consideration. When the minoritized person is the instructor of the class (or the chair of a meeting, or the facilitator of a session), their status of temporary authority will be overridden by their rank as a minoritized group member, and any expertise they bring to the discussion may quickly be dismissed.

In order to constructively interrupt the dynamics of oppression in this scenario the following skills are necessary:

Critical social justice skills:

- See at the group level and understand the saliency of your group memberships and those of others around you.
- Recognize that colorblindness hides, rather than addresses, social injustice.
- Recognize what is lost in homogeneity.
- Move beyond good/bad binaries.
- Work from the knowledge that the societal default is oppression; there are no spaces free of it. Thus, the question becomes, "*How* is it manifesting here?" rather than "*Is* it manifesting here?"
- Lower any defensiveness you may be feeling.
- Educate yourself about groups you have been separated from.
- Build authentic cross-group relationships (authentic means committed, ongoing, reciprocal, and nontransactional, and does not mean seeking out a lone member of the minoritized group to educate you).

UNDERSTAND OUR OWN POSITIONS WITHIN RELATIONS OF UNEQUAL POWER (INTERSECTIONALITY)

Imagine... a workplace meeting with 14 people sitting around the table. Only three in the meeting are men, and all of these men are White. Of the rest of the group, three are women of Color. A White woman is chairing the meeting and opens the discussion by asking for suggestions on a problem the group is working on. One of the men makes the first suggestion. Without waiting for other suggestions to be brought to the table, a second man rebuts the first man's suggestion. They begin a back-and-forth exchange that goes on at length. Every now and then one of the women asks a question for clarification. One of the men occasionally prefaces his comments with, "I know I've been talking a lot, but..." and then continues to talk. Eventually, they wrap up their debate and a woman of Color makes the next suggestion. As soon as she begins speaking, one of the men checks his email and another gets up to refill his coffee.

Let's look at the dynamics of the meeting through a critical social justice lens. The first task is to identify the most salient group memberships at play in a given part of the meeting. Once we've identified them, we can begin to notice what patterns these groups bring and how they might be manifesting in ways that reinforce, rather than interrupt, inequitable outcomes. Then we can decide what actions would be most constructive for each player to take.

Critical social justice perspective: Salient group memberships and the patterns at play. The most salient social group memberships in this scenario are *gender* and *race.* The first pattern manifesting in the meeting is that of male domination of the discussion. Men, and White men in particular, tend to take up an inordinate amount of talk time. They are apt to speak first, speak next, and afford very little if any "wait time" during a discussion (Ridgeway et al., 2022). They may believe that the space is open and free and that other people should just speak up; that is, act like them. The presumption is that anyone can speak if they want to. In reality, however, airtime is a limited resource; due to typical time constraints, not everyone can speak even if they want to, and certainly not for as long as they want to. Further, wait time is subjective—what seems to dominant group members as a very long pause may not feel long to others. And certainly, women overall have not been socialized to "just speak up."

> **STOP:** It is highly unlikely that any of these patterns are conscious or intentional. Remember, from a critical social justice perspective, intentions are not as relevant as impact. Patterns, although enacted by individuals, accrue collectively at the group level and are the result of socialization; they are not our fault, but we are responsible for becoming aware of and interrupting them.

Another pattern in this scenario is that of the men shifting their attention away when a woman begins to speak. The men's behavior reinforces the dominant messages that men's voices are more important than women's, that men are entitled to speak first and most, and that what a woman has to say is not as valuable to men. These messages are reinforced for everyone in the meeting, but are further problematic because the woman who begins to speak is a woman of Color. In addition to what this communicates to women overall, this also communicates to the women of Color that their voices are less valuable and reinforces not only male privilege, but White privilege. While this may seem to be an isolated incident in which the men just happened to get up or check their email at the moment a woman of Color began to speak, it is only one example of the kinds of slights the women of Color endure every day; to the woman of Color this is likely not an isolated experience. Whiteness is also reinforced for the White women. Though they are disadvantaged by the male dominance, they still benefit from the racial dynamics manifesting in the room.

> **STOP:** Remember, injustice is not about numbers, it is about power. Although women were the numerical majority in this scenario, the men were still able to dominate.

Critical social justice perspective: Why these patterns matter. Those who speak first set the agenda, guide the discussion, disproportionately influence decisions, are seen as leaders, and gain more social capital. Social patterns in groups are well documented; dominant groups lead *overall*. While an *individual* member of a dominant group might not be dominating (in this case, the third man who was at the meeting but silent), in proportion to the ratio of men in the meeting, the men *collectively* are still dominating. In fact, the third man sitting silently and not facilitating a more equal sharing of limited airtime in the meeting supports their behavior (e.g., he could say, "I'm curious what other people think; could we hear from others?"). These patterns are independent of individual members' intentions; they are not personal and they are always at play. To challenge social injustice we have to challenge our group's patterns (whether we personally see ourselves participating in them or not).

This scenario also demonstrates a point made earlier in the classroom scenario: Although there were members of minoritized groups present in the meeting, in the absence of critical social justice skills and perspectives on the part of the dominant group members, the environment was not inclusive.

> **STOP:** Remember that we are simultaneously members of multiple social groups. While in one domain we may be oppressed (e.g., as women), in another domain we may enact dominance (e.g., as White women). These identities don't cancel each other out.

Critical social justice perspective: Additional layers of complexity. Now let us add an additional layer of complexity: intersectionality. Imagine that the meeting includes no men and consists instead of 14 women: 11 White women and three women of Color. In this context, the dynamics of race will rise to salience and the White women will tend to dominate. Although the White women have been socialized to defer to the voices of the White men (internalized gender oppression), they have also been socialized to dominate over peoples of Color (internalized racial dominance).

In order to constructively interrupt the dynamics of oppression in this scenario the following skills are necessary:

> **STOP:** It is *always* the primary responsibility of the dominant group members to use their positions to interrupt oppression.

Critical social justice skills:

- Recognize the range of social group memberships in the context.
- Think from the group rather than individual level.
- Remember that patterns are not personal.
- Understand that these patterns are deeply rooted and will not interrupt themselves.
- Understand that although you are in the same room, you are not having the same experience as others due to dynamics of inequitable power. When a member of the minoritized group speaks, be cognizant of your body language and of when you decide to take a break, either mental or physical.

For the dominant group:

- Move your focus from your *intentions*, to taking responsibility for the *impact* of your behavior.
- In general, don't speak first (this guideline may be bypassed if the speaker is making a strategic move to use his or her voice in order to interrupt broader group dynamics, but this is an advanced strategy that is best taken up in consultation with minoritized group members and other allies).
- Self-monitor your participation.
- Build your tolerance for listening.
- Push your wait time beyond your comfort zone (try counting to 10 before speaking).
- Invite different voices into the discussion ("Could we go around the table and hear from each person?" "Before we move on, who haven't we heard from?").
- Stating awareness of your pattern ("I know I'm talking a lot, but . . .") without stopping the pattern is disingenuous, allowing one to appear sensitive while still not letting go of control. If you are aware that you are dominating, stop dominating.

Intersectionality (in this case, the White women):

- Understand that because of racism and White privilege, you and the women of Color do not experience the White men's sexism in the same way.
- While there are always other dynamics at play, use your privilege when you can to support peoples of Color (for example, the White woman chairing the meeting could have taken greater control).

- A powerful step in challenging inequity is to recognize how your own internalized (gender) oppression may be silencing you and thus inadvertently contributing to the oppression of the women of Color.
- Your role is not to protect or save peoples of Color; if you choose to intervene in service of more inclusivity, do so for your own growth and interest in fostering a just society, and not because you expect gratitude or believe yourself to be the most qualified.

Intersectionality (in this case, the women of Color):

- Practice seeing how your group's socialized racial patterns may contribute to upholding racism for people from minoritized racial groups other than your own. Challenge these patterns where they uphold internalized racial oppression for you and other peoples of Color.
- Utilize the privilege you may have in other aspects of your life (e.g., language, religion, class, sexuality, status in the workplace). Use your positions to leverage power and be heard (use your status, e.g., "As the director of this program, I agree that we must address the fact that our students are not prepared to teach in urban schools," or use your rank privilege, e.g., "As a native English-language speaker, I can see the value of actively recruiting more multilingual people into our department").

THINK CRITICALLY ABOUT KNOWLEDGE

Imagine... You have been practicing your critical social justice literacy by working to identify ideology in a range of texts (books in school, news coverage, social media, advertisements, and movies). Over coffee, a friend tells you about an "amazing movie" she just saw called *Saving the Jungle*. The film takes place in the future when climate change has ravaged the planet and made it impossible to breathe without special equipment. Food is manufactured in factories because nothing can grow naturally any longer. Water is especially scarce and roving gangs patrol city streets, violently controlling access and charging exorbitant prices. The plot of the film revolves around a group of five scientists (all White, four men and one woman) looking for seeds that can be developed to grow in harsh conditions. They come upon an area of jungle previously unknown to the outside world that is pristine and untouched. They discover that they can breathe there without any equipment, and safely drink the water and eat the fruit. They also discover a tribe of Indigenous people who live in this jungle and who have never interacted with outside civilization. This tribe calls itself Nazirae. At first the Nazirae are wary and hide from the scientists but over time they come to trust them. Before long, a romance develops between the Nazirae princess and the head scientist, Jude. She shows him how to grow food, fish, and care for the land. Jude has a severe asthma condition due to the pollution he has breathed all his life, but the pure air in the jungle soon cures him. While the rest of the group return to share their findings, Jude decides to stay and never go back to the outside world. Word gets out about the jungle and representatives from a corporation descend and offer the Nazirae laptops and other technology in exchange for access to the land (your friend tells you about a really sweet scene when the Nazirae hear music coming from a laptop for the first time). The Nazirae believe that they are sharing the land, but the corporation plans to ethnically cleanse them and build a factory to bottle and sell the water and patent the seeds of the fruit for huge profits. Jude tries to stop this but the military is brought in, and while the corporation begins to cut down the trees to start work on the factory, the military begin to hunt and kill the Nazirae. Jude stays and fights alongside the Nazirae. He teaches them how to use automatic assault rifles and grenades and they teach him to set traps. Eventually they manage to fight off the invaders. The film ends with Jude and the princess snuggled in a hammock, and the last shot reveals that she is pregnant.

You feel a little uncomfortable with the stereotypes the film seems to reinforce. You raise this concern by cautioning your friend to remember that this film was written, produced, directed, and told from the White perspective, and the Indigenous people are depicted from a White perspective. You tell her that the characters and representations of the Indigenous people are pretty stereotypical.

"But," your friend protests, "the Indigenous people are the good guys!" She seems genuinely confused by your suggestion that this story, which she found so inspirational, could be problematic. After all, she says, it isn't just about bad White people, it is also about Indigenous people and how close they are to the Earth and how much traditional knowledge they hold and are willing to share and work together with good White people.

The following considerations can be useful for thinking about how to respond to your friend.

Critical social justice perspective: Key aspects of the exchange. A central element in this exchange is your friend's belief that the story can't be problematic because the Indigenous characters are presented as sympathetic. As we described in detail in Chapter 2, one of the key skills in adopting a critical social justice perspective is asking questions about the meaning given to any story. In this example we would ask: From whose perspective is the story told? Whose perspectives are missing? What was taken for granted about what the future will look like? What messages do we receive from the depiction of a devastated future planet as inevitable? Who funds Jude's team's research? Why is resistance located in the jungle and led by a lone hero and not organized on the streets of cities? How are the representations of Indigenous people and of White/Settler–Indigenous relationships similar to other representations (in, e.g., *Pocahontas, Tarzan, King Kong, The Lone Ranger, Pirates*

Figure 12.1. Frank Chin (b. 1940)

Author, playwright, and educator Frank Chin is the first Asian American to have had his plays performed on major New York stages with 1972's *The Chickencoop Chinaman* and 1974's *The Year of the Dragon*. Chin is an important figure in American theater, helping establish the Asian American Theatre Company in 1973. His works of fiction often examine the theme of stereotypes about Chinese and Asian Americans in mainstream society. His work brings attention to the importance of thinking critically about any text; all stories are constructed, and audiences must ask questions about what is being reproduced. Chin recognizes that there is a complicated relationship between being presented with the stories and experiences of "others" and actually "knowing" or understanding these experiences.

Source: https://commons.wikimedia.org/wiki/File:FRANKCHIN1975SF.jpg

of the Caribbean, *The Mission*, or *Avatar*)? Asking questions such as these is an important first step in unpacking the social construction of knowledge.

Frank Chin's work (Figure 12.1) illustrates the struggle of peoples of Color to tell their own stories in ways that don't reproduce racist stereotypes in mainstream culture.

Critical social justice perspective: Ideologies and discourses in the text. The plot of *Saving the Jungle* may sound familiar to you because many of us have seen some variation of this story many times. The story is a classic narrative of Whiteness. The following are some of the key elements that are repeated and reinforced in the story:

- The story is told from the perspective of White people.
- White people act as saviors of Indigenous peoples (and other racialized people).
- White people who are willing to save/help BIPOC peoples, at seemingly great personal cost, are noble and courageous.
- BIPOC peoples are politically, socially, and militarily "innocent" and childlike and can only fight a battle with the help of White people.
- Urban spaces and the people living in them are inherently threatening, dangerous, and criminal.

- The most dependable route for escaping "dangerous cities" is to find clean, resourced, and unpolluted land to settle.
- White people who are willing to "live among" and adapt to the way of life of BIPOC peoples are morally superior to other White people.
- There is only one hero, usually a strong White man, and he doesn't collaborate or engage in organizing others.
- The "happy ever after" is a heterosexual nuclear family.

Critical social justice perspective: Economic and social interests in the production of the text. There are social and economic interests in the telling of any story, be it in popular film or school textbooks. In addition to understanding the concept of perspective, it is also important to ask whose interests are best served by a particular story.

- Who wrote and produced the text?
- Who is the primary audience for this text?
- Why will this story appeal to its intended audience? (In the case of a movie, in order to appeal to the masses, it must reinscribe familiar plots and characters. In the case of a textbook, a governing body that represents specific interests must approve it.)
- Who will profit from this text?

Critical social justice perspective: Additional layers of complexity. Now let us add an additional layer of complexity to this vignette by considering how texts are read and interpreted by audiences. From a critical social justice perspective, it is always important to question narratives that are inspirational to a mass audience. Generally, racial narratives will be inspirational to a mass audience only when they reinforce familiar ideologies of White supremacy and moral goodness.

While a text's ideologies and the economics of its production may be fixed, the way that text is interpreted and valued by audiences is not. Herein lies the audience's agency: The more layers of complexity we can recognize in a text, the more critically we can engage with that text.

Critical social justice skills:

Be aware that:

- There is no neutral text; all texts represent a particular perspective.
- All texts are embedded with ideology; the ideology embedded in most mainstream texts functions to reproduce historical relations of unequal power.
- Texts that appeal to a wide audience usually do so because they reinforce dominant narratives and serve dominant interests.
- Identify the ideology and what or whom it serves.
- Expect there to be social consequences for challenging dominant ideology.

- Build your tolerance for the resistance you will likely get when you challenge dominant ideologies.
- Develop the skills to lower your and others' defensiveness and diplomatically provide an alternative perspective. For example, regarding your friend in the opening vignette, you might say, "I read a critical analysis of this film and it gave me a perspective I hadn't considered before. Can I share it with you?"

ACT IN SERVICE OF A MORE JUST SOCIETY

Although all of the previous principles are necessary for critical social justice literacy, they are meaningless without action. We use the term *ally* to refer to a member of the dominant group who understands that oppression is systemic and that they are positioned to benefit from that system, and who interrupts that system whenever and wherever they can. There are several other terms that capture the role of an ally and these terms change over time; others you may have heard include *coconspirator* and *accomplice*. The following are examples of allies: men who work to identify and challenge their internalized gender superiority, work with other men to do the same, and speak out alongside of women; and White people who work to identify and challenge their internalized racial superiority, and work with other White people to do the same.

In general, being an ally means:

- Validating and supporting people who are socially or institutionally minoritized in relation to you, regardless of whether you completely agree with or understand where they are coming from
- Engaging in continual self-reflection to uncover your socialization and internalized superiority
- Working with other members of the dominant group and not positioning yourself as better or more advanced than they are
- Advocating when the oppressed group is absent by pointing out their absence and the impact of that absence on the group's decision-making/process
- Letting go of control and sharing power
- Building authentic relationships with minoritized group members (mutually beneficial and nontransactional)
- Taking responsibility for and repairing harm you cause
- Having humility and being willing to admit not knowing
- Earning trust through action

In institutional spaces, such as meetings, allies can take these actions:

- Validate and back up the contributions and perspectives of members of minoritized groups.

- Pay attention to your position in relation to minoritized colleagues in terms of rank (race, class, gender) and in terms of status (the job title you and they have and their relative power). Use your position strategically.
- Generate a working definition of critical social justice and a way to assess it. Work from this framework and call people back to this commitment when needed. There are many tools available from various organizations, as well as many excellent examples of organizations that have implemented definitions and assessments (such as the United Steelworkers of Canada union's statement, described below, and the American Federation of Labor and Congress of Industrial Organizations [AFL-CIO]'s human rights and equity workplace toolkits).
- Pay attention to the dynamics in meetings and interrupt inequitable patterns.
- Recognize that it matters who is in our environment (such as in the workplace, schools, and neighborhoods) and the roles they play; work to increase representation and create a supportive climate.
- Recognize and affirm the importance of discussing critical social justice issues, even when uncomfortable.
- Be honest about your lack of knowledge while demonstrating your willingness to learn.
- Change the process. For example, move away from depending solely on voluntary participation in large-group discussions (sometimes called "popcorn style"); try calling for a go-around, or working in small groups, or working in pairs.
- Facilitate by inviting other voices in by extending wait time and asking, "Who hasn't had a turn yet?" and then waiting.
- Facilitate dialogue rather than debate, working toward finding common ground, using both/and rather than either/or framework.
- Work in solidarity with others and not in isolation; don't distance yourself from others in your dominant group.
- Be humble about your skills; members of the dominant group are the least qualified to judge their ally effectiveness.
- The "isms" are always operating and thus feedback about something problematic you've done is not an accusation. Appreciate the courage it takes to give feedback, learn from it, and move forward.

While the above are examples of actions an individual can take, the following is an example of action that an organization can take: The United Steelworkers of Canada's diversity statement on gay, lesbian, bisexual, and transgender issues incorporates critical social justice into its mission. Because we find their statement an exceptional example, we quote directly from their handbook below.

In the opening, they state (as many organizations do) that they value diversity:

Proud to represent lesbian, gay, bisexual and transgender workers, Steelworkers are actively working for equality in the workplace, at the bargaining table and in our communities. Steelworkers are helping to raise understanding and respect for the diversity and differences that make us strong, proud and, indeed, Everybody's Union. Human rights are workers' rights. When someone is harassed or isolated in the workplace because of his sexual orientation or her gender identity, their human rights and their rights as workers are violated.

Fear of harassment, violence, isolation and bullying lead many people to hide or deny their sexual orientation or gender identity.

The Steelworkers union must continue to take steps to help create "positive space" for gay, lesbian, bisexual and transgendered workers.

(United Steelworkers of Canada, 2008)

But what distinguishes this diversity statement from most (and makes it exceptional) is that the authors do not stop there. They operationalize (i.e., make concrete) the critical social justice work that is necessary in order to create a "positive space." For example, they identify concrete objectives, state where and how they will act, and explicitly name their goals, which include:

At the bargaining table:

- Negotiate anti-harassment workplace training, policies and procedures. The United Steelworkers' Anti-Harassment Workplace Training Program has reached over 45,000 front line workers, supervisors and managers.
- Bargain for anti-discrimination language to be included into [the] collective agreement.
- Make sure your definition of spouse includes same sex partners. In Canada, it is illegal to deny same-sex spousal benefits.

In the union:

- Start a Steelworker Pride Committee. . . . Pride Committees are opportunities for gay, lesbian, bisexual, transgendered workers and their supporters to talk about issues, and plan how to raise awareness in our workplaces and in the union of gay, lesbian, bisexual and transgendered rights. Steelworker Pride Committees join with other labor and community groups to hold events and parades to both celebrate and educate.

Take action:

- Help fight HIV/AIDS. HIV/AIDS is a union issue. We work with people who have HIV/AIDS and care for people who have HIV/AIDS. We must make sure our workplaces are safe, healthy and harassment free for all

workers. That means preventing harassment and discrimination of people with HIV/AIDS.
- The Steelworkers Humanity Fund is helping to support the work of Stephen Lewis and the United Nations to build a global fund to fight AIDS, tuberculosis and malaria. Canadian workers can demonstrate leadership in raising the resources, and pressuring other countries to do the same, to stop this epidemic.
- The Federal Government is appealing a court decision which granted Canada Pension Plan survivor spousal pensions to persons who lost their same sex partners between 1985–1998. LGBT persons paid into the CPP just like everyone else and are entitled to equal benefits. Let your Member of Parliament know that you disapprove of their wasting tax money to promote inequality. (United Steelworkers of Canada, 2008)

The Steelworkers offer a powerful example of collective action and accountability, and the critical social justice vision that guides them. While these will not be easy goals to achieve given the embedded nature of oppression, their articulation is a fundamental step. Without a framework to keep the organization accountable, it is unlikely that there would be much institutional change.

At the beginning of this chapter we asked the question, "What does it mean, then, to put critical social justice into action?" We offered vignettes to illustrate different elements of critical social justice literacy and discussed them in some depth. Now we ask our readers to use the example of racism (or any other form of oppression), to reflect upon the following and jot down some examples for each:

- Active racism
- Passive racism
- Active antiracism
- Passive antiracism

Perhaps your list looks something like the following:

For *active racism*, your examples might include telling or encouraging racist jokes, committing violence against peoples of Color, name-calling, racial profiling, and accusing peoples of Color of "playing the race card" when they try to bring up racism.

For *passive racism*, your examples might include silence, assuming a person of Color is an unqualified "diversity hire," ignoring incidents and dynamics that you notice, the inequitable funding of schools, lack of interest in learning more about racism, having few if any cross-racial relationships, apathy toward—and lack of awareness about—movements for racial justice, and not getting involved in antiracist efforts or in continuing education.

For *active antiracism*, examples might include working to identify internalized racial dominance if you are White, working to identify internalized racial oppression if you are a person of Color, making sure there are multiple racial perspectives on an issue in the workplace, joining organizations working for racial justice, and seeking out continuing education.

But now we come to *passive antiracism*. If you were able to come up with any examples, reconsider them from the lens of *action* and you will likely find that they don't hold up; antiracism requires action—by definition, it cannot be passive. There really are no examples of passive antiracism. Antiracism, or any other endeavor to challenge injustice, is by definition not passive.

To illustrate the various layers of action, consider this analogy. Most of us know the basic rules of basketball. There are two teams, and each team is trying to get the ball into the opposing team's basket while simultaneously preventing the other team from doing the same. Each player has a position on the team, and novice players focus on their assigned role. However, skilled players are able to see beyond their own position and synthesize all of the dynamics in play. This enables them to think strategically about every move, consider the positions of every other player in relation to their own, and base their next moves on multiple, shifting, and contextual factors. Although these players must know how the game is played and have a familiar style of playing, they do not follow a set plan and likely do not make the exact same decision twice. Instead, they are always taking into account the bigger picture based on their knowledge of the opposing team's players, the rules of the game, and which other players from their team are nearby to support them, as well as their own developing skill level. All of these factors inform the decision they will make about their next move (DiAngelo & Sensoy, 2010).

Developing critical social justice literacy requires a lifelong commitment to an ongoing process. This process challenges our worldview and our relationships to others. It asks us to connect ourselves to uncomfortable concepts such as prejudice, privilege, and oppression. It challenges simplistic dos-and-don'ts such as *"do treat everyone equally"* and *"don't see Color."* Of course it's so much easier when we believe that attaining social justice is as simple as a list of dos and don'ts. We wouldn't have to take account of the history of oppression in our nation-states or trace that history into our present lives. We wouldn't have to think deeply, engage in uncomfortable self-reflection, admit to our socialization into systems of inequality, strive for humility in the face of the unknown, and build relationships with people that we haven't been taught are valuable. We *would* have to acknowledge that our achievements are not simply or solely the result of merit and hard work, for within a society that is socially stratified, most of us benefit in some aspects of our lives from the disadvantages of others. And finally, we would have to take risks, make mistakes, and *act*.

DISCUSSION QUESTIONS

1. Now what? What are your next steps (tomorrow, next week, next year) to continue the work of developing critical social justice literacy? What might be the easiest of these steps to accomplish? What will take longer?

Identify what might be your key challenges. How will you meet these challenges?
2. The authors state that it is always the responsibility of the dominant group to interrupt oppression. Does this mean the minoritized group has no role? If it is the dominant group's responsibility, who should be in charge or lead the effort? How and why? Discuss the assumptions and dynamics involved in the concept of where the problem lies.
3. Revisit the scenario of the meeting, when the two men who have been dominating the discussion choose to get up or open their laptop when a woman of Color begins to speak. Imagine now that these men claim that their timing had nothing to do with the woman speaking. Distinguishing between "intention versus impact," explain why their behavior was problematic, regardless of their intentions. Discuss all of the various dynamics at play in the meeting. Imagine you are at the meeting, and practice responding to interrupt the patterns of dominance. What will you say or do? Take account of your position in relation to the others in the group.

EXTENSION ACTIVITIES

1. Identify someone with whom you share an identity—either dominant or minoritized—and who is also on a social justice learning journey. Make a plan to check in with one another in a month. Decide what you will commit to doing in that month's time in working toward interrupting your internalized superiority or your internalized oppression (depending on what identity you pair around). This could involve reading more deeply about your group in relation to social justice and/or oppression, engaging in self-care (for a minoritized group), identifying resources about your group within your community and connecting with them, or identifying a local issue in your school or community that you want to address/understand from your group's perspective.
2. Produce an essay examining your life through a critical social justice lens. This activity is meant to integrate your personal experiences with the theoretical framework of the book (the activity is *not* meant to be an unanalyzed narrative of your life story or your opinions about the various groups you do or do not belong to). Please draw upon the chapter themes (socialization, oppression, class, gender, racism, privilege, etc.) to provide an analysis of what shapes your perspectives, values, expectations, and beliefs as a member of the various social groups you belong to.

   In your essay, describe how key influences (such as family, friends, schools, communities, ideas, values, your culture(s), and/or the wider society) have been formative in your thinking (or lack of thinking) about your experiences as a member of the groups you belong to.

It may be helpful to focus your analysis on one or two key group memberships (for example, race and gender) or to select one identity in which you experience privilege and one in which you experience oppression (for example, as a White woman).

Some guidelines for working on your essay and questions to stimulate your thinking:

» You must be a member of the groups you are writing about.
» Consider the historical, institutional, ideological, and cultural dimensions of your group's position in U.S. or Canadian society that influence your understanding of your group.
» Name a minoritized group that you are a member of. What is the dominant group in relation to your group? What kind of feelings do you experience as a member of this group? In what ways is your group made visible or invisible? In what circumstances? How has oppression manifested in your life as a member of this group? In what ways does this group membership affect your daily life? How does membership in this group affect your understanding of and attitudes toward the dominant group?
» Name a dominant group that you are a member of. What groups are minoritized in relation to yours? What feelings do you experience as a member of this dominant group? Do you notice a difference in your ability to identify feelings when thinking about dominant group membership compared with minoritized group membership? In other words, is this question harder to answer than the questions relating to your minoritized group identity? If so, what are the implications of that difficulty? How is your group powerful? What forms of power does your group hold? What institutions are used to exert this power? In what ways? What privileges do you have as a member of the dominant group? How does membership in this group affect your daily life? How does membership in this group affect your understanding of and attitudes toward the minoritized group?

(This is a widely used activity called Multicultural Mapping. This version is adapted from Maxwell et al., 2023.)

3. Watch the documentary film *Searching for Anna May Wong* (2020), directed by Denise Chan and Z. Eric Yang. What does the documentary reveal about Whiteness in the film industry? How does the default of Whiteness impact the career opportunities for Asian heritage actors and industry workers? Explore the history of Anna May Wong and watch one of her early films. How are her experiences in Hollywood in the

1920s and 1930s similar to and different from the experiences of Asian American women actors now, in the 2020s?

PATTERNS TO PRACTICE SEEING

1. Notice how strong the pull is for easy answers and any feelings of frustration about not receiving them. Notice too that we can understand critical concepts intellectually, yet still respond at the emotional level from our earlier conditioning. Use insights from your reflections to seek out and plan your next move to support your ongoing learning.

References

Abaied, J. L., Perry, S. P., Cheaito, A., & Ramirez, V. (2022). Racial socialization messages in White parents' discussions of current events involving racism with their adolescents. *Journal of Research on Adolescence, 32*(3), 863–882.

Aberson, C. L. (2019). Friendships with Blacks relate to lessened implicit preferences for Whites over Blacks. *Collabra: Psychology, 5*(1), 16. https://doi.org/10.1525/collabra.195

Abu-Amr, Z. (1993). Hamas: A historical and political background. *Journal of Palestine Studies, 22*(4), 5–19.

Acemoglu, D., Robinson, J. A., & Verdier, T. (2004). Alfred Marshall Lecture: Kleptocracy and divide-and-rule: A model of personal rule. *Journal of the European Economic Association, 2*(2/3), 162–192.

Adair, M., & Howell, S. (2007). *Common behavioral patterns that perpetuate power and relations of domination.* Tools for Change. https://chcnetwork.org/wp-content/uploads/2022/03/Tools-for-Change.pdf

Adams, M., Bell, L., Goodman, D. J., & Joshi, K. Y. (2016). *Teaching for diversity and social justice* (3rd ed.). Routledge.

Adjei, P. B. (2016). The (em)bodiment of Blackness in a visceral anti-Black racism and ableism context. *Race Ethnicity and Education, 21*(3), 275–287. https://doi.org/10.1080/13613324.2016.1248821

Adler, P. S. (2019). *The 99 percent economy: How democratic socialism can overcome the crises of capitalism.* Oxford University Press.

AFL-CIO. (2024a). *2024 executive paywatch.* https://aflcio.org/paywatch#:~:text=Average%20CEO%20Pay%20Is%20Growing,500%20Index%20companies%20in%202023

AFL-CIO. (2024b). *Company pay ratios.* https://aflcio.org/paywatch/company-pay-ratios

Ahmed, S. (2007). A phenomenology of Whiteness. *Feminist Theory, 8*(2), 149–168. https://doi.org/10.1177/1464700107078139

Ahmed, S. (2017). *Living a feminist life.* Duke University Press.

Ajemian, N. (2025). Women run 11% of Fortune 500 companies in 2025—but progress is still slow. *Fortune.*: https://fortune.com/2025/06/02/fortune-500-companies-run-by-female-ceos-women-2025/

Ajour, A. (2025). Unveiling the colonial violence of space in the Gaza genocide. *European Journal of Cultural Studies.* https://doi.org/10.1177/13675494241310778

Alexander, M. (2010). *The new Jim Crow: Mass incarceration in the age of colorblindness.* New Press.

Alfani, G. (2025). Inequality in history: A long-run view. *Journal of Economic Surveys, 39*(2), 546–566.

Ali, M. M., Islam, M. S., Islam, A. R. M. T., Bhuyan, M. S., Ahmed, A. S., Rahman, M. Z., & Rahman, M. M. (2022). Toxic metal pollution and ecological risk assessment in water and sediment at ship breaking sites in the Bay of Bengal Coast, Bangladesh. *Marine Pollution Bulletin, 175*, 113274. https://doi.org/10.1016/j.marpolbul.2021.113274

Aliprandi, G., Busschots, T., & Oliveira, C. (2023). *Mapping the global geography of shell companies* [Report]. EU Tax Observatory. https://www.taxobservatory.eu/publication/mapping-the-global-geography-of-shell-companies/

Allport, G. W. (1954). *The nature of prejudice.* Addison-Wesley.

Almeida, L. (2025, April 24). Trump's meme coin soars after he asks top 220 holders to dinner. *The Guardian*. https://www.theguardian.com/technology/2025/apr/24/donald-trumps-meme-coin-value-surges-after-gala-dinner-invites

Altman, A., & Watson, L. (2018). *Debating pornography*. Oxford University Press.

Amadeo, K. (2018, December 1). *How outsourcing jobs affects the U.S. economy*. The Balance. [Updated June 16, 2022] https://www.thebalance.com/how-outsourcing-jobs-affects-the-u-s-economy-3306279

American Civil Liberties Union (ACLU). (2011). *Banking on bondage: Private prisons and mass incarceration*. https://www.aclu.org/banking-bondage-private-prisons-and-mass-incarceration

American Civil Liberties Union (ACLU). (2017). *Mass incarceration: What's at stake*. www.aclu.org/issues/mass-incarceration

American Civil Liberties Union (ACLU). (2022, February 22). *Smart justice*. https://www.aclu.org/issues/smart-justice

American Civil Liberties Union (ACLU). (2024, October 28). *Mass incarceration: An animated series*. https://www.aclu.org/news/smart-justice/mass-incarceration

Amra & Elma. *100 top kid influencers in 2023*. https://www.amraandelma.com/top-kid-influencers/

Anderson, C. (2017). *White rage: The unspoken truth of our racial divide*. Bloomsbury.

Anderson, C. (2018). *One person, no vote: How voter suppression is destroying our democracy*. Bloomsbury.

Anderson, M., Faverio, M., & Gottfried, J. (2023). *Teens, social media and technology 2023: YouTube, TikTok, Snapchat and Instagram remain the most widely used online platforms among U.S. teens*. Pew Research Center. https://www.pewresearch.org/internet/2023/12/11/teens-social-media-and-technology-2023/#how-much-time-are-teens-spending-online

Androcentrism. (2009). In J. O'Brien (Ed.), *Encyclopedia of gender and society* (p. 32). SAGE Publications. https://doi.org/10.4135/9781412964517

Anker, E. R. (2020). "White and deadly": Sugar, slavery, and the sweet taste of freedom. *Theory & Event*, *23*(1), 169–206. https://doi.org/10.1353/tae.2020.0008

Anyon, J. (1981). Social class and school knowledge. *Curriculum Inquiry*, *11*(1), 3–42.

Anyon, J. (2011). *Marx and education*. Routledge.

Anzaldúa, G. (2009). La conciencia de la mestiza. In R. Warhol-Down & D. Price Herndl (Eds.), *Feminisms redux: An anthology of literary theory and criticism* (pp. 303–313). Rutgers University Press.

Apple, M. W. (1993). *Ideology and curriculum*. Routledge.

Applebaum, B. (2016, June 9). Critical Whiteness studies. *Oxford Research Encyclopedia of Education*. https://oxfordre.com/education/view/10.1093/acrefore/9780190264093.001.0001/acrefore-9780190264093-e-5

Applebaum, B. (2022). Willful hermeneutical ignorance and the "critical race theory" controversy. *Educational Theory*, *72*(6), 689–702. https://doi.org/10.1111/edth.12553

Appleman, L. I. (2022). Bloody lucre: Carceral labor and prison profit. *Wisconsin Law Review*, *22*(3), 619–664.

APTN National News. (2023, January 17). *Wauzhushk Onigum Nation finds 171 anomalies during search of St. Mary's School*. https://www.aptnnews.ca/national-news/wauzhushk-onigum-nation-finds-171-anomalies-during-search-of-st-marys-school-site/

Arneil, B. (2024). Colonialism versus imperialism. *Political Theory*, *52*(1), 146–176. https://doi.org/10.1177/00905917231193107

Aslund, A. (2005). *Comparative oligarchy: Russia, Ukraine and the United States*. CASE Network Studies and Analyses, 296. https://ideas.repec.org/p/sec/cnstan/0296.html

Au, W. (2021). Testing for Whiteness? How high-stakes, standardized tests promote racism, undercut diversity, and undermine multicultural education. In J. H. Writer & H. P. Baptiste (Eds.), *Visioning multicultural education* (pp. 99–113). Routledge. https://doi.org/10.4324/9781003095644-9

Austin, N., & Harper, S. (2019). Quantifying the impact of targeted regulation of abortion provider laws on US abortion rates: A multi-state assessment. *Contraception*, *100*(5), 374–379. https://doi.org/10.1016/j.contraception.2019.06.003

References

Awaya, T., & Tsuboi, Y. (2024). Colonization and imperialism. In R. Sayashi, Y. Matsuda, & W. Aoyama (Eds.), *Asia rising: A handbook of history and international relations in East, South and Southeast Asia* (pp. 31–42). Springer Nature Singapore. https://link.springer.com/book/10.1007/978-981-97-4375-9

Bailey, J., & Burkell, J. (2021). Tech-facilitated violence: Thinking structurally and intersectionally. *Journal of Gender-Based Violence, 5*(3), 531–542. https://doi.org/10.1332/239868021X16286662118554

Baker, E. J., Lake, F. R., & Wilson, C. (2021). Rooted in oppression: Why the U.S. policing and carceral systems are issues of systemic environmental injustice. *Environmental Justice, 14*(6), 411–417. https://doi.org/10.1089/env.2021.0031

Baker, H. A., Jr. (1990). Handling "crisis": Great books, rap music, and the end of Western homogeneity (reflections on the humanities in America). *Callaloo, 13*(2), 173–194.

Baker, S. (2024, April 17). One NBA benchwarmer will earn more than Caitlin Clark's entire team. *Axios*. https://www.axios.com/2024/04/17/caitlin-clark-wnba-salaries-pay-contract

Ballantine, J. H., & Spade, J. Z. (2008). *Schools and society: A sociological approach to education* (3rd ed.). SAGE Publications.

Banaji, M. R., Fiske, S. T., & Massey, D. S. (2021). Systemic racism: Individuals and interactions, institutions and society. *Cognitive Research: Principles and Implications, 6*(1), 82.

Banks, C. A. M. (2005). *Improving multicultural education: Lessons from the intergroup education movement*. Teachers College Press.

Banks, J. A. (1996). The canon debate, knowledge construction, and multicultural education. In J. A. Banks (Ed.), *Multicultural education, transformative knowledge, and action: Historical and contemporary perspectives* (pp. 3–39). Teachers College Press.

Banks, J. A. (Ed.). (2003). *Diversity and citizenship education: Global perspectives*. Jossey-Bass.

Banks, J. A. (2006a). *Cultural diversity and education: Foundations, curriculum, and teaching* (5th ed.). Pearson/Allyn and Bacon.

Banks, J. A. (2006b). *Race, culture, and education: The selected works of James A. Banks*. Routledge.

Banks, J. A. (2008). *An introduction to multicultural education* (4th ed.). Pearson/Allyn and Bacon.

Banks, J. A., & Banks, C. A. M. (Eds.). (1995). *Handbook of research on multicultural education*. Jossey-Bass.

Bassiouni, M. C., & Ben Ami, S. (2009). Antecedents to the League of Nations Mandate for Palestine: 1897–1922. In *A guide to documents on the Arab-Palestinian/Israeli Conflict: 1897–2008* (Vol. 29). Brill.

Battalora, J. (2013). *Birth of a White nation: The invention of White people and its relevance today*. Strategic Book Publishing.

Bem, S. L. (2004). Transforming the debate on sexual inequality: From biological difference to institutionalized androcentrism. In J. C. Chrisler, C. Golden, & P. Rozee (Eds.), *Lectures on the psychology of women* (pp. 3–15). McGraw-Hill.

Benoit, C., Smith, M., Jansson, M., Healey, P., & Magnuson, D. (2019). "The prostitution problem": Claims, evidence, and policy outcomes. *Archives of Sexual Behavior, 48*(7), 1905–1923.

Benson, C. (2023, December 21). *Child poverty rate still higher than for older populations but declining*. Census.gov. https://www.census.gov/library/stories/2023/12/poverty-rate-varies-by-age-groups.html

Bergvall, V. L., Bing, J. M., & Freed, A. F. (Eds.). (1996). *Rethinking language and gender research: Theory and practice*. Longman.

Bertrand, M., & Mullainathan, S. (2004). Are Emily and Greg more employable than Lakisha and Jamal? A field experiment on labor market discrimination. *The American Economic Review, 94*(4), 991–1013.

Bettio, F., Della Giusta, M., & Di Tommaso, M. L. (2017). Sex work and trafficking: Moving beyond dichotomies. *Feminist Economics, 23*(3), 1–22.

Bhargava, A., Arnold, A. P., Bangasser, D. A., Denton, K. M., Gupta, A., Hilliard Krause, L. M., Mayer, E. A., McCarthy, M., Miller, W. L., Raznahan, A., & Verma, R. (2021). Considering sex as a biological variable in basic and clinical studies: An Endocrine Society scientific statement. *Endocrine Reviews, 42*(3), 219–258. https://doi.org/10.1210/endrev/bnaa034

Bhungalia, L. (2024). *Elastic empire: Refashioning war through aid in Palestine*. Stanford University Press.

Bhutta, N., Chang, A. C., Dettling, L. J., & Hsu, J. W. (2020, September 20). *Disparities in wealth by race and ethnicity in the 2019 survey of consumer finances* [FEDS Note]. Board of Governors of the Federal Reserve System. https://www.federalreserve.gov/econres/notes/feds-notes/disparities-in-wealth-by-race-and-ethnicity-in-the-2019-survey-of-consumer-finances-20200928.html

Bilmes, L. J., Hartung, W. D., & Semler, S. (2024). *United States spending on Israel's military operations and related U.S. operations in the region, October 7, 2023–September 30, 2024*. Watson Institute for International and Public Affairs, Brown University. https://watson.brown.edu/costsofwar/files/cow/imce/papers/2023/2024/Costs%20of%20War_US%20Support%20Since%20Oct%207%20FINAL%20v2.pdf

Binnie, J., & Reavey, P. (2020). Development and implications of pornography use: A narrative review. *Sexual and Relationship Therapy, 35*(2), 178–194.

Bishu, S. G., & Alkadry, M. G. (2016). A systematic review of the gender pay gap and factors that predict it. *Administration & Society, 49*(1), 65–104.

Blaut, J. M. (1989). Colonialism and the rise of capitalism. *Science & Society, 53*(3), 260–296. https://www.jstor.org/stable/40404472

Bloomberg. (n.d.). *Billionaires*. Accessed May 11, 2025, from https://www.bloomberg.com/billionaires/

Bonilla-Silva, E. (2006). *Racism without racists: Color-blind racism and the persistence of racial inequality in the United States* (2nd ed.). Rowman & Littlefield.

Bonilla-Silva, E. (2019). Feeling race: Theorizing the racial economy of emotions. *American Sociological Review, 84*(1), 1–25. https://doi.org/10.1177/0003122418816958

Bonilla-Silva, E., & Peoples, C. E. (2022). Historically White colleges and universities: The unbearable Whiteness of (most) colleges and universities in America. *American Behavioral Scientist, 66*(11), 1490–1504. https://doi.org/10.1177/00027642211066047

Bower, B. (2006, April 22). The bias finders. *Science News, 169*(16), 250–251, 253. https://www.proquest.com/magazines/bias-finders/docview/197480531/se-2

Box Office Mojo. (n.d.). *Top lifetime grosses*. https://www.boxofficemojo.com/chart/top_lifetime_gross/?area=XWW

Bradley, B. D. A. (2024). Sex education after Dobbs: A case for comprehensive sex education. *Berkeley Journal of Gender, Law and Justice, 39*, 121.

Brady, D. (2024, August 14). *The rising cost of pensions and perks for former presidents requires reform*. National Taxpayers Union Foundation. https://www.ntu.org/foundation/detail/the-rising-cost-of-pensions-and-perks-for-former-presidents-requires-reform

Brah, A., & Phoenix, A. (2004). Ain't I a woman? Revisiting intersectionality. *Journal of International Women's Studies, 5*(3), 75–86.

Brodkin, K. (1998). *How Jews became White folks and what that says about race in America*. Rutgers University Press.

Brown v. Board of Education of Topeka, 347 U.S. 483 (1954).

Brown, J. D. (2024). *Dismantling White supremacy in counseling*. Emerald Publishing. https://doi.org/10.1108/978-1-83797-492-420241003

Budd, K. M. (2024). *Incarcerated women and girls*. The Sentencing Project. https://www.sentencingproject.org/fact-sheet/incarcerated-women-and-girls/

Budd, K. M., & Napal, D. (2022, December 16). *The color of justice: Racial and ethnic disparity in state prisons*. The Sentencing Project. https://www.sentencingproject.org/reports/the-color-of-justice-racial-and-ethnic-disparity-in-state-prisons-the-sentencing-project/

Budig, M. J. (2002). Male advantage and the gender composition of jobs: Who rides the glass escalator? *Social Problems, 49*(2), 258–277.

Bunn, C. (2022, March 4). *Report: Black people are still killed by police at a higher rate than other groups*. NBC. https://www.nbcnews.com/news/nbcblk/report-black-people-are-still-killed-police-higher-rate-groups-rcna17169

Burczycka, M. (2020). *Students' experiences of unwanted sexualized behaviours and sexual assault at postsecondary schools in the Canadian provinces, 2019*. Statistics Canada. https://www150.statcan.gc.ca/n1/pub/85-002-x/2020001/article/00005-eng.htm

Burns, D. (2025, April 26). Trump-aligned club for the ultra rich launches in Washington. *Politico*. https://www.politico.com/news/2025/04/26/donald-trump-washington-club-00311720
Caleb, A. M. (2022). Darwin and the feminists: Nineteenth-century debates about female inferiority. In C. A. Jones, A. E. Martin, & A. Wolf (Eds.), *The Palgrave handbook of women and science since 1660* (pp. 289–306). Palgrave Macmillan.
Calliste, A. (1996). Antiracism organizing and resistance in nursing: African Canadian women. *Canadian Review of Sociology, 33*(3), 361–390.
Cammaerts, B. (2022). The abnormalisation of social justice: The "anti-woke culture war" discourse in the UK. *Discourse & Society, 33*(6), 730–743. https://doi.org/10.1177/09579265221095407
Campani, G., Fabelo Concepción, S., Rodriguez Soler, A., & Sánchez Savín, C. (2022). The rise of Donald Trump right-wing populism in the United States: Middle American radicalism and anti-immigration discourse. *Societies, 12*(6), 154–179. https://doi.org/10.3390/soc12060154
Canadian Encyclopedia. (2015). *Inuktitut words for snow and ice*. https://www.thecanadianencyclopedia.ca/en/article/inuktitut-words-for-snow-and-ice
Canadian Femicide Observatory for Justice and Accountability. (2022). *#CallItFemicide: Understanding sex/gender-related killings of women and girls in Canada, 2018–2022*. https://femicideincanada.ca/callitfemicide2018-2022.pdf
Canadian Press. (2023, June 16). How ground penetrating radar is used to find unmarked graves at residential schools. APTN National News. https://www.aptnnews.ca/national-news/how-ground-penetrating-radar-is-used-to-find-unmarked-graves-at-residential-schools/
Canadian Press. (2025, Mar 18). Trump administration threatening Canadian researchers. https://www.thecanadianpressnews.ca/globenewswire_press_releases/trump-administration-threatening-canadian-researchers/article_03853d2a-77fb-5f17-b482-dfbf5362fd61.html
Cantillon, S., & O'Connor, M. (2021). Gender, equality and the sex trade. Women's Studies *International Forum, 89*, 102532. https://doi.org/10.1016/j.wsif.2021.102532
Cao, L. (2019). Made in the USA: Race, trade, and prison labor. *NYU Review of Law and Social Change, 43*, 1.
Caron, S. L., & Mitchell, D. (2022, July). "I've never told anyone": A qualitative analysis of interviews with college women who experienced sexual assault and remained silent. *Violence Against Women, 28*(9), 1987–2009. https://doi.org/10.1177/10778012211022766
Castrillon, N. E. (2024, March 14–16). *Undoing White settler designed cities: The agency of mapping with racialized immigrant and refugee women in Canada*. [Paper presentation]. ACSA 112th Annual Meeting: Disrupters on the Edge, Vancouver, BC, Canada. https://www.acsa-arch.org/proceedings/Annual%20Meeting%20Proceedings/ACSA.AM.112/ACSA.AM.112.83.pdf
Cavalli-Sforza, L. L., Menozzi, P., & Piazza, A. (1994). *The history and geography of human genes*. Princeton University Press.
CBC News. (2006, November 10). *Ontario to take back control of private super-jail*. CBC News. https://www.cbc.ca/news/canada/ontario-to-take-back-control-of-private-super-jail-1.586052
CBC News. (2023a, February 23). *17 Potential unmarked graves scanned at former Vancouver Island residential school, First Nation says*. https://www.cbc.ca/news/canada/british-columbia/search-possible-graves-vancouver-island-residential-school-1.6754634
CBC News (2023b, April 20). *Shíshálh nation says 40 unmarked graves believed found at residential school site, more are expected*. https://www.cbc.ca/news/canada/british-columbia/shíshálh-nation-says-40-unmarked-graves-found-at-former-residential-school-expect-more-1.6817021
Celikates, R., & Flynn, J. (2023). Critical theory (Frankfurt School). In E. N. Zalta & U. Nodelman (Eds.), *The Stanford encyclopedia of philosophy*. https://plato.stanford.edu/archives/win2023/entries/critical-theory/
Center for American Women and Politics. (2025). *Current numbers*. https://cawp.rutgers.edu/facts/current-numbers
Center for Policy and Inequality Research. (2018, January). *What are the annual earnings for a full-time minimum wage worker?* University of California–Davis. https://poverty.ucdavis.edu/faq/what-are-annual-earnings-full-time-minimum-wage-worker

Center for Reproductive Rights. (2025, January 27). *The global gag rule and human rights* [Fact sheet]. https://reproductiverights.org/wp-content/uploads/2025/01/Global-Gag-Rule_Fact-Sheet_1-27-25.pdf

Center on Budget and Policy Priorities. (2022, March 1). *Policy basics: Temporary Assistance for Needy Families.* https://www.cbpp.org/research/policy-basics-an-introduction-to-tanf

Charalambous, P., & Negussie, T. (2025, February 18). *"Unadulterated animus": Judge blasts DOJ about transgender military restrictions.* ABC News. https://abcnews.go.com/Politics/judge-poised-block-limitations-transgender-service-members/story?id=118927094

Charalambous, P., Romero, L., & Kim, S. R. (2024, December 17). *Trump has tapped an unprecedented 13 billionaires for his administration. Here's who they are.* ABC News. https://abcnews.go.com/US/trump-tapped-unprecedented-13-billionaires-top-administration-roles/story?id=116872968

Charlesworth, T. E. S., & Banaji, M. R. (2019). Gender in science, technology, engineering, and mathematics: Issues, causes, solutions. *The Journal of Neuroscience, 39*(37), 7228–7243. https://doi.org/10.1523/JNEUROSCI.0475-18.2019

Chatfield, K. (2024). *A 50-state comparison of TANF benefit amounts.* National Center for Children in Poverty. https://www.nccp.org/publication/a-50-state-comparison-of-tanf-amounts/

Chatterjee, S. (2022). Off-shore aesthetics and waste in the ship-breaking literature of Bangladesh. *South Asian Review, 44*(2), 70–84. https://doi.org/10.1080/02759527.2022.2145745

Chayka, K. (2025). How Donald Trump's crypto dealings push the bounds of corruption. *The New Yorker.* https://www.newyorker.com/culture/infinite-scroll/how-donald-trumps-crypto-dealings-push-the-bounds-of-corruption

Cheng, C. I. (2025). Words matter, so does the context of history: On the homeless and the unhoused. *Modern American History, 8*(1), 94–107.

Children's Commissioner. (2025). *"Sex is kind of broken now": Children and pornography.* https://assets.childrenscommissioner.gov.uk/wpuploads/2025/08/cc-sex-is-kind-of-broken-now-children-and-pornography.pdf

Childs, T. M., & Wooten, N. R. (2022). Teacher bias matters: An integrative review of correlates, mechanisms, and consequences. *Race Ethnicity and Education, 26*(3), 368–397. https://doi.org/10.1080/13613324.2022.2122425

Chin, M. J., Quinn, D. M., Dhaliwal, T. K., & Lovison, V. S. (2020). Bias in the air: A nationwide exploration of teachers' implicit racial attitudes, aggregate bias, and student outcomes. *Educational Researcher, 49*(8), 566–578. https://doi.org/10.3102%2F0013189X20937240

Chinn, P. (1979). Curriculum development for culturally different exceptional children. *Teacher Education and Special Education, 2*(4), 49–58. https://doi.org/10.1177/088840647900200409

Cho, E. H. (2025, April 11). *ACLU FOIA litigation reveals information about plans to expand ICE detention facilities nationwide* [Press release]. ACLU. https://www.aclu.org/press-releases/aclu-foia-litigation-reveals-information-about-plans-to-expand-ice-detention-facilities-nationwide

Chopra, S. B. (2021). Healing from internalized racism for Asian Americans. *Professional Psychology: Research and Practice, 52*(5), 503–512. https://doi.org/10.1037/pro0000407

Chronicle of Higher Education. (2009, August 24). *Number of full-time faculty members by sex, rank, and racial and ethnic group, fall 2007.* https://www.chronicle.com/article/Number-of-Full-Time-Faculty/47992/

Cilveti-Lapeira, M., Rodríguez-Molina, J. M., & López-Trenado, E. (2024). Key aspects in the development of gender identity and sexual orientation according to trans and gender diverse people: A qualitative approach. *Culture, Health & Sexuality, 27*(8), 992–1006. https://doi.org/10.1080/13691058.2024.2416541

CIUSSS du Centre-Ouest-de-l'Île-de-Montréal. (n.d.). *Disability-inclusive language.* https://cdn.ciussscentreouest.ca/documents/ciusss-coim/A_propos_de_nous/Diversite_equite_inclusion_et_appartenance/Nouvelles_et_evenements/Disability_inclusive_language.pdf

Clark, K. B., & Clark, M. P. (1950). Emotional factors in racial identification and preference in Negro children. *The Journal of Negro Education, 19*(3), 341–350.

Coates, T. (2015). *Between the world and me.* Random House.

Cockfield, A. (2021, December 28). Secrets of the Panama papers: How tax havens exacerbate income inequality. *Columbia Journal of Tax Law, 13*(1), 45–76.

Collins, P. H. (2000). It's all in the family: Intersections of gender, race, and nation. In U. Narayan & S. Harding (Eds.), *Decentering the center: Philosophy for a multicultural, postcolonial, and feminist world* (pp. 156–176). Indiana University Press.

Collins, P. H., & Bilge, S. (2016). *Intersectionality*. Polity Press.

Conforti, Y. (2014). Searching for a homeland: The territorial dimension in the Zionist movement and the boundaries of Jewish nationalism. *Studies in Ethnicity and Nationalism, 14*(1), 36–54. https://doi.org/10.1111/sena.12077

Conley, D. (1999). *Being Black, living in the red: Race, wealth, and social policy in America*. University of California Press.

Connolly, M., Haeck, C., & Lapierre, D. (2021, February 10). *Trends in intergenerational income mobility and income inequality in Canada*. https://www150.statcan.gc.ca/n1/pub/11f0019m/11f0019m2021001-eng.htm

Connor, D. J., Ferri, B. A., & Annamma, S. A. (2016). *DisCrit: Disability studies and critical race theory in education*. Teachers College Press.

Connors, S. (2023, January 12). *Search finds remains of a child at former Qu'Appelle Indian residential school in Saskatchewan*. APTN National News. https://www.aptnnews.ca/national-news/search-finds-remains-of-a-child-at-former-quappelle-indian-residential-school-in-saskatchewan/

Conroy, S. (2024, April 26). *Recent trends in police-reported clearance status of sexual assault and other violent crime in Canada, 2017 to 2022*. https://www150.statcan.gc.ca/n1/pub/85-002-x/2024001/article/00006-eng.htm

Conte, J. (2018). Sex versus gender. In *Oxford bibliographies: Sociology*. Oxford University Press. https://www.oxfordbibliographies.com/display/document/obo-9780199756384/obo-9780199756384-0153.xml

Conyers, A., Lynn, V., & Leigey, M. (Eds.). (2023). *Mass incarceration in the 21st century: Realities and reflections* (1st ed.). Routledge. https://doi.org/10.4324/9781003274292

Cookney, F. (2019). Porn was legalized 50 years ago, this is how the business has changed. *Forbes*.

Cooley, A., Heathershaw, J., & Sharman, J. C. (2018). The rise of kleptocracy: Laundering cash, whitewashing reputations. *Journal of Democracy, 29*(1), 39–53.

Cooley, C. H. (1922). *Human nature and the social order*. Charles Scribner's Sons.

Cooper, R. S., Kaufman, J. S., & Ward, R. (2003). Race and genomics. *New England Journal of Medicine, 348*(12), 1166–1170.

Cotter, A. (2021, April 26). *Intimate partner violence in Canada, 2018: An overview*. Government of Canada, Statistics Canada. https://www150.statcan.gc.ca/n1/pub/85-002-x/2021001/article/00003-eng.htm

Crenshaw, K. (1989). Demarginalizing the intersection of race and sex: A Black feminist critique of antidiscrimination doctrine, feminist theory, and antiracist politics. *University of Chicago Legal Forum, 1*, 139–167.

Crenshaw, K. (1991). Mapping the margins: Identity politics, intersectionality, and violence against women. *Stanford Law Review, 43*(6), 1241–1299.

Czopp, A. M., Mark, A. Y., & Walzer, A. S. (2014). Prejudice and racism. In F. T. L. Leong, L. Comas-Díaz, G. C. Nagayama Hall, V. C. McLoyd, & J. E. Trimble (Eds.), *APA handbook of multicultural psychology, Vol. 1: Theory and research* (pp. 361–377). American Psychological Association. https://doi.org/10.1037/14189-019

Daigle, L. E., Felix, S. N., Muñoz, R. B., Hancock, K. P., Oesterle, D. W., & Gilmore, A. K. (2025). Examining the risks of multiple types of interpersonal victimization for transgender and gender nonconforming college students. *Journal of Interpersonal Violence, 40*(3–4), 876–905. https://doi.org/10.1177/08862605241254139

Dana, T. (2024). Death dealers: Dynamics of Israel's permanent war economy. *Capital & Class*. https://doi.org/10.1177/03098168241291350

Daneback, K., Ševčíková, A., & Ježek, S. (2018). Exposure to online sexual materials in adolescence and desensitization to sexual content. *Sexologies, 27*(3), e71–e76. https://doi.org/10.1016/j.sexol.2018.04.001

Das, A., Hudson, I., & Hudson, M. (2024). Unionization rates, inequality, and poverty in Canadian provinces 2000–2020. *Capital & Class.* https://doi.org/10.1177/03098168241269173

Da Silva, C., & Gubash, C. (2025, March 5). *U.S. and Israel reject Arab alternative to Trump's Gaza "Riviera."* NBC. https://www.nbcnews.com/news/world/us-israel-reject-arab-alternative-trumps-gaza-riviera-rcna194831

David, E. R., Schroeder, T. M., & Fernandez, J. (2019). Internalized racism: A systematic review of the psychological literature on racism's most insidious consequence. *Journal of Social Issues, 75*(4), 1057–1086.

Davis, A. Y. (1981). *Women, race & class.* Random House.

Davis, K. (Director). (2005). *A girl like me* [Documentary short film]. Reel Works Teen Filmmaking. https://www.youtube.com/watch?v=YWyI77Yh1Gg

Dechief, D., & Oreopoulos, P. (2012). *Why do some employers prefer to interview Matthew but not Samir? New evidence from Toronto, Montreal, and Vancouver* (Working Paper No. 95). Canadian Labour Market and Skills Researcher Network. https://dx.doi.org/10.2139/ssrn.2018047

Decker, S., Ortiz, N., Spohn, C., & Hedberg, E. (2015). Criminal stigma, race, and ethnicity: The consequences of imprisonment for employment. *Journal of Criminal Justice, 43*(2), 108–121. https://doi.org/10.1016/j.jcrimjus.2015.02.002

Dei, G. J. (2008). Anti-racism education for global citizenship. In M. A. Peters, A. Britton, & H. Blee (Eds.), *Global citizenship education* (pp. 477–490). Brill.

Dei, G. J., Karumanchery, L. L., & Karumanchery-Luik, N. (2004). *Playing the race card: Exposing White power and privilege.* Lang.

Dei, G. J., & Vickers, J. (1997). Anti-racism education: Theory & practice. *Journal of Canadian Studies, 32*(2), 175.

DeKeseredy, W. S. (2015). Critical criminological understandings of adult pornography and woman abuse: New progressive directions in research and theory. *International Journal for Crime, Justice and Social Democracy, 4*(4), 4–21.

Delgado, R., & Stefancic, J. (Eds.). (1997). *Critical White studies.* Temple University Press.

DeNavas-Walt, C. & Proctor, B. D. (2015*). Income and poverty in the United States: 2014.* United States Census Bureau. https://www.census.gov/library/publications/2015/demo/p60-252.html

Department of Justice Canada. (2024, November). *The overrepresentation of Indigenous people in the criminal justice system* [Factsheet]. Government of Canada. https://www.justice.gc.ca/eng/rp-pr/jr/jf-pf/2024/nov.html

Derenoncourt, E., Kim, C. H., Kuhn, M., & Schularick, M. (2024). Wealth of two nations: The US racial wealth gap, 1860–2020. *The Quarterly Journal of Economics, 139*(2), 693–750.

Deva, S., & Anand, P. (2024). A global south perspective on labour rights and supply chains for a post-growth world. In N. Bueno, B. P. Haar, & N. Zekić (Eds.), *Labour law utopias: Post-growth and post-productive work approaches* (pp. 90–115). Oxford University Press.

Devereux, C. (2005). *Growing a race: Nellie L. McClung and the fiction of eugenic feminism.* McGill-Queen's University Press.

Diamond, J. B., & Gomez, L. M. (2023). Disrupting White supremacy and anti-Black racism in educational organizations. *Educational Researcher.* https://doi.org/10.3102/0013189X231161054

DiAngelo, R. J. (2006). My class didn't trump my race: Using oppression to face privilege. *Multicultural Perspectives, 8*(1), 51–56.

DiAngelo, R. J. (2011). White fragility. *International Journal of Critical Pedagogy, 3*(3), 54–70.

DiAngelo, R. J. (2016). *What does it mean to be White? Developing White racial literacy* (2nd ed.). Peter Lang.

DiAngelo, R. J. (2018). *White fragility: Why it's so hard for White people to talk about racism.* Beacon Press.

DiAngelo, R. J., & Sensoy, Ö. (2010). "OK, I get it! Now tell me how to do it!" Why we can't just tell you how to do critical multicultural education. *Multicultural Perspectives, 12*(2), 97–102.

Dickason, O. P. (2002). *Canada's first nations: A history of founding peoples from earliest times* (3rd ed.). Oxford University Press.

Di Gironimo, S. (2025). Hardcore and the politics of consent: A woman's stupid smile, or toward *something else. Studies in Gender and Sexuality, 26*(1), 37–51. https://www.tandfonline.com/doi/full/10.1080/15240657.2025.2453287

Dines, G. (2010). *Pornland: How porn has hijacked our sexuality.* Beacon Press.

Dines, G., & Sanchez, M. (2023). Hentai and the pornification of childhood: How the porn industry just made the case for regulation. *Dignity, 8*(1), Article 3. https://doi.org/10.23860/dignity.2023.08.01.03

Disability Justice. (2023). *Sexual abuse.* https://disabilityjustice.org/sexual-abuse/

Dovidio, J., Glick, S., & Rudman, L. (2005). *On the nature of prejudice: Fifty years after Allport.* Blackwell.

Dubey, R. (2023, June 29). Radar search at northern Alberta residential school uncovers 88 suspected graves. CBC News. https://www.cbc.ca/news/canada/edmonton/alta-residential-school-graves-1.6892401

Du Bois, W.E.B. (1937, June 5). The nucleus of class consciousness. *The Pittsburgh Courier,* p. 23.

Du Bois, W.E.B. (1989). *The souls of Black folk.* Bantam Books. (Original work published 1903)

Duckitt, J. H. (1992). *The social psychology of prejudice.* Praeger.

Duncan, P. (2014). Hot commodities, cheap labor: Women of color in the academy. *Frontiers: A Journal of Women Studies, 35*(3), 39–63.

Durou, G., Maroto, M., & Brown, D. (2023). Unpacking the Alberta Advantage through an intersectional lens: Social class, gender and minority groups in Alberta. *Alternate Routes: A Journal of Critical Social Research, 33*(1). https://alternateroutes.ca/index.php/ar/article/view/22549

Dyer, R. (1997). *White.* Routledge.

Eberhardt, J. (2019). *Biased: Uncovering the hidden prejudice that shapes what we see, think and do.* Penguin.

Eberhardt, M., Facchini, G., & Rueda, V. (2023). Gender differences in reference letters: Evidence from the economics job market. *The Economic Journal, 133*(655), 2676–2708. https://doi.org/10.1093/ej/uead045

Eddo-Lodge, R. (2017). *Why I'm no longer talking to White people about race.* Bloomsbury Publishing.

Elaref, A. I. A. (2023). Colonial discourse studies: Uncovering the unfair otherness. *AWEJ for Translation & Literary Studies, 7*(2), 83–92. https://doi.org/10.2139/ssrn.4472912

Ellis, L., Palmer, C. T., Hopcroft, R., & Hoskin, A. W. (2024). *The handbook of sex differences, Vol. IV: Identifying universal sex differences.* Routledge. https://doi.org/10.4324/9781003405290

Elsass, P. M., & Graves, L. M. (1997). Demographic diversity in decision-making groups: The experiences of women and people of Color. *The Academy of Management Review, 22*(4), 946–973.

Erickson-Schroth, L., & Davis, B. (2021). *Gender: What everyone needs to know.* Oxford University Press.

Espinosa, L. L., Turk, J. M., Taylor, M., & Chessman, H. M. (2019). *Race and ethnicity in higher education: A status report.* American Council on Education and the Andrew F. Mellon Foundation.

Ever Accountable. (2024, November 4). *What is OnlyFans and why is it so dangerous?* https://everaccountable.com/only-fans/

Exec. Order No. 14190, 90 FR 8853 (2025). https://www.federalregister.gov/documents/2025/02/03/2025-02232/ending-radical-indoctrination-in-k-12-schooling

Fairbairn, J., Boyd, C., Jiwani, Y., & Dawson, M. (2023). Changing media representations of femicide as primary prevention. In M. Dawson & S. M. Vega (Eds.), *The Routledge international handbook on femicide and feminicide* (pp. 554–564). Routledge.

Falah, G. (1996). The 1948 Israeli-Palestinian War and its aftermath: The transformation and designification of Palestine's cultural landscape. *Annals of the Association of American Geographers, 86*(2), 256–285.

Fanon, F. (2001). *The wretched of the Earth* (C. Farrington, Trans.). Penguin. (Original work published 1961)

Farley, M. (2018). Risks of prostitution: When the person is the product. *Journal of the Association for Consumer Research, 3*(1), 97–108.

Farley, M., & Donevan, M. (2021). Reconnecting pornography, prostitution, and trafficking: The experience of being in porn was like being destroyed, run over, again and again. *ATLÁNTICAS— Revista Internacional de Estudios Feministas, 6*(1), 30–66. https://dx.doi.org/10.17979/arief.2021.6.1.7312

Fausto-Sterling, A. (1992). *Myths of gender: Biological theories about women and men* (2nd ed.). Basic Books.

Fausto-Sterling, A. (2000). *Sexing the body: Gender politics and the construction of sexuality.* Basic Books.

Fausto-Sterling, A. (2019). Gender/sex, sexual orientation, and identity are in the body: How did they get there? *The Journal of Sex Research, 56*(4–5), 529–555. https://doi.org/10.1080/00224499.2019.1581883

Faverio, M., & Sidoti, O. (2024). *Teens, social media and technology 2024.* Pew Research Center. https://www.pewresearch.org/wp-content/uploads/sites/20/2024/12/PI_2024.12.12_Teens-Social-Media-Tech_REPORT.pdf

Feagin, J. R. (2020). *The White racial frame: Centuries of racial framing and counter-framing* (3rd ed.). Routledge. https://doi.org/10.4324/9780429353246

Federation of Canadian Municipalities. (2023). *Women's representation in municipal elected positions.* https://fcm.ca/en/resources/women-in-local-government/women-representation-in-municipal-elected-positions-2023-report

Federer, J. P., Dedyukina, L., & Walker, P. O. (2025). The politics of knowledge, positionality and power: The 'inclusivity' of Indigenous women in peacemaking in Turtle Island (North America). In A. Björkdahl & J. Mannergren (Eds.), *The production of gendered knowledge of war* (pp. 74–86). Routledge.

Fernandez, A. A., França, K., Chacon, A. H., & Nouri, K. (2013). From flint razors to lasers: A timeline of hair removal methods. *Journal of Cosmetic Dermatology, 12*(2), 153–162. https://doi.org/10.1111/jocd.12021

Fiallo, J. (2025, February 20). Vance has "cringe" advice for men suppressed by U.S. culture. *The Daily Beast.* https://www.thedailybeast.com/jd-vance-offers-cringe-advice-to-young-men-suppressed-by-us-culture/

Fields, G. (2020). Lockdown: Gaza through a camera lens and historical mirror. *Journal of Palestine Studies, 49*(3), 41–69.

Findley, M. G., Nielson, D. L., & Sharman, J. C. (2014). *Global shell games: Experiments in transnational relations, crime, and terrorism.* Cambridge University Press.

Fine, M. (1997). Witnessing Whiteness. In M. Fine, L. Weis, C. Powell, & L. Wong (Eds.), *Off White: Readings on race, power, and society* (pp. 57–65). Routledge.

Finkelhor, D., Turner, H., & Colburn, D. (2022). Prevalence of online sexual offenses against children in the US. *JAMA Network Open, 5*(10), e2234471.

Fishbein, H. D. (2002). *Peer prejudice and discrimination: The origins of prejudice* (2nd ed.). Psychology Press. https://doi.org/10.4324/9781410606228

FitzGerald, C., & Hurst, S. (2017). Implicit bias in healthcare professionals: A systematic review. *BMC Medical Ethics, 18*, 19. https://doi.org/10.1186/s12910-017-0179-8

Flanagan, T., & Purnanandam, A. (2024). Did banks pay fair returns to taxpayers on TARP? *The Journal of Finance, 79*(5), 2909–2941. https://doi.org/10.1111/jofi.13367

Flores, A. R., Meyer, I. H., Langton, L., & Herman, J. L. (2021). Gender identity disparities in criminal victimization: National Crime Victimization Survey, 2017–2018. *American Journal of Public Health, 111*(4), 726–729.

Foucault, M. (1995). *Discipline and punish: The birth of the prison* (2nd ed.). Vintage Books. (Original work published 1977)

Fourchard, L., Berg-Schlosser, D., Badie, B., & Morlino, L. (2011). *Colonialism*. In B. Badie, D. Berg-Schlosser, & L. Morlino (Eds.), *International encyclopedia of political science* (Vol. 2, pp. 302–307). SAGE Publications. https://doi.org/10.4135/9781412959636.n79

Fox, M. (2016). Challenging the concept of cultural deficit, through a framework of critical-based education. *Pedagogika, 88*(5), 638–647.

Franco, R., & Webber, V. (2024, September). 'This is fucking nuts': The role of payment intermediaries in structuring precarity and dependencies in platformized sex work. *Porn Studies, 12*(3), 411–428. https://doi.org/10.1080/23268743.2024.2393641

Frankenberg, R. A. E. (1993). *White women, race matters: The social construction of Whiteness*. University of Minnesota Press.

Freire, P. (1970). *Pedagogy of the oppressed*. Continuum.

Frum, D. (2025). The Trump presidency's world-historical heist. *The Atlantic*. https://www.theatlantic.com/ideas/archive/2025/05/trump-golden-age-corruption/682935/

Frye, M. (1983). *The politics of reality: Essays in feminist theory*. Crossing Press.

Gallavan, N. P. (2000). Multicultural education at the academy: Teacher educators' challenges, conflicts, and coping skills. *Equity & Excellence in Education, 33*(3), 5–11.

Garcia, A. M. (1989). The development of Chicana feminist discourse, 1970–1980. *Gender and Society, 3*(2), 217–238.

García-Cuéllar, M. M., Pastor-Moreno, G., Ruiz-Pérez, I., & Henares-Montiel, J. (2023). The prevalence of intimate partner violence against women with disabilities: A systematic review of the literature. *Disability and Rehabilitation, 45*(1), 1–8. https://doi.org/ 10.1080/09638288.2022.2025927

Gatto, J. T. (2002). *Dumbing us down: The hidden curriculum of compulsory schooling* (2nd ed.). New Society Publishers.

Gavey, N., & Brewster, O. (2025, January 15). Is "rough sex" a thing? A survey of meaning. *The Journal of Sex Research*, 1–17. https://doi.org/10.1080/00224499.2024.2438711

Gay, G. (1983). Why multicultural education in teacher preparation programs. *Contemporary Education, 54*(2), 79–85.

Gibraltar Mines v. Harvey, 2022 BCSC 385 (2022). https://www.bccourts.ca/jdb-txt/sc/22/03/2022BCSC 0385.htm

Gillborn, D. (2006). Rethinking White supremacy: Who counts in "White world." *Ethnicities, 6*(3), 318–340. https://doi.org/10.1177/1468796806068323

Gillies, C. (2023). Anti-Indigenous deficit racism and cultural essentialism in K–12 education: We want you to recognize there's a problem. *Journal of Critical Race Inquiry, 10*(2), 68–88.

Giroux, H. (1997). White squall: Resistance and the pedagogy of Whiteness. *Cultural Studies, 11*(3), 376–389. https://doi.org/10.1080/095023897335664

Goldsmith, B., MacKenzie, M., & Wynter, T. (2024). Racial bias in academia: An audit experiment revealing disparities in faculty responses to prospective students. *International Journal of Education Policy and Leadership, 20*(1), 1–23. https://doi.org/10.22230/ijepl.2024v20n1a1401

Gomez, J., & Cataldo, P. (2016). *Private prisons and political contributions: How big money shackles immigration policy*. https://freespeechforpeople.org/bilingual-private-prisons-report/

Gomez, R. A. (2007, Fall). Protecting minors from online pornography without violating the First Amendment: Mandating an affirmative choice. *SMU Science & Technology Law Review, 11*(1). https://core.ac.uk/download/pdf/147643334.pdf

Gonzalez, C. G. (2021). Racial capitalism and the Anthropocene. In S. A. Atapattu, C. G. Gonzalez, & S. L. Seck (Eds.), *The Cambridge handbook of environmental justice and sustainable development* (pp. 72–85). Cambridge University Press.

Gossett, T. E. (1997). *Race: The history of an idea in America*. Oxford University Press.

Gould, S. J. (1996). *The mismeasure of man*. Norton. (Original work published 1981)

Graves, J. L., Jr. (2015). Why the nonexistence of biological races does not mean the nonexistence of racism. *American Behavioral Scientist, 59*(11), 1474–1495.

Green, D. S., & Smith, E. (1983). W.E.B. DuBois and the concepts of race and class. *Phylon (1960–), 44*(4), 262–272. https://doi.org/10.2307/274576

Green, E. C. (1997). *Southern strategies: Southern women and the woman suffrage question*. University of North Carolina Press.

Green, E. L. (2025, March 21). Trump administration dropped policy prohibiting contractors from having segregated facilities. *The New York Times*. https://www.nytimes.com/2025/03/21/us/politics/trump-segregation.html

Greenwald, A. G., & Krieger, L. (2006). Implicit bias: Scientific foundations. *California Law Review*, 94(4), 945–967.

Greenwald, A. G., Poehlman, T. A., Uhlmann, E. L., & Banaji, M. R. (2009). Understanding and using the Implicit Association Test: III. Meta-analysis of predictive validity. *Journal of Personality and Social Psychology*, 97(1), 17.

Gregory, A., Skiba, R. J., & Noguera, P. A. (2010). The achievement gap and the discipline gap: Two sides of the same coin? *Educational Researcher*, 39(1), 59–68.

Grekul, J., Krahn, A., & Odynak, D. (2004). Sterilizing the "feeble-minded": Eugenics in Alberta, Canada, 1929–1972. *Journal of Historical Sociology*, 17(4), 358–384.

Grewal, I., & Kaplan, C. (Eds.). (1994). *Scattered hegemonies: Postmodernity and transnational feminist practices*. University of Minnesota Press.

Griffin, K. A. (2020). Institutional barriers, strategies, and benefits to increasing the representation of women and men of Color in the professoriate: Looking beyond the pipeline. In L. W. Perna (Ed.), *Higher education: Handbook of theory and research* (Vol. 35, pp. 277–349). Springer International Publishing.

Grogan, S. (2016). *Body image: Understanding body dissatisfaction in men, women and children* (3rd ed.). Routledge.

Grosfuguel, R., & Mielants, E. (2006). The long-durée entanglement between Islamophobia and racism in the modern/colonial capitalist/patriarchal world-system: An introduction. *Human Architecture*, 5(1), 1–12. https://digitalcommons.fairfield.edu/sociologyandanthropology-facultypubs/39

Hägerdal, H. (2024). Slaving, colonial diplomacy, and resource extraction in seventeenth-century Maritime Asia. *Journal of Indian Ocean World Studies*, 8(1), 26–49. https://muse.jhu.edu/article/933176.

Hagopian, E., & Zahlan, A. B. (1974). Palestine's Arab population: The demography of the Palestinians. *Journal of Palestine Studies*, 3(4), 32–73.

Haig-Brown, C. (1998). *Resistance and renewal: Surviving the Indian residential school*. Arsenal Pulp Press.

Halperin, J. R. (2025). A service as easy as ordering takeout: Tech, startups, and the business ontology. *The Political Librarian*, 8(1), 39–48. https://doi.org/10.7936/pollib.9016

Halperin, L. (2015). *Origins and evolution of Zionism*. Foreign Policy Research Institute. https://www.fpri.org/article/2015/01/origins-and-evolution-of-zionism/

Hambacher, E., & Thompson, W. C. (2015). Breaking the mold: Thinking beyond deficits. *Journal of Educational Controversy*, 9(1), 7. http://cedar.wwu.edu/jec/vol9/iss1/7

Hamermesh, D. S., & Parker, A. M. (2005). Beauty in the classroom: Professors' pulchritude and putative pedagogical productivity. *Economics of Education Review*, 24(4), 369–376.

Hammond, C. (2024). *The most visited websites every year since 1995*. A2 Hosting. Retrieved March 1, 2025, from https://www.a2hosting.com/blog/the-most-visited-websites-every-year-since-1995/ (Updated June 13, 2025)

Happ, M., Harpenau, F., & Wiewiorra, L. (2024). *Economics and regulation of adult online content* (Working Paper No. 9). Wissenschaftliches Institut für Infrastruktur und Kommunikationsdienst. https://www.wik.org/en/publications/publication/working-paper-nr-9-oekonomie-und-regulierung-von-pornografischen-online-inhalten

Hare, J. (2007). First Nations education policy in Canada: Building capacity for change and control. In R. Joshee & L. Johnson (Eds.), *Multicultural education policies in Canada and the United States* (pp. 51–68). University of British Columbia Press.

Harris, C. I. (1993). Whiteness as property. *Harvard Law Review*, 106(8), 1707–1791.

Harvard University. (n.d.). *Project Implicit*. http://www.projectimplicit.net/

Haskell, L., & Randall, M. (2009). Disrupted attachments: A social context complex trauma framework and the lives of Aboriginal peoples in Canada. *Journal of Aboriginal Health, 5*(3), 48–99.

Heathershaw, J., Pitcher, M. A., & de Oliveira, R. S. (2023). Transnational kleptocracy and the international political economy of authoritarianism. *Journal of International Relations and Development, 26*(2), 215–223.

Helfenbein, R. (2016, September 5). The darker side of "Made in the USA." *The Hill*. https://thehill.com/blogs/pundits-blog/labor/294524-the-darker-side-of-made-in-usa

Heller, J. (2019). Constructed gender but unconstructed sex? Historical roots of sociological practice. *The American Sociologist, 50*(1), 38–62.

Henry, A. (2015). "We especially welcome applications from members of visible minority groups": Reflections on race, gender and life at three universities. *Race, Ethnicity and Education, 18*(5), 589–610.

Henry, F., & Tator, C. (2006). *The colour of democracy: Racism in Canadian society*. Thomson Nelson.

Hernández-Truyol, B. E. (2023). Who's afraid of being woke? Critical theory as awakening to erascism and other injustices. *Journal of Critical Race and Ethnic Studies, 1*(1), 19–52.

Herrnstein, R. J., & Murray, C. (1994). *The bell curve: Intelligence and class structure in American life*. Free Press.

Hickel, J., Dorninger, C., Wieland, H., & Suwandi, I. (2022). Imperialist appropriation in the world economy: Drain from the Global South through unequal exchange, 1990–2015. *Global Environmental Change, 73*, 102467. https://doi.org/10.1016/j.gloenvcha.2022.102467

Hill, L., & Artiga, S. (2023). *What is driving widening racial disparities in life expectancy?* KFF. https://www.kff.org/racial-equity-and-health-policy/issue-brief/what-is-driving-widening-racial-disparities-in-life-expectancy/

Hilliard, A. (1992, January). *Racism: Its origins and how it works* [Paper presentation]. Mid-West Association for the Education of Young Children, Madison, WI, United States.

Holdcroft, A. (2007). Gender bias in research: How does it affect evidence based medicine? *Journal of the Royal Society of Medicine, 100*(1), 2–3. https://doi.org/10.1177/014107680710000102

hooks, b. (1994). *Teaching to transgress: Education as the practice of freedom*. Routledge.

hooks, b. (2000). *Where we stand: Class matters*. Routledge.

hooks, b. (2014). *Talking back: Thinking feminist, thinking Black* (2nd ed.). Routledge.

Hope, D., & Limberg, J. (2022). The economic consequences of major tax cuts for the rich. *Socio-Economic Review, 20*(2), 539–559.

HOPE: Domestic Violence Homicide Help. (n.d.). *Domestic violence statistics*. Retrieved June 24, 2017, from https://domesticviolencehomicidehelp.com/statistics/

House of Commons of Canada. (2025, May 13). *Ministry (Cabinet) as of May 13, 2025*. Parliament of Canada. https://www.ourcommons.ca/members/en/ministries

Howard, J. (2018). The White kid can do whatever he wants: The racial socialization of a gifted education program. *Educational Studies, 54*(5), 553–568.

Huecker, M. R., King, K. C., Jordan, G. A., & Smock, W. (2023, April 9). *Domestic violence*. StatPearls. https://www.ncbi.nlm.nih.gov/books/NBK499891/

Hughes, M., & Thomas, M. E. (1998). The continuing significance of race revisited: A study of race, class, and quality of life in America, 1972–1996. *American Sociological Review, 63*(6), 785–795.

Hulchanski, J. D., & Murdie, R. A. (2013, April 5). *Canada's income polarization trend: An international and a four metropolitan area comparison* [Brief]. www.ourcommons.ca/content/Committee/411/FINA/WebDoc/WD6079428/411_FINA_IIC_Briefs/MurdieRobertAE.pdf

Hunt, C. S., & Seiver, M. (2017). Social class matters: Class identities and discourses in educational contexts. *Educational Review, 70*(3), 342–357. https://doi.org/10.1080/00131911.2017.1316240

Hyatt, J. (2025, May 24). Elon Musk is $170 billion richer since endorsing Trump. *Forbes*. https://www.forbes.com/sites/johnhyatt/2025/05/24/elon-musk-is-170-billion-richer-since-endorsing-trump/

Ignatiev, N. (1995). *How the Irish became White*. Routledge.

International Court of Justice. (2024, July). *Legal consequences arising from the policies and practices of Israel in the occupied Palestinian territory, including East Jerusalem*. https://www.icj-cij.org/node/204176

Inter-Parliamentary Union. (2025). *Women in politics: 2025.* https://www.ipu.org/resources/publications/infographics/2025-03/women-in-politics-2025

Jackson, A. (2021). *The fire and the ashes: Rekindling democratic socialism.* Between the Lines.

Jackson, L. M. (2020). *The psychology of prejudice: from attitudes to social action* (2nd ed.). American Psychological Association.

Jacobson, M. F. (1998). *Whiteness of a different color: European immigrants and the alchemy of race.* Harvard University Press.

Jamal, A. (2017). In the shadow of the 1967 war: Israel and the Palestinians. *British Journal of Middle Eastern Studies, 44*(4), 529–544. https://doi.org/10.1080/13530194.2017.1360010

James, C. E. (2007). "Reverse racism"? Students' responses to equity programs. In T. D. Gupta, C. E. James, R. C. A. Maaka, G. E. Galabuzi, & C. Andersen (Eds.), *Race and racialization: Essential readings* (pp. 356–362). Canadian Scholars' Press.

James, C. E., & Turner, T. (2017). *Towards race equity in education: The schooling of Black students in the Greater Toronto area.* York University. https://edu.yorku.ca/files/2017/04/Towards-Race-Equity-in-Education-April-2017.pdf

Jancsics, D. (2018). Shell companies and government corruption. In A. Farazmand (Ed.), *Global encyclopedia of public administration, public policy, and governance* [Living edition]. Springer. https://doi.org/10.1007/978-3-319-31816-5_3566-1

Jankowski, G. S. (2016). Who stops the sweatshops? Our neglect of the injustice of maldistribution. *Social and Personality Psychology Compass, 10*(11), 581–590.

Jansen, B. (2025, February 19). "Biologically inaccurate": Judge blasts Trump policy to ban transgender people from the military. *USA Today.* https://www.usatoday.com/story/news/politics/2025/02/18/trump-order-banning-transgender-troops-military/78617284007/

Jayakumar, U. M. (2022). Introduction: CRT in higher education: Confronting the "boogeyman" bans, censorship, and attacks on racial justice. *Philosophy and Theory in Higher Education, 4*(3), 1–12.

Jefferson, T. (2002). *Notes on the state of Virginia: With related documents* (D. Waldstreicher, Ed.). Bedford/St. Martins. (Original work published 1787)

Jensen, R. (2021). Men and pornography: Illusions, delusions, and the struggle for intimacy in patriarchy. *Atlánticas, 6*(1), 15–29. https://doi.org/10.17979/arief.2021.6.1.7129

Jensen, R. (2024, November 24). *Feminism is freedom for men: Pornography and sexuality.* Julie Bindel's writing and podcast [Substack]. https://juliebindel.substack.com/p/feminism-is-freedom-for-men

Jhally, S. (Producer & Director). (2007). *Dreamworlds 3: Desire, sex, and power in music video* [Film]. Media Education Foundation.

Jhally, S. (2009). Advertising, gender, and sex: What's wrong with a little objectification? In R. Hammer & D. Kellner (Eds.), *Media/cultural studies* (pp. 313–323). Peter Lang.

Jiang, C., Vitiello, C., Axt, J. R., Campbell, J. T., & Ratliff, K. A. (2019). An examination of ingroup preferences among people with multiple socially stigmatized identities. *Self and Identity, 20*(4), 569–586. https://doi.org/10.1080/15298868.2019.1657937

Jiwani, Y. (2006). Missing and murdered women: Reproducing marginality in news discourse. *Canadian Journal of Communication, 31*(4), 895–918.

Johnson, A. G. (2004). Patriarchy, the system. In G. Kirk & M. Okazawa-Rey (Eds.), *Women's lives: Multicultural perspectives* (3rd ed., pp. 25–32). McGraw-Hill.

Johnson, A. G. (2006). *Power, privilege, and difference* (2nd ed.). McGraw-Hill.

Johnson, H. B., & Shapiro, T. M. (2003). Good neighborhoods, good schools: Race and the "good choices" of White families. In A. W. Doane & E. Bonilla-Silva (Eds.), *White out: The continuing significance of racism* (pp. 173–187). Routledge.

Jones, K. M., & Pineda-Torres, M. (2024). TRAP'd teens: Impacts of abortion provider regulations on fertility & education. *Journal of Public Economics, 234*, 105112. https://doi.org/10.1016/j.jpubeco.2024.105112

Jones, T. (2024). Trans bans expand: Anti-LGBTIQ+ lawfare and neo-fascism. *Sexuality Research and Social Policy, 22*, 69–84.

Jordan-Young, R. M. (2010). *Brain storm: The flaws in the science of sex differences*. Harvard University Press.
Jordan-Young, R. M. (2014). Homunculus in the hormones? In W. Ernst & I. Horwath (Eds.), *Gender in science and technology: Interdisciplinary approaches* (pp. 111–128). transcript Verlag. http://www.jstor.org/stable/j.ctv1xxsrx.8
Joshee, R. (1995). An historical approach to understanding Canadian multicultural policy. In T. Wotherspoon & P. Jungbluth (Eds.), *Multicultural education in a changing global economy: Canada and the Netherlands* (pp. 23–40). Waxmann.
Joshee, R. (2004). Citizenship and multicultural education in Canada: From assimilation to social cohesion. In J. A. Banks (Ed.), *Diversity and citizenship education: Global perspectives* (pp. 127–156). Jossey-Bass.
Joyce, T. J., Kaestner, R., & Ward, J. (2020). The impact of parental involvement laws on the abortion rate of minors. *Demography, 57*, 323–346.
Katz, B. W., Oesterle, D. W., Prince, J. R., Leone, R. M., Davis, K. C., Orchowski, L. M., & Gilmore, A. K. (2025). Examining differences in sexual violence perpetration likelihood by perceived intoxication among sexual and gender minority college students. *Journal of Aggression, Maltreatment & Trauma, 34*(3), 312–330. https://doi.org/10.1080/10926771.2025.2450396
Kazemian, L., & Galleguillos, S. (2025). A global comparison of long prison sentences. *Journal of Criminal Justice, 96*, 102341.
Keister, L. A., & Southgate, D. (2022). *Inequality: A contemporary approach to race, class & gender* (2nd ed.). Cambridge University Press.
Kendi, I. X. (2016). *Stamped from the beginning: A definitive history of racist ideas in America*. Bold Type Books.
Kendi, I. X. (2021). *How to be an antiracist*. One World Press.
Khalidi, R. (2020). *The hundred years' war on Palestine: A history of settler colonialism and resistance 1917–2017*. Henry Holt and Company.
Khalidi, W. (1991). The Palestine problem: An overview. *Journal of Palestine Studies, 21*(1), 5–16.
Kincheloe, J. L. (1999). The struggle to define and reinvent Whiteness: A pedagogical analysis. *College Literature, 26*(3), 162–194.
Kincheloe, J. L. (2008). *Knowledge and critical pedagogy*. Springer Press.
King, M. L., Jr. (1998). *March on Washington: The autobiography of Martin Luther King, Jr.* (Clayborne Carson, Ed.). Warner Books.
Kipling, R. (1899, February). The White man's burden. *McClure's Magazine, 12*(4), 290–291.
Kirmayer, L. J., & Valaskakis, G. G. (Eds.). (2009). *Healing traditions: The mental health of Aboriginal peoples in Canada*. University of British Columbia Press.
Kite, M. E., Whitley, B. E., Jr., & Wagner, L. S. (2022). *Psychology of prejudice and discrimination* (4th ed.). Routledge. https://doi.org/10.4324/9780367809218
Kline, W. (2005). *Building a better race: Gender, sexuality, and eugenics from the turn of the century to the baby boom*. University of California Press.
Knight, B., Birnbaum, J., & Craig, M. (Eds.). (2024, May 16). Forbes 2024 world's highest-paid athletes list. *Forbes*. https://www.forbes.com/sites/justinbirnbaum/2024/05/16/the-worlds-10-highest-paid-athletes-2024/
Kobayashi, A. (2018). Now you see them, how you see them: Women of Colour in Canadian academia. In *Racism in the Canadian university* (pp. 60–75). University of Toronto Press.
Kraus, M. W., & Tan, J. X. (2015). Americans overestimate social class mobility. *Journal of Experimental Social Psychology, 58*, 101–111.
Kujawinski, E. B., Reddy, C. M., Rodgers, R. P., Thrash, J. C., Valentine, D. L., & White, H. K. (2020). The first decade of scientific insights from the Deepwater Horizon oil release. *Nature Reviews Earth & Environment, 1*(5), 237–250.
Kumari, P., & Tiwari, N. (2022). Analyzing the causes of the First World War. *Journal of Studies in Social Sciences, 21*, 1.
Kunjufu, J. (2005). *Keeping Black boys out of special education*. African American Images.

Kwon, S. H., Lao, W. W. K., Lee, C. H., Hsu, A. T. W., Koide, S., Chen, H. Y., & Chang, T. N. J. (2021). Experiences and attitudes toward aesthetic procedures in East Asia: A cross-sectional survey of five geographical regions. *Archives of Plastic Surgery, 48*(06), 660–669.

La Salle, T. P., Wang, C., Wu, C., & Rocha Neves, J. (2020). Racial mismatch among minoritized students and White teachers: Implications and recommendations for moving forward. *Journal of Educational and Psychological Consultation, 30*(3), 314–343.

Lavie, C., De Schutter, A., & Milani, R. (2015). Healthy obese versus unhealthy lean: The obesity paradox. *Nature Reviews Endocrinology, 11*, 55–62. https://doi.org/10.1038/nrendo.2014.165

Lawson, D. (2025, May 3). Trump's presidency is his family's piggybank. *The Sunday Times*. https://www.thetimes.com/comment/columnists/article/trumps-presidency-is-his-familys-piggybank-h3q0hk8nn

Lawson, J. (2024, April 17). Caitlin Clark's $76,000 WNBA salary puts a spotlight on pay disparity. *ABC News*. https://abcnews.go.com/GMA/Living/caitlin-clarks-76000-wnba-salary-puts-spotlight-pay/story?id=109341851

Leach, J. (2013). Citizens United: Robbing America of its democratic idealism. *Daedalus, 142*(2), 95–101.

Leboeuf, C. (2020). The embodied biased mind. In E. Beeghly & A. Madva (Eds.), *An introduction to implicit bias* (pp. 41–56). Routledge.

Leemis, R. W., Friar, N., Khatiwada, S., Chen, M. S., Kresnow, M.-j., Smith, S. G., Caslin, S., & Basile, K. C. (2022). *The national intimate partner and sexual violence survey: 2016/2017 report on sexual violence*. National Center for Injury Prevention and Control, Centers for Disease Control and Prevention. https://stacks.cdc.gov/view/cdc/124646

Leistyna, P. (2009, Fall). Exposing the ruling class in the United States using television and documentary film. *Radical Teacher, 85*, 12–15.

Leonardo, Z. (2004). The color of supremacy: Beyond the discourse of "White privilege." *Educational Philosophy and Theory, 36*(2), 137–152.

Leonardo, Z. (2009). *Race, Whiteness, and education*. Routledge.

Levin, D. E., & Kilbourne, J. (2008). *So sexy so soon: The new sexualized childhood and what parents can do to protect their kids*. Ballantine Books.

Lewis, M., & Lupyan, G. (2019). Language use shapes cultural stereotypes: Large scale evidence from gender. PsyArXiv preprint. https://doi.org/10.31234/osf.io/7qd3g

Li, P. S. (1988). *The Chinese in Canada*. Oxford University Press.

Lindesmith, A. R., Strauss, A., & Denzin, N. K. (1999). *Social psychology*. SAGE Publications.

Lindo, J. M., Myers, C. K., Schlosser, A., & Cunningham, S. (2020). How far is too far? New evidence on abortion clinic closures, access, and abortions. *Journal of Human Resources, 55*(4), 1137–1160. https://muse.jhu.edu/article/771324

List of unarmed African Americans killed by law enforcement officers in the United States. (2005, July 16). In *Wikipedia*. https://en.wikipedia.org/w/index.php?title=List_of_unarmed_African_Americans_killed_by_law_enforcement_officers_in_the_United_States&oldid=1300874068

Little, W. (2016). *Introduction to sociology* (2nd Canadian ed.). BC Campus Open Source Textbook.

Llorens, A., Tzovara, A., Bellier, L., Bhaya-Grossman, I., Bidet-Caulet, A., Chang, W. K., Cross, Z. R., Dominguez-Faus, R., Flinker, A., Fonken, Y., Gorenstein, M. A., Holdgraf, C., Hoy, C. W., Ivanova, M. V., Jimenez, R. T., Jun, S., Kam, J. W. Y., Kidd, C., Marcelle, E. . . . & Dronkers, N. F. (2021). Gender bias in academia: A lifetime problem that needs solutions. *Neuron, 109*(13), 2047–2074. https://www.sciencedirect.com/science/article/pii/S0896627321004177

López, I. F. H. (2000). The social construction of race. In R. Delgado & J. Stefancic (Eds.), *Critical race theory: The cutting edge* (2nd ed., pp. 163–175). Temple University Press.

Lord, H. (2025). Prison labour as modern neoslavery: A Marxist political economy analysis of exploitation and surplus value in the US neoliberal capitalist economy. *Politicus, 11*(2), 56–61. https://ojs.library.queensu.ca/index.php/politicus/article/view/18955

Lorde, A. (1984). *Sister outsider: Essays and speeches*. Crossing Press.

Love, H. R., & Beneke, M. R. (2021). Pursuing justice-driven inclusive education research: Disability critical race theory (DisCrit) in early childhood. *Topics in Early Childhood Special Education*, *41*(1), 31–44. https://doi.org/10.1177/0271121421990833

Lovelace v. Ontario, [2000] 1 S.C.R. 950, 2000 SCC 37 (2000). https://decisions.scc-csc.ca/scc-csc/scc-csc/en/item/1800/index.do

Lucas, D. (2024). How much do guarantees and bailouts cost the government? *Policy Hub*, *2024*(3), 1–29.

Lund, D. E. (2006). Social justice activism in the heartland of hate: Countering extremism in Alberta. *The Alberta Journal of Educational Research*, *52*(2), 181–194.

Lyonga, F. (2021). Shades of homophobia: A framework for analyzing negative attitudes toward homosexuality. *Journal of Homosexuality*, *68*(10), 1664–1684. https://doi.org/10.1080/00918369.2019.1702352

MacDonald, D. (2025). *Company men: CEO pay in 2023*. Canadian Centre for Policy Alternatives. https://www.policyalternatives.ca/news-research/company-men

Mackenzie, J. (2025, February 5). Trump's Gaza "Riviera" echoes Kushner waterfront property dreams. *Reuters*. https://www.reuters.com/world/us/trumps-gaza-riviera-echoes-kushner-waterfront-property-dreams-2025-02-05/

MacKenzie, M., Sensoy, Ö., Johnson, G. F., Sinclair, N., & Weldon, L. (2023). How universities gaslight EDI&I initiatives: Mapping institutional resistance to structural change. *International Journal of Education Policy and Leadership*, *19*(1), 1–18. https://doi.org/10.22230/ijepl.2023v19n1a1303

Mady, S., Biswas, D., Dadzie, C. A., Hill, R. P., & Paul, R. (2023). "A whiter shade of pale": Whiteness, female beauty standards, and ethical engagement across three cultures. *Journal of International Marketing*, *31*(1), 69–89.

Mahomed, S. (2023). When sanctuaries of humanity turn into corridors of horror: The destruction of healthcare in Gaza. *South African Journal of Bioethics and Law*, *16*(3), 77–79.

Mangan, D. (2025). *Trump pardons Nikola founder Trevor Milton in securities fraud case*. CNBC. https://www.cnbc.com/2025/03/28/trump-pardons-nikola-trevor-milton-ceo-securities-fraud-electric-vehicle.html

Mar, L. R. (2010). *Brokering belonging: Chinese in Canada's exclusion era, 1885–1945*. Oxford University Press.

Mast, N. (2025, January 16). *Forced prison labor in the "Land of the Free."* Economic Policy Institute. https://www.epi.org/publication/rooted-racism-prison-labor/

Matheson, K., Seymour, A., Landry, J., Ventura, K., Arsenault, E., & Anisman, H. (2022). Canada's colonial genocide of Indigenous peoples: A review of the psychosocial and neurobiological processes linking trauma and intergenerational outcomes. *International Journal of Environmental Research and Public Health*, *19*(11), 6455. https://doi.org/10.3390/ijerph19116455

Mathieu, X. (2018). The dynamics of 'civilised' sovereignty: Colonial frontiers and performative discourses of civilisation and savagery. *International Relations*, *32*(4), 468–487. https://doi.org/10.1177/0047117818782612

Matias, C. E. (2016). *Feeling White: Whiteness, emotionality, and education*. Springer.

Matias, C. E. (2023). Hysteria, hypermania, & hullabaloo: How White emotionalities manufacture fear of critical race theory & teaching. *Thresholds in Education*, *46*(1), 1–7. https://academyforeducationalstudies.org/wp-content/uploads/2023/03/matiasintrofinal-1.pdf

Maxwell, K. E., Nagda, B. R., & Thompson, M. C. (2023). *Facilitating intergroup dialogues: Bridging differences, catalyzing change*. Taylor & Francis.

M'baye, B. (2006). The economic, political, and social impact of the Atlantic slave trade on Africa. *The European Legacy: Toward New Paradigms*, *11*(6), 607–622. https://doi.org/10.1080/10848770600918091

McGuirk, R. (2024, December 20). Gisèle Pelicot's Australian supporters are moved that their French heroine wore an Aboriginal scarf. *AP News*. https://apnews.com/article/australia-gisele-pelicot-indigenous-scarf-f286d7cd0d15ea9a446d3d9a3899db65

McIntosh, P. (1989). White privilege: Unpacking the invisible knapsack. *Peace and Freedom*, July/August, 10–12.

McLaren, P. (1997). Decentering Whiteness. *Multicultural Education, 5*(1), 4–11.

McMurry, T. B. (2011). The image of male nurses and nursing leadership mobility. *Nursing Forum, 46*(1), 22–28.

McNeil, K., & Enns, T. (2022). *Procedural injustice: Indigenous claims, limitation periods, and laches* [Working paper]. Osgoode Hall Law School of York University. https://digitalcommons.osgoode.yorku.ca/all_papers/336/

Mekay, E. (2025, March 6). *Trump Gaza 'Riviera' scheme 'utterly contrary to international law'*. International Bar Association. https://www.ibanet.org/Trump-Gaza-Riviera-Scheme-utterly-contrary-to-international-law

Menakem, R. (2017). *My grandmother's hands: Racialized trauma and the pathway to mending our hearts and bodies*. Central Recovery Press.

Mentan, T. (2018). *Africa in the colonial ages of empire: Slavery, capitalism, racism, colonialism, decolonization, independence as recolonization, and beyond*. Langaa RPCIG.

Metzgar, J. (2010). Are "the poor" part of the working class or in a class by themselves? *Labor Studies Journal, 35*(3), 398–416.

Milkman, K. L., Akinola, M., & Chugh, D. (2015). What happens before? A field experiment exploring how pay and representation differentially shape bias on the pathway into organizations. *Journal of Applied Psychology, 100*(6), 1678–1712.

Milloy, J. S. (1999). *A national crime: The Canadian government and the residential school system, 1879–1986*. University of Manitoba Press.

Milloy, J. S. (2000). The early Indian Acts: Developmental strategy and constitutional change. In I. A. L. Getty & A. S. Lussier (Eds.), *As long as the sun shines and water flows: A reader in Canadian native studies* (pp. 56–64). University of British Columbia Press.

Mirrlees, T. (2022). Trump and the Alt Right: The mainstreaming of White nationalism. In B. Perry, J. Gruenewald, & R. Scrivens (Eds.), *Right-wing extremism in Canada and the United States* (pp. 67–96). Springer International Publishing.

Mohamed, T., & Beagan, B. L. (2019). 'Strange faces' in the academy: Experiences of racialized and Indigenous faculty in Canadian universities. *Race, Ethnicity and Education, 22*(3), 338–354.

Mohanty, C. T. (1988). Under Western eyes: Feminist scholarship and colonial discourses. *Feminist Review, 30*(1), 61–88. https://doi.org/10.1057/fr.1988.42

Monarrez, T., Kisida, B., & Chingos, M. (2022). The effect of charter schools on school segregation. *American Economic Journal: Economic Policy, 14*(1), 301–340. https://www.jstor.org/stable/27113822

Moraga, C., & Anzaldúa, G. (Eds.). (1981). *This bridge called my back: Writings by radical women of Color*. Persephone Press.

Morrison, T. G., & Halton, M. (2009, Winter). Buff, tough, and rough: Representations of muscularity in action motion pictures. *The Journal of Men's Studies, 17*(1), 57–74.

Motaparthi, K. (2010). Blepharoplasty in Asian patients—Ethnic and ethical implications. *Virtual Mentor: American Medical Association Journal of Ethics, 12*(12), 946–949.

Mukherjee, A., Mukherjee, A., & Godard, B. (2006). Translating minoritized cultures: Issues of caste, class and gender. *Postcolonial Text, 2*(3), 1–23.

Mullaly, R. (2002). *Challenging oppression: A critical social work approach*. Oxford University Press.

Muller, C., & Scrage, D. (2021). The political economy of incarceration in the Cotton South, 1910–1925. *American Journal of Sociology, 127*(3), 828–866. https://www.journals.uchicago.edu/doi/abs/10.1086/718045

Myers, K. (2003). White fright: Reproducing White supremacy through casual discourse. In W. Doane & E. Bonilla-Silva (Eds.), *White out: The continuing significance of racism* (pp. 129–144). Routledge.

Myhre, K.G.T, (2020, November 22). *"White supremacy is not a shark; it is the water." Not a lot of reasons to sing, but enough*. https://guante.info/2020/11/22/nottheshark/

Nair, G., & Hofman, N. G. (2022). Middle-class women and domestic work in India and the United States: Caste, race and patriarchy. *Sociological Bulletin, 71*(1), 24–40. https://doi.org/10.1177/00380229211063157

National Inquiry into Missing and Murdered Indigenous Women and Girls. (2019, May 29). *Reclaiming power and place—Final report*. MMIWG. https://www.mmiwg-ffada.ca/final-report/

National Taxpayers Union Foundation. (n.d.). Pensions and perks for former presidents. https://www.ntu.org/foundation/tax-page/pensions-and-perks-for-former-presidents-archive#:~:text=The%20biggest%20personal%20benefit%20that%20former%20presidents,eligible%20for%20a%20separate%20federal%20pension%20program.

Navarro-Mantas, L., & Sáez-Lumbreras, A. (2025). Sexuality construction, pornography, and gender violence: A qualitative study with Spanish adolescents. *Sexuality & Culture, 29*, 1339–1387. https://link.springer.com/article/10.1007/s12119-025-10326-3

Newman, L. M. (1999). *White women's rights: The racial origins of feminism in the United States*. Oxford University Press.

Nielsen-Reagan, A. (2021). The profitability of inhumanity: How corporate power gives rise to forced labor in privatized immigration detention. *Systemic Justice Journal, 1*. https://systemicjustice.org/article/the-profitability-of-inhumanity/

Nieri, T., Montoya, L., & Carlos, C. (2023). Ethnic–racial socialization of White children by White parents: A systematic review. *Journal of Family Issues, 45*(7), 1735–1763. https://doi.org/10.1177/0192513X231194306

Nieto, L., Boyer, M., Goodwin, L., Johnson, G., Collier Smith, L., & Hopkins, J. P. (2010). *Beyond inclusion, beyond empowerment: A developmental strategy to liberate everyone*. Cuetzpalin.

Nisbett, R. E. (1998). Race, genetics, and IQ. In C. Jencks & M. Phillips (Eds.), *The Black–White test score gap* (pp. 86–102). Brookings Institution Press.

Nocella, R. R. (2024). Global sex work in the twentieth-century gig economy: Empowering adult content creators through labour recognition. In C. Phipps (Ed.), *Histories of sex work around the world* (pp. 214–232). Routledge.

Nonini, D. M. (2005). Making the case for kleptocratic oligarchy (as the dominant form of rule in the United States). *Social Analysis, 49*(1), 177–189.

Novotney, A. (2023, April 24). *7 in 10 human trafficking victims are women and girls. What are the psychological effects?* American Psychological Association. https://www.apa.org/topics/women-girls/trafficking-women-girls

Oakes, J. (1985). *Keeping track: How schools structure inequality*. Yale University Press.

Office of the Assistant Secretary for Planning and Evaluation. (2025). *Poverty guidelines*. U.S. Department of Health and Human Services. https://aspe.hhs.gov/topics/poverty-economic-mobility/poverty-guidelines

Office of Family Assistance. (2024). *Characteristics and financial circumstances of TANF recipients, fiscal year 2023*. https://acf.gov/ofa/data/characteristics-and-financial-circumstances-tanf-recipients-fiscal-year-2023

Office of Government-wide Policy. (2025, February 15). *CAAC consultation to issue a class deviation from the federal acquisition regulation regarding Executive Orders 14173 and 14168* [CAAC letter 2025-01]. U.S. General Services Administration. https://www.acquisition.gov/sites/default/files/caac/CAAC_Letter_2025-01.pdf

Office of Justice Programs. (2024, December). *Understanding and reducing deaths in custody: Interim summary report to Congress*. U.S. Department of Justice. https://www.ojp.gov/pdffiles1/nij/309952.pdf

Olson, J. M., & Maio, G. R. (2003). Attitudes in social behavior. In T. Millon & M. J. Lerner (Eds.), *Handbook of psychology, Vol. 5: Personality and social psychology* (pp. 299–326). John Wiley & Sons.

Oluo, I. (2018). *So you want to talk about race*. Seal Press.

Olwan, D. M. (2019). Pinkwashing the "honor crime": Murdered Muslim women and the politics of posthumous solidarities. *Signs: Journal of Women in Culture and Society, 44*(4), 905–930.

Olwan, D. M. (2021). *Gender violence and the transnational politics of the honor crime*. The Ohio State University Press.

O'Malley, R. L., & Holt, K. M. (2020). Cyber sextortion: An exploratory analysis of different perpetrators engaging in a similar crime. *Journal of Interpersonal Violence, 37*(1–2), 258–283.

Omi, M., & Winant, H. (2014). *Racial formation in the United States: From the 1960s to the 1980s* (3rd ed.). Routledge.

OnlyFans Annual Report. (2023). Parent company Fenix International. https://s3.eu-west-2.amazonaws.com/document-api-images-live.ch.gov.uk/docs/uS16M_KlijllnIEKIzThxkgN4eGDMoMoyBlch6syddM/application-pdf?X-Amz-Algorithm=AWS4-HMAC-SHA256&X-Amz-Credential=ASIAWRGBDBV3KU3HTBZH%2F20250813%2Feu-west-2%2Fs3%2Faws4_request&X-Amz

Ortiz-Martínez, G., Vázquez-Villegas, P., Ruiz-Cantisani, M. I., Delgado-Fabián, M., Conejo-Márquez, D. A., & Membrillo-Hernández, J. (2023). Analysis of the retention of women in higher education STEM programs. *Humanities and Social Sciences Communications, 10*(1), 1–14.

Osei-Tutu, A. A. Z., & Osei-Tutu, K. O. A. (2023). International perspectives on media disinformation: Critical media literacy as antiracist pedagogy. *New Directions for Adult and Continuing Education, 2023*(178), 105–117. https://doi.org/10.1002/ace.20490

Owens, J. (2022). Double jeopardy: Teacher biases, racialized organizations, and the production of racial/ethnic disparities in school discipline. *American Sociological Review, 87*(6), 1007–1048. https://doi.org/10.1177/00031224221135810

Owens, J., & McLanahan, S. S. (2020). Unpacking the drivers of racial disparities in school suspension and expulsion. *Social Forces, 98*(4), 1548–1577.

OXFAM. (2024, July 25). *Top 1 percent bags over $40 trillion in new wealth during past decade as taxes on the rich reach historic lows* [Press release]. https://www.oxfam.org/en/press-releases/top-1-percent-bags-over-40-trillion-new-wealth-during-past-decade-taxes-rich-reach

OXFAM. (2025a, January 20). *Billionaire wealth surges by $2 trillion in 2024, three times faster than the year before, while the number of people living in poverty has barely changed since 1990* [Press release]. https://www.oxfam.org/en/press-releases/billionaire-wealth-surges-2-trillion-2024-three-times-faster-year-while-number

OXFAM. (2025b, June 2). *Do the rich pay their fair share?* https://www.oxfamamerica.org/explore/stories/do-the-rich-pay-their-fair-share/

Page, C. T. (2022). Stop the steal: The history of voter suppression in America, and who is really stealing votes? *Intercultural Human Rights Law Review, 17*, 153.

Pager, D. (2007). *Marked: Race, crime, and finding work in an era of mass incarceration.* University of Chicago Press.

Pailey, R. N. (2020). De-centring the 'White gaze' of development. *Development and Change, 51*(3), 729–745. https://doi.org/10.1111/dech.12550

Palmowski, J., & Riches, C. (2021). Capitalism. In J. Palmowski & C. Riches, *A dictionary of contemporary world history* (6th ed.). Oxford University Press.

Pappé, I. (2006). The 1948 ethnic cleansing of Palestine. *Journal of Palestine Studies, 36*(1), 6–20. https://doi.org/10.1525/jps.2006.36.1.6

Pappé, I. (2017). *The biggest prison on Earth: A history of Gaza and the occupied territories.* Simon and Schuster.

Parliament of Canada. (2025). *Indemnities, salaries, and allowances: Parliament of Canada.* https://lop.parl.ca/sites/ParlInfo/default/en_CA/People/Salaries

Parker, W. C. (2008). Knowing and doing in democratic citizenship education. In L. S. Levstik and C. A. Tyson (Eds.), *Handbook of research in social studies education* (pp. 65–80). Routledge.

Patchin, J. W., & Hinduja, S. (2018). Sextortion among adolescents: Results from a national survey of U.S. youth. *Sexual Abuse, 32*(1), 30–54.

Patek, A. (2012). *Jews on route to Palestine, 1934–1944: Sketches from the history of Aliyah Bet—Clandestine Jewish immigration* (G. R. Torr & T. Williams, Trans). Jagiellonian University Press.

Paton, D., Bullivant, S., & Soto, J. (2020). The impact of sex education mandates on teenage pregnancy: International evidence. *Health Economics, 29*(7), 790–807. https://doi.org/10.1002/hec.4021

Payne, R. K. (2005). *A framework for understanding poverty.* Aha! Process.

Pearl, A., & Valencia, R. R. (1997). Cultural and accumulated environmental deficit models. In R. R. Valencia (Ed.), *The evolution of deficit thinking* (1st ed., pp. 132–159). Routledge.

Pearman, F. A., Curran, F. C., Fisher, B., & Gardella, J. (2019). Are achievement gaps related to discipline gaps? Evidence from national data. *AERA Open, 5*(4). https://doi.org/10.1177/2332858419875440

Pedersen, S. (2015). *The guardians: The League of Nations and the crisis of empire*. Oxford University Press.

Pedulla, D. S., Allen, S., & Baer-Bositis, L. (2023). Can customers affect racial discrimination in hiring? *Social Psychology Quarterly, 86*(1), 30–52. https://doi.org/10.1177/01902725221109533

Perry, L. B., Yoon, E. S., Sciffer, M., & Lubienski, C. (2024). The impact of marketization on school segregation and educational equity and effectiveness: Evidence from Australia and Canada. *International Journal of Comparative Sociology*. https://doi.org/10.1177/00207152241227810

Peterson-Withorn, C. (2024). The Forbes 400: The definitive ranking of America's richest people 2024. *Forbes*. https://www.forbes.com/forbes-400/

Pham, M. T. (2022). A world without sweatshops: Abolition not reform. In A. Bierria, J. Caruthers, & B. Lober (Eds.), *Abolition feminisms: Organizing, survival, and transformative practice*. Haymarket Books.

Picca, L., & Feagin, J. (2007). *Two-faced racism: Whites in the backstage and frontstage*. Routledge.

Pomeranz, K. (2005). Empire & "civilizing" missions, past & present. *Daedalus, 134*(2), 34–45. http://www.jstor.org/stable/20027976

Pontell, H. N., Black, W. K., & Geis, G. (2014). Too big to fail, too powerful to jail? On the absence of criminal prosecutions after the 2008 financial meltdown. *Crime, Law, and Social Change, 61*(1), 1–13.

Popoviciu, A., & Masarwa, L. (2021). *Gaza: What the iron wall built by Israel means for besieged Palestinians*. Middle East Eye. https://www.middleeasteye.net/news/israel-iron-wall-gaza-palestinians-siege

Preston, A., & Eisenberg, R. (2022, July 13). *Profit over people: The commercial bail industry fueling America's cash bail systems*. Center for American Progress. https://www.americanprogress.org/article/profit-over-people/

Pryce, D. K. (2025). Factors affecting the quality of life of residents in the United States: Lessons from Virginia. *International Social Science Journal, 75*(256), 427–437. https://doi.org/10.1111/issj.12561

Public Citizen. (2025, March 4). *Trump guts enforcement, greenlights corporate crime spree*. https://www.citizen.org/news/trump-guts-enforcement-greenlights-corporate-crime-spree/

Quigley, J. (2022). *Britain and its mandate over Palestine: Legal chicanery on a world stage*. Anthem Press. https://doi.org/10.2307/j.ctv307fgnk.17

Quillian, L., & Lee, J. J. (2023). Trends in racial and ethnic discrimination in hiring in six Western countries. *Proceedings of the National Academy of Sciences, 120*(6), e2212875120.

Quillian, L., Lee, J. J., & Oliver, M. (2020). Evidence from field experiments in hiring shows substantial additional racial discrimination after the callback. *Social Forces, 99*(2), 732–759.

Quinan, C. Q. (2025). From criminalization to erasure: Project 2025 and anti-trans legislation in the US. *Crime, Media, Culture: An International Journal, 21*(4), 529–547.

R. v. Kapp, (2008) 2 S.C.R. 483, 2008 SCC 41 (2008). https://decisions.scc-csc.ca/scc-csc/scc-csc/en/item/5696/index.do

Rabuy, B., & Kopf, D. (2016). *Detaining the poor: How money bail perpetuates an endless cycle of poverty and jail time*. Prison Policy Initiative. https://www.prisonpolicy.org/reports/incomejails.html

Radesky, J., Chassiakos, Y. L. R., Ameenuddin, N., Navsaria, D., & Council on Communication and Media. (2020, July 1). Digital advertising to children [Policy statement]. *Pediatrics, 146*(1), e20201681. https://doi.org/10.1542/peds.2020-1681

Rahali, M. (2021, December 8). *(Un)Boxing day: Kidfluencers reprise role as Santa's little helpers*. Parenting for a Digital Future. https://blogs.lse.ac.uk/parenting4digitalfuture/2021/12/08/kidfluencers/

Ramos, J. (2015). Liquid democracy and the futures of governance. In J. Winter & R. Ono (Eds.), *The future Internet: Alternative visions* (pp. 173–191). Springer International Publishing.

Rasmussen, E. E., Riggs, R. E., & Sauermilch, W. S. (2022). Kidfluencer exposure, materialism, and US tweens' purchase of sponsored products. *Journal of Children and Media, 16*(1), 68–77.

Ratliff, K. A., & Smith, C. T. (2024). The Implicit Association Test. *Daedalus, 153*(1), 51–64. https://direct.mit.edu/daed/article/153/1/51/119941/The-Implicit-Association-Test

Razack, S. (2022). *Nothing has to make sense: Upholding White supremacy through anti-Muslim racism*. University of Minnesota Press.

Reich, R. (2023, December 14). Finding moral clarity on campus about the Hamas–Israeli war. https://robertreich.substack.com/p/moral-clarity-on-campus-about-the

Restifo, S. J., & Bostic, A. (2024). Anti-immigrant sentiment and hate: The past as prologue. In J. Hawdon & M. Costello (Eds.), *Research handbook on hate and hate crimes in society* (pp. 142–161). Edward Elgar Publishing.

Rettig, E., & Spanier, B. (2024). Striking energy deals in disputed seas: The case of the Gaza Marine gas field. *The Journal of World Energy Law & Business, 17*(2), 128–135. https://doi.org/10.1093/jwelb/jwad039

Reyna, C., Bellovary, A., & Harris, K. (2022). The psychology of White nationalism: Ambivalence towards a changing America. *Social Issues and Policy Review, 16*(1), 79–124.

Rhode, D. L. (2010). *The beauty bias: The injustice of appearance in life and law*. Oxford University Press.

Ridgeway, C. L., Korn, R. M., & Williams, J. C. (2022). Documenting the routine burden of devalued difference in the professional workplace. *Gender & Society, 36*(5), 627–651. https://doi.org/10.1177/08912432221111168

Roberts, S. O., & Rizzo, M. T. (2021). The psychology of American racism. *The American Psychologist, 76*(3), 475–487. https://doi.org/10.1037/amp0000642

Robey, J., Massoglia, M., & Light, M. (2023). A generational shift: Race and the declining lifetime risk of imprisonment. *Demography, 60*(4), 977–1003. https://doi.org/10.1215/00703370-10863378

Roediger, D. R. (1991). *The wages of Whiteness: Race and the making of the American working class*. Verso.

Roeloffs, M. W. (2023, December 1). New billionaires inherited more than they earned last year, UBS Report says. *Forbes*. https://www.forbes.com/sites/maryroeloffs/2023/11/30/new-billionaires-inherited-more-than-they-earned-last-year-ubs-report-says/

Roscoe, W. (2020). Sexual and gender diversity in Native America and the Pacific Islands. In K. Crawford-Lackey & M. E. Springate (Eds.), *Identities and place: Changing labels and intersectional communities of LGBTQ and Two-Spirit people in the United States* (pp. 58–88). Berghahn.

Ross, M., & Bateman, N. (2019). *Meet the low-wage workforce* [Report]. Metropolitan Policy Program at the Brookings Institute. https://www.brookings.edu/wp-content/uploads/2019/11/201911_Brookings-Metro_low-wage-workforce_Ross-Bateman.pdf

Rothstein, R. (2018). *The color of law: A forgotten history of how our government segregated America*. Norton.

Rudman, L. A., & Kiliansky, S. E. (2000). Implicit and explicit attitudes toward female authority. *Personality and Social Psychology Bulletin, 26*(11), 1315–1328.

Rueschemeyer, D. (1986). *Power and the division of labour*. Stanford University Press.

Rutter, E. R. (2024). Becoming an antiracist in the multiethnic literature classroom. In C. Stanciu & G. Totten (Eds.), *Race in the multiethnic literature classroom* (pp. 161–177). University of Illinois Press.

Said, E. W. (1978). *Orientalism*. Pantheon Books.

Sakala, L. (2014). *Breaking down mass incarceration in the 2010 census: State-by-state incarceration rates by race/ethnicity* [Brief]. Prison Policy Initiative. https://www.prisonpolicy.org/reports/rates.html

Sanders, B. (2024). On democratic socialism in the United States. In T. Ball, R. Dagger, D. I. O'Neill, & J. Kirkpatrick (Eds.), *Ideals and ideologies* (pp. 179–184). Routledge.

Sardinha, L., Yüksel-Kaptanoğlu, I., Maheu-Giroux, M., & García-Moreno, C. (2024). Intimate partner violence against adolescent girls: Regional and national prevalence estimates and associated country-level factors. *The Lancet Child & Adolescent Health, 8*(9), 636–646.

Sawyer, W., & Wagner, P. (2025, March 11). *Mass incarceration: The whole pie 2025*. Prison Policy Initiative. https://www.prisonpolicy.org/factsheets/pie2025_allimages.pdf

Schachner, J. N. (2022). Racial stratification and school segregation in the suburbs: Evidence from Los Angeles County. *Social Forces, 101*(1), 309–340. https://doi.org/10.1093/sf/soab128

Schaeffer, K. (2024). *Key facts about public school teachers in the U.S.* Pew Research Center. https://www.pewresearch.org/short-reads/2024/09/24/key-facts-about-public-school-teachers-in-the-u-s/

Schick, C. (2000). White women teachers accessing dominance. *Discourse: Studies in the Cultural Politics of Education, 21*(3), 299–309.

Schisgall, D., & Alvarez, N. (Directors). (2007). *Very young girls* [Documentary]. Swinging T Productions.

Schmader, T., & Block, K. (2025). Why do women care more & men couldn't care less? *Daedalus, 154*(1), 82–97.

Scholtens, I. (2025, April 26). *Private prison companies are raking in profits from increased deportations.* Truthout. https://truthout.org/articles/private-prison-companies-are-raking-in-profits-from-increased-deportations/

Sciullo, N. J. (2015). Richard Sherman, rhetoric, and racial animus in the rebirth of the bogeyman myth. *Hastings Communication and Entertainment Law Journal, 37,* 201.

Seltzer, M. C., & O'Brien, L. M. (2024). Fostering racial literacy in early childhood contexts. *Early Childhood Education Journal, 52*(1), 181–189.

Sensoy, Ö., & DiAngelo, R. (2006). "I wouldn't want to be a woman in the Middle East": White female student teachers and the narrative of the oppressed Muslim woman. *Radical Pedagogy, 8*(1). radicalpedagogy.icaap.org/content/issue8_1/sensoy.html

Sensoy, Ö., & DiAngelo, R. (2014). "Respect differences"? Challenging the common guidelines in social justice education. *Democracy & Education, 22*(2), Article 1. https://democracyeducationjournal.org/home/vol22/iss2/1/

Seth, S. (2024, August 19). *The world's top 10 news media companies.* Investopedia. https://www.investopedia.com/stock-analysis/021815/worlds-top-ten-news-companies-nws-gci-trco-nyt.aspx

Shanks, T. R., & McLoyd, V. C. (2024). Struggling for economic security: Wealth, race and child development. *Annual Review of Developmental Psychology, 6,* 223–249. https://doi.org/10.1146/annurev-devpsych-120621-034917

Shelley, L. (2024). Post-Soviet oligarchs and kleptocrats: Their rise, their survival, and Western complicity. In R. I. Rotberg & F. O. Hampson (Eds.), *Grand corruption: Curbing kleptocracy globally* (pp. 70–83). Routledge.

Sherman, A., Trisi, D., & Cureton, J. (2024, December 11). *A guide to statistics on historical trends in income inequality.* Center on Budget and Policy Priorities. https://www.cbpp.org/research/poverty-and-inequality/a-guide-to-statistics-on-historical-trends-in-income-inequality

Shin, F., & Judah, B. (2023). *Stopping the kleptocrats: A strategy for the United States and Europe to address weaponized corruption.* Atlantic Council Europe Centre. https://www.atlanticcouncil.org/wp-content/uploads/2023/01/AC_Kleptocracy_EuropeCenter_Final.pdf

Shkembi, A., Smith, L. M., & Neitzel, R. L. (2024). Linking environmental injustices in Detroit, MI, to institutional racial segregation through historical federal redlining. *Journal of Exposure Science & Environmental Epidemiology, 34*(3), 389–398.

Shohat, E. (Ed.). (1998). *Talking visions: Multicultural feminism in a transnational age.* MIT Press.

Shook, J., Goodkind, S., Engel, R. J., Wexler, S., & Ballentine, K. L. (2020). Moving beyond poverty: Effects of low-wage work on individual, social, and family well-being. *Families in Society, 101*(3), 249–259. https://doi.org/10.1177/1044389420923473

Skinner-Dorkenoo, A. L., George, M., Wages, J. E., III, Sánchez, S., & Perry, S. P. (2023). A systemic approach to the psychology of racial bias within individuals and society. *Nature Reviews Psychology, 2*(7), 392–406.

Sleeter, C. E. (1989). Multicultural education as a form of resistance to oppression. *Journal of Education, 171*(3), 51–71. https://doi.org/10.1177/002205748917100305

Sleeter, C. E. (1994). The value of a multicultural education for all students. In B. McLeod (Ed.), *Language and learning: Educating linguistically diverse students* (pp. 107–128). SUNY Press.

Sleeter, C. E. (2017). Critical race theory and the Whiteness of teacher education. *Urban Education, 52*(1), 155–169.

Smallwood, S. E. (2019). Reflections on settler colonialism, the Hemispheric Americas, and chattel slavery. *The William and Mary Quarterly, 76*(3), 407–416. https://doi.org/10.5309/willmaryquar.76.3.0407

Smith, L. (1949). *Killers of the dream*. Reynal & Hitchcock.

Smith, S., Oates, C. J., & McLeay, F. (2024). Slimy tactics: The covert commercialisation of child-targeted content. *Journal of Strategic Marketing, 32*(3), 304–316.

Snyder, T. (2017). *On tyranny: Twenty lessons from the twentieth century*. Tim Duggan Books.

Social Rise. (2024, October 9). *OnlyFans terms of service: What you can and can't do*. https://social-rise.com/blog/onlyfans-terms-of-service#

Society for Adolescent Health and Medicine. (2017). Abstinence-only-until-marriage policies and programs: An updated position paper of the Society for Adolescent Health and Medicine. *Journal of Adolescent Health, 61*(3), 400–403. https://doi.org/10.1016/j.jadohealth.2017.06.001

Solorzano, D. G. (1992). An exploratory analysis of the effects of race, class, and gender on student and parent mobility aspirations. *The Journal of Negro Education, 61*(1), 30–44. https://doi.org/10.2307/2295627

Statista. (2025). *Global ad expenditure 2022–2024* [Dataset]. https://www.statista.com/statistics/1174981/advertising-expenditure-worldwide/

Statistics Canada. (2021, April 26). *Intimate partner violence in Canada, 2018*. https://www150.statcan.gc.ca/n1/en/daily-quotidien/210426/dq210426b-eng.pdf?st=8_zY_C4l

Statistics Canada. (2023). *Canada's Indigenous population*. https://www.statcan.gc.ca/o1/en/plus/3920-canadas-indigenous-population

Statistics Canada. (2024). *Distributions of household economic accounts for income, consumption, saving and wealth of Canadian households, first quarter 2024*. https://www150.statcan.gc.ca/n1/daily-quotidien/240717/dq240717a-eng.pdf

Steele, C. M. (1997). A threat in the air: How stereotypes shape intellectual identity and performance. *American Psychologist, 52*(6), 613–629.

Steet, L. (2000). *Veils and daggers: A century of National Geographic's representation of the Arab world*. Temple University Press.

Stepan, N. (1982). *The idea of race in science*. Macmillan.

Stewart, P., & Ali, I. (2024, November 13). Hegseth, advocate for firing "woke" military leaders, picked for Defense secretary. *Reuters*. https://www.reuters.com/world/us/trump-says-he-will-nominate-fox-news-host-pete-hegseth-defense-secretary-2024-11-13/

Sue, D. W. (2010). *Microaggressions in everyday life: Race, gender, and sexual orientation*. Wiley.

Sun, C., & Picker, M. (Director and Producer). (2008). *The price of pleasure: Pornography, sexuality, and relationships* [Film]. Media Education Foundation.

Sundquist, E. J. (Ed.). (1996). *The Oxford W. E. B. Du Bois reader*. Oxford University Press.

Supernant, K. (2025). From the archaeology of violence to the violences of archaeology. In B. A. Stewart, R. A. Beck, T. C. Fryer, M. L. Galaty, R. Garvey, H. Hoover, J. O'Shea, & A. Ventresca-Miller (Eds.), *100 years of archaeology at the University of Michigan* (pp. 125–138). University of Michigan Press.

Talbott v. Trump, 1:25-cv-00240 (D. D.C. 2025).

Tappan, M. B. (2006). Reframing internalized oppression and internalized domination: From the psychological to the sociocultural. *Teachers College Record, 108*(10), 2115.

Tatum, B. (1997). *"Why are all the Black kids sitting together in the cafeteria?" And other conversations about race*. Basic Books.

Taub, G. (2013). Zionism. In G. Claeys (Ed.), *Encyclopedia of modern political thought* (Vol. 2, pp. 869–872). SAGE Publications. https://doi.org/10.4135/9781452234168.n346

Taylor, D. E. (2024). Prisons, jails, and the environment: Why environmentalists should care about mass incarceration? *American Behavioral Scientist, 68*(4), 449–485.

Tehranian, J. (2000). Performing Whiteness: Naturalization litigation and the construction of racial identity in America. *Yale Law Journal, 109*(5), 817–848.

Thobani, S. (2007). *Exalted subjects: Studies in the making of race and nation in Canada*. University of Toronto Press.

Thompson, H. A. (2012). The prison industrial complex: A growth industry in a shrinking economy. *New Labor Forum, 21*(3), 38–47.

Thorneycroft, R., Nicholas, L., & Smith, E. K. (2025). Young people's perspectives of the 'male gaze' and matters of representation in online pornography. *Australian Feminist Studies, 39*(122), 442–457. https://doi.org/10.1080/08164649.2025.2498648

Tomiyama, A., Hunger, J., & Nguyen-Cuu, J. (2016). Misclassification of cardiometabolic health when using body mass index categories in NHANES 2005–2012. *International Journal of Obesity, 40*, 883–886. https://doi.org/10.1038/ijo.2016.17

Toprani, A. (2019). *Oil and the great powers: Britain and Germany, 1914 to 1945*. Oxford University Press.

Tranchese, A., & Sugiura, L. (2021). "I don't hate all women, just those stuck-up bitches": How incels and mainstream pornography speak the same extreme language of misogyny. *Violence Against Women, 27*(14), 2709–2734.

Trepagnier, B. (2010). *Silent racism: How well-meaning White people perpetuate the racial divide* (2nd ed.). Paradigm.

Tsakiropoulou-Summers, T., & Kitsi-Mitakou, K. (2018). Introduction: The ideological construct of the 'inferior female.' In T. Tsakiropoulou-Summers & K. Kitsi-Mitakou (Eds.), *Women and the ideology of political exclusion* (pp. 1–30). Routledge.

Tuana, N. (Ed.). (1989). *Feminism and science*. Indiana University Press.

Tunamsifu, S. P. (2022). The colonial legacy and transitional justice in the Democratic Republic of the Congo. *African Journal on Conflict Resolution, 22*(2), 85–110.

Tyack, D. (1976) Ways of seeing: An essay on the history of compulsory schooling. *Harvard Educational Review, 46*(3), 355–389.

Uggen, C., Larsen, R., Shannon, S., & Pulido-Nava, A. (2022*). Locked out 2020: Estimates of people denied voting rights due to a felony conviction*. The Sentencing Project.

Ukanwa, K., Jones, A. C., & Turner, B. L., Jr. (2022). School choice increases racial segregation even when parents do not care about race. *Proceedings of the National Academy of Sciences, 119*(35), e2117979119.

UNICEF. (2023, December). *Child poverty in the midst of wealth* [Innocenti Report Card 18]. UNICEF Innocenti—Global Office of Research and Foresight. https://www.unicef.org/innocenti/media/3296/file/UNICEF-Innocenti-Report-Card-18-Child-Poverty-Amidst-Wealth-2023.pdf

UNICEF. (2024). *Over 230 million girls and women alive today have been subjected to female genital mutilation—UNICEF* [Press release]. https://www.unicef.org/press-releases/over-230-million-girls-and-women-alive-today-have-been-subjected-female-genital

United for a Fair Economy. (2020). *State of the dream 2020*. http://www.faireconomy.org/dream20

United Nations. (2024a). *Global report on trafficking in persons 2024*. https://digitallibrary.un.org/record/4069246?v=pdf

United Nations. (2024b). *One woman killed every 10 minutes: The harrowing global reality of femicide*. https://news.un.org/en/story/2024/11/1157386

United Nations. (2025, March). *Understanding human trafficking*. https://www.un.org/en/peace-and-security/understanding-human-trafficking

United Nations General Assembly (UNGA). (1947). *Resolution 181 (II). Adoption of the plan of partition with economic union*.

United Nations Office for the Coordination of Humanitarian Affairs—Occupied Palestinian Territory (UNOCHA). (2025, March 25). *Reported impact snapshot: Gaza Strip*. https://www.ochaopt.org/content/reported-impact-snapshot-gaza-strip-25-march-2025

United Nations Office of the High Commissioner for Human Rights (UNOHCHR). (2022, March 25). *Israel's 55-year occupation of Palestinian Territory is apartheid—UN human rights expert* [Press release]. https://www.ohchr.org/en/press-releases/2022/03/israels-55-year-occupation-palestinian-territory-apartheid-un-human-rights

United Nations Regional Information Centre for Western Europe (UNRIC). (2024). *Women and girls are disproportionately affected by conflict-related sexual violence*. https://unric.org/en/women-and-girls-are-disproportionately-affected-by-conflict-related-sexual-violence/

UN Women. (2024). *Femicides in 2023: Global estimates of intimate partner/family member femicides.* https://www.unwomen.org/sites/default/files/2024-11/femicides-in-2023-global-estimates-of-intimate-partner-family-member-femicides-en.pdf

UN Women. (2025, July). *Facts and figures: Women in sport.* https://www.unwomen.org/en/paris-2024-olympics-new-era-for-women-in-sport/facts-and-figures-women-in-sport

UN Women. (n.d.). *Facts and figures: Women's leadership and political participation.* Retrieved March 11, 2025, from https://www.unwomen.org/en/articles/facts-and-figures/facts-and-figures-womens-leadership-and-political-participation

United States v. Bhagat Singh Thind, 261 U.S. 204 (1923).

United Steelworkers of Canada. (2008). *Statement on gay, lesbian, bisexual and transgender issues.* https://usw.ca/wp-content/uploads/2022/04/Pride_jan08-1.pdf

USAGov. (n.d.). *Minimum wage.* U.S. General Services Administration. https://www.usa.gov/minimum-wage

U.S. Air Force. (2025, April). *Biography: General Charles Q. Brown, Jr.* https://www.af.mil/About-Us/Biographies/Display/article/108485/charles-q-brown-jr/

U.S. Department of Labor. (2025). *State minimum wage laws.* https://www.dol.gov/agencies/whd/minimum-wage/state

U.S. Department of State. (2023). *2023 country reports on human rights practices—Turkmenistan.* https://www.state.gov/reports/2023-country-reports-on-human-rights-practices/turkmenistan/

U.S. House Appropriations Committee. (2024, December 12). *Cole, First Native American to chair House Appropriations: "Data indicates that Native women and girls experience a murder rate 10 times higher than the national average"* [Press release]. https://appropriations.house.gov/news/press-releases/cole-first-native-american-chair-house-appropriations-data-indicates-native

U.S. House Committee on the Judiciary. (2025). *New Judiciary Democrats analysis reveals Trump's corrupt pardon spree cheated crime victims of $1.3 billion.* https://democrats-judiciary.house.gov/media-center/press-releases/new-judiciary-democrats-analysis-reveals-trump-s-corrupt-pardon-spree-cheated-crime-victims-of-13-billion

U.S. Sentencing Commission. (2024, August 13). *2023 demographic differences in federal sentencing.* https://www.ussc.gov/research/research-reports/2023-demographic-differences-federal-sentencing

Valenti, A. (2021). LGBT employment rights in an evolving legal landscape: The impact of the Supreme Court's decision in *Bostock v. Clayton County, Georgia. Employee Responsibilities and Rights Journal, 33,* 3–23.

Van Anders, S. M., Steiger, J., & Goldey, K. L. (2015). Effects of gendered behavior on testosterone in women and men. *Proceedings of the National Academy of Sciences, 112*(45), 13805–13810.

Van Ausdale, D., & Feagin, J. (2001). *The first R: How children learn race and racism.* Rowman & Littlefield.

van der Linden, M. (2022). *The world wide web of work: A history in the making.* UCL Press.

Wagner, P., & Rabuy, B. (2017). *Following the money of mass incarceration.* Prison Policy Initiative. https://www.prisonpolicy.org/reports/money.html

Warner, J. A. (2011). Sweatshop labor. In J. P. Rodriguez (Ed.), *Slavery in the modern world: A history of political, social, and economic oppression* (Vol. 1, pp. 60–68). Bloomsbury Publishing.

Warren, E. (2025, June). *Special interests over the public interest: Elon Musk's 130 days in the Trump Administration.* https://www.warren.senate.gov/imo/media/doc/130_days_of_elon_musk_report.pdf

Washington Post. (2024, December 31). *Fatal Force Database 2015–2024.* https://www.washingtonpost.com/graphics/investigations/police-shootings-database/?itid=lk_inline_manual_1

Watson, D. (2011). "Urban, but not too urban": Unpacking teachers' desires to teach urban students. *Journal of Teacher Education, 62*(1), 23–34.

Watson, R., & De Gelder, B. (2017). How White and Black bodies are perceived depends on what emotion is expressed. *Scientific Reports, 7*(1), 41349. https://doi.org/10.1038/srep41349

Watts, C., & Zimmerman, C. (2002). Violence against women: Global scope and magnitude. *The Lancet, 359*(9313), 1232–1237.

References

Weiner, D. I., & Lau, T. (2025). *Explainer: Citizens United explained*. Brennan Center for Justice. https://www.brennancenter.org/our-work/research-reports/citizens-united-explained

Weis, L., & Fine, M. (1996). Notes on "White" as "race." *Race, Gender & Class, 3*(3), 5–9. http://www.jstor.org/stable/41675332

Weisbord, R. G. (2003). The King, the Cardinal and the Pope: Leopold II's genocide in the Congo and the Vatican. *Journal of Genocide Research, 5*(1), 35–45. https://doi.org/10.1080/14623520305651

Weiss, T. C. (2012, November 20). *People with disabilities and sexual assault*. Disabled World. http://www.disabled-world.com/disability/sexuality/assaults.php#ixzz2SXMEQWra

Westlake, B. G., Kusz, J., & Afana, E. (2025). A double-edged sword: The role of pornography in learning about BDSM. *Sex Education, 25*(1), 23–37.

White, B. (2014). *Israeli apartheid: A beginner's guide* (2nd ed.). Pluto Press.

White House. (2025a, January 20). *Initial rescissions of harmful executive orders and actions*. https://www.whitehouse.gov/presidential-actions/2025/01/initial-rescissions-of-harmful-executive-orders-and-actions/

White House. (2025b, February 9). *Fact sheet: President Donald J. Trump eradicates anti-Christian bias*. https://www.whitehouse.gov/fact-sheets/2025/02/fact-sheet-president-donald-j-trump-eradicates-anti-christian-bias/

Wieberneit, M., Thal, S., Clare, J., Notebaert, L., & Tubex, H. (2024). Silenced survivors: A systematic review of the barriers to reporting, investigating, prosecuting, and sentencing of adult female rape and sexual assault. *Trauma, Violence, & Abuse, 25*(5), 3742–3757. https://doi.org/10.1177/15248380241261404

Wiesenthal, S. (1976). *The sunflower: On the possibilities and limits of forgiveness*. Schocken.

Wight, M., & Yost, D. (2023). *History and international relations* (1st ed.). Oxford University Press. https://doi.org/10.1093/oso/9780192867476.001.0001

Williams, H. A. (2014). *American slavery: A very short introduction*. Oxford University Press. https://doi.org/10.1093/actrade/9780199922680.003.0001

Willis, H. A., Sosoo, E. E., Bernard, D. L., Neal, A., & Neblett, E. W. (2021). The associations between internalized racism, racial identity, and psychological distress. *Emerging Adulthood, 9*(4), 384–400.

Wilson, W. J. (2011). The declining significance of race: Revisited & revised. *Daedalus, 140*(2), 55–69.

Winks, R. W. (1997). *The Blacks in Canada: A history* (2nd ed.). McGill-Queen's University Press. (Original work published 1971)

Wires, N. (2024, December 19). *Dominique Pelicot sentenced to 20 years in French mass rape trial*. France 24. https://www.france24.com/en/live-news/20241219-ex-husband-of-gisele-pelicot-found-guilty-in-france-mass-rape-trial

Woodson, C. G. (1933). *The mis-education of the Negro*. Associated Publishers.

World Bank. (n.d.). *Annual GDP rankings*. https://data.worldbank.org/indicator/NY.GDP.MKTP.CD?name_desc=false

World Health Organization. (2021). *Violence against women prevalence estimates, 2018*. https://www.who.int/publications/i/item/9789240022256

World Health Organization. (2024). *Violence against women*. https://www.who.int/news-room/fact-sheets/detail/violence-against-women https://www.who.int/mediacentre/factsheets/fs239/en/index.html

Wyatt-Nichol, H. (2016). The enduring myth of the American dream: Mobility, marginalization, and hope. *International Journal of Organization Theory and Behavior, 14*(2), 258–279.

Yassin, S., Petit, G., & Abraham, Y. (2024, July 18). *The troubling rise of income and wealth inequality*. Policy Options. https://policyoptions.irpp.org/magazines/july-2024/income-wealth-inequality

Yazdani, K., & Castro, C. (2023). Capitalisms of the "Global South" (c. 10th to 19th centuries): Old and new contributions and debates. *Historia Crítica, 89*, 3–41. https://journals.openedition.org/histcrit/12906

Yendell, O., Claus, C., Bonefeld, M., & Karst, K. (2024). "I wish I could say, 'Yeah, both the same'": Cultural stereotypes and individual differentiations of preservice teachers about different low socioeconomic origins. *Social Psychology of Education, 27*(3), 777–812.

Young, F. L., III. (2021). *World Christianity and the unfinished task: A very short introduction.* Wipf and Stock Publishers.

Yourish, K., Daniel, A., Datar, S., White, I., & Gamio, L. (2025, March 7). These words are disappearing in the new Trump administration. *The New York Times.* https://www.nytimes.com/interactive/2025/03/07/us/trump-federal-agencies-websites-words-dei.html

Zeppegno, P., Gramaglia, C., di Marco, S., Guerriero, C., Consol, C., Loreti, L., Martelli, M., Marangon, D., Carli, V., & Sarchiapone, M. (2019). Intimate partner homicide suicide: A mini-review of the literature (2012–2018). *Current Psychiatry Reports, 21*(3), 13.

Zhang, S. (2024). *Major brands like McDonald's, Kroger and Coca-Cola linked to forced prison labor.* Truthout. https://truthout.org/articles/major-brands-like-mcdonalds-kroger-and-coca-cola-linked-to-forced-prison-labor/

Ziegerhofer, A. (2019). League of Nations. In U. Daniel, P. Gatrell, O. Janz, H. Jones, J. Keene, A. Kramer, & B. Nasson (Eds.), *International encyclopedia of the First World War.* https://doi.org/10.15463/ie1418.11382

Ziegler, R. D. (2020). *The nexus of business and human rights: Challenging corporate profiteers in the United States immigration detention industry* [Doctoral dissertation]. University of Minnesota. https://conservancy.umn.edu/server/api/core/bitstreams/f42fe93e-a817-47bd-8079-a65dd221c0d7/content

Zinn, H. (2010). *A people's history of the United States* (Rev. ed.). HarperCollins. (Original work published 1980)

Zinn, H. (2018). *You can't be neutral on a moving train: A personal history of our times.* Beacon Press.

Zweig, M. (2000). *The working class majority: America's best kept secret.* Cornell University Press.

Glossary

Because language is infused with ideology, it is a significant area of attention for critical social justice scholars. Definitions, connotations, and terms vary between lay and academic usage, as well as among social groups. The terms we do or do not use at any given moment in history play a fundamental role in dynamics of visibility and invisibility, legitimacy and illegitimacy, normalcy and deviancy. For these reasons, it is important to be thoughtful about the political and evolving nature of language. Our goal with this glossary of terms is to provide guidance that is responsive to all of these complexities and avoids essentializing categories (making it appear that they are stable and natural). Regarding terms that refer to social groups in this glossary, not all people who identify with a specific group will agree to the terms here for that group. It is best to continually educate yourself about the politics of language in general, and how specific individuals identify in particular.

Ableism or Disableism: The systematic oppression of people with (perceived) disabilities. Ableism is based on the assumption that there is a physical, intellectual, and emotional standard for human beings and that this standard is the only one accepted as "normal." All other variations of the human body are considered abnormal, deviant, and inherently inferior. This norm is institutionalized in architectural structures, school policies and practices, and legal segregation of persons with disabilities. Some activists prefer the term *disableism* because it centers the reason for the oppression—one's disability status.

Aboriginal: People who are Indigenous to (native or the original habitants of) a specific continent or geographic region. *See also Indigenous peoples.*

African American, African Canadian, African Heritage, Caribbean, or Black: The range of terms used to indicate someone who identifies and is identified as having origins in the Black populations of Africa. A person of Black or Black African heritage.

American Indian: Native or Indigenous people of the United States. This term is used interchangeably with Native American. In Canada, the preferred term is Indigenous. Please note that it is best to refer first to the person by their tribal nation, such as Cherokee, Sioux, and so forth. *See also Indigenous peoples.*

Androcentrism: The term used to describe a male-centered society and institutions, in which men are positioned as superior to women. Androcentrism is not simply the idea that men are superior to women, but a deeper premise that supports this idea—the definition of males and male experience as the norm or standard for human, and females and female experience as a deviation from that norm.

Anecdotal Evidence: Anecdotes (personal stories) that are based on single, isolated or non-representative incidences that cannot be verified. They are offered as counter evidence for group-level dynamics. e.g. "I know a guy that . . . and that proves that not all . . ."

Antiracism: A framework for ending racism that goes beyond tolerating or celebrating racial diversity and addresses racism as a system of unequal institutional power between White people and peoples of Color.

Asian or Asian Heritage: Refers to people of Asian ancestry. This broad category includes South Asian (including Indian, Sri Lankan, Pakistani, Nepalese), East Asian (including Chinese, Japanese, Korean), and Southeast Asian (including Filipino, Thai, Hmong, Vietnamese, Cambodian, Burmese, Laotian). The term Asian or Asian Heritage is preferred when speaking of macro level dynamics. However, the multitude of groups under the broad category of Asian have very different histories, languages, and experiences. Due to these differences, some find the term *Asian* problematic because it collapses this wide range of groups into a unified collective.

Authoritarianism: Referring to a type of governance that demands obedience to authority, typically in the form of one supreme leader. Authoritarian regimes usually engage in surveillance to engender fear and control the population.

Binary: An either/or construct. Presenting only two options, which are seen as polar opposites, for example, male/female, young/old, gay/straight, good/bad.

BIPOC: Black, Indigenous, and People of Color. See also IBPOC.

Biracial: A person with parentage or grandparentage from two distinct racial groups.

Capitalism: A political and economic system that prioritizes profit through control of the means of production, private ownership, and control of supply and demand. Capitalism is not simply an economic system but also influences social structures, political institutions, and cultural norms.

Caucasian: This term originally referred to people from the Caucasus mountain range. These people were thought to be a "pure" race of humans by early race scientists. Today it is primarily used to refer to people of White European ethnic heritage, but because the term is from outdated race science classifications that included *Negroid*, *Mongoloid*, and *Caucasoid*, it is a problematic term and *should be avoided*. *White* is the preferred term.

Cisgender: The term for people whose sex category given at birth and subsequent gender socialization are the same as their own gender identity. *See also Gender, Transgender.*

Classism: The systematic oppression of poor and working people by those who control resources (including jobs, wages, education, housing, food, services, medicine, and cultural definitions). Classism has economic, political, and cultural dimensions.

Class Terminology: The terms commonly used to identify the various class positions, for example, working class, middle class.

Colonialism: The name given to European nations' political and economic exploration, settlement, occupation, and exploitation of large areas of the world beginning in the 15th century (sometimes called the "Age of Discovery"). Colonialism resulted in the spread of White European institutional and cultural domination over the global majority.

Colored or Colored People: This term is connected to legal racial segregation and is considered extremely outdated and derogatory. *People* or *Peoples of Color* is the preferred term when referring to racialized peoples. Please note: We have included these terms in the glossary only as an opportunity to inform those with limited racial awareness that the terms *should not be used*.

Commodification: The action of treating a person, place, or culture as an object that can be bought, sold, privately owned, profited from, and consumed.

Critical Theory: A body of scholarship that examines how society works. This scholarship offers a critique of society by engaging with questions of social justice and change.

Culture: The norms, values, practices, patterns of communication, language, laws, customs, and meanings shared by a group of people in a given time and place.

Discourse: The academic term for meaning that is communicated through language in all of its forms. Discourses include myths, narratives, explanations, words, concepts, body language, mannerisms, and ideology. Discourses are not universal; they represent a particular cultural worldview and are shared among members of a given group. Discourse is different from ideology because it refers to all of the ways in which we communicate ideology, including verbal and nonverbal aspects of communication, symbols, and representations.

Discrimination: Action based on prejudice. When we act on our prejudices, we are discriminating.

Dominant Group: The group at the top of the social hierarchy. In any relationship between groups that define each other (men/women, nondisabled person/person with disability), the dominant group is the group that is valued more highly. This higher value is created and maintained through legal, historical, social, and institutional authority. It is sustained by how the group is represented, their degree of access to and control of resources, and how that access is rationalized. Dominant groups set the norms by which the minoritized group is understood and found lacking. Dominant groups benefit from the existence of the inequality. Avoid referring to a minoritized group as a "non" dominant group, for example, "non-White."

Enlightenment: An intellectual movement that emerged in Europe in the late 17th century and that elevated science and rationality over superstition and religion. Also referred to as the *Age of Reason*.

Fascism: In the modern era, this term refers to a political ideology rooted in state authoritarianism. Characteristics of fascism include ultra–right-wing nationalism and militaristic control of the population.

Feminism: The advocacy for the social, economic, and political equality of all sexes. Sometimes heard as *feminisms*, to capture the plurality of ways that feminist theorizing and critique have occurred (e.g., Marxist feminism, transnational feminism, Black feminist thought, and so on).

First Nations: First Nations (or sometimes First Peoples) refers to the various groups of Indigenous peoples first present during the colonization of the North American continent. Examples of First Nation communities include the Blackfoot Nation (primarily in parts of Montana and Alberta), the Cherokee Nation (primarily in the southern United States), and the Ojibwe Nation (north and south of the Great Lakes region). The term First Nations refers to these groups collectively.

Framework: A fundamental theory, paradigm, or thought pattern through which we make meaning of a given phenomenon; a particular way of seeing and knowing.

Gender: The socially prescribed and enforced roles, behaviors, and expectations that are assigned to us at birth based on our presumed sex. These roles determine how you are "supposed" to feel and act based on your body.

Gender Diverse (or Genderfluid, non-Binary): People who do not identify in binary terms and/or whose gender identity and expression is fluid and dynamic. *See also Sex* and *Gender*.

Gender Identity: The development of one's self in relation to the categories male or female.

Globalization: The process by which corporations and other large enterprises exert international influence. In exerting this influence, they channel resources away from local communities and usually erode local industry, culture, environment, and identity.

Hegemony: The imposition of dominant group ideology onto everyone in society. Hegemony makes it difficult to escape or to resist believing in this dominant ideology, thus social control is achieved through conditioning rather than physical force or intimidation.

Heterosexism: The values, attitudes, beliefs, and behaviors that support the primacy of male–female intimate relationships. Heterosexism is enforced by institutions and the creation of laws, social policies, and everyday practices that maintain heterosexuality as the innate norm for human intimacy. Heterosexism rests on the assumption that male–female bonding is superior to any other form of intimacy, and anything other than heterosexuality is deviant or nonexistent.

Hispanic: There is great diversity and complexity within the category that dominant culture terms Hispanic. For example, according to the U.S. Census, a person who is Hispanic can be of any race, therefore the Census asks for race identification as well as identification as Hispanic or Latino/a. Generally this group includes peoples of Cuban, Mexican, Puerto Rican, Central American, and South American heritage, and/or of other Spanish culture. *Hispanic is not a preferred term* for critical scholars because its roots are colonialist ("of Spain") and thereby merge diverse communities of people through the language of the colonizers. Latino/a can be problematic because it also merges many diverse countries together. Chicano/a is a self-applied political term for Mexican Americans who want to acknowledge that they live on lands stolen from Mexico by the United States.

Homophobia: The prejudice, fear, contempt, and hatred of gay, lesbian, bisexual, and transgender people and associations. Homophobia includes misinformation about and prejudice against people who do not perform the expected gender roles assigned to them at birth. Homophobia affects all people in that it is a powerful tool for enforcing gender roles.

IBPOC: Indigenous, Black, and People of Color. *See also BIPOC.*

Ideology: The big, shared ideas of a society that are reinforced throughout all of the institutions and thus are very hard to avoid believing. These ideas include the stories, myths, representations, explanations, definitions, and rationalizations that are used to justify inequality in society. Individualism and Meritocracy are examples of ideology.

Indigenous or Indigenous Peoples: The United Nations defines Indigenous peoples as pre-colonial inhabitants of any settler society, such as Canada and the United States. There are differences in the terms used, which are related to the colonial context. In Canada, it is acceptable to use the terms Indigenous and Aboriginal. Indigenous Peoples are defined under three prominent subgroups: First Nations (various distinct tribal communities), Inuit (the distinct groups of the Northern continent), and Métis (referring to Indigenous peoples of mixed ancestry). In the United States, it is acceptable to use the terms Indigenous and Native American. Indigenous Peoples are defined under prominent subgroups including: American Indian (various distinct tribal communities) and Alaska Native (various distinct tribal communities in the northern part of the continent). *We use Peoples here in plural to acknowledge that myriad distinct and diverse groups are included under this broad umbrella term.*

Native and Native American are terms that are sometimes used in the United States. However, Indigenous serves as the most universal term. While the term "Indian" in the context of "American Indian" is in use in the United States, in Canada "Indian" was used predominantly in the past, and has very important legal connotations. To be a status or nonstatus Indian (as defined by government) gave/denied certain rights. Today, the term *Indian* should be avoided (especially by outsiders). It is best to refer to Indigenous communities by their specific tribal affiliation.

In either country, *avoid using the term Eskimo*, as it is not what people of the north call themselves and it is considered derogatory.

Institutional, Institutionalized: Embedded into the policies, practices, norms, traditions, and outcomes of institutions. When a form of social bias is institutionalized, it is reproduced automatically and no longer depends on the intentions or awareness of individuals; it is the default or status quo outcome of that institution's work.

Institutions: Large-scale organization within a society. Examples of institutions are media, criminal justice, economics, marriage and family, education, religion, medicine, government, and military.

Internalized Dominance: Internalizing and acting out (often unawarely) the constant messages circulating in the culture that you and your group are superior to whichever group is minoritized in relation to yours and that you are entitled to your position, resources, and conferred advantages.

Internalized Oppression: Internalizing and acting out (often unawarely) the constant messages circulating in the culture that you and your group are inferior to whichever group is dominant in relation to yours and that you are deserving of your position, lesser access to resources and advantages.

Intersectional, Intersectionality: The understanding that we simultaneously occupy multiple social positions and that these positions do not cancel each other out; they interact in complex ways that must be explored and understood.

Kleptocracy, Kleptocrat: Refers to a governance system wherein corrupt leaders (kleptocrats) expropriate the wealth, the land, and the people they govern, typically by embezzlement or misappropriation of government resources and funding. A system controlled and run for the benefit of an individual or small group who use their power to transfer society's resources to themselves.

Mainstream Society: The dominant culture that is circulated across all institutions and that all members of society are exposed to. This culture is circulated via mechanisms such as films, TV shows, advertisements, public school curriculum, holidays, and the stories, myths, representations, explanations, definitions, theories, and historical perspectives that are used to rationalize and hide inequality.

Meritocracy: The ideology that everyone succeeds on their own effort or merit. In a system presumed to be a meritocracy, each individual is believed to have earned what they have through their own talent and hard work. Everyone is presumed to have the same opportunities in this system.

Métis or Métis Nation: A group of people who are of mixed European and Indigenous ancestry. *See also Indigenous peoples.*

Microaggressions: A term coined by Dr. Derald Wing Sue to capture the everyday slights and insults that minoritized peoples endure in mainstream society and that dominant groups don't notice or take seriously. The term is specific to dominant harm towards minoritized people and is not meant as a stand-in for any "small insult" that anyone across any situation experiences.

Minoritized Group: A social group that is devalued overall in society in relation to the relative dominant group. This devaluing is created and maintained through legal, historical, social, and institutional authority. It is sustained by how the group is represented, what degree of access to resources it is granted, and how the unequal access is rationalized. Traditionally, a group in this position has been referred to as a "minority" group. However, this language has been replaced with the term "minoritized" (making it a verb and thus active) in order to capture the dynamics that create the lower status in society. The term also signals that a group's status is not necessarily related to how many or few of them there are in the population at large. Inequality between groups is based on power, not numbers—minoritized groups can be larger in numbers than dominant groups.

Misogynoir: A term coined by Dr. Moya Bailey to capture the specific intersection of racism and sexism, particularly as it manifests in popular and digital culture. The term describes how anti-Blackness informs the way misogyny is directed towards Black women.

Misogyny: The contempt for and hatred of women and characteristics that are associated with women or femaleness.

Multiracial or Mixed Race: A person of mixed (or multiple) racial heritage. This term refers to people with parentage or grandparentage from two or more racial (rather than ethnic) groups.

Native Hawaiian and Pacific Islander: According to the U.S. Census, this term refers to Indigenous peoples originating from the territories of Guam, Hawaii, Samoa, or other Pacific Islands.

Net Worth: What you have when you subtract what you owe from what you own free and clear. What is left is your net worth.

Normalized (Norm, Normative): Taken for granted and seen as normal, natural, unremarkable, and universal.

Objective: The perception that some knowledge is factual and not informed by social or cultural interpretations; a universal truth outside of any particular framework. A person or position that is seen as objective is seen as having the ability to transcend social or cultural frameworks and engage without bias or self-interest.

Oligarchy, Oligarch: A political system where a small group of the richest people in society (called oligarchs) protect and expand their material wealth by using that wealth to influence the political system.

Oppression: The discrimination of one social group against another, backed by institutional power. Oppression results when one group is able to enforce its prejudice throughout society because it controls the institutions. It occurs at the group or macro level, and goes well beyond individuals. Sexism, racism, classism, ableism, and heterosexism are specific forms of oppression.

Oriental: In a general sense this term means "of the East," with the referent being Europe; that which is east in relation to Europe. It is a term that was used to refer to people of Asian ancestry and of the Asian continent and Near, Middle, or Far East. Please note: The term Oriental is considered derogatory. We have included this term in the glossary only as an opportunity to inform those with limited racial awareness that the term *should not be used.*

Orientalism: The term Orientalism is not derogatory, as it refers to the specific study of how racism was institutionalized by Western European colonial powers toward people of "the Orient." Scholars who study Orientalism (such as Dr. Edward Said) study the representations of the history, culture, language, and literature of the Near, Middle, or Far East by Western European nations and how those representations have impacted historical and current relations.

Patriarchy: The system built from the concept of male superiority and the power relations by which men dominate over women. The organization of society and the family based on this system. Patriarchy includes the belief that men's superiority is natural and/or ordained by a male God.

Peer Review: The evaluation of scholarly work—often done anonymously to ensure fairness—by peers with expertise in the same field in order to maintain or enhance the excellence of the work in that field and to advance knowledge.

People of the Global Majority (PGM): A term to capture the reality that demographically the majority of the world is made up of people who are not considered White. The term also subverts the term "minority" and makes the point that they are in fact the majority. It is often a term of empowerment against "Third World" or "Developing World" discourses.

Peoples of Color (People of Color; Person of Color; IBPOC; BIPOC): The term used to describe people who are racialized (seen by dominant White society as having race) based on phenotypical features (such as hair texture, bone structure, and skin color). The term is useful in that it acknowledges the racial binary that organizes society under White supremacy, and the overall shared experiences of racism and internalized racial oppression for people who are racialized. However, the term is also problematic in that it conflates the wide range of very diverse groups of people into one group and thus obscures their specific histories, experiences, and challenges under White supremacy. Therefore, BIPOC and IBPOC are also used. They stand for *Black, Indigenous, and People of Color,* or *Indigenous, Black, and People of Color* and are meant to communicate that there is no unified experience and that distinction should be acknowledged. As with all racial terms, the interplay between self-identity and identification within the social political context must be taken into account. *We use it here in plural to acknowledge that myriad distinct and diverse groups are included under this broad term.*

Platitude: A trite, simplistic, and meaningless statement, often presented as if it were significant, original, and meaningful e.g., "People just need to take personal responsibility" or "Anyone can make it if they have a good attitude."

Positionality: The recognition that where you stand in relation to others within a hierarchical society shapes what you can see and understand about the world.

Positivism: A perspective or philosophy of the scientific method as objective, neutral, and the ideal approach to studying the world.

Prejudice: Learned prejudgment about members of social groups to which we don't belong. Prejudice is based on limited knowledge or experience with the group. Simplistic judgments and assumptions are made and projected onto everyone from that group.

Racialized: Perceived in racial terms; seen as having race.

Racism: In the United States and Canada, racism refers to White racial and cultural prejudice and discrimination, supported by institutional power and authority, used to the advantage of White people and the disadvantage of peoples of Color. Racism encompasses economic, political, social, and institutional actions and beliefs that perpetuate an unequal distribution of privileges, resources, and power between White people and peoples of Color.

Sex: The biological, genetic, or phenotypical markers that are presumed to distinguish male and female bodies. While not fully understood scientifically, socially sex categories refer to characteristics of a person's genitals, body structure, and hormonal system. *See also Gender.*

Sexism: The systematic oppression of women under patriarchy. Sexism is based on the belief that men are inherently superior to women. Sexism encompasses economic, political, social, and institutional actions and beliefs that perpetuate an unequal distribution of privileges, resources, and power between men and women.

Signifier: A sign or symbol that conveys specific cultural meaning. Signifiers connect to larger discourses that work together to construct that meaning.

Social Capital: Social resources other than money that are valuable and grant status (such as education, physical appearance, linguistic capacity, ability to navigate dominant culture, and so on).

Socially Constructed: Meaning that is not inherently true, but widely circulated and acted upon by society as if it were true, becoming real in its consequences for people's lives.

Social Stratification: The concept that social groups are relationally positioned in a hierarchy of unequal value (e.g., people without disabilities are seen as more valuable than people with disabilities). This ranking is used to justify the unequal distribution of resources among social groups.

Structural: Built into the foundation of society; norms, traditions, culture, institutions, ideologies, economics, politics, attitudes, and so forth.

Subjective: An individual's personal perspective, feelings, beliefs, interests, or experience, as opposed to a perspective arising from sources considered independent, unbiased, universal, and objective. A person or position that is considered subjective is assumed to be biased and/or self-interested, while a person or position that is considered objective is seen as unbiased and outside of any cultural influences.

Transgender: A person whose gender does not match the sex category assigned at birth (male or female); they may feel themselves to be neither like a woman or a man, that they are a combination of both genders, or that their gender is opposite to their sex. A transgender person can appear to others to partially, occasionally, or entirely perform their gender in a way that does not conform to traditional gender roles. *See also Gender.*

Two-Spirit: An Indigenous concept that recognizes that someone has both (or multiple variations of) feminine and masculine identity. While many worldviews acknowledge that everyone has both feminine and masculine qualities, this term is specifically used to indicate someone who is not primarily heterosexual, or does not identify as male or female. The English term, as a translation, is incomplete in that in using the word "two," the idea that gender and sexuality are binaries is reinforced. Two-spirit is a cultural term used by some within Indigenous communities. The term should not be used as an identity by outsiders to those communities.

White: People whose ancestry is or is perceived to be from Europe. While there are no true biological races, being perceived as White has very real privileges within the system of White supremacy.

White Adjacent, White Assumed, White Passing, White Presenting: Terms used to capture the complexity for persons who are not White (or not fully White) but appear to be White (are "light skinned") and who are therefore more accepted within the system of White supremacy. As with all identity terms, the interplay between self and group identity within the social political context must be taken into account.

White Fragility: A term coined by Dr. Robin DiAngelo to describe the inability of White people to tolerate any challenge to the White position or perspectives. It manifests in emotions such as anger, resentment, fear, and "hurt feelings," and behavior such as crying, arguing, or withdrawing and/or leaving the situation. White fragility functions to block the challenge and regain White racial equilibrium. White fragility is not weakness. Rather, it is a means of racial control wherein White people leverage historical and institutional power to reject any suggestion of White advantage.

Whiteness: The academic term used to capture the all-encompassing dimensions of White privilege, dominance, and assumed superiority in society. These dimensions include: ideological, institutional, social, cultural, historical, political, and interpersonal. Whiteness grants material and psychological advantages (White privilege) that are often invisible and taken for granted by White people.

White Supremacy: A sociological term to indicate the comprehensive system of conferred White racial dominance and centrality and the mechanisms that uphold and enforce this system. The deployment of institutional and cultural forces to protect, define, defend, and center White people's interests. White supremacy positions White people as the standard for and measure of who is fully human.

Index

Abaied, J. L., 151
Abercrombie & Fitch, 194
Aberson, C. L., 45
Ability. *See also* Ableism
 ability privilege, 97–98
 discrimination based on, 61–62
 group identity based on, 49–50, 51
 intersectionality and, 220
Ableism
 ableism, defined, 93
 disability-inclusive language, 105
 example of, 93
 group identities across relations of power, 68
 intersectionality and, 108–109
 popular culture and, 103
 schools and, 95–97
Abraham, Y., 204
Abu-Amr, Z., 186
Acemoglu, D., 200
Achievement gap, 156, 193
Active antiracism, 257–258
Active racism, 257
Adair, M., 82–84
Adams, M., 80
Adjei, P. B., 97
Adler, P. S., 203
Adorno, Theodor, 30
Advertising, sexism in, 125–126
Afana, E., 133
Affirmative action (U.S.), 12, 165–166
AFL-CIO, 194, 255
African Americans. *See also* Peoples of Color
 incarceration of, 149, 208
 need for government assistance and, 223–224
 police violence in the U.S. and, 166–167
 prison labor and, 208–210, 216–219
 slavery and, 141–142, 144, 166, 175–178, 219, 229
Agent groups. *See* Dominant/agent groups
Ahmed, A. S., 208
Ahmed, Sara, 91, 135, 175, 188–190
Ajemian, N., 127
Ajour, A., 186
Akinola, Modupe, 47, 48, 104
Alarcón, Norma, 219

Alexander, M., 12, 149
Alfani, G., 197
Ali, I., 166
Ali, M. M., 208
Aliprandi, G., 202
Alkadry, M. G., 78
Allen, Paula Gunn, 220
Allen, S., 46
Allport, Gordon W., 57
Almeida, L., 200
Alphabet, 127
Altman, A., 132
Alvarez, Nina, 138
Amadeo, K., 210
Amazon, 127, 197
Ameenuddin, N., 125–126
American Civil Liberties Union (ACLU), 216
American Dream myth, 212
Americans with Disabilities Act (ADA) of 1990, 94
Amra & Elma, 125
Anand, P., 207, 208
Anderson, Carol, 159, 165
Anderson, M., 125
Anderson, Tanisha, 167
Androcentrism, 72–73, 77, 78, 126
Anecdotal evidence, patterns versus, 11–13, 170–171
Anisman, H., 178
Anker, E. R., 175
Annamamma, S. A., 97
Antiracism
 active, 257–258
 passive, 258
Anyon, Jean, 18, 26–27, 86–87, 206, 211
Anzaldúa, Gloria, 1, 157, 219
Apple, M. W., 211
Applebaum, B., 104, 172
Apple Inc., 127, 194
Appleman, L. I., 209
APTN National News, 144
Armstrong, Thomas, 97
Arneil, B., 181
Arnold, A. P., 42
Arrogance, 104

301

Arsenault, E., 178
Artiga, S., 141
Ashton, Niki, 203
Asians/Asian heritage. *See also* Peoples of Color
   Asian feminists, 219–220
   Chinese exclusion from U.S. citizenship, 144
   institutional racism and, 149, 168, 172–173
   intelligence and, 109
   Japanese internment, 173
   Orientalism and, 178–179
   skin color and, 163
   U.S. railways and, 149
Aslund, A., 199
Au, W., 170
Austin, N., 35
Australian Older Women's Network, 136
Awaya, T., 177

Badie, B., 181
Baer-Bositis, L., 46
Bagley, Alonzo, 167
Bailey, J., 122
Baker, E. J., 218
Baker, H. A., Jr., 6
Baker, S., 128
Ballantine, J. H., 211
Ballantine, K. L., 150
Banaji, Mahzarin, 44–46, 79, 152
Bangasser, D. A., 42
Banks, C.A.M., 170–171
Banks, James A., 25–26, 170–171
Barnes, Crystalline, 167
Bassiouni, M. C., 182
Bateman, N., 150
Battalora, J., 141
Beagan, B. L., 16
Beauty standards, 60
Bell, L., 80
The Bell Curve (Herrnstein & Murray), 92
Bellier, L., 79
Bellovary, A., 165
Bem, S. L., 77
Ben Ami, S., 182
Beneke, M. R., 97
Benjamin, Walter, 30
Benoit, C., 129
Benson, C., 196
Berg-Schlosser, D., 181
Bergvall, V. L., 42
Bernard, D. L., 155
Bernard, Nora, 237, 238
Bertrand, M., 12, 46, 156
Bettio, F., 129
Bezos, Jeff, 196, 197
Bhargava, A., 42
Bhaya-Grossman, L., 79

Bhungalia, L., 187
Bhutta, N., 167
Bhuyan, M. S., 208
Bidet-Caulet, A., 79
Bigelow, Bill, 36
Bilge, S., 219
Bilmes, L. J., 187
Binary identities
   gender, 41–42, 67–68, 116, 117
   racist/not racist, 145–146, 147, 148
Bing, J. M., 42
Binnie, J., 132
BIPOC. *See* Peoples of Color
Birdcage metaphor, 79
Birnbaum, J., 128
Birthright citizenship, 159
Bishu, S. G., 78
Biswas, D., 163
Black, W. K., 218
Black Lives Matter, 167
Black people. *See* African Americans
Blaut, J. M., 178
Block, K., 42
Bloomberg, 196
Boggs, Grace Lee, 219
Bonefeld, M., 26
Bonilla-Silva, E., 97, 104, 108, 146, 152
Bostic, A., 142
Bourdieu, Pierre, 30
Bourgeoisie, 193–194
Bower, B., 45
Bowman, Jamaal, 203
Box Office Mojo, 153
Boyd, C., 124
Boyer, M., 80, 108
BP Deepwater Horizon oil spill, 218
Bradley, B.D.A., 35
Brady, D., 203
Brah, A., 219
Brewster, O., 133
Brief, Arthur, 48
Briggs v. Elliott (1952), 156–157
Broadcom, 127
Brodkin, K., 142
Brooks, Clifford, 167
Brown, Charles Q., Jr., 166
Brown, D., 141
Brown, J. D., 171
Brown, Michael, 167
Brown v. Board of Education (1954), 156–157, 229
Budd, K. M., 167–168, 208
Budig, M., 78
Bullivant, S., 35
Bunn, C., 167
Burczycka, M., 130
Burkell, J., 122
Burns, D., 200

Bush, Cori, 203
Busschots, T., 202

Caleb, A. M., 72
Calliste, A., 108
Cameron, James, 36
Cammaeris, B., 160
Campani, G., 142
Campbell, Aaron, 167
Canada
  class categories, 204–206
  criminal justice system, 168
  Gradual Civilization Act of (1857), 143
  history of social construction of race in, 142–144
  income polarization in, 194–197, 202–203
  "mosaic" analogy for, 144
  protections for LGBTQ+ people, 87
  racial hierarchy in, 140
  residential schools for Indigenous students, 118, 143–144, 166–167, 211, 223, 229, 238
  sexism in, 120–121, 130
  voting rights in, 73, 75–76
  women in public office, 75–76, 90, 109
  worker rights in, 208
Canadian Centre for Policy Alternatives, 194–196
Canadian Encyclopedia, 116
Canadian Femicide Observatory for Justice and Accountability, 120
Canadian Press, 144, 161
Canonized knowledge, 26
Cantillon, S., 129
Cao, L., 210
Capitalism
  class and, 206
  defined, 181
  democratic, 203
  Global North versus Global South and, 175–181, 187–188, 197, 206–208
  prison labor force, 208–210, 216–219
  pyramid of, 207
  wealth versus income and, 206
Carli, V., 120
Carlos, C., 151
Caron, S. L., 124
Castille, Philander, 167
Castrillon, N. E., 158
Castro, C., 178
Cataldo, P., 217
Cavalli-Sforza, L. L., 141
CBC News, 144, 217
Celikates, R., 29, 30
Center for American Women and Politics (CAWP), 75
Center for Poverty and Inequality Research, 198
Center for Reproductive Rights, 223

Center on Budget and Policy Priorities, 224
Chacon, A. H., 43
Chang, A. C., 167
Chang, T.N.J., 163
Chang, W. K., 79
Charalambous, P., 200
Charlesworth, T.E.S., 79
Chassiakos, Y.L.R., 125–126
Chatfield, K., 224
Chatterjee, S., 208
Chávez, Cesar, 74
Chayka, K., 200
Cheaito, A., 151
Chen, H. Y., 163
Cheng, C. I., 235
Chessman, H. M., 16
Children. *See also* Schools/schooling
  female genital mutilation, 119
  internalized racial oppression and, 156–157
  "kidfluencers" and, 125
  naturalization of sexism and, 121–122
  popular culture and, 157
  pornification of childhood, 132–133
  subjective evaluations of child behavior, 97
  as unhoused people, 235
Children's Commissioner, 132, 133
Childs, T. M., 156
Chin, Frank, 252
Chin, M. J., 45
Chingos, M., 152
Chinn, P., 170
Chopra, S. B., 155
Chugh, Dolly, 47, 48
Churchill, Winston, 184
Cilveti-Lapeira, M., 42
Cisgender, 41–42, 116
Citizens United v. F.E.C. (2010), 199
CIUSS, 105
Civil Rights movement, 74, 80, 150, 159, 164, 170
Clare, J., 124
Clark, Kenneth B., 156–157
Clark, Mamie P., 156–157
Classism, 191–227
  class socialization, 210–212
  common classist beliefs, 222–226
  common misconceptions about class, 212–219
  defined, 203–204
  examples of class privilege, 221–222
  government assistance and, 223–224
  group identities across relations of power, 68
  income polarization and, 194–197, 202–203, 204
  intersectionality and, 219–221
  kleptocracy and, 200–203

Classism (*continued*)
  media and, 211–212
  Mr. Rich White/Mr. Poor White vignette, 191–193, 225–226
  nature of class, 193–203
  oligarchs and, 197, 199–200, 202
  prison labor force, 208–210, 216–219
  race and, 214–215
  wealth and, 197–199
Class/social class. *See also* Classism
  class, defined, 204
  class categories, 204–206
  common class terms, 203–210
  common misconceptions about class, 212–219
  divisions of labor and, 193–194
  group identity based on, 49–50, 51
  intersectionality and, 219–221
  in knowledge construction, 10, 15–17, 26–27, 86–87, 211
  meritocracy and, 205–206
  minimum wage and, 194–199, 205, 210, 215–216
  Mr. Rich White/Mr. Poor White vignette, 191–193, 225–226
  nature of, 193–203
  political power and, 197, 202–203
  poverty and, 198, 214, 215, 223–224, 235
  privilege and, 221–222
  racism and, 157–158
  school tax base and, 168, 211
  social mobility and, 212–213
  social stratification and, 67–69
  stereotypes concerning, 198
  voting rights and, 73–74
Class warfare, 224
Claus, C., 26
Clements, R., 36
Climate change, 178
Coates, Ta-Nehisi, 177–178
Cockfield, A., 202
Cohen, Cathy, 219
Colburn, D., 129
Collier Smith, L., 80, 108
Collins, P. H., 158, 219
Colonialism, 15, 29, 116, 149, 163, 174, 175–178
  African slavery and, 141–142, 144, 166, 175–178, 219, 229
  Canadian residential schools for Indigenous students, 118, 143–144, 166–167, 211, 223, 229, 238
  defined, 181
  group identities across relations of power, 68
  Indigenous populations and, 177, 183
  kleptocracy and, 200–203
  in Palestine/Israel conflict, 181–187
  transnational feminism and, 219
Colorblind racism, 14, 80, 140, 147, 150, 152, 246

Colored/Colored People. *See* Peoples of Color
Columbus, Christopher, 15, 28
Combahee River Collective, 219
Communism, 203
Community Service Organization (CSO), 74
Conejo-Márquez, D. A., 79
Conformity, cultural norms and, 43–44
Conforti, Y., 182
Conley, D., 158
Connolly, M., 213
Connor, D. J., 97
Connors, S., 144
Conroy, S., 130
Consol, C., 120
Conte, J., 114
Continental school/philosophy, 30
Conyers, A., 149
Cook, Tim, 127
Cookney, F., 132
Cooley, Alexander, 201, 202
Cooley, Charles H., 51–53
Cooper, R. S., 141
CoreCivic, 216–217
Cotter, A., 120
Council on Communication and Media, 125–126
COVID-19 pandemic, 206–208
Craig, M., 128
Crenshaw, Kimberlé, 158, 219
Criminal justice system
  incarceration rates, 33, 167–168
  police violence in the U.S. and, 166–167
  prison labor force, 208–210, 216–219
Critical action, 24
Critical analysis, 24
Critical race theory (CRT), 160
Critical self-reflection, 24
Critical social justice, xxi–xxiii
  acting in service of more just society, 254–258
  being an ally, 254–258
  common rebuttals in, 228–241
  considerations, 243–246
  critical thinking in. *See* Critical thinking
  dismissed as opinions of woke radicals, 230
  in negotiating unequal social power, 243–246
  perspectives, 243–248, 251–253
  practicing, xxii
  principles of, xxii
  skills, 246, 249–250, 253–254
  social justice and, xxi–xxii. *See also* Social justice
  understanding personal positions within unequal social power, 246–250
Critical social justice literacy, 1–21
  anecdotal evidence versus patterns and, 11–13, 170–171
  as blend of action and understanding, xxiii

critical theory and. *See* Critical theory
developing, xxvii–xxix
grading in, 17–20
guidelines for developing, 5, 6–17
intellectual humility and, 6–9, 103–104, 117–118
open letter to students, 3–5
opinions versus informed knowledge and, 3–4, 5–6, 9–11, 140, 165–166, 230
planets/astronomy analogy and, 5–7, 9, 11, 14, 16–17
positioning as "extra," 237–238
reactions as entry points for deeper self-knowledge, 13–15, 171–172
social positionality in, 15–17, 172–173
vocabulary in, 1–2
Critical stance, defined, 1
Critical theory
defined, 24
expanding and deepening, 31–32
knowledge construction in, 29–33
nature of, 29
schools of, 29–30
in teaching practice, 32–33
Critical thinking
about knowledge in critical social justice, 24, 28–29, 250–255
about opinions, 9–11
nature of, 24
Cross, Z. R., 79
Crutcher, Terence, 167
Cultural capital, 86
Cultural deficit theory, 92, 149
Cultural knowledge, 25
Culture
class socialization and, 210–212
cultural norms, 43–44
deep, 39, 40, 77–78
defined, 39
fish metaphor for, 16, 39, 49, 91–92, 111–113
gender norms in, 43–44
iceberg of culture metaphor, 39, 40, 77–78
oppression and, 77–79
prejudice and discrimination in, 62–63
surface, 39, 40
Culture of poverty (Payne), 92
Cunningham, S., 35
Cureton, J., 197
Curran, F. C., 97
Czopp, A. M., 45

Dadzie, C. A., 163
Daigle, L. E., 44
D'Amelio, Charli, 125
Dana, T., 187
Daneback, K., 132
Daniel, A., 159
Das, A., 204

Da Silva, C., 187
David, E. R., 155
Davis, Angela, 219
Davis, A. Y., 73
Davis, Benjamin, 114–115
Davis, K. C., 44
Davis, Kiri, 157
Dawson, M., 124
Dechief, D., 12
Decker, S., 165
Dedyukina, L., 144
Deep culture, 39, 40, 77–78
Defensiveness, 244–245
De Gelder, B., 97
Dei, G. J., 6, 104, 171
DeKeseredy, W. S., 132
Delgado, R., 172
Delgado-Fabián, M., 79
Della Giusta, M., 129
Democracy
capitalism and, 203
democratic socialism, 203
DeNavas-Walt, C., 204
Denton, K. M., 42
Denzin, N. K., 57
De Oliveira, R. S., 200
Department of Justice Canada, 168
Derenoncourt, E., 167
Derrida, Jacques, 30
De Schutter, A., 60
Dettling, L. J., 167
Deva, S., 207, 208
Devereux, C., 73
Dhaliwal, T. K., 45
Diamond, J. B., 97
Di Angelo, Robin J., 10, 98, 124, 147, 148, 152, 172, 175, 215, 258
Dickason, O. P., 142–143
Di Gironimo, S., 133
Di Marco, S., 120
Dines, Gail, 131–133
Disability Justice, 130
Discourse. *See also* Language
concerning oppression, 79–80, 106–107
defined, 80
denying the politics of language, 235–236
of sexism as empowerment, 126–137
in the text, 252–253
Discrimination, 56–65
ability and, 61–62
defined, 61
gender, in hiring process, 47–48, 56–57, 63–64, 66–67, 78–79, 87–88
"isms" and, 68, 75–80. *See also* Ableism; Classism; Racism; Sexism
oppression versus, 71–72
prejudice and, 56–60, 62–64, 71–72
prevalence of, 62–64

Discrimination (*continued*)
  protections for LGBTQ+ people, 87, 112, 117
  racial/ethnic, in hiring process, 46–48
  racism versus, 145
Di Tommaso, M. L., 129
Diversity
  additional layers of complexity, 245
  backlash against DEI and, 135, 159–161, 210
  in considering multiple perspectives, 244
  in critical social justice versus mainstream lens, 243–244
  defensiveness for lack of, 244–245
  formal diversity statements, 255–256
  multiculturalism and, 144, 170–171, 193
Dobbs v. Jackson Women's Health Organization (2022), 134
Dominant/agent groups. *See also* Oppression; Privilege; Racism; White supremacy
  biological differences as socially constructed, 94–97
  claims of oppression as oversensitivity, 236–237
  critical social justice skills for, 249–250
  defined, 69
  discourse and, 80
  institutions and, 107–108, 112–113
  internalized dominance and. *See* Internalized dominance
  as "just human," 172, 175, 232
  nature of, 4
  oppression and, 68, 122, 123, 126–137
  perspectives of, 4, 96
  politics of language and, 235–236
  positionality and, 15–17
  reactions as entry points for self-knowledge, 13–14
  refusing to recognize structural and institutional power, 234–235
  relationship with minoritized groups, 153–154
  social stratification and, 68
Dominguez-Faus, R., 79
Donevan, M., 129
Dorninger, C., 175–176
Dorsey, Carl, 167
Double consciousness (DuBois), 78, 79
Dovidio, J., 29, 61, 104
Dred Scott v. Sandford (1857), 199
Dronkers, N. F., 79
Dubey, R., 144
Du Bois, W.E.B., 10, 78, 79, 141, 172, 225
Duckitt, J. H., 57
Duncan, P., 108
Durkheim, Emile, 30
Durou, G., 141
Duvalier, Jean-Claude, 202
Dyer, R., 148, 172

Eberhardt, J., 46, 61
Eberhardt, M., 46

Economic issues. *See also* Capitalism; Classism; Class/social class
  advantages of Whites/Whiteness, 142
  backlash against DEI and, 135, 159–161
  bailout of banks versus student loan forgiveness, 218–219
  in critical social justice perspective, 253
  gross national product, 197
  income polarization, 194–197, 202–203, 204
  kleptocracy, 200–203
  minimum-wage labor, 194–199, 205, 210, 215–216
  oligarchs, 197, 199–200, 202
  prison labor force, 208–210, 216–219
  racism and, 158–159
  taxes and, 168, 202, 211
Eddo-Lodge, R., 98
Education. *See* Schools/schooling
Eisenberg, R., 216
Elaref, A.I.A., 178
Ellis, L., 113, 115
Elsass, P. M., 108
Employment equity (Canada), 12, 165–166
Engel, R. J., 150
Enns, T., 178
Environmental racism, 178, 208, 218
Equal opportunity, privilege and, 101, 106
Equal Rights Amendment (ERA), 129
Erevelles, Nirmala, 220
Erickson-Schroth, Laura, 114–115
Espinosa, L. L., 16
Ethnic cleansing, 184–185
Ethnicity. *See also* Race; Racism *and specific groups*
  defined, 50
  discrimination in hiring and, 12, 46–48
  group identity based on, 49–50, 51
  interaction with race, 51–52
  prejudicial beliefs concerning, 57–58
  race versus, 50–52
Eugenics, 92, 109, 141–142, 177, 179
Ever Accountable, 129

Facchini, G., 46
Fairbairn, J., 124
Falah, G., 185
Fanon, F., 155
Farley, M., 129
Fascism, 203
Fausto-Sterling, A., 42
Faverio, M., 125
Feagin, J. R., 104, 150, 152, 156, 157
Federation of Canadian Municipalities, 76
Federer, J. P., 144
Felix, S. N., 44
Feminism, 112, 157, 164, 219, 220
Fernandez, A. A., 43

Fernandez, J., 155
Ferri, B. A., 97
Fiallo, J., 130
Fields, G., 186
Findley, M. G., 202
Fine, M., 151, 172
Finkelhor, D., 129
Fishbein, H. D., 45
Fisher, B., 97
Fish metaphor, for socialization, 16, 39, 49, 91–92, 111–113
Fiske, S. T., 152
FitzGerald, C., 61
Flanagan, T., 218
Flinker, A., 79
Flores, A. R., 120
Floyd, George, 165, 167
Flynn, J., 29, 30
Fonken, Y., 79
Foucault, Michel, 30, 82–84
Fourchard, L., 181
Fox, M., 149
Fragrance, 126
Frame of reference glasses metaphor, 49–50, 66–67
França, K., 43
Franco, R., 129
Frankenberg, R.A.E., 157, 172, 175
Frankfurt School, 29–30
Freed, A. F., 42
Freire, P., 80
Frum, D., 200
Frye, Marilyn, 79
Fujimori, Alberto, 202

Gabriel, M., 36
Gallavan, N. P., 3
Galleguillos, S., 208
Gamio, L., 159
Garcia, A. M., 219–220
García-Cuéllar, M. M., 119
García-Moreno, C., 119
Gardella, J., 97
Garner, Eric, 167
Gatto, John Taylor, 10–11
Gavey, N., 133
Gay, G., 170
Gay and Lesbian Alliance Against Defamation, 117
Geis, G., 218
Gender. *See also* Sexism
  as binary system, 41–42, 67–68, 116, 117
  defined, 41
  discrimination in hiring and, 47–48, 63–64, 66–67, 78–79, 87–88
  female beauty standards and, 60
  gender norms, 43–44, 72–73
  intersectionality of, 220
  sex versus, 41–42, 113–118
  social construction of, 115–116
  understanding personal positions within unequal power relations, 246–250
  women in public office, 75–76, 90, 109
Gender identity. *See also* LGBTQ+ people
  group identity based on, 49–50, 51
  sexuality versus, 116, 118
  terms for, 41–42, 116–117
Gender roles
  in leadership positions, 72, 74, 75–77, 87–88, 90, 109, 127–128
  sexism and, 133
  stereotypes concerning, 56–57, 59–60, 63, 121–122
Gender socialization, 40–42
  androcentrism and, 72–73, 77, 78, 126
  binary construct, 41–42.67–68.116.117
  in frame of reference glasses metaphor, 49–50, 66–67
GEO Group, 217
George, M., 151
Gibraltar Mines v. Harvey (2022), 89
Gillborn, D., 171
Gillies, C., 156
Gilmore, A. K., 44
A Girl Like Me (film), 157
Giroux, Henry, 172, 203
GLAAD Law, 117
Glick, S., 29, 61, 104
Global Gag Rule (1981), 222–223
Glover, Henry, 167
Goldberg, E., 36
Goldey, K. L., 42
Goldsmith, B., 47
Gomez, J., 217
Gomez, L. M., 97
Gomez, R. A., 132
Gonzalez, C. G., 178
Goodkind, S., 150
Goodman, D. J., 80
Goodwin, I., 80, 108
Gorenstein, M. A., 79
Gossett, T. E., 142
Gottfried, J., 125
Gould, S. J., 92
Grading, 17–20
Gramaglia, C., 120
Grant, Oscar, 167
Graves, J. L., Jr., 141
Graves, L. M., 108
Gray, Freddie, 167
Great Britain, 50, 180, 182–184
Green, D. S., 225
Green, E. C., 77
Green, E. L., 164–165
Greenwald, A. G., 29, 61, 104
Greenwald, Tony, 44–46

Gregory, A., 97
Grekul, J., 95
Grewal, Inderpal, 219
Griffin, K. A., 16–17
Grogan, S., 60
Grosfuguel, Ramón, 175, 177
Gross domestic product, 197
Gubash, C., 187
Guerriero, C., 120
Guilt, paralysis of, 238–240
Gupta, A., 42
Gurley, Akai, 167

Habermas, Jürgen, 30
Haeck, C., 213
Hägerdal, H., 177
Hagopian, E., 184
Haig-Brown, C., 143
Hall, D., 36
Hall, Kim Q., 220
Halperin, J. R., 181, 201
Halton, M., 122
Hambacher, E., 92
Hamermesh, D. S., 58
Hammond, C., 132
Hancock, K. P., 44
Haney-López, I., 182
Happ, M., 133
Harden, Joel Davison, 203
Hare, J., 143
Harpenan, F., 133
Harper, Robert, 167
Harper, S., 35
Harris, Cheryl I., 142
Harris, K., 165
Hartung, W. D., 187
Haskell, L., 144
Hawking, Stephen, 10
Healey, P., 129
Health care
  HIV/AIDS crisis, 220, 224–225
  reproductive rights, 111, 124, 130, 134, 135, 222–223
Heathershaw, John, 200–202
Hedberg, F., 165
Hegemony, 70
Hegseth, Peter B., 117, 166
Helfenbein, R., 210
Heller, J., 42
Henares-Montiel, J., 119
Henry, A., 16
Henry, F., 145
Herman, J. L., 120
Hernández-Truyol, B. E., 160, 164
Herrnstein, R. J., 92
Herzl, Theodor, 182, 184
Heterosexism, group identities across relations of power, 68

Hickel, J., 175–176
Hicks, Christopher, 167
Hill, L., 141
Hill, R. P., 163
Hilliard, A., 144
Hilliard Krause, L. M., 42
Hinduja, S., 129
Hispanics/Latinos. *See* Latinos/Hispanics
HIV/AIDS crisis, 220, 224–225
Hodja, Nasreddin, xxvii–xxix
Hofman, N. G., 150
Holdcroft, A., 72
Holdgraf, C., 79
Holt, K. M., 129
hooks, b., 10, 175, 215, 219
Hopcroft, R., 113, 115
Hope, D., 196
HOPE: Domestic Violence Homicide Help, 130
Hopkins, J. P., 80, 108
Horkheimer, Max, 30
Hoskin, A. W., 113, 115
House of Commons of Canada, 76
Housing discrimination, 167
Howard, J., 151
Howell, S., 82–84
Hoy, C. W., 79
Hsu, A.T.W., 163
Hsu, J. W., 167
Huang, Jensen, 127
Hudson, I., 204
Hudson, M., 204
Huecker, M. R., 120
Huerta, Dolores, 74, 89
Hulchanski, J. D., 196
Human nature, privilege and, 101–102, 106
Humility, intellectual, 6–9, 103–104, 117–118
Hunger, J., 60
Hunt, C. S., 26
Hurst, S., 61
Husayn, Sharif, 183
Husserl, Edmund, 188
Hyatt, J., 201

IBPOC. *See* Peoples of Color
Iceberg of culture metaphor, 39, 40, 77–78
Ideology
  in construction of knowledge, 29
  defined, 2, 77
  hegemony and, 70
  melting pot versus mosaic, 144
  privilege and, 101–102
  role in oppression, 77
  in the text, 252–253
Ignatiev, N., 142
Immigration
  backlash against DEI and, 135, 159–161, 210

birthright citizenship and, 159
classist misconceptions of, 222
detention of immigrants, 216–217
ICE deportations, 142, 159, 210, 217
Imperialism, in Palestine/Israel conflict, 181–187
Implicit Association Test (IAT), 44–46
Implicit bias, 44–48, 58
Indigenous/Indigenous People
  colonialism and, 177, 183
  fetishized depictions of, 179
  Indigenous feminists, 220
  need for government assistance and, 223–224
  in North America, xx (map)
  in popular culture, 154
  prison labor and, 216
  residential schools in Canada, 118, 143–144, 166–167, 211, 223, 229, 238
  sex and gender in, 51, 68, 116, 130
  slavery of, 144, 149, 166, 178
Individualism
  diversity through lens of, 243–244
  individual versus group identity, 48–52
  in negotiating unequal social power, 243
  privilege and, 101, 106
  racism and, 147–148, 161–164
  sexism and, 122
Inequality
  open letter to students, 3–5
  perspectives on, 4
  resistance to, 2
Institutions/institutional power
  dominant culture and, 112–113
  institutional racism, 149, 168, 172–173
  nature of institutions, 112–113
  oppression and, 71, 72, 77, 107–108
  panopticon metaphor (Foucault) and, 82–86
  privilege and, 107–108
  refusal to recognize, 234–235
Intellectual humility, 6–9, 103–104, 117–118
Internalized dominance. *See also* Dominant/agent groups
  acceptance of, 80
  defined, 81
  examples of, 81
  messages of superiority, 102–103, 104, 106
  microaggressions and, 81
  patterns of, 81, 83–84
  refusing to recognize structural and institutional power, 234–235
Internalized oppression, 82–83. *See also* Minoritized/target groups
  acceptance of, 80
  defined, 82
  examples of, 82
  patterns of, 82, 83–84
  racism and, 155–157

refusing to recognize structural and institutional power, 234–235
sexism and, 123
International Court of Justice, 186–187
International Labour Organization (ILO), 208
Inter-Parliamentary Union (IPU), 76
Intersectionality
  additional layers of complexity, 248
  classism and, 219–221
  in critical social justice skills, 249–250
  defined, 158, 219
  ignoring, 233
  key tenets of, 220–221
  knowledge and, 15–17, 26–27
  language to discuss, 4
  oppression and, 72, 108–109
  privilege and, 108–109
  racism and, 108–109, 157–161
  sexism and, 157–158
  sexuality and, 220
  understanding positions within relations of unequal power, 246–250
Invisible knapsack metaphor, 100–101
Islam, A.R.M.T., 208
Islam, M. S., 208
Israel, in Palestine/Israel conflict, 181–187
Ivanova, M. V., 79

Jackson, A., 203
Jackson, L. M., 57
Jacobson, M. F., 142
Jails, 217
Jamal, A., 185
James, C. E., 145, 156
James, Kendra, 167
Jancsics, D., 202
Jansson, M., 129
Jassy, Andy, 127
Jayakumar, U. M., 161
Jefferson, Thomas, 141
Jensen, Robert, 129, 131
Jews
  era of conquest and, 177
  in Palestine/Israel conflict, 181–187
Jews on Route to Palestine (Patek), 184
Ježek, S., 132
Jhally, Sut, 131
Jiang, C., 45
Jimenez, R. T., 79
Jiwani, Y., 124
Johnson, Allan G., 71, 91, 98
Johnson, G., 80, 108
Johnson, G. F., 47–48, 104
Johnson, H. B., 152
Johnston, Kathryn, 167
Jones, A. C., 157
Jones, K. M., 35, 112
Jones, T., 112

Jordan, G., 120
Jordan-Young, Rebecca, 114, 137
Joshee, R., 144
Joshi, K. Y., 80
Joyce, T. J., 35
Judah, B., 202
Jun, S., 79

Kaestner, R., 35
Kam, J.W.Y., 79
Kaplan, C., 219
Karst, K., 26
Kassie, Emily, 169
Katz, B. W., 44
Kaufman, J. S., 141
Kazemian, L., 208
Keister, L. A., 147
Kendi, Ibram X., 145, 146, 149, 150
Khalidi, R., 183, 184
Khalidi, W., 185
Kidd, C., 79
Kilbourne, Jean, 60, 131
Kim, C. H., 167
Kim, S. R., 200
Kincheloe, J. L., 3, 16, 172
King, K. C., 120
King, Martin Luther, Jr., 150
Kipling, Rudyard, 179
Kirmayer, L. J., 144
Kisida, B., 152
Kite, M. E., 45
Kitsi-Mitakou, K., 72
Klein, Naomi, 203
Kleptocracy, 200–203
Kline, W., 95
Knight, B., 128
Knowledge, 22–37
  class in construction of, 10, 15–17, 26–27, 86–87
  critical theory and, 29–33
  critical thinking about, 24, 28–29, 250–255
  multipartisanship and, 33–36
  opinions versus informed, 3–4, 5–6, 9–11, 140, 165–166, 230
  power in schools and, 86–88
  process for finding common ground, 33–36
  reactions as entry points for deeper self-knowledge, 13–15, 171–172
  schools in transmission of, 23
  as socially constructed, 22–29
  typology of (J. Banks), 25–26
Kobayashi, A., 16
Kochiyama, Yuri, 220
Koide, S., 163
Kopf, D., 216
Korematsu, Fred, 172–173
Korn, R. M., 247
Kraus, M. W., 212

Krieger, L., 29, 61, 104
Kuhn, M., 167
Kujawinski, E. B., 218
Kumari, P., 180
Kunjufu, Jawanza, 97
Kusz, J., 133
Kwon, S. H., 163

Lacan, Jacques, 30
Lake, F. R., 218
Landry, J., 178
Langton, I., 120
Language. *See also* Discourse
  denying the politics of, 235–236
  disability-inclusive, 105
  in discourse on oppression, 79–80, 106–107
  for gender identity, 41–42, 116–117
  vocabulary in critical social justice literacy, 1–2
Lao, W.W.K., 163
Lapierre, D., 213
Larsen, R., 168
La Salle, T. P., 16–17
Lasseur, D., 54
Latinos/Hispanics, 50, 74, 89, 149, 208, 219–220. *See also* Peoples of Color
Lau, T., 199
Lavie, C., 60
Lawson, D., 200
Lawson, J., 128
Lawson, Max, 198
Lazarenko, Pavlo, 202
Leach, J., 199
Leadership
  gender roles in, 72, 74, 75–77, 87–88, 90, 109, 127–128
  racism and, 214
Leboeuf, C., 45
Lee, C. H., 163
Lee, J. J., 46
Leemis, R. W., 120, 130
Legacy students, 213–214
Leigey, M., 149
Leistyna, P., 211
Leonardo, Zeus, 108–109
Leone, R. M., 44
Levin, Diane E., 60, 131
Lewis, M., 45
LGBTQ+ people
  and attitudes about sex and gender, 117
  discrimination protections and reversals, 87, 112, 117
  gender socialization and, 41–42
  gender stereotypes and, 56–57, 59–60, 63, 87, 121–122
  sex/gender and science, 113–118
Li, P. S., 144
Liberal humanism, 30–31

Light, M., 167–168
Limberg, J., 196
Lindesmith, A. R., 57
Lindo, J. M., 35
Little, W., 193
Llorens, A., 79
Lloyd, Rachel, 134, 138
Loku, Andrew, 167
Looking glass self (Cooley), 52, 53
Lopez, Andy, 167
López, I.F.H., 141
López-Trenado, E., 42
Lord, H., 209
Lorde, Audre, 17, 219
Loreti, L., 120
Love, H. R., 97
Lovelace v. Ontario (2000), 89
Lovison, V. S., 45
Lubienski, C., 157
Lucas, D., 218
Lululemon Athletica, 194
Lund, D. E., 144
Lupyan, G., 45
Lyles, Charleena, 167
Lynk, Michael, 185–186
Lynn, V., 149
Lyonga, E., 112

MacDonald, D., 196
MacKenzie, J., 187
MacKenzie, M., 47–48, 104
Mady, S., 163
Magnuson, D., 129
Maheu-Giroux, M., 119
Mahomed, S., 186
Mainstream academic knowledge, 25
Maio, G. R., 57
Makey, E., 187
Mamdani, Zohran, 203
Management & Training Corporation (MTC), 217
Mangan, 201
Mar, L. R., 144
Maracle, Lee, 220
Marangon, D., 120
Marcelle, E., 79
Marcos, Ferdinand, 202
Marcuse, Herbert, 30
Mark, A. Y., 45
Maroto, M., 141
Martelli, M., 120
Martin, Trayvon, 167
Marx, Karl, 30
Masarwa, L., 185
Massey, D. S., 152
Massoglia, M., 167–168
Mast, N., 218
Matheson, K., 178

Mathieu, X., 178
Matias, C. E., 161, 172
Mattel Inc., 194
Maxwell, K. E., 260
Mayer, E. A., 42
M'Baye, B., 176
McCarthy, M., 42
McDonalds Corp., 194
McGuirk, R., 136
McIntosh, Peggy, 100–101
McLanahan, S. S., 97
McLaren, P., 172
McLeay, F., 125
McLoyd, V. C., 149
McMurry T. B., 78
McNeil, K., 178
Media
  consolidation of, 211–212
  stereotypical racial representations, 153–154
"Melting pot" ideology, 144
Membrillo-Hernández, J., 79
Menakem, Resmaa, 156, 175
Menozzi, P., 141
Mentan, T., 175
Meritocracy
  class and, 205–206
  privilege and, 101, 106, 199
Meta, 127, 187
Metzgar, J., 204
Meyer, I. H., 120
Microaggressions, 81
Microsoft, 127
Middle class, 204, 205, 212
Mielants, Eric, 175, 177
Milani, R., 60
Military service
  LGBTQ+ people and, 117
  male leadership and, 72, 77
Milkman, Katherine L., 47, 48, 104
Miller, Terrell, 167
Miller, W. L., 42
Milloy, J. S., 143
Milošević, Slobodan, 202
Milton, Trevor, 201
Minimum-wage jobs, 194–199, 205, 210, 215–216
Minoritized/target groups
  defined, 69
  discourse and, 80
  exceptions to the rule, 230–231
  multicultural education and, 144, 170–171
  nature of, 4
  oppression and, 48, 68, 78, 108–109, 122, 123, 126
  perspectives of, 4
  politics of language and, 235–236
  positionality and, 15–17

Minoritized/target groups (*continued*)
  reactions as entry points for self-knowledge, 14
  relationship with dominant groups, 153–154
  schools for, 243
  social stratification and, 68
  Whites as, 162–163, 215–216
Mirrlees, T., 165
Misogyny, 132, 133, 136
Mitchell, D., 124
Mobly, Corey, 167
Mohamed, T., 16
Mohanty, Chandra T., 219
Monarrez, T., 152
Monroe, Marilyn, 58
Montoya, I., 151
Moore, Leroy, Jr., 106, 107, 110
Moraga, C., 157
Morlino, L., 181
Morrison, T. G., 122
"Mosaic" ideology, 144
Mossack Fonseca, 202
Mullainathan, S., 12, 46, 156
Mullaly, R., 155
Muller, C., 210
Multiculturalism, 144, 170–171, 193
Multipartisanship
  nature of, 33
  process for finding common ground, 33–36
Muñoz, R. B., 44
Murdie, R. A., 196
Murray, C., 92
Musk, Elon, 127, 196, 197, 201
Musker, J., 36
Muslims
  era of conquest and, 177
  in Palestine/Israel conflict, 181–187
Myers, C. K., 35
Myers, K., 104
Myhre, K. G. Tran, 146

Nadella, Satya, 127
Nagda, B. R., 260
Nair, G., 150
Napal, D., 208
National Center for Lesbian Rights, 117
National Inquiry into Missing and Murdered Indigenous Women and Girls, 120
Nationalism
  group identities across relations of power, 68
  White, 31, 164–165, 172, 175
Nationality, group identity based on, 49–50, 51
National Taxpayers Union Foundation, 203
The Nature of Prejudice (Allport), 57
Navarro-Mantas, L., 133
Navsaria, D., 125–126
Neal, A., 155
Neblett, E. W., 155
Negussie, T., 200

Neitzel, R. L., 158
Netflix, 127
Net worth, 213, 216
Newman, L. M., 73
Nguyen-Cuu, J., 60
Nicholas, L., 133
Nichols, Tyre, 167
Nielsen-Reagan, A., 217
Nielson, D. L., 202
Nieri, T., 151
Nieto, L., 80, 108
Nieves, Jose, 167
Nike Inc., 194
Nisbett, R. E., 92
Nocella, R. R., 132
Noguera, P. A., 97
NoiseCat, Julian Brave, 169
Non-binary gender categories, 41
Nonini, D. M., 202
Norms, cultural, 43–44
North Atlantic Treaty Organization (NATO), 166, 209
Notebaert, L., 124
Nouri, K., 43
Novotney, A., 119
Nvidia, 127

Oakes, J., 18
Oates, C. J., 125
Obama, Barack, 12, 164, 165
O'Brien, L. M., 157
Ocasio-Cortez, Alexandria, 203
O'Connor, M., 129
Oesterle, D. W., 44
Office of Family Assistance (OFA), 224
Office of Government-wide Policy, 164–165
Office of Justice Programs, 167
Office of the Assistant Secretary for Planning and Evaluation, 198
Oligarchs, 197, 199–200, 202
Oliveira, C., 202
Oliver, M., 46
Olson, J. M., 57
Oluo, I., 156
Olwan, D. M., 124
O'Malley, R. L., 129
Omi, M., 141
O'Neil, Keita, 167
OnlyFans, 129, 133
Opinions
  about social justice topics, 3, 230
  critical thinking about, 9–11
  informed knowledge versus, 3–4, 5–6, 9–11, 140, 165–166, 230
  nature of, 9
  social justice scholarship dismissed as, 230
Oppression, 71–74. *See also* Power; Privilege
  androcentrism and, 72–73, 77, 78, 126

birdcage metaphor for, 79
as cultural, 77–79
as deeply embedded system, 93–94
defined, 71
discourse concerning, 79–80, 106–107
discrimination versus, 71–72
dominant group and. *See* Dominant/agent groups
gender norms and, 43–44, 72–73
as historical, 76
as human nature, 231
as ideological, 77
institutional power in, 71, 72, 77, 107–108
internalized. *See* Internalized oppression
intersectionality and, 72, 108–109
"isms" in, 68, 75–80. *See also* Ableism; Classism; Racism; Sexism
language as political, 79–80
minoritized group and. *See* Minoritized/target groups
need for government assistance and, 223–224
oversensitivity claims, 236–237
prejudice versus, 71–72
Orchowski, L. M., 44
Oreopoulos, P., 12
Orientalism (Said), 178–179
Ortiz, N., 165
Ortiz-Martínez, G., 79
Osei-Tutu, A.A.Z., 179
Osei-Tutu, K.O.A., 179
Oversensitivity claims, 236–237
Owens, J., 97
Owning class, 204, 205, 212, 215
OXFAM, 196, 197, 198–199

Page, C. T., 159
Pager, D., 165
Pailey, R. N., 91
Palestine/Israel conflict, 181–187
Palmer, C. T., 113, 115
Palmowski, J., 181
Panama Papers, 202
Panopticon metaphor (Foucault), 82–86
Pappé, I., 185, 186
Parker, A. M., 58
Parker, Walter, 205–206
Parliament of Canada, 202–203
Passive antiracism, 258
Passive racism, 257
Pastor-Moreno, G., 119
Patchin, J. W., 129
Patek, Arthur, 184
Paton, D., 35
Patriarchy, 71, 111–113, 121, 125, 129, 134, 136, 183–184, 219, 220
Patterns
    anecdotal evidence versus, 11–13, 170–171
    critical social justice, 248

Paul, R., 163
Payne, Ruby K., 92
Pearl, A., 92
Pearman, F. A., 97
Pedersen, S., 183
Pedulla, D. S., 46
Peer review, 7, 230
Pelicot, Dominique, 135–137
Pelicot, Giselle, 135–137
Peoples, C. E., 146
Peoples of Color. *See also* Race; Racism; Slavery *and specific groups*
    cultural deficit theory, 92, 149
    discrimination in hiring, 12, 46–48
    HIV/AIDS crisis, 220, 224–225
    housing discrimination and, 167
    ICE deportations, 142, 159, 210, 217
    oversensitivity claims concerning, 236–237
    "playing the race card," 163–164
    prejudicial beliefs about, 97
    as racist, 164–166, 234–235
    racist/not racist binary, 145–146, 147, 148
    stereotypical representations by media, 153–154
    as term, 139–140
    voting rights and, 73–74
Perry, L. B., 157
Perry, S. P., 151
Personal knowledge, 25
Peters, Greg, 127
Peterson, Bob, 36
Peterson-Withorn, C., 127, 213
Petit, G., 204
Pew Research Center, 125
Pham, M. T., 206, 207, 209
Phoenix, A., 219
Piazza, A., 141
Picca, L., 104, 150, 156
Pichai, Sundar, 127
Picker, Miguel, 131
Pickering, Charmene, 167
Pikes, Baron, 167
Pineda-Torres, M., 35, 112
Pitcher, M. A., 200
Pitchford, Eugene, 167
Planets/astronomy analogy, 5–6
Platitude, defined, 2
Poehlman, T. A., 45
Pomeranz, K., 177
Pontell, H. N., 218
Poor class, 205
Popoviciu, A., 185
Popular knowledge, 25
Pornography, 128–129, 131–134, 179
Positionality
    defined, 15, 188
    individual versus group identity, 48–52
    privilege and, 101

Positionality (*continued*)
  in reactions to course content and instructor, 15–17
  in social construction of knowledge, 24–25, 26–27
  in social justice literacy, 63
Positivism, 24, 30
Poverty. *See* Class/social class
Power, 66–89. *See also* Dominant/agent groups; Minoritized/target groups; Oppression; Privilege
  critical social justice in negotiating, 243–246
  defined, 70
  as hegemony, 70
  institutional, 71, 72
  myth of female, 130–131
  panopticon metaphor (Foucault) and, 82–86
  racism and, 172
  refusing to recognize structural and institutional, 234–235
  sexism as empowerment, 126–137
  social stratification and, 67–69
  understanding, 69–71
  understanding personal positions within unequal, 246–250
  wealth and, 197, 202–203
Preferences, in frame of reference glasses metaphor, 49–50, 66–67
Prejudice, 56–65
  defined, 57
  discrimination and, 56–60, 62–64, 71–72
  female beauty standards, 60
  nature of, 57–60
  oppression versus, 71–72
  prevalence of, 62–64
  racism versus, 145
  search committee vignette, 56–57, 63–64
  social group and, 58, 60, 63
  stereotypes and, 57–60
  unlearning, 64
Preston, A., 216
Prince, J. R., 44
Prison labor force, 208–210, 216–219
Prison Policy, 216
Privilege, 90–110
  ability privilege, 97–98
  attitudinal dimensions of, 98–106
  class, 221–222
  defined, 91
  denial of, 105–106
  dominant group misconceptions about, 97–98, 106–109
  external dimensions of, 92–98
  internal dimensions of, 98–106
  invisibility of, 97–98, 100–101, 104–106
  meritocracy and, 101, 106, 199
  nature of, 91–92
  paralysis of guilt and, 238–240
  structural dimensions of, 92–98, 234–235
  White privilege, 100–101
Proctor, B. D., 204
Project Implicit, 45–46
Proletariat, 193–194
Prostitution, 119, 128–129, 134
Pryce, D. K., 167
Public Citizen, 200
Pulido-Nava, A., 168
Purnanandam, A., 218

Quigley, J., 183
Quillian, L., 46
Quinan, C. Q., 112
Quinn, D. M., 45

Rabuy, B., 216
Race. *See also* Racism
  class and, 214–215
  defined, 50
  discrimination in hiring and, 12, 46–48
  ethnicity versus, 50–52
  group identity based on, 49–52
  history of social construction in Canada, 142–144
  history of social construction in the U.S., 141–142
  interaction with ethnicity, 51–52
  intersectionality of, 220
  nature of, 141
  understanding personal positions within unequal power relations, 246–250
Racism, 139–169. *See also* White supremacy
  active, 257
  antiracism and, 257–258
  challenges to understanding, 145–148
  class and, 157–158
  colorblind, 14, 80, 140, 147, 150, 152, 246
  common White misperceptions about, 161–168
  current issues in, 148–151
  defined, 139, 144, 146
  discrimination versus, 145
  dynamics of internalized racial oppression, 155–157
  economic issues and, 158–159
  environmental, 178, 208, 218
  group identities across relations of power, 68
  individualism and, 147–148, 161–164
  institutional, 149, 168, 172–173
  intersectionality and, 108–109, 157–161
  leadership and, 214
  of low expectations, 156–157
  nature of, 144–145, 177–178
  passive, 257
  of Peoples of Color, 164–166, 234–235
  in popular culture, 153–154
  power and, 172
  prejudice versus, 145

prison labor force, 208–210, 216–219
racial segregation, 152, 156–157
racist/not racist binary, 145–146, 147, 148
reverse, 75, 78, 164, 165
scientific (eugenics), 92, 109, 141–142, 177, 179
structural, 149, 234–235
voting rights and, 73–74
Radesky, J., 125–126
Rahali, M., 125
Rahman, M. M., 208
Rahman, M. Z., 208
Ramirez, V., 151
Ramos, J., 199
Randall, M., 144
Rank
  defined, 108
  status versus, 108, 245
Rasmussen, E. E., 125
Ratliff, K. A., 45
Razack, S., 175
Raznahan, A., 42
Reavey, P., 132
Reddy, C. M., 218
Regents of University of Southern California v. Bakke (1978), 89
Reich, R., 34
Religion. *See also* Jews; Muslims
  group identity based on, 49–50, 51
  religious oppression and group identities across relations of power, 68
Reproductive rights, 111, 124, 130, 134, 135, 222–223
Restifo, S. J., 142
Restitution, 201
Rettig, E., 187
Reverse racism, 75, 78, 164, 165
Reverse sexism, 75, 78, 128
Reyes, Ana C., 117
Reyna, C., 165
Rhode, D. L., 58
Rice, Tamir, 167
Riches, C., 181
Ridgeway, C. L., 247
Riggs, R. F., 125
Rizzo, M. T., 152
Roberts, S. O., 152
Robey, J., 167–168
Robinson, George, 167
Robinson, J. A., 200
Rocha Neves, J., 16–17
Rodgers, R. P., 218
Rodriguez-Molina, J. M., 42
Roediger, D. R., 142, 172, 225
Roeloffs, M. W., 199
Roe v. Wade (1973), 134
Romero, L., 200
Roscoe, W., 116
Ross, M., 150

Rothstein, R., 158
Royal Dutch/Shell, 183
Rudman, L., 29, 61, 104
Rueda, V., 46
Rueschemeyer, D., 193
Ruiz-Cantisani, M. L., 79
Ruiz-Pérez, I., 119
Rutter, E. F., 146
R. v. Kapp (2008), 89
Rwanda, women in public office, 76

Sáez-Lumbreras, A., 133
Said, E. W., 178–179
Salyers, Jacqueline, 167
Sanchez, Mandy, 131–132
Sánchez, S., 151
Sanders, Bernie, 203
Sarandos, Ted, 127
Sarchiapone, M., 120
Sardinha, L., 119
Sauermilch, W. S., 125
Sawyer, W., 208, 216
Schachner, J. N., 141
Schaeffer, K., 156
Schick, C., 6
Schisgall, David, 138
Schlosser, A., 35
Schmader, T., 42
Scholtens, I., 217
School knowledge, 25–26
Schools/schooling. *See also* Critical social justice literacy
  achievement gap and, 156, 193
  antiracism education in, 171
  Canadian residential schools for Indigenous students, 118, 143–144, 166–167, 211, 223, 229, 238
  claims that schools are politically neutral, 229
  class in construction of knowledge, 26–27, 86–87, 211
  compulsory mass schooling, 211
  critical theory in teaching practice, 32–33
  diversity hires and, 159
  education as key to getting ahead, 213–214
  gender in hiring process, 47–48, 56–57, 63–64, 66–67, 78–79, 87–88
  knowledge and, 86–88
  for minoritized/target groups, 243
  multicultural education in, 144, 170–171
  as panopticons, 84–86
  positioning social justice education as "extra," 237–238
  school tax base and, 168, 211
  segregation in, 95–97, 152, 156–157, 229, 243
  sexism as a personal choice, 125
  special education in, 96–97
  White teachers and, 156–157, 168

Schroeder, T. M., 155
Schularick, M., 167
Sciffer, M., 157
Sciullo, N. J., 161
Scott, Walter, 167
Scrage, D., 210
Segregation, in schools, 95–97, 152, 156–157, 229, 243
Seiver, M., 26
Self-knowledge, reactions as entry points for deeper, 13–15, 171–172
Seltzer, M. C., 157
Semler, S., 187
Sensoy, Özlem, 10, 47–48, 104, 124, 258
Sese Seko, Mobutu, 202
Seth, S., 211
Ševčíková, A., 132
Sex
  defined, 41
  gender versus, 41–42, 113–118
  prostitution and, 119, 128–129
Sexism, 111–138
  in advertising, 125–126
  androcentrism and, 72–73, 77, 78, 126
  in Canada, 120–121
  discourse concerning empowerment and, 126–137
  dominant culture and, 68, 122, 124, 126–137, 220
  example of, 118–121
  feminism and, 112, 157, 164, 219, 220
  gendered smell and, 126
  gender norms and, 72–73
  gender roles and, 133
  in global context, 119–120
  group identities across relations of power, 68
  ideology of the "West" versus "East" and, 124–125
  intersectionality and, 157–158
  invisibility of, 121–126
  leadership and, 75–76, 87–88, 90, 109, 127–128
  naturalization of, 121–122
  patriarchy and, 71, 111–113, 121, 125, 129, 134–135, 136, 183–184, 219, 220
  in popular culture, 121, 122–123, 125–126, 129, 132, 133–134
  pornography and, 128–129, 131–134, 179
  prostitution and, 119, 128–129, 134
  reproductive rights, 111, 124, 130, 134, 135, 222–223
  reverse, 75, 78, 128
  as a socializing force, 124–125
  statistics concerning, 127–128, 130
  in the U.S., 120–121
  violence against women, 120, 130–133, 135–137
  voting rights and, 72, 75, 77, 118

Sexuality
  female genital mutilation, 119
  gender versus, 116, 118
  group identity based on, 49–50, 51
  intersectionality of, 220
  reproductive rights, 111, 124, 130, 134, 135, 222–223
  sexual orientation versus, 116
Sexual orientation. *See* Gender identity
Seymour, A., 178
Shame, paralysis of guilt and, 238–240
Shanks, T. R., 149
Shannon, S., 168
Shapiro, Ben, 165
Shapiro, T. M., 152
Sharman, J. C., 201, 202
Shell company, 202
Shelley, L., 202
Sherman, A., 197
Shimizu, Celine Parreñas, 220
Shin, F., 202
Shkembi, A., 158
Shohat, E., 219
Shook, J., 150
Sidoti, O., 125
Signifiers, 123
Sign language, xxvii–xxix
Silverheels, Jay, 154
Sims, James, 167
Sinclair, N., 47–48, 104
Skiba, R. J., 97
Skinner-Dorkenoo, A. L., 151
Slavery
  of African Americans, 141–142, 144, 166, 175–178, 219, 229
  of Indigenous people, 144, 149, 166, 178
  prison labor as, 208–210, 216–219
Sleeter, C. E., 170, 171
Smallwood, S. E., 176
Smith, C. T., 45
Smith, E., 225
Smith, E. K., 133
Smith, Lillian, 191n, 225
Smith, L. M., 158
Smith, M., 129
Smith, S., 125
Smock, W., 120
Snyder, Timothy, 82–84
Social class. *See* Class/social class
Social construction
  of crime, 218–219
  of gender, 115–116
  of knowledge, 22–29
Social groups. *See also* Dominant/agent groups; Minoritized/target groups
  as binaries, 67–68
  in frame of reference glasses metaphor, 49–50, 66–67

Index   317

group identities, 49–52
group identity based on, 49–50, 51
prejudice and, 58, 60, 63
Socialism, 203
Socialization, 39–42
  class, 210–212
  conformity and, 43–44
  cultural norms in, 43–44
  culture and, 39
  defined, 39
  discrimination in hiring and, 46–48, 56–57, 63–64, 66–67, 87–88
  fish metaphor for, 16, 39, 49, 91–92, 111–113
  frame of reference glasses metaphor and, 49–50, 66–67
  gender. *See* Gender socialization
  iceberg of culture and, 39, 40, 77–78
  implicit bias and, 44–48, 58
  individual versus group identity and, 48–52
  insisting on immunity from, 232–233
  institutions in, 112–113
  prejudice and, 60, 62
  social stratification and, 67–69
  vignette, 38–39, 52
Social justice
  critical social justice and, xxii. *See also* Critical social justice
  defined, xxi–xxii
  gap between ideals and practices, xxii
  goal of, 3
  positioning social justice education as "extra," 237–238
  practicing, xxii
Social mobility, 212–213
Social Rise, 129
Social stratification, 67–69
Society for Adolescent Health and Medicine, 35
Socioeconomic status (TIES), 204. *See also* Classism; Class/social class
Solorzano, D. G., 92
Sosoo, E. E., 155
Soto, J., 35
Southgate, D., 147
SpaceX, 197
Spade, J. Z., 211
Spanier, B., 187
Spohn, C., 165
Sports
  female empowerment in, 128
  sexism and, 128–129
  as way out of poverty, 214
Standard Oil, 183
Starbucks Corp., 194
Statista, 125–126
Statistics Canada, 120, 130, 143, 196
Status
  defined, 108
  rank versus, 108, 245

Steele, Claude M., 156
Steet, Linda, 179
Stefancic, J., 172
Steiger, J., 42
Stepan, N., 141
Stereotypes
  class and, 198
  defined, 58–59
  gender role, 56–57, 59–60, 63, 87, 121–122
  implicit bias and, 44–48, 58
  kernel of truth to, 59
  in media representations of Peoples of Color, 153–154
  prejudice and, 57–60
Stereotype threat, 156
Sterling, Alton, 167
Stewart, P., 166
Strauss, A., 57
Structural dimensions
  of privilege, 92–98, 234–235
  refusing to recognize, 234–235
Structural racism, 149, 234–235
Student loan forgiveness, 218–219
Students for Fair Admissions v. Harvard (2023), 89, 166
Sue, Derald Wing, 81
Sugiura, L., 132
Suharto, 202
Sun, Chyng, 131
Sundquist, E. J., 172
Supernant, K., 144
Surface culture, 39, 40
Suwandi, I., 175–176
Sweatshop labor, 121

Talbott v. Trump (2025), 117
Tan, Hock E., 127
Tan, J. X., 212
Tappan, M. B., 80
Target groups. *See* Minoritized/target groups
Tatge, C., 54
Tator, C., 145
Tatum, Beverly Daniel, 146, 152, 155, 239
Taub, G., 181
Taxes
  school tax base and, 168, 211
  shell companies and, 202
Taylor, D. E., 218
Taylor, M., 16
Tehranian, J., 142
Temporary Assistance for Needy Families (TANF), 224
Tesla, 127, 197
Thal, S., 124
Thobani, S., 142–143
Thompson, H. A., 218
Thompson, M. C., 260
Thompson, W. C., 92

Thorneycroft, R., 133
Thrash, J. C., 218
Tiwari, N., 180
Tlaib, Rashida, 203
Tokenism, 244
Tomiyama, A., 60
Toprani, A., 183
Traditional Chinese Medicine (TCM), 11–12, 25
Tranchese, A., 132
Transformative academic knowledge, 26
Transgender, 41, 42, 116, 117, 118
Trepagnier, B., 145, 146
Trisi, D., 197
Troubled Assets Relief Program (TARP), 218
Trump, Donald J., 87, 117, 200, 201
Truth, Sojourner, 219
Tsakiropoulou-Summers, T., 72
Tsuboi, Y., 177
Tuana, N., 72
Tubex, H., 124
Tunamsifu, S. P., 176
Turk, J. M., 16
Turner, B. L., Jr., 157
Turner, H., 129
Turner, T., 156
Tyack, D., 211
Tzovara, A., 79

Uggen, C., 168
Uhlmann, E. L., 45
Ukanwa, K., 157
Unhoused people, 235
UNICEF, 119, 196
United for a Fair Economy, 196
United Nations, 119, 184–186
United Nations Children's Fund (UNICEF), 119, 196
United Nations Office for the Coordination of Humanitarian Affairs–Occupied Palestinian Territory (UNOCHA), 186
United Nations Office for the High Commissioner for Human Rights, 185–186
United Nations Regional Information Centre for Western Europe (UNRIC), 119
United States
  class categories, 204–206
  criminal justice system, 167–168
  history of social construction of race in, 141–142
  housing discrimination, 167
  income polarization in, 194–197, 202–203, 204
  kleptocracy in, 200–203
  loss of protections for LGBTQ+ people, 87
  "melting pot" analogy for, 144
  oligarchs and, 197, 199–200, 202
  in Palestine/Israel conflict, 187
  police violence against African Americans, 166–167
  racial hierarchy in, 140
  sexism in, 120–121, 130
  voting rights in, 73–77, 118, 159, 164–165, 168
  wealth gap in, 199–200
  women in public office, 75, 76
  worker rights in, 208
U.S. Air Force, 166
U.S. Department of Education, 159
U.S. Department of Government Efficiency (DOGE), 201
U.S. Department of Labor, 198
U.S. Department of State, 208
U.S. House Appropriations Committee, 130
U.S. House Committee on the Judiciary, 201
U.S. Immigration and Customs Enforcement (ICE), 142, 159, 210, 217
U.S. Sentencing Commission, 168
United States v. Bhagat Singh Thind (1923), 142
United Steelworkers of Canada, 255–257
UN Women, 76, 119, 128
USAGov, 194

Valaskakis, G. G., 144
Valencia, R. R., 92
Valenti, A., 87
Valentine, D. L., 218
Van Anders, S. M., 42
Van Ausdale, D., 157
Vance, JD, 130, 159
Van der Linden, M., 175
Vázquez-Villegas, P., 79
Ventura, K., 178
Verbinski, Gore, 36
Verdier, T., 200
Verma, R., 42
Vickers, J., 171
Voting rights
  class and, 73–74
  sexism and, 72, 75, 77, 118
  in the United States, 73–77, 118, 159, 164–165, 168
Voting Rights Act (1965), 73, 76, 118, 159, 164–165

Wages, J. E., III, 151
Wagner, L. S., 45
Wagner, P., 208, 216
Walker, Alice, 219
Walker, Jason, 167
Walker, P. O., 144
Walton, Alice, 196
Walzer, A. S., 45
Wang, C., 16–17
Ward, Corey, 167
Ward, J., 35

Index

Ward, R., 141
Warner, J. A., 121
Warren, E., 201
Warren, Earl, 157
Warren, Patrice, 167
Washington Post, 167
Watson, D., 152
Watson, L., 132
Watson, R., 97
Watts, C., 119
Wealth, 197–203. *See also* Class/social class
   classism and, 197–199
   income versus, 206
   kleptocracy, 200–203
   net worth, 213, 216
   oligarchs and, 197, 199–200, 202
   political power and, 197
Webber, V., 129
Weber, Max, 30
Weiner, D. I., 199
Weis, L., 172
Weisbord, Robert G., 175–177, 178
Weiss, T. C., 130
Weldon, L., 47–48, 104
Westlake, B. G., 133
Wexler, S., 150
White, B., 182–184, 185
White, H. K., 218
White, I., 159
The White House, 87, 159
White privilege, 100–101. *See also* Privilege; White supremacy
   backlash against DEI and, 135, 159–161
White supremacy, 170–190. *See also* Colonialism
   common White misperceptions about racism, 161–168
   defined, 171, 172
   dynamics of, 151–155
   examples of, 174
   in global context, 174–189, 197
   Global North versus Global South and, 175–181, 187–188, 197, 206–208
   "modern" versus "primitive" societies and, 180–181
   multicultural education and, 144, 170–171
   nature of Whiteness, 139–140
   in Palestine/Israel conflict, 181–187
   White nationalism, 31, 164–165, 172, 175
Whites/Whiteness. *See also* Dominant/agent groups; White supremacy
   "body within a room" metaphor and, 188–189
   construction of racism as individual acts, 163–164
   as "just human," 172, 175, 232
   as minority position, 162–163, 215–216
   misperceptions about racism, 161–168
   Mr. Rich White/Mr. Poor White vignette, 191–193, 225–226
   naming/not-naming dynamic and, 153–155, 158
   nature of Whiteness, 142, 172
   as property, 142
   racist/not racist binary, 145–146, 147, 148
   reduction of cultural tolerance and, 182
   social and economic advantages of, 142
   teachers in schools and, 156–157, 168
   as term, 140, 142
Whitley, B. E., Jr., 45
Wieberneit, M., 124
Wieland, H., 175–176
Wiesenthal, Simon, 54
Wiewiorra, L., 133
Williams, C., 36
Williams, H. A., 176
Williams, J. C., 247
Willis, H. A., 155
Wilson, C., 218
Wilson, W. J., 167
Winant, H., 141
Winks, R. W., 144
Wires, N., 135–136
"Wokeness," 164, 230
Woodson, C. G., 155–156
Wooten, N. R., 156
Working class, 204, 205, 212
World Bank, 196
World Health Organization (WHO), 119
World War I
   global empire building after, 180
   industrialization after, 180
   League of Nations and, 183, 184
   support for Zionism after, 182
World War II
   origins of Palestine/Israel conflict and, 181–182
   rebuilding after, 200
   United Nations and, 184–186
Wu, C., 16–17
Wyatt-Nichol, H., 212
Wynter, T., 47

XX chromosomes, 42, 113–115
XY chromosomes, 42, 113–115

Yassin, S., 204
Yatim, Sammy, 167
Yazdani, K., 178
Yendell, O., 26
Yoon, E. S., 157
Yost, D., 182
Young, F. L., 178
Yourish, K., 159
Yüksel-Kaptanoğlu, I., 119

Zahlan, A. B., 184
Zeppegno, P., 120

Zhang, S., 218
Ziegerhofer, A., 183
Ziegler, R. D., 216
Zimmerman, C., 119

Zinn, Howard, 36, 146, 166
Zionism, 181–185
Zuckerberg, Mark, 127, 196, 197
Zweig, M., 205

About the Authors

The authors are often asked, "How did you two come to write this book together?" Robin and Özlem met when they were doctoral students at the University of Washington in Seattle, where they were both in the Multicultural Education Program with advisor Dr. James Banks. Each recognized in the other a commitment to the ideals of social justice and a willingness to speak out boldly when necessary. They soon became close friends, supporting each other as they navigated the rigors of their PhD program. After graduating in 2004, while teaching university courses and interacting with colleagues, they noticed a gap between the belief in versus the practice of social justice. They began a program of co-writing peer-reviewed journal articles to support students and teachers to address this gap. During one of their writing sessions, they brainstormed the possibility of creating an accessible Dummies-style handbook addressing foundational social justice concepts. *Is Everyone Really Equal?* is the result!

Robin DiAngelo is an affiliate associate professor of education at the University of Washington. Her scholarship is in Critical Discourse Analysis and Whiteness Studies. She is a two-time winner of the Student's Choice Award for Educator of the Year at the University of Washington's School of Social Work. In 2011, she coined the term *White fragility* in an academic article which has influenced the international dialogue on race. Her book *White Fragility: Why It's So Hard for White People to Talk About Racism* was released in June of 2018 and was on the *The New York Times* Bestseller List for over 3 years. It has been translated into 12 languages and adapted for young adults. Her work or interviews have been featured in *The New York Times, The Guardian*, CNN, MSNBC, CBS, NPR, PBS, and the BBC, among many other forums. Dr. DiAngelo has been a consultant, educator, and facilitator for over 25 years on issues of racial and social justice.

Özlem Sensoy is professor of education and director of the Cassidy Centre for Educational Justice in the Faculty of Education at Simon Fraser University, on unceded Coast Salish territories in British Columbia, Canada. She is also an associate faculty member of the Department of Gender, Sexuality and Women's Studies, and an affiliated faculty member with the Centre for Comparative Muslim Studies at SFU. Her research articles have appeared in journals including *Gender & Education, Discourse: Studies in the Cultural Politics of Education*, and *Democracy & Education*. A university educator and researcher for over two decades, her work focuses on pathways for advancing a more just society through education.